The Voice of a Writer

Honoring the Life of Katie Funk Wiebe

Doug Heidebrecht and Valerie G. Rempel, editors

The Voice of a Writer

Honoring the Life of Katie Funk Wiebe

Goessel, Kansas

Winnipeg, Manitoba

Copyright ©2010 by Kindred Productions, Winnipeg, Manitoba, Canada

All rights reserved. With the exception of brief excerpts for reviews, no part of this book may be reproduced, stored in a retrieval system or transmitted in whole or in part, in any form, by any means, electronic, mechanical, photocopying, recording or otherwise without prior permission of Kindred Productions.

Published simultaneously by Kindred Productions, Winnipeg, Manitoba R3M 3Z6
and Kindred Productions, Goessel, Kansas 67053.

Cover and Book Design: Fred Koop
Printed by Friesens

Library and Archives Canada Cataloguing in Publication

The voice of a writer : honoring the life of Katie Funk Wiebe / Doug Heidebrecht and Valerie G. Rempel, editors.

Includes bibliographical references.
ISBN 978-1-894791-22-9

1. Wiebe, Katie Funk. 2. Wiebe, Katie Funk--Criticism and interpretation.
3. Mennonite authors--Biography. 4. Mennonite women--Kansas--Biography.
5. College teachers--Kansas--Biography. 6. Feminists--Kansas--Biography.
7. Mennonites--Kansas--Biography. I. Wiebe, Katie Funk II. Heidebrecht, Doug, 1961 III. Rempel, Valerie G

BX8143.W43V63 2010   289.7092   C2010-900600-3

Visit our website at www.kindredproductions.com
Printed in Canada

Katie Funk Wiebe

Contents

Introduction ix

Chapter 1
Katie's Pilgrimage – Doug Heidebrecht 1
    Katie Funk Wiebe – "The Barriers Are Not Real" 19

Chapter 2
Katie in Context – Valerie G. Rempel 25
    Katie Funk Wiebe - "A Problem Without a Name" 41
    Katie Funk Wiebe - "A Pilgrimage in Books" 43

Chapter 3
What Would Mother Do? – Joanna Wiebe 45
    Katie Funk Wiebe - "To You, My Father" 63

Chapter 4
A Widow's Journey – Darlene Klassen 67
    Katie Funk Wiebe - "To Be a Widow" 78

Chapter 5
Finding Her Voice in the Church
– Doug Heidebrecht 83
    Katie Funk Wiebe - "The Image is Wrong" 105
    Katie Funk Wiebe - "Freedom for All" 108
    Katie Funk Wiebe - "Who Should Be Ordained?" 111

Chapter 6
Katie's Viewpoint – Wally Kroeker 115
    Katie Funk Wiebe - "Why I Write This Column" 128
    Katie Funk Wiebe - "Convenience…or Murder?" 130

Chapter 7
A Woman among the Brethren – Harold Jantz 133
    Katie Funk Wiebe - "If You're a Mennonite" 148
    Katie Funk Wiebe - "Who Decides?" 151

Chapter 8
An Intellectual High – Don Isaac 153

    Katie Funk Wiebe - "The Conflict of Peace" 164
    Katie Funk Wiebe - "Tipping over the Tub" 167

Chapter 9
Lifting the Fog – Marlene Epp 171

    Katie Funk Wiebe - "Come Higher Friends" 182

Chapter 10
Stories into Books – Peggy Goertzen 185

    Katie Funk Wiebe - "Why Do You Sneeze?" 197

Chapter 11
The World of Mennonite Writing - Daniel Hertzler 201

    Katie Funk Wiebe - "Open Season on Writers" 212
    Katie Funk Wiebe - "Why Mennonites Can't
                      Laugh at Themselves" 215

Chapter 12
Aging with Spirit – Delores Friesen 219

    Katie Funk Wiebe - "Time for Purple with Red" 231
    Katie Funk Wiebe - "After 30 Years,
                      It's Time for a Change" 234

Chapter 13
Yielding and Reaching – Valerie G. Rempel and
                      Lorraine Dick 237

    Katie Funk Wiebe - "Sorting Prayer Thoughts" 249
    Katie Funk Wiebe - "I've Changed My Mind" 252

**The Writings and Oral Presentations of
Katie Funk Wiebe: A Comprehensive Bibliography**
    – David Giesbrecht, Doug Heidebrecht
    and Susan Huebert 255

Contributors 353

Introduction

For more than fifty years, Katie Funk Wiebe has given voice to her thoughts while sitting alone at her typewriter. It is hard to imagine the effort she devoted to the task. By her own estimation, she wrote 525,000 words during the thirty years she composed her column for *The Christian Leader*.[1] Yet this represents only a fraction of the thousands of words that found their way into her articles, chapters, reviews, books, and unpublished presentations, not to mention those discarded on crumpled sheets of paper thrown into the corner wastepaper basket. These words become even more remarkable when set in the context of her life as a single parent, her commitment to a productive teaching career, and the challenge of serving the church in an era of significant debate regarding the roles of women in the church. It seems hard to imagine but the words almost didn't come. Many years ago, as a young mother living in a small village in Saskatchewan, Katie wrestled with her longing to write:

> Today I have been doing a lot of thinking about writing. Is it worthwhile considering seriously or shall I just forget the thing altogether? The whole problem seems to resolve itself around the matter of having something to write about. If I have nothing to say, there is no use in writing that bit of nothing down on paper.[2]

Fortunately, Katie found her writing voice and a conviction that she did, indeed, have things to say.

In choosing to write for the church, Katie encouraged and challenged several generations to think more deeply about their faith and to walk more faithfully with God. She has been particularly adept at opening up her life to others and "wrapping words" around her thoughts, questions, doubts, and struggles.[3] By doing so, she invites her readers not only to listen but to recognize themselves in her stories. In her courage to express her own thoughts she articulates what we may often find difficult to acknowledge, let alone express. It does not take long, when reading Katie, to recognize a powerful and gifted voice.

Katie's significance, however, moves beyond the actual words on the page. In accepting an offer to write "the woman's column" for a small denominational magazine, Katie embarked on a path that put her at the center of the debate over women in ministry. That column became *Viewpoint*, and in it Katie began exploring questions as diverse as what constitutes a Mennonite, to the emergence of feminism within the larger culture. Yet, while Katie quickly became a symbol of the woman's movement and one of its leading voices in the Mennonite Brethren church, an assessment of her contribution cannot be limited to this single issue. Katie has been a pioneer voice, not only for women in the church, but also for widows silenced by their loss and older adults set aside because of their age. Katie deserves to be acknowledged for her important role in challenging the church to open avenues of service for all who have been neglected or have had their gifts overlooked.

The Voice of a Writer emerged as an idea in June 2007. Linda Huebert Hecht and David Giesbrecht, both members of the Mennonite Brethren Historical Commission, had been talking with each other about the possibility of proposing a book project to the Commission regarding Katie's contribution to the Mennonite Brethren. Unbeknownst to them, we had also discussed the idea of putting together a collection of articles highlighting Katie's work. Our paths converged in Fresno that June when we discovered our joint interest in such a project. The Historical Commission then asked the four of us to develop a proposal for an edited collection of essays.

Our vision was to provide an opportunity to reflect on Katie's contribution to the thought and life of both the Mennonite Brethren and the larger Mennonite community. Rather than publish a collection of unrelated essays, we decided to invite a variety of writers to assess the significance of Katie's writings. A thematic approach allowed us to engage the varied concerns reflected across her extensive writing career. The resulting essays range from thoughtful reflections on the personal impact of Katie's life and work, to assessments of her contributions to the broader life of the church.

We believe that reflections about Katie as a writer would be incomplete without the opportunity to hear Katie's own voice. To that end, we have included a selection of Katie's writings interspersed between the chapters. These have been

Introduction | xi

chosen primarily from her *Christian Leader* column to complement the theme of each section and to introduce readers to the wide spectrum of issues Katie addressed. We have also included Katie's bibliography as an acknowledgement of the tremendous gift she has given us and as an invitation to readers to listen for themselves to Katie's voice.

We are very appreciative of how the Mennonite Brethren Historical Commission embraced the vision to honor the life and work of Katie Funk Wiebe. In particular we are thankful for the encouragement of the executive directors, Ken Reddig and Abe Dueck, as well as the board chair, Peter Klassen. We are in debt to Linda Huebert Hecht and David Giesbrecht for helping visualize what this book could look like.

We also wish to thank each of the contributors who have immersed themselves in Katie's writings in order to engage with her thoughts and respond to her challenge. We are very grateful for the support of the staff at Kindred Productions, specifically Marilyn Hudson whose patience and diligence has brought this project to completion. Thank you to Tamara Dyck for her work formatting Katie's columns and to Kathie Ewert for compiling the list of Provident Book Finder reviews.

Finally, we wish to express our deep gratitude to Katie Funk Wiebe, who has chosen to live honestly, courageously, and creatively. Thank you for sharing your life with us and for openly modeling the walk of a faithful disciple of Jesus Christ.

Doug Heidebrecht and Valerie G. Rempel

• • •

Endnotes

1. Katie Funk Wiebe, "After 30 Years, It's Time for a Change," Viewpoint, *The Christian Leader*, December 31, 1991, 9.
2. Katie Funk Wiebe, "The Barriers Are Not Real," in *The Ethnic American Woman: Problems, Protests, Lifestyle*, ed. Edith Blicksilver (Dubuque: Kendall/Hunt, 1978), 180.
3. Katie Funk Wiebe, *You Never Gave Me a Name: One Mennonite Woman's Story* (Telford: DreamSeeker Books, 2009), 114.

Chapter 1

Katie's Pilgrimage

Doug Heidebrecht

Katie's story arises within the context of a larger narrative: a Mennonite journey across continents and cultures. At first glance she appears to be an inconsequential member—a woman, a mother, a widow—of a small immigrant people easily overlooked as they attempted to faithfully follow God within a larger North American society. Yet the significance of Katie's story emerges through her willingness to give voice to her own loss, uncertainty, and hope. It is a voice that resonates far beyond her own particular experiences.

Childhood - 1924-1942

Katie's parents, Jacob and Anna (Janzen) Funk immigrated from Rosenthal, South Russia to Canada in July 1923 as part of a Mennonite exodus following the Russian Revolution (1917-1918). The Funks traveled to Montreal via Southhampton, England with two daughters; Elfrieda (born February 1921) and Anna (born January 1923). Once in Canada, they settled in Hague, Saskatchewan, however, because of the assurance of a job with Jacob's uncle, Abram David Schellenberg, they soon relocated to Laird, a small village about 40 miles north of Saskatoon.[1] Katie was born on September 17, 1924 in Laird.[2] From Laird the family moved to Saskatoon in the spring of 1925 and then to Bruno, Saskatchewan that fall, where Jack was later born in February 1927.[3] Jacob managed a grocery store in Bruno, but asked for a transfer from the solidly Catholic community once Elfrieda had reached school age.[4]

In the spring of 1928 the Funk family moved to Blaine Lake, Saskatchewan where Jacob continued to manage an OK Economy grocery store. With the exception of just a few years, when he owned his own store, Jacob spent his entire Canadian working life in the employ of Central Wholesale. Blaine Lake was an ethnically diverse community of mainly first generation immigrants: Russian, English, Scottish, Irish, French, Ukrainian, Indian, Polish, German, and now one Mennonite family.[5] A fourth daughter, Susan, was born in April 1929, the same month a fire destroyed a large part of the business section on Main Street, yet left the grocery store Jacob managed virtually untouched.[6] Katie has described her childhood in *The Storekeeper's Daughter: A Memoir*, in which she also tells the story of her parents' experiences in Russia.[7]

The Funk family faithfully attended the Laird Mennonite Brethren church during the summer months when the weather would allow. During the winter the children went to Sunday school at the United Church of Canada in Blaine Lake while the parents attended the Russian Baptist Church just south of town or Russian services held in their home.[8] Katie grew up with a mix of theological influences ranging from a forthright Mennonite Brethren evangelicalism, which focused on crisis conversion, missions, and eschatology, to the less confining views of the United Church, which centered around loving God and doing good.[9]

Katie's teen years were relatively uneventful. She worked in her father's store, did well in school, and read as much as she could. She graduated from high school in 1942 and was awarded the Governor General of Canada Bronze Medal for earning a 93% average in grade twelve.[10]

Young Adulthood - 1942-1947

Katie turned down a small physics scholarship following high school, moved to Saskatoon and attended the Saskatoon Technical Institute for six months, where she learned typing, stenography, and bookkeeping.[11] She took a job at the Swift Canadian Meat Packing Company as an order clerk during the spring and summer of 1943, but she soon bored of taking requests for lunchmeat.[12] For the next two years, Katie worked as a bookkeeper and stenographer with Stevenson, McLorg and Company, a law firm in Saskatoon.

Initially Katie lived a directionless "happy-go-lucky" lifestyle with no goals for the future except the anticipation of romance, marriage, and a family.[13] While she called herself a Christian, she reflected later that she wasn't really a disciple until she encountered God at the age of 19 through a random reading of the September 1 daily devotional by Oswald Chambers in *My Utmost for His Highest*.[14] At this point "a rebellious spirit yielded to a Master" and Katie found both purpose and passion in life.[15]

Katie began reading her Bible avidly and spoke openly in youth meetings regarding her newfound zeal, so much so that she was soon elected president of the youth group at the Mennonite Brethren church.[16] It wasn't long, though, before she was asked to step down at the request of the pastor and church council. Katie readily consented without giving much thought as to why a woman would not be allowed to do the Lord's work if she was the best person suited for the task.[17] Katie was baptized near the end of the summer in 1945, just before her 21st birthday, by H.S. Rempel from Saskatoon Mennonite Brethren Church (known later as Central Mennonite Brethren Church). Rempel baptized her in a font because he was reluctant to go into the cold river.[18]

Katie left for Winnipeg in August 1945 to attend Mennonite Brethren Bible College (MBBC), which had just begun offering classes a year earlier. She had been recruited as a student by J.B. Toews, president of the college, who also asked her to serve as his personal secretary.[19] Katie registered for the religious education program and studied under J.B. Toews (New Testament and Systematic Theology), A.H. Unruh (Old Testament), J.H. Quiring (religious education and philosophy), and Ben Horch (music).[20] The move was difficult. The clear conservative social boundaries reinforced by strict rules were foreign to the sense of freedom that had been fostered by Katie's experiences growing up in the religious and ethnic diversity of Blaine Lake and Saskatoon.

When Katie joined the staff of the student publication, *The Harbinger*, she began working with its new editor, Walter Wiebe, a student from Yarrow, B.C. who had arrived late after serving for almost the entire Second World War as a conscientious objector in both Alberta and B.C. Although Walter had been born in Borden, Saskatchewan (October 3, 1918), his family had moved to Coaldale in 1930, where he had finally completed his high school education in 1940.[21] Walter's father, Peter P., had collapsed emotionally following several difficult experiences and continued to suffer ill health for many years. The family moved again to Yarrow, B.C. while Walter's father spent a winter at Bethesda Home in Vineland, Ontario. Walter headed to Winnipeg to attend MBBC, knowing his father would be taken care of.[22]

Walter proposed to Katie in the spring of 1946, while leaning over the counter in the college office.[23] When Katie returned to Saskatoon for the summer months she began to have second thoughts about their relationship and she broke off the engagement.[24] In fall, Katie returned to MBBC while Walter remained in Yarrow to care for his father, who had recently returned from Ontario, and to teach at the Elim Bible School. Katie invited Walter to Blaine Lake for Christmas and their renewed engagement was announced on January 12, 1946.[25]

That spring Walter was invited by J.H. Epp to supervise short-term high school students at Bethany Bible Institute in Hepburn, Saskatchewan. Katie left Winnipeg for Blaine Lake in July in order to prepare for their wedding while Walter attended summer school in Saskatoon. Katie and Walter were married on a Thursday evening, August 21, 1947, in the Saskatoon Mennonite Brethren Church.

Marriage and Ministry - 1947-1958

On the day following their wedding, Katie and Walter travelled to Yarrow, B.C. by train, where they settled into a duplex that housed the Elim Bible School.[26] Walter taught at the school on a reduced salary due to low enrollment and Katie struggled through one of the most difficult years of her life; surrounded by "cramped quarters, limited budgets, and lonely days."[27] In April 1948 they returned to Hepburn, Saskatchewan, with Katie seven months pregnant, so Walter could again teach the short-term high school program offered at Bethany Bible Institute.[28]

Joanna Katherine was born in Saskatoon on June 15, bringing a ray of joy to Katie amidst her difficult circumstances.[29] Katie and Joanna spent the summer with Katie's parents in Blaine Lake while Walter again attended summer school at the University of Saskatchewan in Saskatoon.[30] That fall, Walter began teaching at the one-room Hudson Bay School located a few miles north of Hepburn, while Katie made a home of the teacher's residence.[31] It was during this time that Katie and Walter sought to determine what they thought God wanted of their life together. One evening they knelt beside the kitchen table and committed themselves to a literature ministry within the church.[32]

In the summer of 1950 Walter and Katie moved to Winnipeg in order for Walter to return to his theological studies at Mennonite Brethren Bible College.[33] They moved into the student residences at Ebenezer Hall, which consisted basically of one room that served both as a bedroom and a kitchen, with shared washrooms down the hall.[34] A year later, Susan Helene was born on July 28 in Winnipeg.[35] Walter graduated with a Bachelor of Theology degree on June 20, 1952, a few months after his father passed away at the age of 65.[36]

Bethany Bible Institute offered Walter a teaching position and so Katie and Walter, along with their two daughters, moved back to Hepburn, Saskatchewan in September, where they lived at one end of a new dormitory.[37] Walter taught courses in Bible, theology, and homiletics. Their dream of a literature ministry found expression that same fall when Walter began editing *The Youth Worker*, a publication of the Canadian MB Youth Committee, which sought to support a growing focus on youth work within churches. As a result of Walter's busy teaching and preaching schedule, Katie began to take on some of the editing work, to the point that she was soon producing the entire publication under Walter's name.[38] It was an uncomfortable arrangement for both of them.

The Hepburn M.B. Church ordained Walter to the ministry in October 1953, and Katie reflected later that the imprint of the preacher's sweaty fingers on her new black velvet hat left her with the sign of ordination but no assignment or recognition.[39] Walter provided regular pulpit supply for the Laird M.B.

6 | The Voice of a Writer

Church beginning in March 1954 until May 1956 and this gave Katie a welcomed opportunity to reconnect with people from her childhood church.[40] A third daughter, Christine Ruth, was born on November 19, 1954 in Waldheim and their growing family precipitated a move out of the Bethany dormitory into a teacherage. Walter continued to enroll in courses at the University of Saskatchewan each summer. Katie continued to care for the family and edit *The Youth Worker*.

In March 1956, Hepburn M.B. Church called Walter to serve as their pastor, a call he accepted on the condition that he was allowed to continue his part-time studies.[41] This new ministry entailed both a move into the parsonage, but brought with it the accompanying expectations of a pastor's wife. Still, Katie was able to continue her editorial work for *The Youth Worker* and in September 1957 her name was added as a co-editor.[42] Katie increasingly began to sign her name to the work she was doing, often with a "kfw." She also began writing news releases for *The Canadian Mennonite*.[43]

It wasn't long, though, before both Walter and the Hepburn Church grew uneasy about the "student-pastor" relationship and so Walter resigned in March 1958 in order to devote himself more fully to his studies and the vision of a wider literature ministry.[44] In August, with Katie six months pregnant, they packed up their household and moved to Virgil, Ontario where once again they settled into dormitory accommodations.[45]

Preparation Time - 1958-1962

Walter began teaching at Eden Christian College in September 1958, but felt ill all fall. Katie could only watch as his joy and energy began to dissipate.[46] Their son, James Philip, was born on November 23, 1958 in Niagara-on-the-Lake. Shortly after Christmas, Walter travelled to Winnipeg and then on to Hillsboro, Kansas for both Canadian and General Conference Mennonite Brethren Publication Board meetings. While in Hillsboro he collapsed and emergency surgery revealed a ruptured appendix, which likely had happened already in September.[47] Katie rushed to Hillsboro to visit Walter, who then returned to Ontario where he spent several months recuperating, during which time they were without an income.[48] These challenges created a soul searching crucible around whether God had actually called them to a literature ministry. In the summer of 1959, Walter and Katie moved to Kitchener where Walter could study at Waterloo Lutheran College as well as teach at the Ottawa Street M.B. Bible School.[49] Walter finally completed the requirements for a Bachelor of Arts degree in 1961, which he received from the University of Saskatchewan. Unfortunately, Walter continued to experience health complications. A large cyst was removed from his abdomen in May and his appendix taken out in July.[50]

After nine years, Katie and Walter ended their time as joint editors of *The Youth Worker* in June 1961.[51] That fall Walter enrolled at Syracuse University in New York State in order to pursue a Master of Arts degree in religious journalism. He left Katie and the children behind in Kitchener where she was able to support the family by working for a temporary secretarial service. She continued to write and published several freelance articles in *Christian Living* and *The Canadian Mennonite*.[52] Katie had been invited by Orlando Harms in 1960 to write a column, "Women and the Church," for *The Christian Leader*.[53] Now she accepted the invitation and in January 1962 she began writing for five dollars a column.[54]

As Walter was finishing his first year of studies at Syracuse, Orlando Harms invited him to come to Hillsboro to work at the Mennonite Brethren Publishing House as the book and literature editor. Katie was offered a job with the General Conference Board of Missions as a research assistant, a job that later turned into bookkeeping.[55] Even though Walter noticed another growth in his abdomen, doctors approved their immigration visas to the United States and in September 1962 Walter and Katie moved to Hillsboro, Kansas with great anticipation. Their vision for a literature ministry was finally becoming a reality.

New Beginnings - 1962-1972

A few weeks after arriving in Hillsboro, Walter began to feel ill again and a rapidly growing tumor was discovered in his abdomen. In the early morning of November 17, 1962 Walter died of *pseudo mucinous myxoma peritonei*, a rare non-cancerous growth.⁵⁶ He was forty-four years old. Katie, at thirty-eight years of age, was now a widow in a foreign country surrounded by strangers, faced with the prospect of raising her four children alone. She was plagued with questions. Why did God not heal Walter? Had God really led them to this place only to abandon them? Slowly she realized that God had been developing in her a sense of trust during the last four difficult years; "not as a strong blinding light, but as a glimmer of hope in the gathering darkness."⁵⁷

Much later, Katie would characterize Walter's death as the one "experience that probably had the most far-reaching effect on me, my faith, my outlook on life, and my vocation" because "widowhood changed the road signs and sent me down a new path."⁵⁸ As a widow, Katie experienced a profound loss of identity that prompted her to re-examine her role as a mother within her family but also as a woman in the church.

Katie's first priority was the care of her family, which meant that she now needed to work full time in order to pay for groceries and the rent. She decided to stay in Hillsboro and in January 1963, began working at the Mennonite Brethren Publishing House as an editorial assistant doing copy editing and proofreading.⁵⁹ Katie also continued to write. She published freelance articles alongside her regular *Christian Leader* column, "Women and the Church." She attended writers' conferences at Moody Bible Institute in Chicago in 1964 and at Green Lake, Wisconsin in 1966, where she caught the vision that writing in the church needed to be of superb quality to be effective.⁶⁰ She began speaking to women's groups, and she taught a mixed group of young adults at the Parkview Mennonite Brethren Church; a daring thing for a woman to do at that time.⁶¹ A new identity was being formed and on February 18, 1964, Katie changed the signature on her column from Mrs. Katie Wiebe to Katie Funk Wiebe.⁶²

In the fall of 1966, Wes Prieb, acting dean at Tabor College in Hillsboro, offered Katie a position teaching one section of Freshman English, despite her lack of a degree or formal teaching experience.⁶³ Katie embarked on her new career at Tabor College during her lunch break at the Publishing House and was soon offered a full-time position at the College, beginning in the fall of 1967. Her new job included teaching additional sections of Freshman English, working as the College's Publicity Director, and the opportunity to finish a bachelor's degree.[64] Her role as Publicity Director, which she held until 1970, included editing the *Tabor College Alumni Magazine* and serving as an advisor to the student paper, *The Tabor College View*.[65]

Katie threw herself into her work and her studies, graduating with a Bachelor of Arts degree from Tabor College in May 1968. She immediately began work towards a master's degree in English at Wichita State University. As always, she continued to write and her own comprehension of her identity as a person, not just a widow or even a woman, presented her with the challenge "to write as a person to persons, not just as a woman to women."[66] On March 28, 1967, Katie changed the name of her column in *The Christian Leader* from "Women and the Church" to "Viewpoint" in an attempt to engage both men and women in the discussion regarding the changes in society affecting women.[67] Her own experience had created an awareness of the need for the Mennonite Brethren constituency to hear the voice of the lay person "who hasn't all the background information but who is sometimes concerned, sometimes bewildered, sometimes ready to offer an insight."[68]

Katie completed her master's degree in 1972 and was then recognized as an Assistant Professor of English at Tabor College. At forty-eight years of age, ten years after the death of Walter, Katie was in many ways just beginning her work.

Avenues of Ministry - 1973-1990

Katie served as head of the Tabor College English Department from 1973 to 1976 and again from 1985 until 1990, and was promoted to Associate Professor in 1981. She was also elected chair of the Associated Colleges of Central Kansas English Committee in 1974, a position she held for two years.[69] Katie had high expectations for her students and sought to encourage them to take writing and literature seriously. She especially enjoyed teaching upper level English courses, particularly "Black Literature" and "The Bible in Literature."[70]

Tabor College not only provided Katie with employment and the opportunity to influence the next generation, it also offered her many opportunities for personal and intellectual growth. During a sabbatical year from her teaching at Tabor College in 1977, Katie toured India, Bangladesh and Nepal for six weeks. She attended the first all-India Mennonite Women's Conference, where she gave an address, "Women's Work in the Light of Our Heritage and Mission."[71] She traveled again in 1979, exploring Germany, Holland, Belgium, Austria and Switzerland with an Anabaptist church history tour. A decade later she was able to travel to the former Soviet Union, visiting St. Petersburg, Moscow, and Mennonite villages in the Ukraine. On that trip she had the opportunity to visit her aunt Neta in Moscow for the first time.[72]

During the 1970s Katie's involvements diversified in other areas as well, and her influence began to spread far beyond the Mennonite enclave in Hillsboro, where she taught and lived. Katie started to expand her writing beyond columns and short articles. Her first book, *Have Cart, Will Travel*, was a 1974 adaptation of Mennonite Brethren missionary Paulina Foote's autobiography, *God's Hand Over My Nineteen Years in China*.[73] Then, in the summer of 1976, Katie took on two book assignments: *Alone: A Widow's Search for Joy*, which was the story of her husband's death and her experience as a widow; and *Day of Disaster: The Story of Modern-Day Samaritans*, a history of Mennonite Disaster Service.[74] *Alone* sold thousands of copies, reflecting the way readers resonated with Katie's vulnerable reflections about her experience.[75] As Katie regularly told her own students, "writing is often an exercise in self-revelation…the more personal the writing, the more universal."[76]

These initial books reflected two major themes that Katie would address throughout her career. First, Katie sought to reveal the "underside" of history and tell stories, particularly those of women who were often overlooked because they were not part of official historical accounts. This is exemplified in her history of the Bethel Deaconess Hospital School of Nursing in Newton, Kansas and the collection of stories of Mennonite Brethren and Krimmer Mennonite Brethren women who made significant though undocumented contributions to the life of the church.[77] Katie also wrote *Who Are the Mennonite Brethren?*

which was widely used as an introduction to the history and beliefs of her denomination.[78]

The second theme was Katie's use of autobiographical narrative to share her own story. As she put it, "I cherish the opportunity to share my stumbling through life with others. After I have lived it, why hang on to it?"[79] Katie has written several autobiographical accounts including *Bless Me Too, My Father* (1988), which featured her reflections about change, particularly theological change, during middle adulthood.[80] It won the prestigious Silver Angel award.

Katie's growing success prompted invitations to conduct writing workshops. Since 1979 she has conducted numerous workshops across Canada and the United States. She has also sought to provide practical resources for those wishing to write their own memoirs and family histories.[81]

In 1973, after writing about women in the church for over a decade, Katie attended her first conference on the topic. It was the Evangelical Perspectives on Women's Role and Status sponsored by the Conservative Baptist Theological Seminary in Denver.[82] Several years later, in 1975, Katie participated in the Evangelical Women's Caucus in Washington D.C., where evangelical women came together to study the biblical basis for Christian feminism, examine the historical record of women's roles, and explore women's gifts.[83] These were exhilarating experiences and Katie delighted in the spiritual and intellectual stimulation they provided.

It was during this period that women were beginning to be recruited to sit on the boards and committees of Mennonite agencies. Katie began to be involved at a number of levels within the Mennonite Brethren conference. She was appointed a board member for the Center for Mennonite Brethren Studies in Hillsboro in 1974, a position she continues to hold. Katie was also appointed to the Mennonite Central Committee Taskforce for Women in the Church and Society in 1975, where she represented Mennonite Brethren until 1977, even though no Mennonite Brethren board took responsibility for her involvement.[84]

Katie served on the editorial board of *Direction*, a journal sponsored by Mennonite Brethren higher education institutions. From 1978 to 1980 Katie was hired as the part-time literature coordinator for the Board of Christian Literature, where she was responsible for encouraging writers, soliciting manuscripts for publication, and promoting published materials.[85] She also served on the publicity committee for the Mennonite World Conference in 1978.

The church's reluctance to welcome more women into leadership troubled Katie. In May 1976 she presented a paper entitled, "Voices of Liberation," at the Anabaptist and Mennonite Brethren History and Practice Symposium on Women in the Church in Fresno.[86] This was followed in 1978 by two papers, "Jesus and Womanhood" and "The Church's Response to Changing Roles for Men and Women," which she presented at an MCC conference on Biblical Perspectives on Women in the Church, in Clearbrook, B.C.[87] There, Katie observed that the church could take one of two approaches: "it can become a leader, speaking forth in power, with love and with understanding on the matter of changing roles or it can speak with fear and continue to set up barriers and structures, limiting the role and contribution, thereby, of both men and women."[88]

Katie found herself increasingly at the center of the conversation about women in the Mennonite Brethren church. In 1986 she was appointed to the Board of Reference and Counsel's Women in Ministry Task Force, which drafted the first resolution on women in the church to be prepared by both men and women.[89] The following year Katie was invited to be the first woman to address a General Conference convention as a plenary speaker.[90] She also agreed to co-edit *Your Daughters Shall Prophesy: Women in Ministry in the Church* (1992), which was used by Mennonite Brethren congregations as a study guide for reflecting on the issue of women in church leadership.[91]

In 1990, after a twenty-four year career, Katie retired from teaching at Tabor College and was honored with the appointment of Professor Emeritus. The years had been rich but Katie was ready for new challenges.

Retirement and Beyond - 1990-present

In 1991 Katie moved from Hillsboro to Wichita, Kansas to begin her retirement years. She also completed her last "Viewpoint" column for *The Christian Leader* on December 31, 1991, acknowledging that the "columns have, in a sense become a journal of my life and concerns."[92] The column was a remarkable achievement. For thirty years Katie had served as a lay theologian addressing issues and concerns and asking questions that others didn't have the opportunity to ask.

Even though Katie helped establish a Wichita chapter of Christians for Biblical Equality in 1993, her attention began to shift toward the needs of older adults as she started to think about her own aging. She deliberately began doing some hospice volunteer work related to death and dying.[93] These were not abstract issues for Katie as she faced the loss of her parents; her father Jacob in 1986 and her mother Anna in 1994; and the death of her daughter Christine in 2000 after a lengthy illness.

Katie now embraced a new challenge, "I want to be a catcher in the rye for older adults before they fall off the cliff and think of themselves as nobodies. I want them to keep growing."[94] She began to write both about her own experience of growing older as well as the role of older adults in the church.[95] Soon she was being invited to lead workshops on aging and speak at older adult retreats. Katie joined the Adventures in Learning program sponsored by East Wichita Shepherd's Center, where she eventually taught a number of courses on writing and storytelling.[96]

Retirement did not stop Katie from writing or continuing to pursue her vision of a literature ministry. Katie served as editor of *Rejoice!*, an inter-Mennonite devotional guide, from 2000-2005 and in 2000, she filled in as interim editor for six months for *The Christian Leader*. Katie also began sharing more of her own story through the medium of autobiographical narrative. She wrestled with her experience of aging in *Border Crossing: A Spiritual Journey* (1995) and looked back on her childhood and Mennonite roots in *The Storekeeper's Daughter: A Memoir* (1997). In 2009 Katie shared the struggles and joys of her journey as an adult, from a naïve college student to octogenarian in *You Never Gave Me a Name: One Mennonite Woman's Story*. She also continued to travel and in 2002 went to Central America on an MCC Learning Tour to study political and religious persecution.

Katie has been recognized and honored for her significant contribution to the life of the church. In February 1993 the Mennonite Health Association honored Katie with the Anabaptist Healthcare Award in recognition of her "tireless, dedicated and joyful service to the church as a teacher, writer, and resource person in many areas including health care, mental health, women's issues and aging."[97] The fall 1995 issue of *Direction*, a Mennonite Brethren academic journal, was dedicated to Katie who modeled "a life of writing with skill and integrity."[98] In 2000 Katie was given the Tabor College Alumni Merit Award for "bringing meaning to life through writing and encouraging others to do the same."[99] Also in 2000, Katie was chosen by *The Mennonite* editorial staff as one of the top twenty Mennonites who significantly influenced the life and belief of Mennonites during the twentieth century.[100] She was recognized as "a pioneer and inspiration for women seeking greater roles in church leadership...for raising the credibility of Mennonite writing and...[giving] voice to widowhood."[101]

Katie and Walter's persistence in following their sense of God's call to a literature ministry took a much different route than they had anticipated, yet it has also born fruit far beyond their expectations. Katie has published over two thousand articles, columns, and book reviews, and written or edited twenty books.

She has openly shared her life and by doing so has invited others not only to listen but to recognize themselves in her story. Katie's courage to express the thoughts of an ordinary woman has given voice to the marginalized and her example as a disciple on a journey has challenged the church to be more faithful. Katie recently wrote, "although I am eighty-three, it is not yet time to pull back. I tell myself it is important to keep reaching for goals I personally will not win...I want to die climbing."[102]

…

Endnotes

1. Katie Funk Wiebe, "We Arrive," in *Growing Up in Blaine Lake*, by Elfrieda Schroeder et al. (1991), 1, and Katie Funk Wiebe email to Doug Heidebrecht, June 10, 2009.
2. There is some discrepancy about the exact date of Katie's birth. Katie's birth certificate, which she received as an adult, identifies September 15 as her birth date, yet church records list September 17. Throughout her childhood and young adulthood, Katie had always thought her birthday was on September 17. See Katie Funk Wiebe email to Doug Heidebrecht, June 8, 2009. See also "Familien Register, Mennonite Brethren Church, Saskatoon," Vol. 1170, Membership Records 1940-49, CMBS (Winnipeg); and "Laird MB Church Membership and Family Register II," Vol. 638, CMBS (Winnipeg).
3. Anna Janzen Funk's Story (Wichita, Kansas, 1996), 6.
4. *Ibid.*, 2.
5. Katie Funk Wiebe, *Alone: A Search for Joy* (Winnipeg: Kindred Press, 1987), 196.
6. Katie Funk Wiebe, "The Big Fire," in *Growing Up in Blaine Lake*, by Elfrieda Schroeder et al. (1991), 5.
7. Katie Funk Wiebe, *The Storekeeper's Daughter: A Memoir* (Scottdale: Herald Press, 1997).
8. Katie Funk Wiebe, *Border Crossing: A Spiritual Journey* (Scottdale: Herald Press, 1995), 67.
9. *Ibid.*, 67-68.
10. "Miss Katie Funk Wins Governor General's Medal for High Marks," *Blaine Lake Echo*, 1942.
11. Wiebe, *Border Crossings*, 41.
12. *Ibid.*, 42.
13. *Ibid.*, 43.
14. Wiebe, *Alone*, 197. See also Wiebe, *Border Crossings*, 87.
15. *Ibid.*, 197.
16. *Ibid.* 198
17. *Ibid.* 198.
18. "Familien Register, Central Mennonite Brethren Church, Saskatoon," Vol. 1170, Membership Records 1940-49, CMBS (Winnipeg) and Katie Funk Wiebe email to Doug Heidebrecht, June 8, 2009. The Mennonite Brethren Church records list her baptism on September 12, 1945, yet Katie was already in Winnipeg at that time. For a baptismal date of September 17 see "Laird MB Church Membership and Family Register II," Vol. 638, CMBS (Winnipeg).
19. Katie Funk Wiebe, *You Never Gave Me a Name: One Mennonite Woman's Story* (Telford: DreamSeeker Books, 2009), 21.
20. *Ibid.*, 25.
21. *Ibid.*, 45, 46.
22. *Ibid.*, 48.

23. *Ibid.*, 50.
24. *Ibid.*, 50, 51.
25. *Ibid.*,, 53.
26. *Ibid.*,, 57.
27. *Ibid.*; Wiebe, *Alone*, 199.
28. *Ibid.*, 61.
29. *Ibid.*, 62.
30. *Ibid.*, 63.
31. *Ibid.*, 63.
32. *Ibid.*, 165.
33. *Ibid.*, 65, 80.
34. *Ibid.*, 65-66.
35. *Ibid.*, 66.
36. *Ibid.*, 67.
37. *Ibid.*, 68.
38. See Walter Wiebe's acknowledgement of Katie's involvement in "How It Came About." *Youth Worker Program Helps: Volume One* (Winnipeg: Youth Committee of the Canadian Conference of the Mennonite Brethren Church of North America, 1960), 6.
39. Wiebe, *You Never Gave Me a Name*, 68-69.
40. *Ibid.*, 69.
41. *Ibid.*, 71.
42. See *Youth Worker*, September 1957, 2.
43. See "Sask. Mennonite Brethren Plan New Mission Work." *The Canadian Mennonite*, June 14, 1957, 4, and "Bethany Institute Family Commemorates Thirty Years." *The Canadian Mennonite*, August 23, 1957, 7.
44. Wiebe, *You Never Gave Me a Name*, 78, 79.
45. *Ibid.*, 80-81.
46. *Ibid.*, 81, 82.
47. *Ibid.*, 82.
48. *Ibid.*, 83.
49. *Ibid.*, 86.
50. *Ibid.*, 90, 91.
51. See Katie and Walter Wiebe, "Good-bye for Now," *The Youth Worker*, June 1961, 3.
52. For example, see Katie Funk Wiebe, "A Pilgrimage in Books," *Christian Living*, April 1962, 19 and Katie Funk Wiebe, "Church Secretarial Services for K-W Ministers." *The Canadian Mennonite*, March 23, 1962, 5.
53. Katie Funk Wiebe, *Born Out of Season: A Short biography of Walter William Wiebe 1918-62*, unpublished manuscript, 1997, 71. See also Katie Wiebe to Orlando Harms, September 5, 1960.
54. See Katie Wiebe, Women and the Church, *The Christian Leader*, January 9, 1962, 21.
55. Wiebe, *You Never Gave Me a Name*, 98.
56. *Ibid.*, 102-103.
57. Katie Funk Wiebe, "When God Does Not Heal," *The Christian Leader*, December 12, 1972, 7.
58. Katie Funk Wiebe, "Growing with the Seasons of Life," *Direction* 24, no.2 (Fall 1995): 77; Wiebe, *Alone*, 207.

59. Katie Funk Wiebe, "Why I Went to Work When I Was Working," in *Who Am I? What Am I?: Searching for Meaning in Your Work*, ed. Calvin Redekop (Grand Rapids: Academie Books, 1988), 97.
60. Wiebe, *You Never Gave Me a Name*, 119.
61. Katie Funk Wiebe email to Doug Heidebrecht, June 13, 2009.
62. See Katie Funk Wiebe, "You Can Be a Literature Evangelist," Women and the Church, *The Christian Leader*, February 18, 1964, 29.
63. Wiebe, *You Never Gave Me a Name*, 121.
64. *Ibid.*, 125.
65. *Ibid.*
66. Wiebe, *Alone*, 59, 206. See also Katie Funk Wiebe, "Color Me a Person," *Mennonite Brethren Herald*, December 28, 1973, 2-5, 7.
67. Katie Funk Wiebe, "A Voice for the Layman," Viewpoint, *The Christian Leader*, April 25, 1967, 21. See also Katie Funk Wiebe, "Courting Women for Church Work." Viewpoint, *The Christian Leader*, March 28, 1967, 21.
68. *Ibid.*
69. Wiebe, *You Never Gave Me a Name*, 141.
70. *Ibid.*
71. Katie Funk Wiebe, *Bless Me Too, My Father* (Scottdale: Herald Press, 1988), 38.
72. Wiebe, *Border Crossing*, 129.
73. Katie Funk Wiebe, *Have Cart, Will Travel* (Hillsboro: North American Conference of Mennonite Brethren Churches; Board of Christian Literature, 1974). See also Paulina Foote, *God's Hand Over My Nineteen Years in China* (Hillsboro: M.B. Publishing House, 1962).
74. See Katie F. Wiebe, *Alone: A Widow's Search for Joy* (Wheaton: Tyndale House, 1976) and Katie Funk Wiebe, *Day of Disaster: The Story of Modern-Day Samaritans* (Scottdale: Herald Press, 1976).
75. Wiebe, *You Never Gave Me a Name*, 168.
76. *Ibid.*, 170.
77. See Katie Funk Wiebe, *Our Lamps Were Lit: An Informal History of the Bethel Deaconess Hospital School of Nursing* (Newton: Bethel Hospital School of Nursing; Alumnae Association, 1978); and Katie Funk Wiebe, ed., *Women among the Brethren: The Story of Fifteen Mennonite Brethren and Krimmer Mennonite Brethren Women* (Hillsboro: General Conference of the North American Mennonite Brethren Churches; Board of Christian Literature, 1979).
78. Katie Funk Wiebe, *Who Are the Mennonite Brethren?* (Hillsboro: Kindred Press, 1984).
79. Wiebe, *You Never Gave Me a Name*, 170.
80. Katie Funk Wiebe, *Bless Me Too, My Father* (Scottdale: Herald Press, 1988).
81. See Katie Funk Wiebe, *Good Times with Old Times: How to Write Your Memoirs* (Scottdale: Herald Press, 1979) and Katie Funk Wiebe, *How to Write Your Personal or Family History: If You Don't Do It, Who Will?* (Intercourse: Good Books, 2009).
82. Wiebe, *You Never Gave Me a Name*, 200.
83. *Ibid.*, 201.
84. William Keeney to Katie Funk Wiebe, April 7, 1975. See "Members of the Task Force/Committee on Women's Concerns," *MCC Committee on*

18 | The Voice of a Writer

Women's Concerns Report, July-August, 1983, 7. See also Wiebe, *You Never Gave Me a Name*, 203.
85. "Wiebe Coordinates MB Literature," *The Christian Leader*, December 19, 1978, 20.
86. See Katie Funk Wiebe, "Voices of Liberation" (paper presented at Symposium: Women and the Church, Fresno, CA, May 6-7, 1976).
87. See Katie Funk Wiebe, "Jesus and Women" (paper presented to Biblical Perspectives on Women in the Church, Clearbrook, B.C., November 18, 1978); and Katie Funk Wiebe, "The Church's Response to Changing Roles for Men and Women" (paper presented to Biblical Perspectives on Women in the Church, Clearbrook, B.C., November 18, 1978).
88. Wiebe, "The Church's Response to Changing Roles for Men and Women," 4.
89. "Resolution on Women in Ministry," *Yearbook: 57th Session General Conference of Mennonite Brethren Churches of North America* (August 7-11, 1987): 46-47.
90. "Love in the Church," *Yearbook: 57th Session General Conference of Mennonite Brethren Churches of North America* (August 7-11, 1987), 70.
91. John E. Toews, Valerie Rempel, and Katie F. Wiebe, eds., *Your Daughters Shall Prophesy: Women in Ministry in the Church* (Hillsboro: Kindred Press, 1992).
92. Wiebe, *Bless Me Too, My Father*, 221. See Katie Funk Wiebe, "After 30 Years, It's Time for a Change," Viewpoint, *The Christian Leader*, December 31, 1991, 9.
93. Wiebe, *Border Crossing*, 174.
94. *Ibid.*, 179.
95. Katie Funk Wiebe, *Life After Fifty: A Positive Look at Aging in the Faith Community* (Newton: Faith and Life, 1993); Wiebe, *Border Crossing*; Katie Funk Wiebe, *Prayers of an Omega: Facing the Transitions of Aging* (Scottdale: Herald Press, 1994); Katie Funk Wiebe, *Older Adults and Faith: Their Spiritual Development and Relationship to the Church* (Newton: Faith and Life, 1995); and Katie Funk Wiebe, *Bridging the Generations* (Scottdale: Herald Press, 2001).
96. Wiebe, *You Never Gave Me a Name*, 240-241.
97. John Bender, "Health Association Recognizes Katie Funk Wiebe," Mennonite Health Association News Release, March 9, 1993.
98. Jean Janzen, "From the Editors," *Direction* 24, no. 2 (Fall 1995): 4.
99. Katie Funk Wiebe email to Doug Heidebrecht, July 9, 2009.
100. "20 for the 20th Century," *The Mennonite*, February 22, 2000, 4-7.
101. *Ibid.*, 7.
102. Wiebe, *You Never Gave Me a Name*, 225.

The Barriers Are Not Real

Katie Funk Wiebe

A few years ago I found an old notebook full of clippings and letters in the bottom of the trunk my parents had given me when I finished high school. On a loose sheet I had written:

> I'm afraid to be a writer…I'm afraid to put things down on paper, things I might regret later on, as if these things really applied to me. But then they do; these things that I want to write are my thoughts, the things that keep me going, the things that slow me up and make me wish I was anywhere but where I am. I shouldn't be afraid. I know I shouldn't. No one will ever see these things I write. No one will ever know they belonged to a girl who once had hopes and dreams, but who never saw them realized.

Were those my words? Had this pressure to write started when I was still absorbed in boyfriends and suntans? I thought it had been the product of my middle years. But there it was, "I want to write…"

Now, several decades later, I am writing. Did anyone in my family have the same longing? Most of my Mennonite ancestors had been farmers for centuries, poking the ground, making green things grow. I never knew my grandfather, the one who was a miller in South Russia. But my father? Did he ever want to describe with words how it felt to clomp around his father's mill in the village of Rosenthal on wooden *Schlorren*? Or to spend Christmas in a train boxcar as a homesick medic in the Russian army? Or to begin life anew in Canada with a red-haired wife, two toddlers, and twenty-five cents in his Russian-style trousers? Why do I know these stories as if I had seen pictures of them?

My paternal grandmother kept a genealogy. My forefathers were members of the group of Mennonites who settled, in peaceful villages in the Ukraine in Russia about 1786 upon the invitation of Empress Catherine the Great. They came from Prussia. And before that from Germany and Holland. Always they were wandering, wandering, in search of freedom to worship God according to the way they knew Him in the Bible.

Catherine the Great had promised the Mennonites religious privileges in exchange for becoming colonists in her country. She needed them. They had the reputation of being honest, hard-working thrifty farmers. They settled and developed the rich steppes of the Ukraine. At various periods when this precious freedom seemed threatened, they left Russia for other lands, many going to America about 1874. My German-speaking parents, who could also speak the language of their adopted country, left with hundreds of others for Canada in 1923 after the Russian revolution. It seemed certain Catherine's *Privilegium* would no longer be honored by the new regime: pacifist Mennonite young men would have to take up arms against their convictions.

So I was born in Canada. I was a New Canadian, my parents told me. I lived in a community that worked hard at the melting pot theory, yet I emerged as a member of an ethnic minority dominated by strong religious beliefs and barnacled by the cultural accretions of four hundred years of wandering from country to country.

But why, if I had received all my education in this new land of promise, did writing remain a silent wish, an undreamt dream, an unarticulated hope—something I could not personally envision happening to me?

Mennonites have always been an agrarian people. Only in the last decades have they moved in large numbers into business and the professions. On the traditional farm work was divided between husband and wife out of necessity. The men worked outside on the land. They were leaders in church and community, especially in Russia, where the government allowed them to regulate life in their own villages. Mennonites were a strongly patriarchal society, like many other Protestant groups developing out of the Reformation.

During the Mennonite interlude in Russia, women worked inside the home baking the *Zwiebach* and *Roggebrot* in the wall oven fired with straw. Sometimes a woman worked in the fields beside her men. The framework for the picture of the ideal Mennonite woman in Russia and in the early years in America was one most Mennonites found comfortable: silence, modesty, and obedience.

I can still see my father walking to church, about three steps ahead of Mother, and Mother calling to him to wait. She wanted the American way, but he had no patience with it. Men moved ahead, took the risks, and women followed. Men walked into church in one door and women in the other. They sat in separate pews. The Bruderschaft (council) was represented only by men. This was the way it had always been done, and it seemed right and normal.

Women's place was not with the men. Not with thinking. Not with dreaming, declaring, determining sin, disciplining, deciding to stay or leave Russia. Her place was at home kneading the soft dough with strong hands; stripping milk from soft, warm udders; serving *Prips* and *Schinkefleisch* to tired men when they came home from the fields; cradling children into quietness; loving deeply without open words; praying silently with head covered. The poetry of living had no real attachment to the poetry of words, as Mennonites in their search for a pure God-life isolated themselves from society through language, customs, and geography.

But I knew very little of this when I left high school. I had inherited a strong mixture of values—the freedom entrusted to one of the top students in a school where sex was never considered a deterrent to any vocational goal. Yet, at the same time, I had unconsciously absorbed the values of my Mennonite home in other areas. Mother, while she ladled sour cream gravy and fried Russian pancakes drew the family together through her open acceptance of her role as keeper of the home. Father, who had attended school for about three years, knew the hardships of earning a living without an education. He encouraged economic survival for me and my sisters. He had eaten gophers and crows during the famine in Russia of 1921-22. This new land would provide better for his family. But his limited understanding of what lay ahead in the New World for his daughters could not push me over the hurdles into writing.

I left our heterogeneous community for the outside world and plummeted into the Mennonite world instead. I became an active member of the Mennonite Brethren youth group in the city where I began work after high school. In school I had been accustomed to speaking out and arguing with the boys, so I aired my ideas freely in the youth group. As a result I was elected president. Within a matter of weeks though, some of my "young brethren" asked me to resign at the request of pastor and church council. Something about my shape and bodily functions made it impossible for them to allow me to be president. I agreed. Perhaps my interest in leadership had only been a passing fancy.

About 1956 I typed myself a little note again:

> Today I have been doing a lot of thinking about writing. Is it worthwhile considering seriously or shall I just forget the thing altogether? The whole problem seems to resolve itself around the matter of having something to write about. If I have nothing to say, there is no use in writing that bit of nothing down on paper.

By this time I was married, had three children, and a preacher-husband who was studying religious journalism, and I had penetrated the Mennonite world even more deeply. But I did set up a desk in the corner and began to write. My first writing attempts led to helping my husband in his work of editing a small periodical for youth workers in the church. I enjoyed the creative activity, and, as my husband became busy in other activities, the editing became mostly my effort. When he suggested to the administrative committee that because I was doing most of the work and apparently quite successfully, I be appointed editor, their reaction was negative. In the Mennonite world, women did not teach nor usurp authority over the men, even in writing. I was crushed.

For a time I fought a battle against two enemies, both of whom should have been my best friends—God and myself. I felt guilty questioning what seemed right and pure: that a woman should find complete fulfillment in her role as wife and mother and never expect God to require anything more of her. She had her sphere of service. Was I trying to wiggle out from under the authority of God's Word by considering a sideline venture? My Mennonite conscience told me I should find sufficient meaning in life as the wife of Rev. Walter Wiebe, without making any specific contribution of my own. Most Mennonite women had done so. My mother had never had any other aspirations. Or had she? The thought dumbfounded me. Had she buried her longings for creative expression deep inside her as she baked pan after pan of *Zwiebach* and *Platz*?

If I fought what seemed to be the voice of God, I fought myself also. The craving inside me to write was part of me, yet I couldn't acknowledge it as mine. The men in the black suits and open Bible said it shouldn't be in me, and I did want to please them.

My perplexity is true for many women, ethnic and non-ethnic, in Protestant groups. It stems from the subtle leeching of her belief in her own power to think, to create, to choose, and to contribute as a person in her own right, especially in the arts, for this is part of the public sphere, which belongs to men by tradition. Women lack the psychic strength to give utterance to areas of life about which they have been trained to be silent. In social groups, I recall my husband drifted to the men's corner and the interesting talk about church and world politics. We women had to content ourselves with hemline lengths, new knitting patterns, canning successes and failures, and how to potty-train a child.

I wanted to write. I wanted to discover through writing the meaning of my life and to let others know how I felt. I needed a mentor, someone to encourage me, to stroke, to guide, to support my dreams and help put them into effect. My role models were loving, generous women who made excellent *Vereniki* and sewed fine stitches in quilts, but understood little of my longing to give myself away on paper. Writing was a frill, a luxury—not important for frugal, practical people. Further, it was unseemly for women to move into any field which might put them into competition with men or where they might judge masculine fields of endeavor.

As I began to write, both fear of success and fear of failure haunted me. Fear sat close to me every time I opened my typewriter. *How do you think you can write with authority?* Mennonite women aren't an authority in any matter except familial concerns. Desperately I wanted the opportunity for insight and comprehension which would make me an authority, but instead I was offered another coffeemaker to attend to.

Any woman wanting to write, coming from a culture which values family life highly, will battle her conscience in other areas. If fear sat on one side, guilt moved in close on the other. *Shouldn't you be baking another batch of cookies for the children?* What will the family say if they get casserole again tonight? Writing can seldom be a first for women, if they are wives and mothers. Mothers don't have a secretary. They don't have a wife. They can be interrupted by children, husband, plumber and paperboy. So they are eased out of writing early, unless they make peace between family concerns and writing.

In "The Red Line," a short story of Rudy Wiebe, a young Mennonite girl on the ship crossing the ocean to her new home, becomes bored with life behind the barrier (a red line on the floor) which separates the immigrants from the first-class passengers. Boldly she crosses the red line into their life.

In a critical review of the story I wrote, "In defiance of her Mennonite-trained conscience she sets out to explore this new world and finds that the barriers are not real—only man-made. She can easily pass each one."

24 | The Voice of a Writer

Though for a while every time I sat down to write, a jury of six solemn men in dark suits with large black thumb-indexed Bibles open to I Timothy watched me work, I slowly realized the barriers before me were not divine interdicts. The barriers were man-made, but they were also in me. I had to be persistent with my own creativity. With the help of editors, friends, and children, I moved toward the barrier once again. Bumping, blundering, blustering, battering, bluffing and blessing, I crossed over.

Katie Funk Wiebe, "The Barriers Are Not Real," in *The Ethnic American Woman: Problems, Protests, Lifestyle, ed. Edith Blicksilver* (Dubuque: Kendall/Hunt, 1978), 178-181.

Chapter 2

Katie in Context

Valerie G. Rempel

Writing, like life itself, always emerges in a context. There is the give and take of events that shape a writer's perspective, the particularities of geography, education, family background and the political and cultural environment in which the writer lives and works. Whether subtle or profound, these form the well from which the writer draws ink.

Katie Funk Wiebe grew up with one foot in the Canadian Mennonite experience and the other in the ethnic mosaic of Blaine Lake, Saskatchewan. She married and began a family in the years immediately following World War II. And she came of age, intellectually, in the heady mix of the mid-twentieth century when voices were calling for new ways of thinking about a host of issues, not the least of which were the roles of women and men in society and the church.

Katie's identity as a woman and as a writer was formed in relationship to these events. When she set up her typewriter and began to arrange *her* words on the page rather than order the words of others, she drew on these experiences to develop what would become one of the most influential Mennonite voices of the twentieth century.[1]

A Different Kind of Mennonite

Katie has written extensively about her childhood in Blaine Lake.[2] Though small by today's standards of urban life, it was remarkably diverse. Immigrants from many parts of the world settled the area bringing with them a variety of folkways and religious traditions. As the daughter of a storekeeper, Katie interacted not only with children but the adults of the community as she helped her father stock shelves and wait on customers. She learned the town secrets and the value of honesty and hard work.

Her father had a mixed relationship with the Mennonite Brethren church that dated back to his youth. In Russia, he had been disciplined by the church for taking communion with members of an Alliance church whose practice was sprinkling rather than baptism by immersion.[3] He was excommunicated when he married Katie's mother in the Alliance church. Though they would later join the Mennonite Brethren congregation that met across the river from Blaine Lake, he was never entirely at home there.[4] He found it easier to fellowship across denominational lines than many Mennonites of his day. While he and Katie's mother worshiped with a local Russian Baptist congregation, their children spent winters in the United Church of Canada, a decision that helped accelerate their acculturation into Canadian life. They quickly became comfortable with "Canadian clothes, haircuts, activities, and customs."[5] They often found themselves uncomfortable in more conservative Mennonite Brethren settings.

What Katie could not have fully understood as a child was the level of concern many Mennonites had about acculturation into Canadian life. Church discipline was often focused on the need to be separate, even if that included separation from other Christians. The World Wars tested that commitment, pushing congregations and leaders to wrestle with questions of identity, language, and national loyalty. Mennonite Brethren reactions were complicated by the patterns of migration. The first wave of immigrants came in the 1870s, settling primarily in the United States. Relatively few chose to settle in Canada but those who did usually settled in agricultural communities. Their communities remained small and isolated.[6] When the next wave of immigrants began arriving in the 1920s, relationships between the two groups were quickly strained. The earlier *Kanadier* were often viewed as too simple and unsophisticated by the new arrivals. The new immigrants, the *Russländer*, were far more willing to settle in cities, to work in business and industry, and to take advantage of the educational opportunities offered by their new homeland. Not surprisingly, the *Russländer* quickly moved to the center of Mennonite Brethren church life in ways that sometimes left the *Kanadier* feeling as if they were losing their church.

As a conference of churches, Mennonite Brethren struggled to keep the two groups together. Leaders worried about how to best handle the transition from German to English so that it might not be the "ruin of all that is good."[7] Resources were quickly channeled toward the establishment of Bible schools and religious publications in order to train a new generation of church leaders who could help preserve a distinct theological (and cultural) identity.

Katie's parents were among the *Russländer* and in Katie's accounts of her childhood it is easy to see the family's openness to the new culture. Katie tells of reading poetry with her mother, recalls the movie projector and large radio her father brought home and used, and her experience of enrolling in the cooking classes offered by the local agricultural office.[8] These were symbols of a new life, a new Canadian life. When Katie briefly changed her name to Kay, she was identifying herself more as a Canadian than as a Mennonite. She writes that she left Blaine Lake in 1942 with "Kay" inscribed on a gold bracelet, a name that "matched the image I had developed for myself—sleek pageboy haircut, camel-hair coat with fox-fur collar, bright red lipstick when Dad wasn't watching, high heels and boyfriends."[9] "Katie" was Mennonite; "Kay" was "English."

Eventually, Katie's Mennonite identity would re-emerge when she chose to attend the Mennonite Brethren Bible College (MBBC) in Winnipeg, Manitoba, and then to marry a young *Kanadier* who was preparing for ministry within the denomination. Marriage to Walter Wiebe effectively moved her across the river from Blaine Lake and into the kind of Mennonite community she had really only visited as a child. Her blonde pageboy and "blue beanie with the soaring feather" were replaced by braids carefully wrapped around her head as Katie sought to fit into a conservative, mostly German-speaking community.[10] It would truly become her own many years later when, as an adult, she embraced Mennonite Brethren theology by choice.[11] Though she has not always found the fit comfortable (she has compared it to a coat that "prickles") she has chosen to stay.[12]

Still, she remains a different kind of Mennonite, one who reflects her family's uneasiness with artificial boundaries. A

1991 column in *The Christian Leader* speaks of the second class status of many in the church, "minorities, the disabled, the elderly, the people who never can find a church-going wardrobe that matches and is whole and who speak evangelical jargon with difficulty."[13] She pushed the church to re-imagine first class status as not for those "zealous for the traditions of the brethren," but for those willing to commit to dialogue and honest reflection "about the place of Christian faith in modern life," and who were willing to be "servants who listen to and enter into the pain of those who feel rejected."[14]

Katie's openness to other ways of living and thinking has been a hallmark of her work. Throughout her career her impulse has been to examine and then test new ideas and even new ways of living. She has regularly pushed against theological and cultural boundaries that seem illogical or ill-conceived.

This instinctive openness to the world has been nurtured by her love of books. As a child, she fed her hunger for reading material at a traveling library that was sponsored by a grain company. The choice was limited and so she read almost indiscriminately—from Elsie Dinsmore to the classics of literature.[15] Much later, she would work her way through theologians and devotional writers, historians and cultural analysts, and an array of secular and religious novelists. These would further shape her thinking and then her writing.

But first, she had to grow up.

Becoming a Woman

Like many young women of her day, Katie moved quickly from girlhood to marriage. She was young and unprepared. She met her future husband when she was twenty-one, married him at age twenty-two and bore her first child some ten months later. The decision to marry Walter had not been entirely easy. Walter worried that she loved her office work more than him; Katie's boss, J.B. Toews, fretted over the loss of his secretary and sought ways to keep her; and Katie was uneasy about marrying a man "without a vocation or fixed income."[16] Still, what else was there? As Katie writes, "like most other young women of my generation…I had never seen myself beyond the age of nineteen or twenty. Then a knight in shining armor (over his slacks and sports shirt, of course) would gallop down the gravel road past our wooden fence, sweep me off my size 8 1/2 spectator pumps, and ride off with me into the golden sunset...What was going to happen after twenty-one didn't really matter."[17]

Of course, what happened after twenty-one did matter. Finding herself unprepared for marriage and motherhood, Katie went to work in the way she knew best—she began to read.

In her most recent memoir, Katie lists authors and titles that began to nurture her soul during the early years of her marriage as she struggled to sort out what it meant to be a wife and mother at home and in the church.[18] Reading those books today makes it clear, however, that more than her soul was being nurtured. Her ideas were being formed, ideas that would be worked out in length when she began a serious writing career. The sense of herself as an individual, the need to develop her own interests and identity, the push to take her place as an adult in a complex world and to handle aging with grace are all themes she has explored at length in her autobiographical works.[19] These ideas are clearly present in the authors she names as some of her conversational partners during this period.

British physician Eustace Chesser published *Love Without Fear* in 1947, the same year Katie married Walter.[20] A marriage manual, Chesser's book was "far less conservative" than other similar works and focused on "what might be called the psychology of love and marriage."[21] He defined a "free marriage" as "the coming together of two persons, emotionally mature, to share their lives and to unite for mutual enrichment in the closest possible manner open to human beings. There must be a basis of equality, and each must contribute towards the common weal. Thus, the ideal marriage is an ideal community in miniature."[22] Here was a balance to the language of submission in marriage offered by leading Mennonite Brethren pastors and teachers. At MBBC, Katie had been taught that a preacher's wife was there "to bear the burdens, to cook and darn for her husband. A missionary's wife did not go to the mission field to be a missionary but to be her husband's caretaker."[23] Katie found it odd that so many women were studying at the College if they were only to be caretakers, but strove to fit the image of Christian womanhood that was being offered. Walter took note, writing that he had observed a "tender tone of submission" in her letters and attributing it to what was being taught at the College. "I wonder just from what angle or method of approach has been used," he dared to ask.[24]

Years later, Katie would write eloquently of the need to understand herself as a full person rather than "a mere feminine appendage to male endeavors." Failure to do so "was to deny myself the way God had made me, and therefore in some sense was to deny God himself."[25] She seems to have recognized herself in Chesser's admonition that a good marriage required maturity on the part of both partners. "Sensible people face up to the fresh problem, with all its unpleasantness and difficulty. They adopt a constructive attitude. They weigh advantages and disadvantages in an adult manner."[26] Here were words that helped push her toward adulthood, moving her beyond the youthful romanticism of their courtship. They also suggest an approach to problem-solving that would stand her in good stead when she found herself facing an uncertain future as the head of a young family.

Katie's reflections on her early days of marriage often reveal her own sense of herself as young and partially unformed. The comment of a Slavic neighbor woman cut her to the core. Seeing Walter bring a breakfast tray to Katie, struggling with morning sickness during her first pregnancy, elicited the amused observation that "in America women are like children."[27] Katie was hurt but seems to have recognized some element of truth. "Her statement humiliated me but also pushed me," Katie wrote. "I had chosen marriage. I would make it through this time of misery."[28]

While the immediate misery was a bad bout of morning sickness, the more encompassing misery was boredom and the growing realization that she did not fit easily into the cultural and theological restrictiveness of the tightly knit Mennonite community she was living in. Used to a challenging job and the stimulation of college life, Katie longed for books and conversation. A new community and the birth of her first child were only temporary fixes.

By 1952, when Walter accepted the editorship of *The Youth Worker*, Katie was more than ready to assist in the work. She quickly became the editor in everything but name. The work met a need in her life, she has written, providing her the creative outlet she longed for.[29] Later, when Katie began to read Marion Hilliard's work, she must have recognized a kindred spirit. Hilliard wrote:

> Women must work, all women must work. There is no place in our society for an indolent woman. But as a doctor I am certain that it is good health therapy to work and that women must work for values other than purely economic. Women need to work to gain confidence. Women need to work in order to know achievement. Women need to work to escape loneliness. Women need to work to avoid feeling like demihumans, half woman and half sloth.[30]

Finally, here was someone who offered the kind of encouragement Katie needed.

Hilliard, a medical doctor with an obstetrics and gynecology practice in Toronto, had begun writing a column for the popular Canadian woman's magazine, *Chatelaine*.[31] Her first book was published in 1957 and was followed by a second book, published posthumously, in 1958. Katie counts them as important for shaping her thinking about women. It is easy to see why. Hilliard identified the "current mood of nameless longing...sweeping modern housewives" as a problem of too many "so-called blessings" that left women with little demand on their time or intellect.[32]

> This is the deep dark water under the thin ice of a married woman's composure. Frittering away the scant years before she marries, she learns no trade. She comes to marriage with little ability beyond a certain flair for looking attractive in strong sunlight. On this house of cards she builds her self-assurance.[33]

Hilliard knew this was not enough. Katie did, as well. She had a trade of course, but she was living in a world that expected her to subsume it under her husband's name. Only a few years later Katie would write about the "grave sin of this age" that was "sacrificing our girls to this image of emptiness." "To rescue them from it the church will have to stress the biblical image of women, an image which shows that women have many roles in life to fill…not only wife, and mother, but also citizen, friend, neighbor, worker in the labor force, creator of the beautiful or cultural, and also servant in the church."[34]

Hilliard, like Chesser, wrote for a secular audience but another early favorite, Argye M. Briggs, was a Baptist novelist. Her book, *Christ and Modern Woman*, lodged women's need for identity in a relationship to Christ. Briggs wrote that the modern woman "must begin with the realization that, as a Christian, her place in the scheme of things is not accidental; it is her own because God has assigned it to her. She must know that she has a work to do, that no one else can do that work, and that if she does not do it, He may see fit to let it remain undone."[35]

Briggs' influence can be seen in Katie's first book, *Alone: A Search for Joy*. In it, Katie writes that prior to Walter's death she had already begun formulating "certain tenants of my own faith and life philosophy, writing them down, revising them as new light came to me." She had discovered that she "couldn't hide behind the merits of a father, a husband, or children, much as I would like to at times…I had learned that I was responsible to God for all my life, all of it."[36]

Katie could not have known how important these formational years would be or how often she would return to the ideas that were taking root during this period. She was about to face a significant crisis in the death of her husband, and she would need courage to forge a teaching and writing career while raising a family. Hilliard's advice, read in light of Katie's life, seems remarkable prescient. She strongly encouraged women to step out, to keep trying new things, to be brave in the face of advancing years.

> I don't mean to give the impression that fear can be conquered at one gulp, forever. It

never can. Everyone who is sensitive to life is afraid. The danger in fear is that it can make itself at home in our minds and sit there, breeding nightmares, doubts, terror, pain and suspicion. It must be met whenever it occurs and beaten, if only for the moment.[37]

Katie could not have known how much she would need these words in the years ahead.

Coming of Age

"I had never really found out who Katie was until I was well into my forties."[38] The words leap off the page and a little arithmetic suggests a time period—the late 1960s when Katie was well into the first years of widowhood juggling a teaching position, her studies, and the column she was writing for *The Christian Leader*.

Katie may have been coming to know herself but she was living in a world that seemed far less certain of its identity. The years immediately following World War II were years of rapid prosperity and growth. Church attendance and membership boomed, fueled in part by the rapid rise in birth rates following the end of the war. Robert Ellwood has called it "a fine time to go to church;" Gallup polls put average Sunday attendance in the U.S. as high as forty-seven percent.[39]

The 1950s celebrated the nuclear family, built the suburbs, and encouraged young families to buy the consumer goods being turned out by retooled factories. Gender roles were clear—men went to work and women stayed home. It was not completely true of course; many women continued to work after the war, but the economic prosperity of those years meant that middle class women could be expected to stay home and pour their energies into their husbands and their children. The ravages of the Great Depression were not forgotten and many business and political leaders worried that returning soldiers would not find the jobs they needed. Women were expected to leave "real" jobs to men. When they ventured out they were encouraged to simply volunteer in church and community organizations. Youth culture was becoming an identifiable movement while the popular new television sets portrayed happy families whose domestic ills were minor enough to be easily resolved in a half-hour show. As historian Nancy Cott has observed, the period between 1940 and 1960 was "a unique twenty-year era of domesticity."[40]

There were, of course, tensions underneath the surface. The McCarthy trials gave witness to new political rigidities while the ongoing Cold War left thoughtful people uneasy about the future. Some evangelical leaders chaffed under the old restrictions of the fundamentalist movement and sought to reinstate their reputations, working hard to establish new institutions such as Fuller Seminary and the popular *Christianity Today* magazine. A year before the U.S. Supreme Court ruled school segregation unconstitutional, Billy Graham daringly instructed ushers to let African Americans attending his crusade in Chattanooga, Tennessee, sit wherever they wanted.[41]

And then the 1960s arrived. The Civil Rights Movement, which had been simmering under the surface of American life, came to a boil in the heated summer of 1963. The Viet Nam war began to be a regular feature of the evening news where images of soldiers fighting a new kind of war vied with film from antiwar protests. John F. Kennedy and Martin Luther King, Jr. were both assassinated. It was the era of Woodstock, the Jesus Movement and Women's Lib. Katie, the columnist, had a great deal to write about.

The book that seems to have launched Katie into the 1960s was Betty Friedan's *The Feminine Mystique*, first published in 1963. Like Hilliard before her, Friedan spoke movingly about the restlessness of a generation of women who found themselves isolated in the new suburban landscapes. Hilliard had written of the "nameless longing" of contemporary housewives; Friedan famously called it "the problem that has no name." Katie described it as

> a sense of dissatisfaction, that yearning of modern women, who though established in a house with a husband and children, are still asking, "Is this all? Is life just housekeeping and chauffeuring and shopping? Can my

> life be lived only through the lives of a husband or children? Why don't women have the same unlimited opportunities as men for personal fulfillment through their individual talents?"[42]

Here, finally, was an author who seems to have identified Katie's own restless desire for something more.

Friedan's book quickly became a bestseller and helped pave the way for the establishment of the National Organization of Women (NOW) in 1966. It was an organization "comparable to the NAACP, ready to fight through the media, the courts, and the Congress for the same rights for women that the NAACP sought for blacks."[43] NOW actively supported the Equal Rights Amendment (ERA) and pushed President Johnson for women's inclusion in his affirmative action policies.[44]

This growing activism on the part of American women during the 1960s actually represented a second wave of feminist activity. The first wave grew out of the nineteenth century abolitionist movement and eventually brought about passage of the 19th Amendment to the U.S. constitution, guaranteeing women the right to vote. The second wave arose in the context of the civil rights struggle and called for an end to the discrimination women faced in social and economic life. For a time, it "showed every sign of becoming a true mass movement" as it revitalized efforts to pass the ERA and called for equality both at home and in the workplace.[45]

Not surprisingly, many Christians found the language of "women's rights" not only offensive but biblically unsound. Katie astutely observed, however, that the church could not "simply disregard this revolution, much as it would like to, because an upheaval in society's view of women will affect home and religious life."[46] She encouraged the church to consider the possibility of liberation for both men and women from stereotypes that limited participation in the life of the church. Slowly, Mennonite Brethren began to wrestle with the question of women's roles in church and society. Katie became both a symbol of the movement and a thoughtful translator of its ideas.

In 1973 Katie attended the Evangelical Women's Perspective on Women's Role and Status, held in Denver, Colorado. It was the same year that a group calling themselves the Evangelicals for Social Action (ESA) met in Chicago to discuss Christian faith and its relationship to issues of social and economic justice. Only a few women attended the meeting but a year later a seminar at the second ESA gathering gave rise to the Evangelical Women's Caucus and "biblical" feminism was born.[47]

The move to define a "biblical" feminism arose among women who considered themselves a part of the evangelical movement. More mainstream Christians had already begun to incorporate feminist ideas in their theological writings but tended to ground them in liberation theology. By contrast, evangelical women who formed the Caucus supported the authority of Scripture and sought to use "contemporary hermeneutics to reinterpret traditional understandings of women's roles in the church and home."[48] It was an important distinction that, for a time, allowed them to draw support from organizations such as ESA and to publish in popular evangelical periodicals such as *Eternity* and *Christianity Today*. Katie, writing about women's issues in *The Christian Leader*, was in good company and when she was able to attend the 1975 Caucus meeting in Washington, D.C., found it to be "a huge women's red tent of Old Testament times, a place of rest and spiritual mentoring for women."[49]

As the Evangelical Women's Caucus matured it increasingly moved toward the progressive wing of the evangelical community. During the hotly contested debates over the inerrancy of Scripture that preoccupied much of the 1970s, they attempted to articulate a "modified view" of inerrancy and infallibility.[50] But members of the Caucus were actually torn in their view of Scripture and the organization eventually split. The more conservative movement formed Christians for Biblical Equality in the late 1980s. Katie supported the new organization and worked unsuccessfully to establish a branch in Wichita, Kansas during the early 1990s.[51]

Organizations such as ESA and the Evangelical Women's Caucus helped spur various gatherings of Mennonite women and men to explore women's roles in church and society from a consciously Anabaptist perspective. Katie was frequent participant, and as always, she read. Dr. V. Mary Stewart joined her shelf of "favorites," and helped Katie think through the question of roles for both men and women.[52] In her own writing, Katie began to suggest that questions of submission were rightly directed toward submission to God. All else was idolatry. As a regular columnist for *The Christian Leader*, Katie was in a unique position to translate the issues and concerns of these organizations to a lay audience. Their influence can be seen in articles as varied as "Honky Hermeneutics" and "The Proof-Text Game," to "Freedom for All."[53] Repeatedly, Katie made the case that Scripture should never be used as a kind of bat to club people into submission but rather it should be used to liberate all who felt oppressed by the expectation that they stay silent in the affairs of the Christian community. Her writing generated a great deal of passionate response and even "hate" mail. It also opened up new avenues for service as Katie quickly became perceived as the "voice" for the women's movement within the Mennonite Brethren church. There was a cost, of course. Katie writes:

> What was the cost? The whole gamut of women being gently ridiculed for joining a secular fad to being harshly accused of heresy for having fallen prey to the sin of interpreting the Bible to fit personal preferences and cultural demands. The cost included losing the esteem of one's peers and of jeopardizing local political and spiritual influence.[54]

Still, Katie kept writing.

Writing Her Life

Katie, an inveterate reader, once admitted that when she could not "find the exact book I need I write it, for writing pushes one into being."[55] It is a curious statement suggesting that for Katie, the act of writing gives form and shape to her life.

If it is true that writing her life has given it form, it seems also true that the experiences of her life have directed its content and meaning. The girl who grew up with a love of books and openness to new ideas, became the trail-blazing columnist who dared to explore with her readers issues as diverse as abortion and aging. The young woman who struggled to find her place as a wife and mother became the single adult who carved out a successful career as a teacher and writer. And the mature woman who weathered the cultural shifts of the mid-twentieth century became the articulate spokesperson for a generation of women who wanted to actively participate in all the ministries of the church.

We should be very glad Katie kept writing.

• • •

Endnotes

1. In 2000 Wiebe was named one of the most influential Mennonites of the twentieth century by the editors of *The Mennonite*. See "20 for the 20th Century," *The Mennonite*, February 22, 2000, 4-7.
2. See Katie Funk Wiebe, *The Storekeeper's Daughter: A Memoir* (Scottdale: Herald Press, 1994). The Alliance was another group of evangelical Mennonites.
3. *Ibid.*, 104.
4. *Ibid.*, 105.
5. *Ibid.*, 170.
6. Abe Dueck, "Coming to North America: the Immigrants of the 1920s-1940s," in *For Everything a Season: Mennonite Brethren in North America, 1874-2002, an Informal History*, eds. Paul Toews and Kevin Enns-Rempel (Winnipeg: Kindred Productions, 2002), 32.
7. B.B. Janz, quoted in Gerald C. Ediger, "Canadian Mennonite Brethren and Language Transition," in *Bridging Troubled Waters: The Mennonite Brethren at Mid-Twentieth Century*, ed. Paul Toews (Winnipeg: Kindred Productions, 1995), 247.
8. Wiebe, *The Storekeeper's Daughter*, 20, 121, 162.
9. Katie Funk Wiebe, *You Never Gave Me a Name: One Mennonite Woman's Story* (Telford: DreamSeeker Books), 12.
10. Ibid., 60.
11. Katie Funk Wiebe, ""If You're a Mennonite," Women and the Church, *The Christian Leader*, November 10, 1964, 21.
12. *Ibid.*
13. Katie Funk Wiebe, "Who is a First-class Mennonite Brethren?" Viewpoint, *The Christian Leader*, April 9, 1991, 14.
14. *Ibid.*
15. Katie Funk Wiebe, "A Pilgrimage in Books," *Christian Living*, April 1962, 19.
16. Wiebe, *You Never Gave Me a Name*, 51-53.

17. Katie Funk Wiebe, *Bless Me Too, My Father* (Scottdale: Herald Press, 1988), 28-29.
18. Wiebe, See *You Never Gave Me a Name*, 96.
19. See especially *Bless Me Too, My Father* and *You Never Gave Me a Name*.
20. The book was first published in a two-volume set in England in 1940, and then published in hardback and paperback versions by American publishing houses in 1947. See M.E. Melody and Linda M. Peterson *Teaching America About Sex: Marriage Guides and Sex Manuals from the Late Victorians to Dr. Ruth* (New York: New York Univ. Press, 1999), 125.
21. *Ibid.*, 126.
22. Eustace Chesser, *Love Without Fear: How to Achieve Sex Happiness in Marriage* (New York: Signet, 1947), 13.
23. Wiebe, *You Never Gave Me a Name*, 55.
24. *Ibid.*, 53.
25. Katie Funk Wiebe, *Alone: A Search for Joy* (Winnipeg: Kindred Press, 1987), 4.
26. Chesser, *Love Without Fear*, 39.
27. Wiebe, *You Never Gave Me a Name*, 59.
28. *Ibid.*
29. *Ibid.*, 7.
30. Marion Hilliard, *A Woman Doctor Looks at Love and Life* (Garden City: Doubleday & Co., 1957), 104.
31. *Ibid.*, 11.
32. *Ibid.*, 103
33. *Ibid.*, 105.
34. Katie Funk Wiebe, "The Image is Wrong," Women and the Church, *The Christian Leader*, March 1, 1966, 21.
35. Argye M. Briggs, *Christ and Modern Woman* (Grand Rapids: Wm. B. Eerdmans, 1958), 33.
36. Wiebe, *Alone: A Search for Joy*, 4.
37. *Ibid.*, 131.
38. Wiebe, *You Never Gave Me a Name*, 216.
39. Robert S. Ellwood, *The Fifties Spiritual Marketplace: American Religion in a Decade of Conflict* (New Brunswick: Rutgers University Press, 1997), 1.
40. Nancy Cott, *No Small Courage: A History of Women in the United States* (New York: Oxford University Press, 2000), 492.
41. *Ruth and Billy Graham: What Grace Provides* at http://www.unctv.orgruthandbillygraham/timelinetext.html, accessed February 8, 2010.
42. Katie Funk Wiebe, "A Problem Without a Name," Women and the Church, *The Christian Leader*, April 13, 1965, 25.
43. Cott, *No Small Courage* , 548.
44. *Ibid.*
45. Ellen Willis, "Radical Feminism and Feminist Radicalism," in *The 60s Without Apology*, ed. Sohnya Sayres, et al. (Minneapolis: University of Minnesota Press, 1984), 91-92.
46. Katie Funk Wiebe, "Liberation—For Men and Women." Viewpoint, *The Christian Leader*, November 3, 1970, 19.
47. Pamela Cochran, *Evangelical Feminism: A History* (New York: New York University Press, 2005), 2.

48. *Ibid.*, 22-23.
49. Wiebe, *You Never Gave Me a Name*, 201.
50. *Ibid.*, 70-71.
51. *Ibid.*, 209.
52. *Ibid.*, 215.
53. See Katie Funk Wiebe, "Honky Hermeneutics." Viewpoint, *The Christian Leader*, September 28, 1976, 19; Katie Funk Wiebe, "The Proof-text Game." Viewpoint, *The Christian Leader*, October 23, 1979, 17; Katie Funk Wiebe, "Freedom for All," Viewpoint, *The Christian Leader*, February 18, 1975, 19.
54. Wiebe, *You Never Gave Me a Name*, 223.
55. Wiebe, *Bless Me Too, My Father*, 12.

A Problem Without a Name

Katie Funk Wiebe

The best seller, *The Feminine Mystique,* by Betty Friedan, is a book which has either confused, or disturbed or aroused scores of American women. Her weighty tome (384 pages) deals with the problem which has no name, which women are afraid to face squarely, and which men do not think is real. She calls it the "Feminine Mystique."

This is her term for that sense of dissatisfaction, that yearning of modern women, who though established in a house with a husband and children, are still asking, "Is this all? Is life just housecleaning and chauffeuring and shopping? Can my life only be lived through the lives of a husband or children? Why don't women have the same unlimited opportunities as men for personal fulfillment through their individual talents?"

Betty Friedan has tried to hold a thermometer to the inner life of modern woman, to explain the reasons for this gnawing hunger she claims to have which food cannot satisfy, and to prescribe a remedy.

Some people lay the blame for the root of this unrest on the increased educational opportunities for women or on their supposedly increasing loss of femininity due to heavy competition with men in all fields, or even on the very heavy demands of domesticity which our standards of living thrust upon housewives.

Betty Friedan, however, points out that from her research she concludes that society has combined forces within the past 15 to 20 years to keep women from growing to their full human capacity. Modern mass media have created an image of woman as young, almost childlike, passive, gaily content in a world of sex, babies, kitchen and house with never a deep thought to her credit. Women have accepted this image as their goal and have lived down to it with the result that they are now experiencing a dearth in their lives. They are hungry for something which will challenge their whole being.

She points out that women have been brainwashed of any purpose for life unrelated to sex—that there is anything worthwhile in life beyond sexual relationships. One of the results of this brainwashing is the hundreds of high school girls who rush to the marriage altar and only too soon find themselves in the housewife trap, void of any inner resources. As these girl-brides mature they begin to discover they have capacities, abilities which have been left trailing in the dust.

The author gives as the key to the problem not less education for women, but more education. She insists that educators must see to it that women make a lifetime commitment to a field of thought ("career" being a dirty word). To avert the mass burial of women she feels there will need to be "drastic reshaping of the cultural image of femininity that will permit women to reach maturity, identity, completeness of self, without conflict with sexual fulfillment." By this she means finding a life plan, fitting in the love and children and home that have defined women's role in the past.

Although the book has not been written from a Christian standpoint, and while it is impossible to generalize and say that the problem she describes *is* every woman's problem, it does make clear that there is a problem.

The simple fact is that women are traveling the road of transition in today's society. Their role which was so clear and well-defined a century ago, circumscribed by home and church, is now a much wider one. Women are being pushed by social pressures many cannot cope with. Increased education and work opportunities have sharpened the hunger to be able to "stretch and stretch in every aspect, never holding themselves down just to stay feminine." It is a problem which needs the careful guidance of church leaders instead of a gentle patting into submissiveness back to the kitchen and the sewing circle.

If the world as Betty Friedan points out has asked too little of women in this century, has the church also been guilty of the same error? If modem society has an image of women as gay, kittenish, and empty, has the church also fallen short by building an image for women which includes mostly silence and submission—a silence which *is* empty, and a submission which too often has been a negation of individuality? Has the church appealed to women to use their total resources in a creative ministry for Christ within biblical concepts, making full use of the talents of leadership, intellect, love, concern, and special skills which they have?

Perhaps we need to thank Betty Friedan for pointing out to us, even if it makes us feel uncomfortable, that as women we are underselling ourselves. Above all, we need to come to a new understanding of the biblical teaching of the role of women in a changing society, a society which needs more women like Priscilla, Lydia, Mary and Dorcas.

Katie Funk Wiebe, "A Problem Without a Name," Women and the Church, *The Christian Leader*, April 13, 1965, 25.

A Pilgrimage in Books

Katie Funk Wiebe

I moved from a child's world of dreams into the world of books when I learned to spell out the words of "Little Half Chick," a story in our first grade reader. I have never left it.

Up through the primary grades and into high school I explored this wonderful world. But the world of books to which I had access in those days had narrow limits. The three short shelves of well-worn volumes at school were finished all too soon. A row of musty, tattered books in a forgotten corner of an old church, I read in the few short weeks of one summer holiday shortly after they were discovered. The only constant supply of books was the Traveling Library of one of the grain companies, which had a turnover of several dozen books every month. Not all the books in the solid wooden case were suitable for young girls, but they were books and without them I could not live.

They took me on long adventures with the Overland Girls, made me weep copious tears with Elsie Dinsmore at the harsh treatment of her father, and laugh through the homely experiences of L. M. Alcott's *Little Women*. I felt a soul agony with the bleeding French masses of Victor Hugo's *Les Miserables*. Books were the warp and woof of my life in those days. Through them I learned that life is more than eating and drinking, and buying and selling. Life was more than that, but what was it more?

By a strange set of circumstances I found myself living in an older folks' convalescent home shortly after I left home to work in the city. I, a young lady of nearly 20, just entering adult life, was a paying guest in a home where most of the other inmates had already lost their firm grasp on life.

Perhaps it was living so close to the waning edge of life that caused me to do some serious thinking that summer.

One Saturday morning I walked into the large, sunny reading room hoping there would be someone there to help me while away the time. It was empty. With nothing better to do I rummaged through some untidy shelves of books and papers. There I found it—the book that was to change my life. It wasn't a very exciting-looking book. A quick glance at its contents revealed no interesting conversation sprinkled here and there. I did notice it was a religious book, and I usually found it wise not to read seriously of the life of discipleship. It might implicate my life. But any book to read was better than no book.

It turned out to be a volume of daily devotional readings, and so, much in the same manner as I had often sought a penny fortune in a slot machine, I turned to September 1, to read what was written for this day. The words of Scripture leaped from the page to arrest me: "You shall be holy, for I am holy" (I Peter 1:16, RSV). The introductory paragraph began, "Continually restate to yourself what the purpose of your life is. The destined end of man is not happiness nor health, but holiness." These were the intensely right words for me. Here was the answer to my problem. I had lacked purpose to my life and this book which I held in my hand was telling me what the purpose of life was. I read eagerly to the end of the page.

That day a weak, faltering faith received strengthening, and aimless feet were put on course. A life without ambition was given a goal. A rebellious spirit yielded to a Master.

Much as I would have liked to have kept the book for myself—it had no owner's name on the cover—my new concept of the life of a Christian forbade my keeping the book. I made a copy of the reading which had so impressed me and returned it to the shelves in the common room. Perhaps some weary pilgrim, nearing the end of life's journey, found strength and comfort from the reading of that book. I did not want to rob him of it.

Shortly after this experience I left this convalescent home for a more suitable boarding place. I had neglected to take down the name of the book and sorrowed over my loss.

Several years later a close friend presented *My Utmost for His Highest*, by Oswald Chambers, to my husband and me as a wedding gift. When within a few weeks I came upon the familiar selection for September 1, I recognized immediately the book I thought was lost to me. I rejoiced as at the return of a long-lost friend. For many years now I have read in it with great inspiration and help.

Katie Funk Wiebe, "A Pilgrimage in Books," *Christian Living*, April 1962, 19.

Chapter 3

What Would Mother Do?

Joanna Wiebe

The auctioneer nodded as I held up my bid card. The quilt was mine.

A sunburst of three-inch multi-colored vintage-fabric parallelograms, I owned a new quilt, hand-pieced by the women of the Julesburg Mennonite Church. My elation over my winning bid was shared by my sister Susan as we sat on the aluminum bleachers in a fair barn at the Hamilton County Fairgrounds in Aurora, Nebraska. We had met at this Mennonite Central Committee auction on an April Saturday to share our love of quilts and to do some homework. Susan had agreed to help me think about what to write about our mother.

"People want to know that she was as great a mother as she is a great woman in her public life," Susan said.

I didn't immediately respond, as I paused to witness an especially fine king-sized quilt raise almost $5,000 for the Mennonite Central Committee.

"Hmmm," I said, hunting for a pen to take notes on the back of my bid card. "Of course she was a great mother. Just look at her children!"

Susan listened patiently while I mused on the excellence of Katie's children. James is a technological innovator and businessman. Christine, who died in 2000, was a nurse and writer. Susan is a physician practicing General Internal Medicine. I am a writer and software designer. We have nurtured seven children, and so far, two grandchildren. We have followed our mother's example of ethical behavior, and positive, energetic involvement in our families and the world.

"By measure of her children, I'll agree she was a great mother," Susan said, breaking into my monologue. "But she did not nurture us in a way that was typical of a Mennonite mother of the 1950s and 60s."

> **EXPLORING**
>
> I find my mother's old Dutch oven.
> Heavy, black, spherical—
> I imagine it looked like this
> when father gave it to her 40 years ago.
> Now as I study that black hole in my kitchen,
> I feel conditions must be right
> to slip through this density of memories
> to their time, or at the very least,
> by some chance tilting,
> to snatch compressed messages
> from that dark space before my birth.
>
> *Christine Wiebe - January 1989*

The main thing that was different was that she wrote. I first became aware of this unusual behavior in the mid-1950s, when we were living in the white frame parsonage in Hepburn, Saskatchewan. Slipped in among all the other things Mommy did in a week, sometimes she put pieces of soft yellow foolscap into a typewriter, and rapidly tapped her fingers on the black keys. At other times, she tailored clothes for her three girls and herself (I will always be thankful for that beautiful blue dress with the black velvet trim and sparkly buttons). She ironed our clothes, including our father's starched shirts (he almost always dressed up). She gardened and canned. She baked light, delicious bread in a wood- and coal-fired stove. Visiting church dignitaries and missionaries would roll up their sleeves and tuck their ties into their white shirt-fronts before giving themselves to her chicken soup, sucking every bit of meat off the bones, slurping the homemade noodles. My mother helped me struggle through my math homework and engineered wild Easter egg hunts. She tuned into *Saturday Afternoon at the Opera* on CBC radio, while we slid around on old woolen socks to polish the hardwood floors. We were proud to hear how she had once won a prize for her handwriting, a medal for being smart, a scholarship to study physics. For a treat, Mother would open her cedar chest and let us look at a watercolor she had painted, her wedding dress, photos of herself as a confident, beautiful young woman. She played the piano. She sang popular songs like "The Happy Wanderer," and recited Wordsworth, Keats, Shelley, and other romantic poets: "I wandered lonely as a cloud that floats on high o'er vales and hills. When all at once I saw a crowd, A host, of golden daffodils..." Oh, I loved my mother. And she loved us. She was always available for questions and confidences. Except—when she was typing at her small desk under the stairs, by a window looking north over the prairie. When she was writing.

My entire memory of my father, Walter William Wiebe, is of a man intensely focused on educating himself to take a role as a religious journalist in the church. I had a feeling that our family was special because our father was preparing to step into this greatness. There was a dark side to this focus on his education. I experienced a chronic and growing family tension around money. I was desolated by his absences when he attended summer school, conferences and church meetings. But I was excited when he said that we were going to move to a place with lots of books, because by the fifth grade, I had read every book in the Hepburn, Saskatchewan public school library, and could finish in one day the two books doled out by the traveling bookmobile.

• • •

> **LETTING GO**
>
> This is how it should be:
> Christmas vacation, and I am six;
> Daddy and I are driving outside the city
> to a great hill with untouched snow.
> Sun warms the car.
>
> I climb up the tracks Daddy makes
> hearing the crunch each time the first time.
> We stand at the top, just Daddy and I, breathing,
> and the sparrows laugh.
> "I'm afraid," I say.
>
> But then we're sailing
> and I'm safe on a narrow strip of wood
> clinging to his broad back,
> a solid thing in a swaying world,
> and I'm laughing and wishing
>
> we could fall like this forever
> into the sun sparkles and whipping wind
> and the white snowdrift
> waiting to embrace us
> over and over and over.
>
> *Christine Wiebe - September 19, 1985*

So we left the parsonage and moved to Virgil, Ontario. Our family expanded to include a friendly little brother, James. My father was very ill for a time. The six of us then moved to Kitchener, Ontario. After studying at Waterloo University and finishing his bachelor's degree, our father moved to Syracuse University in New York state to pursue a master's degree in religious journalism. The rest of the family stayed behind in our little rented brick house on Bournemouth Street. Mother continued to write articles and joined the Christian Writers Club. Additionally, she worked in temporary secretarial jobs. Because she was gone from home more now, she began teaching us the formulas for making basic foods. Under her direction, we continued to keep ourselves and our home clean and attractive. However, she did not teach us that any of the domestic arts were an end in themselves. For example, we did not quilt, or even consider quilting. Free time was for reading and writing. My sisters and I took the bus downtown to the public library and came home with stacks of exciting, delighting books. There were never any restrictions on what we could read. While my father was dubious whether I would gain anything from reading Boris Pasternak's *Dr. Zhivago*, he let me plow through it. I took a touch-typing course.

 I begged for my own room, which Mother created by partitioning a corner of the basement with blankets. Here, a narrow beam of sunlight illuminated a thirteen-year-old girl perched before a small desk, like her mother's, with a typewriter and a stack of soft yellow paper. I wrote long stories about First Nations' princesses and lost children; poems featuring dead birds and bare trees. Late at night, when I was supposed to be sleeping, I read most of Dickens under the blankets with a flashlight.

 I am looking at a photo of our family, taken in late 1961 in our Kitchener living room. Although we are living on next to nothing, we're impeccably dressed and coiffed. Mommy holds the baby. Daddy is home from Syracuse for Christmas. We face the photographer solemnly. We are about to change our lives, yet again. For our father is almost done with his education and is about to take the important church position our whole lives have been about, for as long as I can remember.

       • • •

One year later, in mid-November, 1962, we are living in a drafty rented house in Hillsboro, Kansas. Our father is gone. Months after having achieved his life's dream, he finally died of that mysterious thing that was growing inside him for many years. Mrs. Walter Wiebe is now a single parent of four children: I am fourteen, Susan is eleven, Christine is seven, and James is three, just days away from his fourth birthday.

> **CHILDREN UNDER FOURTEEN NOT ADMITTED**
>
> I climb down the stairs in Daddy's shoes.
> Mother gives me some death words.
> They don't fit anyway.
> Take them back, Mother.
>
> Relatives fly to our house like black birds.
> Circled in uncle's lap I watch.
> "What did that mean?"
> "We're talking German, Chrissie."
>
> At the back of the church a long box
> With a person in it.
> I want to look inside
> But I'm too far away.
>
> Under the fir trees: a stone and a hole.
> Is it really six feet?
> Why is the lid shut?
> May I move closer, Mother?
>
> *Christine Wiebe*

We all missed—unspeakably—the vibrant presence of Walter William Wiebe. We didn't feel like a family any more. But in our bereavement and isolation, our family could not turn to counselors, psychotherapists, or school psychologists, for there weren't any. We heard Christian platitudes about death. We hid our bewilderment and pain from Hillsboro, our church, and often, even from each other. I cried alone.

But we had our Mother.

The week after my father's funeral, mommy sat down at her typewriter to write dozens of well-composed letters to caregivers, community members, friends, and family. She vividly told the story of our father's illness and death, carefully explained our circumstances, warmly thanked people for their cards and letters, their gifts and visits. Even in such a time, she had the presence of mind to make carbon copies of her letters, which, years later, she shared with us. The letters reveal a person struggling with great challenges, extremely short of money, yet gracious, determined and scarcely revealing the immense feeling of being overwhelmed. In the letters, as she enters a period of mighty grief for the loss of her beloved husband, she nonetheless appears to be organized, thinking logically, communicating expressively, and in touch with some inner vision of how our lives could be re-ordered to become more efficient and sensible.

These are some of the talents Katie used—at last—to create a settled, coherent home for her family. I was greatly relieved when she said our moving-around days were over and that we would stay in Kansas. She went to work full-time. Within two years, we were living in our own modern ranch-style home with a yard, a garage, and large trees. I graduated from Hillsboro High School, and studied two years at Tabor College while living at home. During those five years, I also was participant, support system, and witness of my mother's approach to single parenting. I had not previously known a single parent, so I had no expectations. I took it for granted that she was only doing what any mother would do if left with four children. Now I see how exceptional she was.

One of her challenges was that as a fatherless family of three girls and a toddler boy, few knew how to relate to us. Our mother felt like "an incomplete social unit." I saw that we were not invited to visit at my friends' homes, the homes that had both a mother and a father.

Being urban Canadians, we did not fit into the local culture. The Low German Mennonite Brethren town of Hillsboro, Kansas was all at once more lowbrow, more rural, and worldlier than the Russian-German Mennonite culture we had known in Kitchener, although these Kansas Mennonites had come to America several generations earlier. I walked into school wearing dresses which had been sewn by Mother, with love and skill. But these girls in Hillsboro wore store-bought skirts and sweaters, nylon stockings and high heels, jewelry and makeup. They teased their hair into bouffant beehives. I'd never had a date. Some of the girls here made out with boys; a few were going steady. Our family didn't even have a television set and never listened to popular radio. But some of my new classmates got up early to do farm chores before coming to school, singing along to Loretta Lynn and Patsy Cline on KFDI, and the Beach Boys, the Crystals, the Shirelles, and the Chiffons on KEYN. They talked about what they had seen last night on The Beverly Hillbillies, Candid Camera, and The Ed Sullivan Show. Nobody had heard of any of the poets Mother had brought into my life. In the Kitchener Memorial Auditorium, I had been part of the Mennonite World Conference and a Billy Graham revival, as well as in the audience for the Vienna Boys Choir from Austria. Here in Hillsboro, I was invited to football games, pajama parties, and hay rides.

Because we were different, our family became emotionally interdependent. We turned to our mother for our support, encouragement, affirmation, and friendship, and Mommy leaned on us too; to the point where we became very sensitive to one another's moods. Mommy sometimes felt despondent and said she was afraid she couldn't do a good job with us as a single parent. She said to us, "You have no father but our Father in Heaven." We read an article by Billy Graham which seemed to suggest that it is very harmful for children to grow up with only one parent. Some in the community suggested strongly that Mother should remarry as soon as possible. I coldly told her, "I don't mind at all if you would ever want to get married again, but the day you did, I would leave home." Then I felt bad for what I had said and tried hard to make her happy, to behave well, to obey her. I memorized jokes to tell at the dinner table.

What Would Mother Do? | 53

I slowly awoke from the fog of my grief to realize with horror that I was now living in a dull town of 2400 persons stuck out in the middle of what seemed like nowhere. As I finished high school, I often felt alone and angry, and almost always unchallenged by my schoolwork. I invented an imaginary friend and became obsessed with boys. I did my chores sluggishly, carelessly. I thought about killing myself. I blamed myself for my father's death and fantasized about bringing him back to life. I ate too much. I experienced stress-induced coronary artery spasms and chest pains. I began to butt heads with Mother over abstract topics such as existentialism and pantheism, and wrestled with her over the power issues that emerged because I would take care of the children until five-thirty, when she arrived home from work to take back the reins of authority. Once I complained that Jamie was getting spoiled because she wouldn't discipline him, and I didn't know how, and she cried. She told me she longed to spend more time with him. Sometimes, Mother and I would clash against each other so hard that we would both wind up in tears. Memories of these times are now still painful to us, especially James, who was so young when he witnessed them.

The other children were more even-keeled. However, Mother had other kinds of challenges with them. For example, Susan had two operations for a ruptured appendix, and Christine became ill with what was initially diagnosed as *rheumatoid arthritis*, then *systemic lupus erythematosus*.

Where should Mother turn for support? What could she offer her children as a way to work with their emotions? What would strengthen our family? Hillsboro offered us narrow resources. The Parkview Mennonite Brethren Church was an emotionally inhibited environment, although some of the members loved us well, particularly John B. and Susie Jost, and P.B. and Hannah Willems. Mother received the gift of their friendship, which gave us all a happy, safe haven where we could relax and be ourselves. However, despite the generous warmth of some of its members, the church in general was not a place to go for emotional healing. It also was not a place to wonder out loud about existentialism and pantheism.

To nurture us emotionally and spiritually, Mother re-invigorated our practice of family worship. Every evening after supper, we prayed together and read Bible verses and sections from books like Oswald Chambers' *My Utmost for His Highest*: "Never reserve anything. Pour out the best you have, and always be poor. Never be diplomatic and careful about the treasure that God gives. This is poverty triumphant!"

Mother also encouraged us to write and journal, practices Christine and I adopted. By example, she taught us how to see the stories in our lives, and tell them.

She thought carefully about the new cultural influences we were encountering, and used her discrimination to make choices about where we would engage and where we would hold firm to our family's values. She filled in the low-cut bodice of my party dress with frothy chiffon trim. She bought a television set and we watched Star Trek. We attended football games, and afterwards, talked about how silly we felt when we joined the others in cheering out loud.

Mother was often not at home, and when she was, she kept office hours. This was because she was gaining her bachelor's, and then master's degrees, while working full time. James remembers how special he felt when she put aside the papers she was grading to give him time and attention. He remembers that his Mom was very protective of her youngest child.

"She had a very good mommy radar—she knew where the dragons lay," he told me recently.

· · ·

> **TELL NO MAN**
>
> My mother seduced me with quiet
> while she carried me in utero.
>
> I can see her now reading,
> a book propped on her silently swelling stomach,
> as they shifted in the wind.
> And then long evenings without speech,
> her knitting needles clicking a counterpoint to the clock,
> while Daddy wrote under the gooseneck lamp.
> They drank a pot of tea before bedtime,
> and while Daddy explained
> Mother said, "Yes," and "uh huh." She listened.
>
> In the night I woke her with my kicks
> Because I could not shout in the womb
> that I had fallen in love
> with the silence between her breaths.
> Because she was wise she waited
> until I had learned not to speak.
>
> *Christine Wiebe*

After working for awhile at the same publishing company that had enlisted my father to move to Kansas, Mother became a professor of English at Tabor College. And she continued to write. In the 1950s, her first published articles had been bylined, "Mrs. Walter Wiebe." Now her work was under her own name: Katie Wiebe. She discussed with us children whether she should include her maiden name in her byline, too. So we witnessed her evolution into the writer, "Katie Funk Wiebe."

Recently, I found an instructive photo on the website of the Canadian Conference of Mennonite Brethren Churches. This photo depicts a group of women attending a session of the 1966

Canadian Conference of Mennonite Brethren Churches. The women sit apart from the men in the back rows of the Eden Christian College gymnasium.

The year that photo was taken, women around the world were taking a front seat. Indira Gandhi was elected India's third prime minister. Betty Friedan founded the National Organization for Women (NOW), Roberta Bignay became the first woman to run in the Boston Marathon, Janis Joplin gave her first live concert, and Billie Jean King won her first Wimbeldon singles title. And in Kansas, Katie Funk Wiebe was saying, "women can no longer look for safe, easy roles away from the social and intellectual ferment of our age." In May of 1966, she attended the Maranatha Christian Writers Conference at Winona Lake, Indiana and returned ready to do something with her writing.

Our family dinners became excited explorations of Big Ideas. Daring questions were asked. For months, Betty Friedan's *The Feminine Mystique* took the place of honor on top of our bookshelf in the dining room! Mother wrote many articles relating to the liberation of women, inviting understanding by being open about her own experience as a widow on the fringes of Hillsboro, Kansas society. At the same time that she advocated for changing roles for women in the church, she valued the Mennonite Brethren church and looked for ways to broaden her role there. This created both an inner and outer tension, which played out in our family dynamics.

It was a big day for the family when *our Mother!!!* was invited to speak in the "Big" Hillsboro Mennonite Brethren church (although not from the pulpit). In the church, we four sat near the front, eagerly watching her. She looked poised and beautiful in her dark blue dress, and spoke fluently, with many interesting stories, making complete sense, in words that anyone could understand. I was proud to be her daughter. Then we went home to eat Sunday dinner, a pot roast with potatoes, carrots and onions, which had been slowly mellowing into tender wonderfulness in the oven as she had been speaking. We were all elated. Mother had preached!

"No, children, it wasn't preaching," she said, "I didn't speak from the pulpit, and that's an important difference."

"I don't see any difference," I said.
She smiled, ruefully.
The phone rang.
We all stopped chewing to listen. She answered buoyantly, but in a minute, her voice lost its confident ring, slowed.
She came back to the table, looking uncomfortable and tense.
She said that the caller—a man in the church—had criticized her sharply for wearing a dress with such a short skirt, just below the knees. She was being provocative, he had said.
"It isn't a thing for a Christian woman to do, sister," he had chided her. "Bad enough that you stand in front of the church and speak. But in such a dress...."
I wanted so much to comfort Mother, help her feel better.
"He's *weird*," I said, using the nastiest word I could think of. "What difference does it make what you wear?"
Susan spoke up. "You made a very good sermon," she said. "I could understand every word. That's the main thing. That guy is crazy."
"That's not kind," said Mother.
"He was not kind to you," said Christine, softly, and got up from her chair to hug her mommy. Jamie joined them as Susan and I sat stiffly in our dining room chairs, not knowing what to say, angrily looking out the window at the road. I closed my eyes and pretended I was little again, on holiday in northern Saskatchewan, Daddy driving our brown Chevy through piney, rocky landscapes painted by a glowing sunset.
"It's alright, children," said Mother. "Let's not let that man make us bitter. Let's eat dinner. Then after dinner, Joanna, will you watch Jamie so I can finish grading those papers? Christine, can you work with Susan on your science homework? Then at ten to three, we'll leave for the play at Tabor College."
Now the quilt auction was almost over. The late afternoon sky was turning yellow-grey; a storm was brewing. I knew I should get on the highway if I was going to beat the weather. Susan admired a quilt purchased by her friend's mother, then turned back to me with a summary of our discussion.
"That's how Mother was," Susan said. "She gave us the knowledge that we can do hard work. She was telling us: 'I can

do things that are unpleasant, difficult, and tedious. I can do things atypical for my social group, even when I am criticized or misunderstood. I can handle the internal conflict between my need for acceptance and my need to be true to my self and what I am called to do. And I can do those hard things for years.'"

In 1967, at the age of 19, I explored the borders of a wider world as I interned at Reba Place Fellowship in Evanston, Illinois. In the fall, I enrolled at the University of Kansas. I had been helping with the younger children for so long that I now felt conflicted about abandoning the family and striking out on my own. James coveted my affection and seeing me when I came home from college was very important to him. Christine clung to me emotionally, and was distressed at some of my new behaviors. She was afraid that I wasn't a Christian any more. She prayed for me and worried about me. Mother drove three hours north to visit me at university, bringing the children, and picnics. She began the practice of writing me a weekly letter, with detailed news, encouragement, support, jokes, and family updates. But despite all that she did, I was temporarily lost to the family and myself. After a year and a half, I dropped out of school and stayed for a few months at the Salvation Army Home for Unwed Mothers in Wichita, until my son Matthew William was born. Just stating those bare facts does not begin to describe the experience.

In 1970, I launched a commune with my boyfriend, on St. Francis Street in Wichita, blocks away from our friends at the Mennonite Voluntary Service house. Christine worried about letting slip any information about my living arrangements to Mother's friends in Hillsboro. "I wouldn't care if my friends knew," Chris wrote. "But if some of the people in the Parkview church knew there would be a big stink. What kind of a church is that? We put on a front as if everything is just fine. We never really communicate about what bothers us most deeply with the people in the church. We never get past the surface."

Mother struggled to understand my actions, an unsteady mixture of individuation, rebellion, and stepping in her feminist footsteps. She had written about how men and women in the church "need each other's support, but not at the expense of one another." I was not patient enough to work through that struggle in the Mennonite Brethren Church, or in any church, for that matter.

In 1971, at the age of 19, Susan moved to Omaha to go to nursing school; she married a year later. Christine's illness was diagnosed as *lupus* and she spent a summer at the National Institutes of Health, then moved into a Tabor College dormitory in September of 1972.

Christine was intrigued by my experiment in communal living. While she was at Tabor she took a trip to explore Christian intentional communities. Mother told Christine that communal living held no appeal for her because she cherished her privacy and independence.

Nonetheless, with James as the only child still at home, Mother often told Christine that she was lonely. She also told Christine that she was feeling the pull to write more, but that she was "not willing to stake her financial security on her writing talent." Christine commented, "I would like her to do what she wants to do." By April of 1976, Katie Funk Wiebe was writing a book about her experiences as a widow.

At the MCC quilt auction, the grey-haired quilt bidders in the paid chairs at the front of the room were getting to their feet, showing off their purchases, finding their families, debating whether to go back to the food building to get one more paper bag of warm, sugar-dusted, raisin-studded *portzelky*. The sky was darkening and a stiff wind was rattling the metal roofs of the fairground buildings.

However, I had one more topic to bring up with Susan before we parted.

"When you were young, did Mother ask you if you would take Jesus into your heart?"

"Yes," she said, "I was around five."

Christine also told me about how Mother had introduced her to Jesus, not just as an idea, but "as a living Person who is interested deeply in me."

"For me," I said, "when I was about six years old, Mother asked me if I would like Jesus to come into my heart. I said yes, not knowing what I was choosing. I remember that she prayed with me, the Saskatchewan prairie wind tossing our hair as we stood in the back yard with our eyes closed and hands folded.

As I grew up, I read the Bible and went to Sunday School, but most importantly, I watched her live, to see how a follower of Jesus did things."

Mother eventually became my guru, modeling the way, as I strained to live with the difficult consequences of my earlier choices. For example, for many years, my every day was tinged with despair that the Kansas legal system would forever keep me from my son, who had been adopted. Then one day, as a new mother of my second son, David Miguel, and living a hard life in a new city, working ten to twelve hours a day, I realized that I had a key to making things work for me. I decided that when in difficult circumstances, I would ask myself, "What would Mother do?" Mothering my sons David and Zachary, working in the corporate world, writing and expressing myself, and at last, after twenty-seven years, meeting and learning to know my son, Bill, this was my mantra: *What would Mother do?*

IN THE BLUE WILLOW PLATE

I have walked miles on narrow paths
to this place in the story where I sit
encircled by the willow's green serenity,
I gaze across the pond at a gazebo
and recognize at last it is the one
in Mother's plate, the one she placed
above the rest, "because it tells a story."
I know now who I am
that messengers are on their way,
the lovers plan their flight
and I need wait for nothing
but the wind to ripple willow wands
and startle words from me
like birds surprised in flight.

Christine Wiebe

What Would Mother Do? | 61

Upon asking this question, I would feel the tears dry on my face, my spine straighten, my brain swing into high gear, my confidence strengthen. Solutions would begin to appear. I would build relationships. Make friends. Think logically. Be gracious. Organize my calendar. Make lists and prioritize. Write letters. Reach out for help. Have faith in positive outcomes. Pray. Persevere. Create a better world.

Some of these gifts came more naturally than others. Along the way, I developed my own strengths, and integrated them with these gifts from Mother.

And she's still ahead of me on the path, my mother. I have gained wisdom by watching how she has managed her aging process. As I approach retirement, I reflect on the style in which she downsized her career, home, and possessions when she still had lots of energy to do it. I learn how to manage loss and change as I see how she responds as one after another dear friend or family member weakens, dies. I see that she grieves and then makes new friends, deepens other connections.

On July 5, 1964, when we were all struggling to learn how to live without Walter William Wiebe, I wrote a prayer in my journal for my Mother:

> Eternal Father of us all, I come unto thee in prayer
>   for my Mother.
> For the rich gifts of life that she has freely bestowed
>   upon me, I give thee now these words of thanks.
> For the measureless gift of physical life itself –
> For patience through long nights of illness –
> For an understanding heart when my feet stumbled
>   in finding the true path –
> For guidance against shipwreck and for freedom in
>   which to grow –
> For these gifts of a wise Mother I give my thanks to
>   thee and to her.
> Grant me patience and understanding when her
>   thoughts are not the same as my thoughts.
> Lead me slowly though it be, into the larger
>   wisdom that she has gained from life.
> Make me a steady support for her, in these years of

maturing hopes.
In the name of Him who said to his earthly parents, 'Did ye not know that I must be about my Father's business?'"

At the age of sixteen, when I wrote this prayer, I had a Mother who was diligent, concerned, questing, wise, organized, gracious, perseverant, driven to express herself in written and spoken word. She still has these qualities, but they don't define her now as they did then. The Mother I have now is also relaxed and celebratory, with a twinkle in her eye and a ready hug.

Katie is now well-known in certain circles, admired, studied. She made a measurable impact on the role of women in the church. Through teaching, writing, and speaking publicly, she has helped people learn how to tell their stories, how to age more gracefully, how to grow spiritually. But these achievements happened out in the world. At home, she is Mother.

To You, My Father

Katie Funk Wiebe

I have written this column often in my mind. When my father dies, I have asked myself, what will I say about this man whose life placed a burden on me, at once both light and heavy? Last week he died.

During recent visits to my parents there was less and less of the kind of stuff scholars now call oral history. But after I returned to Kansas, memories often rushed in how I, the middle child of five, spent many hours as his Saturday helper in the store.

I saw again the man who carried out hundred-pound sacks of flour on his shoulder, who whistled as he moved quickly from task to task, and who was caught up with a love of the ingenious—schemes for perpetual motion and the way the pyramids might have been erected. These images replaced those of the thin, stooped, silent man I had just visited.

Only in recent years when I saw the forest instead of the trees, could I generalize about my father's influence on my life. He admired punctuality, thoroughness and excellence in others. He yearned for harmony in his life, in the church, and in society. Therefore he struggled with problems of disunity, ecclesiastical posturing and war.

He was generous with his money almost to a fault, particularly to people in need. He had never learned to openly show his feelings, so love often took the form of a gift left behind or casually handed over.

I recognize I inherited some of his puzzlements about life: the divisions in the church, the struggle between tradition and change. My file of his longer letters indicates that questions about scriptural interpretation interested him even after retirement.

When I started writing on behalf of the greater use of women's gifts in the church, he cautioned, "If you go against the wind, Katie, you'll get sand and dust in your face." He knew of life's storms, for he had stood in the midst of disrupted patterns of life often.

Only in later years did I think to ask him how he had become a Christian. To my surprise I learned that the turnaround in his life had occurred while he had been a conscientious objector in the army during World War 1. Amid the regular involvement with death, he had become convicted of his sinfulness and need for eternal life.

This action was followed by obeying God's call to become a deacon evangelist. He found he enjoyed public work, but during the depression in Canada he had had to decide between evangelism on the road and taking care of a growing family. He opted to become a lay minister.

Once, as we sat together in my parents' retirement home in Clearbrook, B.C., I asked him to tell me about his favorite sermon. Without hesitation, he recalled most of it, point for point.

As he talked I knew he was back in Rosental, in the Ukraine, in his father's windmill on the hill at the end of the village. He had grown up as a miller's son. Each son in turn had had to learn to sharpen the two-yard wide millstone and to operate the mill as each of us children had had to learn to serve customers and fill shelves.

His text was from John 3:8: "The wind bloweth where it listeth and thou hearest the sound thereof, but canst not tell whence it cometh, and whither it goeth; so is every one that is born of the Spirit."

Because each wind has its own characteristics, a miller in the Ukraine had to know the winds intimately to make them work for him. In British Columbia, Father often sat and watched the wind circle along the valleys, unlike the winds of his youth. But in the prairies, the winds were the same as in Russia.

"I never knew when the West wind would begin, for it starts slowly," he told me. "I would wet my finger and turn it in the air to feel the wind even before I could see branches moving. When it cooled my finger, I knew it was time to prepare the blades of the mill. The wind would be steady, dependable for several days at a time.

"And like this West wind, many people cannot say the exact time of their spiritual birth. Though you can't see the wind, you can feel it. You can see its activity—the branches waving. You can't see the Spirit working in a life, producing the new birth, but you can see the deeds of the Spirit."

He compared the South wind, one which worked well during the day, but then stopped suddenly at nightfall and blew hard from the opposite direction, to Christians who start the Christian life well, but then suddenly change direction to go their own way.

The stormy East wind often blew many directions at once, making it an unsatisfactory wind to harness for the mill. Some people are like this wind—directionless—experiencing confusion as a result.

The North wind, which blew long and strong for weeks, like the fair weather Christian, lost its strength when the warm spring weather arrived. Similarly, prosperity saps the Christian's strength.

Someone said to me today, "You look like him, Katie." I hope that along with his physical characteristics I may have passed along his inquiring attitude and giving spirit to my children.

Katie Funk Wiebe, "To You, My Father," Viewpoint, *The Christian Leader*, May 27, 1986, 13.

66 | The Voice of a Writer

Chapter 4

A Widow's Journey

Darlene Klassen

Exposing the Journey

So many words could describe the season of widowhood: a season of winter, of grief, of darkness, of a fog, of being lost. It is both a private and unique journey, marked differently for each woman, colored by the particular person who has gone and the nature of their relationship; as well as a common journey, inhabited always by some new and alien realities—new isolation, new identity, new horizons, new expectations, and new challenges. It is often a silent journey, a silence that comes not only because of the male voice that disappears, but also from the fear of judgment for choices made. Moving too quickly, moving too slowly, remembering too much, remembering too little; looking for the "right" way to do things and finding that none of the current options fit that description. The "right" way disappeared along with the husband and they wonder if they are locked forever in a second choice, in a "flat" world. This is the way Katie Funk Wiebe describes women left silent with their widowhood: looking outwardly for cues, or looking inwardly—finding little congruence between the two perspectives.[1]

Katie Funk Wiebe gives voice to the widow as she exposes and examines her own widow journey. She has the courage to step out of the shadows, revealing the loss, the shockwaves, and her particular path to another side of life. Her voice invites others into the conversation, whether to question or to affirm, as she processes loss and reflects on the God who was her companion on this journey. In giving voice to her season of grief and naming some of the realities of widowhood, she creates a space for others to speak. And as Katie continues to reflect, to study and to write, she goes beyond creating space. She helps to build a platform for widows to speak, a place for widows to belong. As she struggles with the realities of identity and a name, as she reveals the struggle after the loss, and then marks the end of widowhood, she articulates a path forward.

Gaining Her Own Voice

Katie has written at some length of her early struggles to fit her thoughts and gifts into the constraints of the world around her. Her latest autobiography, *You Never Gave Me a Name*, reflects many of the conflicts she experienced as she sought to discover her role as a female student, as the wife of a pastor in rural Saskatchewan Mennonite Brethren churches, and as an editor and writer.[2]

Her husband Walter struggled with her. When he became the editor of a new publication, *The Youth Worker*, in 1952, she began to work with him. As his work and commitments took up more of his time over the years, Katie became involved in the production and eventually did the bulk of the editing and writing for this periodical. Their futile attempts to attach her own name to her work resulted in their resignation from this position in 1961, as Walter "became uncomfortable" with taking credit for work that belonged to his wife.[3]

Katie names the fall of 1961 as the beginning of the "kindergarten" of her grief. Walter was accepted by New York's Syracuse University in the religious journalism sequence of a master's program. "I didn't know then that that winter would be my kindergarten lesson in living alone. In another year that experience would be mine as a widow."[4] In January of this kindergarten year, Katie began to write the biweekly column "Women and the Church" for *The Christian Leader*. Walter's ongoing illness, and then his death in November of 1962 quickly led her to the brink of widowhood, then past kindergarten into a new and stark reality.

Although we stand on the other side of Katie's many reflections on widowhood, her writings in the 1960s are remarkably silent on the topic. A bit of math and a bit of digging through a massive bibliography reveals a wide span of time between her initiation into widowhood and the reader's invitation to peer into the journey. In the months leading up to and following Walter's death her column refers only occasionally and generally to losses that may have been experienced by readers in their lives, losses that may cause them to question God or to wrestle with him. As she moves through the days and months of raw grief she chooses not to write of this grief, but of ideas and issues, encouraging women to read, to think, and to be informed.

Though she kept her grief out of the printed domain for a season, it began to leak out in carefully guarded words: "*Who can measure the darkness* which comes with the loneliness when a loved one is taken through death, or as you daily watch a child, a wife or husband grow weaker through physical suffering."[5] Ten months later in a still guarded reflection called "When You Sorrow," she addressed the choice to be made between bitterness and acceptance in a time of sorrow.[6] In July of 1964, another publication, *Christian Living*, published her article "To Be a Widow."[7] Then, after almost eight years, a sudden increase:

- "Memo from a Widow," *Mennonite Brethren Herald*;
- "Widowhood is Coming," *Christian Living*;
- "Widowhood Without Worry," *The Messenger*;
- "Women Alone in a Couples World," *Canadian Mennonite Reporter*;
- "Can A Widow Survive in Today's Church?" *Eternity*;
- "Widows and Singles…Pushed Out of Noah's Ark," *The Christian Leader*.[8]

Finally, in 1976, fourteen years after Walter's death, her book, *Alone, A Widow's Search for Joy* was published.[9]

Katie's initiation into grief was also her initiation into a prolific writing career, but, for a time, she kept these domains separate. She developed her voice as a writer before adding to it the shades of widowhood. It is remarkable to read the columns of 1962 and 1963 in *The Christian Leader* together with Katie's later reflections in *Alone*. The latter reveals the journey, the former barely gives the reader a nod as to its existence.

The German poet Rainer Maria Rilke speaks rather violently of exposing an inward journey: "For I still didn't understand fame," he writes, "that public demolition of someone who is in the process of becoming, whose building-site the mob breaks into, knocking down his stones."[10] Perhaps it is easier to restrain the words and the emotions, so that no one can comment on them, or even to try prematurely to help you out of the struggle. As Katie has noted, "writing is a form of giving oneself away, of standing in the public square without clothes."[11]

Ironically, widowhood often provides a platform for women to speak, if they so choose, of this place; revealing the darkness, and the ways that God is able to heal and give strength for the journey. The loss of my own husband resulted in opportunities to speak of my life, telling the story of loss and then healing. Over time, I found that it is more acceptable for a Mennonite Brethren widow to speak publicly from pain and healing than from passion and conviction. It has been surprisingly difficult to find a voice to speak words of conviction and theology from a platform of loss.

In developing a voice that spoke first of issues and ideas, and then of grief, Katie built a foundation for a different voice for the widow. Her uniqueness is found in her ability to write broadly, while at the same time allowing grief to have its way with her—not to abort the process, but to face it honestly, and to continue to deal with it. Later, when the time came to write of widowhood, she was able to revisit her grief, examining it from different angles, and using it to color her thinking in other areas of life.

Choosing A Name

In the shadows of her early struggle to write under her own name rather than that of her husband, the various renditions of Katie's name suggests the inner wrestling with identity. From the first issues of the column "Women and the Church" in *The Christian Leader*, "Mrs. Katie Wiebe" stands in a strong font at the beginning of each column just below the title. Fifteen months after Walter's death, a new name, "Katie Funk Wiebe" appears in a smaller, italicized font at the bottom of the page.[12] In the following issue, the old name, "Mrs. Katie Wiebe," reappears, but in the changed font at the bottom of the page.[13] Finally, on March 17, 1964, "Katie Funk Wiebe" becomes the permanent title of the columnist, located at the bottom of the page.[14]

Twelve years later we are told of the profound inner turmoil that swirled behind the scenes of this small visible shift. A small deletion ("Mrs." disappears), a small addition ("Funk" inserted), and the position and font shift. In *Alone* Katie pulls back the curtain:

> After Walter's death, some persons insisted on calling me Mrs. Walter Wiebe, because Amy Vanderbilt said that's the way a widow should be referred to. Yet I knew, and they knew, that I was no longer Mrs. Walter Wiebe. Walter was dead. How could I be the wife of a dead man? Suddenly I had lost my role. I retained the name, but it was an empty title. I had no concept of my true identity. I was a nothing. A total blah. I couldn't answer the question, Who are you? I never answered "Mrs. Walter Wiebe" as I heard other widows do, for that answer shrieked a lie. He was dead, dead, dead.[15]

The public documentation of the name change only hinted at the inner struggle for identity, but the shift reflected a new direction, a new identity, a determined and single widowed voice.

Revealing the Struggle

Katie's first book, *Alone: A Widow's Search for Joy*, reveals much of the private struggle of life after Walter's death. The second edition, *Alone: A Search for Joy*, published in 1987, gives a different perspective. A profound snapshot of a widow's journey is found in the first few pages as Katie vividly combines the specific details of her loss with the universal realities of widowhood.[16] These five pages chart the path of hope with sorrow, perspective with intimacy, the practical as well as the theological struggle. Katie speaks intensely of the darkness of widowhood: the desolation of the new "widow" name which is not a name, the struggle to forge a new identity and direction, the treatment of widows as less than a person, and the challenge of singly taking on the work that was previously shared by two.[17] Her writing reveals a recurring struggle against bitterness as she gives voice to the ongoing nature of significant pain, and to the effort required to let it change and shape us, not by bitterly struggling against it, but by wrestling to accept it.[18]

While part of the struggle of widowhood is connected to identity, a significant part of the wrestling can be connected to direction. The path through the early years of widowhood becomes a prism that changes the entire trajectory of a life. Sometimes the change is deliberate as the one who is left examines an earlier direction and decides not to continue. Sometimes the trajectory changes because one person's gifts and energies are simply not sufficient to continue to move forward on a path that previously required both partners to be fully engaged in contributing gifts and energies in a single direction. Sometimes the trajectory changes because the partner who is gone held the keys to the dreams and goals and the one who is left behind was the support, the enabler, the enhancer. When the key-holder is gone, the gifts of the helper can be frustrating rather than enabling. Some, when examining their previous goals, choose to lay down the gifts they were using to pursue these goals and look for a new direction; others simply stop seeking.

Katie faced this search for direction as well. With Walter's death, their joint goal of pursuing religious journalism was quickly buried beneath the responsibility of being the only parent left to provide both care and income for her family. She wrote:

> The experience of widowhood probably caused the greatest change in my thinking… As a widow, I had to accept this truth: Faithfulness to God is more important than faithfulness to tradition, or to earlier maps one had made for one's life. I had accepted as my role in life, as the will of God, that I should be a housewife and mother. I never planned to leave that comfy spot. God had put me there. I liked my place. Then I was forced to change my role. Widowhood changed the road signs and sent me down a new path. When my hus-

band died, I thought I was lost again—but God has helped me find my way.[19]

Yet, when two job offers were presented to Katie after Walter's death, one with the Board of Missions, and one with the Publishing House, Katie chose the Publishing House and began to move in a similar direction as before.[20] Her role and the particular path have changed, it is clear that the trajectory has been tested by separation, but it is still pursued. She continued to write for *The Christian Leader* and slowly steered herself toward the newly shaped goals of "becoming a better writer," and clarifying for herself her "role as a woman in the church."[21]

Marking the End

Twenty years after becoming a widow, Katie's identity changed again. *Today's Christian Woman* carries an article in 1982 with the title, "No Longer a Widow," and *Christian Living* (December 1983) carries "Widowhood is Not a Lifelong Sentence."[22] The second edition of *Alone* begins with the words: "Twenty Years Later: NO LONGER A WIDOW."[23]

> God didn't expect you to be a widow the rest of your life. Widowhood was a psychological state and a term used in business and legal documents, but not a lifelong sentence…The question no longer was what did life owe you as a widow with young children, but what did you owe life as a Christ-believer. What had God expected of a wife with a husband and four children in a coupled society? The same as he now expected of a widow with four children in the same society. Discipleship, of course. That never ends with death—or marriage.[24]

These were new, untried words in their time. What other way was there out of widowhood than remarriage? Katie suggested a path and proceeded to map it in "Password: Discipleship, not Widowhood."[25]

What is the significance of this? Why does it stick in my mind as a particularly significant marker? If we examine the time frame set by Katie's names, there is an immediate change in identity during the first months, and then a relatively long term in which she comes to grips with the deeper implications of the loss. She writes that she was thinking about this ending to widowhood for quite a long time before saying it out loud, and that new widows to whom she spoke did not understand how she could leave widowhood behind without remarrying.[26] Katie took twenty years for doing the work of widowhood, engaging in a new life and direction before coming to the conclusion that she was no longer a widow. In doing so, she gives voice to the widow's journey and struggle to acknowledge the joy and the life that was, while moving forward to the new life and joy that God holds out. Katie did it at one level the first time she changed her name. But she added a new level to it the second time, when she substituted the name "disciple" for "widow."

The spring of 2009 marked twenty years since my first husband died. As I read Katie Funk Wiebe's writings, I revisited many of the places of grief blanketed by the layers of life and years. While Katie had to figure out how to leave her widowhood behind, I struggled to carve a place for it. Re-marriage created a new identity, but did not prevent the need for the long-term work of integrating loss and life. This work of grief—the processing of loss, the integration of life with death, the wrestling with an all-powerful God who somehow still allows tragedy and still asks us to pray, the conflict of rediscovering joy when death claimed your first chosen life's partner—all of this requires more than you could ever foresee, even as you walk through the first intense season of pain. That is not to say that the twenty years are years of intense grief. That is not to say that there is not life abundant and joy in these years. But it is to say that it takes longer than the first round of rebuilding to deal with the fault lines and foundational damage of a massive earthquake. And it is the revisiting of the foundations that requires courage, both for those who endure the earthquake as well as those who decide to stick around to help with the rebuilding project.

Katie's courage in the rebuilding, and her courage in deciding what would define her, astounds me. She dared to write under her own name when it was highly controversial to do so. She publicly changed her name fourteen months after Walter dies. She declared, twenty years later, that she was a widow no longer, and she gives a clarion call to the widow to lay aside fear, and take up creativity. For Katie, courage is a secondary companion, and creativity the main goal. It is a fascinating contrast that Katie explores in a chapter of *Alone* titled "Beyond Widowhood":

> A creative widow will also need courage. We can't be creative with fear as our keeper. Fear demands too much. I know. Every time I sit down to write, I struggle with the fear of what people will think about what I've written. Fear knows how to use my typewriter, often better than I do. "Play it safe" he says... When fear is finished, I'm left with a mess of words resembling wallpaper paste.[27]

I believe that creativity was the driving force through Katie's widowhood—before, through and after this season. Creativity, strengthened by courage, motivated her to find new ways to explore and inhabit the unnamed territory beyond widowhood.

> Grief is a process, a work that must be done. To grieve is natural, but to grieve for years and years is not healthful. The time must come to finish grieving and move on. Ahead lies the challenge to learn new skills, sometimes in a vocation, more often in decision-making or new types of services, always to choose between the good and better.[28]

In Conclusion

Katie Funk Wiebe has sometimes reflected on her quiet voice when speaking in public, and the unavoidable reality that she will need a public address system in order to be heard.[29] As I have studied the writings of this "quiet" voice, I find that it has reached me quite clearly, not because she demands a hearing with the volume of her voice, but by gently speaking volumes into the lives of those who care to listen. She has written pervasively, constantly, frequently, and honestly; and in this way, has provided a voice for those who often have no voice. Strange, really, to discover a new companion on a journey you took long ago...to wonder if this companion by her writing and speaking had changed your very path.

• • •

Endnotes

1. Katie Funk Wiebe, *Bless Me Too, My Father* (Scottdale: Herald Press, 1988), 163, 170.
2. Katie Funk Wiebe, *You Never Gave Me a Name: One Mennonite Woman's Story* (Telford: DreamSeeker Books, 2009), 21-105.
3. *Ibid.*, 76-77.
4. Katie Funk Wiebe, *Alone: A Search for Joy* (Winnipeg: Kindred Press, 1987), 28.
5. Katie Funk Wiebe, Women and the Church, *The Christian Leader*, November 12, 1963, 21. (emphasis Klassen's)
6. Katie Funk Wiebe, "When You Sorrow," Women and the Church, *The Christian Leader*, September 15, 1964, 21.
7. Katie Funk Wiebe, "To Be a Widow," *Christian Living*, July 1964, 12-13.
8. Katie Funk Wiebe, "Memo from a Widow," *Mennonite Brethren Herald*, April 17, 1970, 5-7; Katie Funk Wiebe, "Widowhood Is Coming," *Christian Living*, December 1970, 12-15; Katie Funk Wiebe, "Widowhood Without Worry," *The Messenger*, March 1, 1971, 10-12; Katie Funk Wiebe, "Women Alone in a Couples World," *Canadian Mennonite Reporter*, November 1, 1971, 5; Katie Funk Wiebe, "Can A Widow Survive in Today's Church?" *Eternity*, September 1972, 20-21; Katie Funk Wiebe, "Widows and Singles...Pushed Out of Noah's Ark," *The Christian Leader*, November 11, 1975, 2-5.
9. Katie F. Wiebe, *Alone: A Widow's Search for Joy* (Wheaton: Tyndale House, 1976).
10. Stephen Mitchell, ed. and trans., *The Selected Poetry of Rainer Maria Rilke* (New York: Random House, 1982), 101.
11. Wiebe, *You Never Gave Me a Name*, 171.
12. Katie Funk Wiebe, "You Can Be a Literature Evangelist," Women and the Church, *The Christian Leader*, February 18, 1964, 29.
13. Katie Wiebe, review of *Growing with Your Children* by Ray F. Koonce, *The Christian Leader*, March 3, 1964, 21.
14. Katie Funk Wiebe, review of *The Spirit of Holiness* by Everett Lewis Cattell, *The Christian Leader*, March 17, 1964, 21.
15. Wiebe, *Alone* (1987), 53.
16. *Ibid.*, 9-13.

17. Wiebe, *Alone* (1987), 51-68; Katie Funk Wiebe, "Galloping, Naked, in the Night," *DreamSeeker Magazine*, Summer 2002, 16-23; and Wiebe, *Bless Me Too, My Father*, 164-165.
18. Wiebe, "When You Sorrow," 21.
19. Wiebe, *Alone* (1987), 196, 207.
20. Wiebe, *You Never Gave Me a Name*, 104.
21. *Ibid.*, 114.
22. Katie Funk Wiebe, "No Longer a Widow," *Today's Christian Woman*, Summer 1982, 97-99; Katie Funk Wiebe, "Widowhood Is Not a Lifelong Sentence," *Christian Living*, December 1983, 8-10.
23. Emphasis Katie's.
24. Wiebe, *Alone* (1987), 12-13.
25. Wiebe, *Bless Me Too, My Father*, 162-172.
26. Wiebe, *Alone* (1987), 9.
27. *Ibid.*, 190.
28. Wiebe, *Bless Me Too, My Father*, 172.
29. Wiebe, *You Never Gave Me a Name*, 178.

To Be a Widow

Katie Funk Wiebe

"To be a widow is pure humiliation." The speaker was a young widow with three small children. She spoke with sureness and yet without malice.

I stared at her unbelievingly. Surely she meant lonely? I was sure the life of a widow was starkly empty of rich life relationships. Or perhaps she meant difficulty? But humiliating?

I had only begun my novitiate as a widow when I understood what she meant. She had called it humiliation. The Apostle James spoke of it as affliction. To me the death of my husband meant being "ceremoniously" ushered out of the life I had known and enjoyed into a completely new way of living. This new way seemed to be a continual stepping down and away from life ... an emptying and a vast emptiness.

When a person dies, and particularly if that person is a young father or mother, the community and church stands aghast at this monstrous deed which God has permitted. Quickly friends and loved ones rally around the bereaved person and family and bear them up in prayer. Such spiritual support is a great strength in the first weeks of sorrow when many decisions and adjustments must be made.

But life doesn't stand still because someone died. Friends and relatives must return to their own responsibilities. Gradually the strong undergirding of prayer, the visits, the words of comfort, the letters and the cards thin out. One day, usually a dull day when everything has gone wrong, the widow realizes that she is now alone—yet not all alone, for perhaps at no other time in her life will she have such an opportunity to learn to trust God so completely.

What word conveys the image of destitution and loneliness as surely as the word "widow"? "I just hate that word," one woman who had lost her husband said vehemently. "I wish there was another word that could be used."

Any story writer or speaker who wishes to depict a character who has the whole world pitted against him chooses a widow's son. In Biblical times widows knew real affliction. Frequently they were left without material support or even the opportunity to earn a living. Without a spokesman of any kind, they became the prey of ruthless moneylenders. The plight of widows in past centuries and even now in underprivileged countries is very dismal.

Widows in our country are not usually faced with starvation. Their affliction takes on a different pattern.

During the days of our marriage I often looked with pitying eyes upon the single girls and widows in the community. While most married people would not admit it openly, being married does make them feel superior to the single persons.

The Couple Status

In our sex-dominated society the acceptable standard in social life is a couple—not necessarily married. Single girls will admit that our society does not fully accept or make room for the single person, whether that single status is voluntary or not. Such people eventually learn that they must be content to live on the periphery of society, out of the mainstream. "Substitute living," is what one single girl termed it. "I feel like a little girl with her nose pressed flat against the window of a candy shop," explained another. "The church is geared to couples' classes, and mothers' classes, husbands' night at the sewing circle, and family night. Where do I fit in? Nowhere!"

Most widows find the fact that they are now an incomplete social unit one of the first difficult adjustments. Many hearts are big enough to accept her with her children into family gatherings, but there are too few who will help widows or single girls find their place as individuals in church and community. A widow who was part of a social group by reason of her husband's profession and who because of his death was thrust out, speaks of frustrating "withdrawal pains." One day Mrs. Jacqueline Kennedy was the First Lady in the land. The next day she was sitting on the side lines, a spectator to the activities in which she had been a participant. This hurts.

Loneliness is one of the most crushing emotions. The battle of most widows against loneliness is constant. It takes working at, for you have a heart hunger to share your life with someone you love and need and who loves and needs you.

"We're sure lonely now, aren't we?" asked my little son quietly one hot summer evening as he and I sat down to supper. His three sisters had left that afternoon for a lengthy vacation.

Tears stung my eyes. Lonely? Even a little fellow could sense that one mother and one little boy don't make a family, and yet to keep that family feeling is all important or the family which has been broken by death may suffer complete breakdown.

There is nothing which helps so much to the readjustment and rehabilitation of a widowed person as solid, long-range support. We were complete strangers in the community in which my husband died only two months after we had moved there. "Give us your burden," said newfound friends in the community at the time. Some are still bearing it now.

One older man takes time to swing Jamie gleefully over his shoulder and stuff his pockets with candy each time he sees him. His wife is grandmother to the girls and friend to me. An older woman picks up the laundry each week and slips it into the house again beautifully folded and ironed, and says, "I am doing this for my Lord. I will not take money." How do you say thanks to the missionary, now returned to the field, who was willing to fix balky furnaces and lawn mowers if the conversation between his wife and me drifted too much into woman's talk? As others opened their hearts to me, I learned one thing: I have never loved enough.

Privilege of Sharing

Most widows do not miss the security of life with a husband, nor the big exciting moments of life. I find what I miss most is the privilege of sharing life with someone—at the end of a weary day to know again the gentle touch of a dear hand, and to tell someone what the day has been.

One family had for years been burdened by a nagging debt which in spite of careful budgeting could not be paid. When the father in the home was suddenly taken from them, his insurance covered this debt. The day his wife came into the house with the canceled note in her hand the urge to tell him overcame her. "Henry," she shouted, "I've paid it. We don't owe that money any more." She longed to share this high moment with him, but the words fell empty.

Widows, such as Mrs. Kennedy, whose husbands were statesmen, writers, or leaders in their field, have another burden: the question of what their husband might have been able to achieve had God permitted him to live. These are questions without answers.

Young couples contemplating married life plan for years of life together. They leave one factor almost entirely out of their consideration. It is simply this. Barring a motor accident or other act of universal disaster in which both husband and wife are killed instantaneously, the day will come when one will be left alone. Statistics reveal that in most cases it will be the wife. Not only do women have a longer life expectancy than men, but because they frequently marry men older than themselves, the husband usually dies first. So, as one writer put it, the bride who has not made a study of widowhood is in many ways less prepared for life than the one who does not know how to diaper a baby.

Social security, insurance, job opportunities take care of most of the financial needs of the woman left alone. But these are not insurance against the needs of the spirit when faced with the question of the ultimate destiny of the soul of the departed person, or the pressing problems of life without his physical presence.

Part of the answer to the affliction of the widow lies in herself and God. "Now she that is a widow indeed, and desolate, trusteth in God" (I Tim. 5:4). To accept her new role in life without bitterness requires divine grace. Spiritual vision is very myopic when life is lived only in dull shades of gray. Only the knowledge that sovereign God cradles the world in the palm of His hand brings life into proper perspective when the spirit protests, "Life isn't fair."

The other answer to her need lies in the church of Jesus Christ who accepts her as an individual and makes room for her even though society does not. I have often heard ministers complain of the burden of "visiting widows." This was considered unproductive time on their schedule. As long as widows are merely spectators, or faces pressed against a window, this will be true. The dividends will come when such people who have met the sting of death with the truth, "I am the resurrection, and the life," are enabled to turn affliction into victory.

Katie Funk Wiebe, "To Be a Widow," *Christian Living*, July 1964, 12-13.

Chapter 5

Finding Her Voice in the Church

Doug Heidebrecht

Katie Funk Wiebe is almost synonymous with Mennonite women's struggle to find their place within the ministry and leadership of the church. While the diversity of Katie's own interests defies reductionism to a single issue, the question of women's role in the church has been a prominent theme in her writing and speaking for over fifty years.[1] Katie has truly been a pioneer on behalf of women in the church. Katie courageously chose to give voice to her own thoughts and feelings when others were silent or no one seemed to be listening. She challenged the church, not from a position of authority or expertise, but as an ordinary woman whose experience did not fit the constraints of longstanding tradition or widespread practice. Behind her concerns about women in ministry is her concern for the nature of the church itself.

A Woman in the Church

As a young adult, Katie was blissfully naïve about the incongruity between how the church viewed women and her own sense of freedom growing up in a home and community where she "never knowingly met discrimination" because she was a girl.[2] She readily consented to the Saskatoon Mennonite Brethren Church council's request that she relinquish her recent election as president of the youth group without giving much thought as to why a woman would not be allowed to do the Lord's work if she was the best person suited for the task.[3] When Katie enrolled as a student at Mennonite Brethren Bible College, she didn't question why women were directed towards the religious education track, rather than theology, because she also shared the assumption that most women would become housewives whose opportunities for ministry would be limited to Sunday school teaching, women's circles, or child evangelism.[4]

Katie began married life in 1947 willing to give up working outside the home. Her husband, Walter Wiebe, felt strongly that it was a man's responsibility to provide for his family and Katie assumed that she would find complete fulfillment in her idealized conception of marriage. Despite keeping herself busy with the domestic tasks that came with a growing family, Katie encountered an unexpected barrenness:

> As a young married woman I felt part of me was living in a void, but I numbed myself to the emptiness because I thought I shouldn't feel that way. The problem was with me…I was doing what I had always dreamed about—being married. Why should I ask for more? I couldn't grasp that the spirit, the mind, the imagination, the inner life, must also be satisfied or its hunger pains can lead to another kind of death.[5]

These feelings were intensified when Walter was pastoring the Hepburn Mennonite Brethren Church during the late 1950s. It began to dawn on Katie that although they were both members of the same church, Walter seemed to have first-class citizenship while she had second-class citizenship.[6] Despite being actively involved in Sunday school teaching, women's sewing circles, and children's work, Katie sensed "a certain frustration and bitterness creeping in" when the church categorized her "only as a woman (who should ask no questions), not as a person (who happened to be female)."[7]

Katie rightly perceived that the church's concern with keeping women "in their place" contributed to women's own lack of excitement about their spiritual and intellectual growth. She was distressed about the tremendous waste of women's gifts because the church failed to see them as a significant spiritual force.[8] Katie was saddened to see her own women's fellowship essentially reduced to encouraging each other to hang a Scripture verse above the kitchen sink: "I can't do much else for the

Lord, but as I wash dishes I can think nice thoughts."[9] So Katie went to work. In her first published letter to the editor (in *The Canadian Mennonite*) she encouraged the coordination of women's groups in order to create greater awareness of what women were doing in their congregations.[10]

Katie discovered that her desire to write offered an alternative avenue for service outside the traditional expectations for women in the church. In 1952 she began assisting Walter in editing *The Youth Worker*, a publication of the Canadian Mennonite Brethren Youth Committee, which sought to support a growing interest in youth work in churches. However, due to Walter's busy teaching and preaching schedule, Katie took on more of the writing and editing responsibility until she was eventually producing the entire publication under Walter's name.[11] Although the Youth Committee agreed in 1957 to list Katie as a co-editor on the masthead, she remained uncomfortable with the arrangement.[12]

When Katie was asked by Orlando Harms to write a women's column for *The Christian Leader*, she proposed a decided shift from the triteness of the previous column, "Pots, Pans and Patter."[13] Katie had begun to read more daringly about the role of women and was cognizant of the changes taking place regarding the status of women within society. In her 1962 introductory column, now titled "Women and the Church," Katie expressed her desire to address questions about the relevancy of the church and women's organizations in the midst of profound societal change. She intended to explore the "very practical and pressing problems" women faced.[14]

As a young woman, Katie's sense of dissonance regarding the role of women in the church gradually emerged as she began to give voice to her experience. Even though Katie desperately wanted to do what the church taught about women, she could not reconcile what felt like empty rhetoric with her own uneasiness and disappointment.[15] For example, when Katie offered to teach a young mother's class at the Ottawa Street Mennonite Brethren Church, she was turned down because "women were not to teach."[16] The opportunity to write a women's column provided Katie with a unique forum in which to raise questions that were not being addressed publically by anyone else among the Mennonite Brethren.

A Person in the Church

When Walter died in November 1962, Katie experienced a profound loss of identity that forced her to re-examine not only her role as a mother within her family but also as a woman in the church. As Katie put it, "no other event has forced me to change patterns of living and thinking so suddenly, so rapidly, so violently."[17] She soon realized that her long-time interest in the work of the church had been experienced through her husband's position, and that now she found herself completely disconnected from the church's decision-making processes.[18] She found herself resisting the subtle pressure to accept the inactive and subdued role of a widow and began to assess the impact of the church's teaching that women "needed only to be submissive and passive."[19]

Katie was anything but passive and she had acquired a platform few Mennonite women had. In her column, "Women and the Church," Katie began to confront traditional Mennonite Brethren concepts of women's involvement in the church in four specific ways.

First, Katie challenged women to take responsibility for their own spiritual growth, in particular, by reading widely.[20] She encouraged women to take an interest in theology and the "overall message of the Scriptures," as well as to emulate the lives of both biblical and historical women as examples of "disciples of God" who could provide models for today.[21]

Second, Katie promoted the revitalization of women's organizations within the Mennonite Brethren church.[22] While Katie initially offered suggestions intended to promote greater effectiveness, she soon began to question the traditional purpose and goals of women's sewing circles and wondered whether there were new opportunities that could be explored.[23]

Third, Katie shared her observations of Mennonite conventions. She reported on the women's sessions at the 1962 Mennonite World Conference, work that was also carried in *The Canadian Mennonite* for the wider Mennonite community.[24] She warned that if the church did not take seriously the "vast reservoir of untapped potential of its women" and provide greater opportunities for service, then women would "become less and less involved in the church."[25] In 1966 Katie expressed disappointment over the lack of integration of women's involvement in relation to the overall concerns of the church, particularly evident at Mennonite Brethren conventions where men participated as delegates and women attended as visitors or went to separate sessions.[26] Two years later women attended the Canadian Mennonite Brethren 1968 convention as delegates for the first time, visibly raising questions regarding women's involvement in the practice of decision making within the church.[27]

Finally, Katie sought to raise awareness in the church regarding the implications of the changing status of women in North American society. She called on the church to stop responding to women who challenged traditional patterns of ministry with "a gentle patting into submissiveness back to the kitchen and the sewing circle."[28] She urged Mennonite Brethren leaders and pastors to "try to close the gap between what women of the church are capable of doing and what there is available to do."[29]

The *Mennonite Brethren Herald* began publishing her writing in 1966 in its revised women's column, the "Wayside Inn," which gave her an opportunity to engage with Canadian Mennonite Brethren. Here, Katie encountered readers who were more willing to interact as well as other columnists who challenged traditional Mennonite Brethren practices that ignored women and did not treat them as "full fledged church members."[30]

Katie discovered that Betty Friedan, in *The Feminine Mystique* (1963), vocalized the dissatisfaction and yearning that she had been experiencing for years.[31] In concert with Friedan, Katie asked whether the church has also asked too little of women by creating "an image for women which includes mostly silence and submission—a silence which is empty, and a submission which too often has been a negation of individuality?"[32] While Katie recognized the "need to come to a new understanding of the biblical teaching of the role of women in a changing society," her approach to women in the church essentially mirrored Friedan's concern for women's rights and her underlying liberal political philosophy which sought to free women from discrimination in the public sphere and provide equal opportunity within current structures. Yet Katie still struggled at this time (1965) with moving beyond what the church espoused, as demonstrated by her contention that "men and women were never intended to be equal, for it is not in their nature to be equal" since they each have a specific purpose and function to fulfill.[33]

Nevertheless, Katie's developing comprehension of her identity as a person, not just a widow or even a woman, presented her with the challenge "to write as a person to persons, not just as a woman to women."[34] She realized, "if what I had to say was worthwhile, it couldn't be pushed into a corner just for women. I could see women only as an integral part of the whole church, not a secondary group who required separate treatment."[35] This realization prompted her to change the name of her column in *The Christian Leader* to "Viewpoint." It was a deliberate attempt to engage the entire church, from a lay perspective, in the discussion regarding the changes in society affecting women.[36]

Katie's first issue of the new "Viewpoint" column, "Courting Women for Church Work," set the stage for her ongoing reflection on women's involvement in the church and the Mennonite Brethren conference.[37] Katie wondered, "Why does the church usually wait for the dust to settle and for the lines to become well defined before it moves in to inform and guide regarding pertinent social issues?"[38] She continued to call on the church to be alert to the "vast reservoirs of intelligent women who…are sitting idle," including those working at tasks below their potential who do not aspire high enough.[39]

Katie's Challenge

In "Viewpoint," Katie questioned women's lack of participation in Mennonite Brethren conference proceedings. After attending the business sessions of the 1968 convention of the United States Mennonite Brethren Conference, Katie surmised that scheduling women's sessions at the same time as the conference sessions would not happen if women attended conventions as delegates instead of as visitors.[40] Yet the scheduling of separate sessions persisted for several years despite a growing number of women registering as delegates.[41] Even with the ability to participate at conventions, Katie was still concerned that women were being "shut out from the more important decision-making processes of the church or been given only token membership in them."[42] Katie often wondered, "what our women, who represent more than half of the church, would have said… Too rarely does the feminine way of viewing life and church work get a hearing."[43]

By 1970, Katie was calling for a Mennonite Brethren study conference on "the position of women in the church."[44] Despite her appeal, Mennonite Brethren conferences in the United States were only stirred to study the issue after receiving a concerned letter from Waldo Wiebe (no relation) a year and a half later.[45] Katie's challenge, as she continued to highlight the need for a study conference, was "when that time comes, I hope it won't be just men studying women. Can't it be done together?"[46] Katie recognized that the deeply emotional response demonstrated by both men and women towards the women's movement required open discussion within the church.[47] Eventually, in 1974, the Canadian Mennonite Brethren Conference held a study conference where Herbert Brandt addressed the role of women in the home and community, while David Ewert focused on the role of women in the church and conference.[48] Two women, Elfrieda Duerksen and Esther Wiens, were among those who responded to these papers.[49]

Katie's practice of submitting her *Leader* columns to other Mennonite periodicals carried her reflections about women in the church beyond her Mennonite Brethren context. In the *Gospel Herald*, Katie's 1970 column, "Liberation—For Men and Women," was "the first article that made a blatant plea for [Old] Mennonites to consider ideas coming out of the feminist movement."[50] Sometimes the names of her columns were changed to reflect a more pointed agenda, as was the case when her column, "I Am Confused," was reprinted in *The Canadian Mennonite* with the title, "Of the Total Integration of Women."[51]

At other times, what she had written for a broader audience, like her reflection on Mennonite attitudes toward women published in the final issue of *The Canadian Mennonite*, was reprinted for Mennonite Brethren readers.[52] Katie challenged Mennonites to recognize the multiple roles women could fill beyond that of wife and mother and to stop emphasizing women's limitations, thus conditioning women to quit growing as persons. While Katie did not find "a desire among women to gain prominence or position—only to make a contribution, to be considered a worthwhile person," she did acknowledge that women were often their own worst enemy because they missed taking hold of opportunities for spiritual growth.[53] Katie boldly suggested that the "church will need to disentangle biblical teaching from cultural accretions," in order to take the initiative in providing opportunities and support for women's involvement.[54]

Prior to 1970, Katie had resonated with the changes in society promoted by the "women's rights" movement which encouraged broader participation of women beyond their traditional roles. After 1970 Katie began using the language of "Women's Liberation" or "Women's Lib," thus reflecting her engagement with the popular grass-roots liberation movement, which emerged spontaneously in 1967 and overshadowed the earlier women's rights movement. Katie struggled with how to call for positive change regarding women's involvement in the church, and continue to be heard given the negative perception many Christians had of this revolutionary movement.

At first, Katie refused to identify too closely with the feminist movement, although she clearly affirmed its underlying plea to "examine the basic attitudes which exist between men and women."[55] She repeatedly challenged the church to move beyond the question of whether women should keep silent or speak up, and recognize that the real issue was whether women were "treated like persons and not like objects."[56] She understood that this liberation movement carried repercussions for both men and women: "men need to reassure women that they have more to offer than the stereotyped patterns many have been forced into; women to reaffirm that men have a contribution to make other than through power and dominance."[57]

In 1973 Katie acknowledged the discomfort she felt: "occasionally when the subject of women's liberation comes up, I find that people drop me into that category, albeit with an apologetic laugh. I wince a little, for I have never considered myself a feminist...They would find it hard to believe that I am not a feminist, knowing that I openly advocate that women join the human race."[58] Yet, in the very next sentence Katie could also claim to be a feminist, "I consider myself a believer in persons. If I am a feminist, I must testify that Christianity has influenced my feminism."[59] Katie's approach to reconciling this incongruity was to appeal to her own story and the journey of discovery she experienced. Katie did not attribute her convictions regarding women's active participation in the church to the influence of the feminist movement, but to her reading of Scripture and in light of her own journey.[60] Katie's use of autobiographical narrative became a means by which she could invite readers to enter into her experience and, at the same time, develop a greater awareness of their own attitudes and assumptions.

Katie was sometimes critiqued by readers for making "her experience rather than Scripture" the judge of women's place in the church. "Scripture firmly establishes the primacy of man over woman," wrote one couple in a letter to the editor, "It matters not whether a woman is ten times as gifted for leadership; the Divine order is inflexible. It may not be emptied of its absolutism to curry favor with a relativistic generation."[61] Yet Katie challenged the church not to read its prejudices onto the Bible and "then promote that as God's truth."[62] She observed, "We tend to forget that sometimes what we consider to be the absolute truth of the Word of God is but a thin slice of our particular culture thickly frosted by a few Scripture verses."[63] Often Katie felt that "writing about the issue was a monologue, not a discussion."[64]

Repeatedly, Katie served as a link to the conversation that was taking place in the larger North American evangelical world concerning women's roles in the church. She participated in the ground-breaking conference, "Evangelical Perspectives on Women's Role and Status," sponsored by the Conservative Baptist Theological Seminary in Denver in 1973. Katie reported on several of the key presentations that wrestled with whether Scripture taught the inferiority of women and how to relate biblical truth to cultural and social change, and suggested that this kind of "dialogue and study should be continued in Mennonite church circles."[65] Katie also attended the 1975 Evangelical Women's Caucus in Washington, D.C., where she did not find any stereotypical "raging, hostile, aggressive, anti-male" feminists, but rather "very calm, level-headed women" attempting to study the biblical basis for Christian feminism, examine the historical records regarding women's roles, and affirm women's gifts.[66] Here, Katie encountered women who shared common concerns and connected with Mennonite women who did not judge her for her views.[67]

In 1975 Katie was elected as a member-at-large to the Mennonite Central Committee (MCC) Peace Section and, more specifically, was appointed to the Taskforce for Women in the Church and Society, which provided an inter-Mennonite forum to discuss the position of women in the church.[68] She represented Mennonite Brethren on this taskforce until 1977, even though no Mennonite Brethren board was willing to take responsibility for her involvement.[69]

Katie Among the Mennonite Brethren

In February 1974 the Southern District Faith and Life Commission met with a group of five women, including Katie, in an attempt to hear women's perspectives regarding their role in the church.[70] These women were asked, "How can we help women use their gifts more fully without taking leadership away from men?"[71] After this one meeting, the Commission suggested women should continue the conversation among themselves at the next annual Women's Missionary Service convention.[72] There was no indication of any further follow-up by the Commission.

Despite admitting her hesitancy to write about the role of women in the church because she was so often misunderstood, Katie began to boldly set out a vision for the church:

1. The development of an aggressive program of education in churches;
2. A readiness to accept the gifts of all members, both men and women, even if they don't fit the traditional gender roles;
3. An emphasis on strengthening the home;
4. A greater readiness to lend a loving, listening ear to one another;

5. The deliberate decision to include more women in decision-making roles in the church.[73]

Katie lamented the inability of those opposed to the women's movement "to feel so little of the hurt which women in the church express because of their limited role."[74]

Katie was increasingly being viewed as the voice of the women's movement among Mennonite Brethren. In a 1976 paper, "Voices of Liberation," presented at a symposium on women in the church sponsored by the Mennonite Brethren Biblical Seminary in Fresno, Katie challenged the church not to dismiss the Christian feminist movement as unspiritual.[75] She now used "liberation" language to call for a change in attitude towards women that would recognize their own identity and gifts instead of alienating them with rigid gender roles, dehumanizing sexist language, and oppressive structures. Katie argued that change in a broken world would not be found in either authority or autonomy; but only when "the oppressors begin to identify with the oppressed."[76]

In 1978 Katie and David Ewert were both asked to present papers at a MCC sponsored symposium ("Biblical Perspectives on Women in the Church") in Clearbrook, B.C., which was intended to facilitate conversation within the wider Mennonite constituency.[77] In her first paper, Katie highlighted the implications of Jesus' relationship with women, set in contrast to the patriarchal attitudes of first century Judaism, for contemporary churches.[78] In her second paper, Katie identified five ways in which the church should lead regarding changing roles for women:

1. Be ready to discuss and deal with problems arising from change;
2. Avoid formula answers, capsule statements, proof texts, and half truths;
3. Study the Scriptures to discover what the various passages in combination may have to say;
4. Affirm women's gifts by opening the door for them to move into new areas of service;
5. Reject male-oriented language which ignores the experience of women and excludes them.[79]

Katie suggested that "any solutions coming from either men or women, with or without support of Scriptures, which seek to retain power and control for one sex and to deny the privilege to the other...[were] unacceptable."[80]

Several weeks after the MCC symposium, David Ewert wrote to John A. Toews, moderator of the Mennonite Brethren General Conference, expressing his discomfort with Katie's perceived push for women's ordination and suggesting that it was time the Mennonite Brethren General Conference considered addressing the issue of women in the church.[81] Unbeknownst to Katie at the time, she had become the spark that prompted North American Mennonite Brethren to formulate their first official position on women in the church.

Without realizing that the Board of Reference and Counsel had already developed plans to address the issue, Katie wrote the board in 1979 asking whether "the question of women's roles in church structures...[could] become part of the ongoing agenda of some conference board or committee."[82] She wondered if it would "be possible for the board to meet with a representative group of women from various areas to discuss this matter at length."[83] Instead, the board asked David Ewert to prepare a paper, which essentially was a revision of his symposium presentation, for the 1980 Board of Reference and Counsel study conference.[84] Ewert's paper eventually became the basis for the 1981 Mennonite Brethren General Conference resolution that affirmed women's ministry in the church with the exception of ordination to pastoral leadership.[85]

Katie perceived that the lack of recognition for women's involvement in the church was linked in part to the "almost total absence of the contribution of women to the church in recorded church history, particularly Mennonite history," and so she began researching and then telling stories of women in the church.[86]

In 1986, Katie was among several women who were asked to respond to a proposed Mennonite Brethren position paper on women in ministry written by Waldo Hiebert and Edmund Janzen.[87] Katie offered several ideas that could "facilitate more constructive dialogue": appoint congregational task forces, encourage nomination and program committees to include women, develop a conference networking system for women, encourage women to attend seminary, and use inclusive language in public. Katie expressed the hope that "eventually women will be included in the process of deciding what happens to them."[88]

It appears that Katie's suggestion to include women in the conversation was taken to heart by the General Conference Board of Reference and Counsel, which decided to involve women in a task force charged with developing a resolution on women in ministry.[89] In Katie's report to the task force, which met in March 1987, she observed that only three women were functioning in church leadership positions, thus indicating that women still had limited representation within church and conference structures.[90] The resolution proposed by the task force sought to present a positive affirmation of women's gifting and involvement in the church as well as provide more specificity regarding what that could entail.[91] After spirited debate, convention delegates were unable to agree until the Board of Reference and Counsel eliminated the specific references to various ministries, which consequently failed to address the ambiguity of the 1981 resolution or the pressing questions regarding church leadership.[92] At the 1987 convention, Katie Funk Wiebe was also the first woman to speak at a General Conference convention in a main session.[93]

The task force had also proposed the development of study material for Mennonite Brethren congregations. A book was commissioned by the Board of Reference and Counsel in 1987 with John E. Toews, Katie Funk Wiebe, and Valerie Rempel as co-editors.[94] *Your Daughters Shall Prophesy* was eventually published in 1992 and served as a congregational study guide in preparation for the 1993 General Conference convention.[95] In Katie's contribution, "Women in the Mennonite Brethren Church," she observed that in the history of the Mennonite Brethren, "women have never been absent—only officially unrecorded—and that has made them invisible to later generations."[96]

In her reflections on the first time Mennonite women gathered together at a "Women Doing Theology" conference in 1992, Katie recognized, "women bring with them to the task of theologizing fears about speaking out, about breaking the silence, of finding their own voice, of making theological decisions."[97] She observed that contributing to women's struggle was their uncertainty about the role of both personal and shared experience in theologizing, which has often been rejected as invalid.[98] Katie called on women and men to develop new models for doing theology together that would reflect the contributions of both within the hermeneutical community.[99]

Following the failed 1993 Mennonite Brethren General Conference recommendation, which proposed allowing diversity of conviction and practice among congregations regarding their approach to women in church leadership, Katie wrote "A Pastoral Letter to Mennonite Brethren Women."[100] While Katie agonized with younger women who felt cut off, alone, and didn't know what direction their lives should take, she also challenged women to "live with hope for what God will do."[101] Katie concluded,

> I tell myself it is important to keep fighting battles I personally will not win. I do not want the next generation of women to know the pain and indecision my generation has known. I want them to enjoy greater freedom in exploring their gifts and finding opportunities for partnership in ministry in both home and congregation.[102]

Katie's Voice

For more than five decades, Katie Funk Wiebe has expressed the concerns and aspirations of women in the church. Her own thinking about the role of women in the church has changed over time in what Katie admits has been a painful process.[103] Yet this change has been motivated by a vision of the church where the gifts God has given each person, whether male or female, are valued and affirmed. Katie recognized,

> I was the only one who knew of the pain gnawing inside me when I thought of the large reservoir of women whose gifts remained unused simply because they

were women. It didn't seem right. Finally I couldn't silence the voice that told me that to describe women's role only in terms of limitations, rather than opportunities, was wrong. If something is evil and sinful, it should be spoken against.[104]

Katie called on the church to extend to women "the rights, privileges and responsibilities of full membership in the body of Christ so they can make full use of their skills and potential for service. And not be set aside because they are women."[105] At the heart of Katie's critique was her sensitivity for people who were marginalized within the church; not only women but also young people, widows, and older adults.

Katie's challenge of the church's traditional teaching and practice regarding women in the church highlights concerns about the validity of experience in the interpretation of Scripture. While Katie consistently appealed to her own experience and that of women in general, she also questioned why women's experience should be rejected as invalid when men also approach Scripture from a particular perspective. The critical issue, Katie recognized, was not the influence of experience itself, but rather how one relates his or her experience to the biblical text Katie's own struggle as a woman in the church as well as her encounter with the women's rights movement paradoxically kept pushing her back to the Scriptures. It was through her reading of the Bible, particularly the life and teaching of Jesus, that Katie found her experience as a woman validated. Even though Katie did not attempt to exegete the key biblical texts regarding women's involvement in the church, her plea to involve women alongside men is permeated with Scripture's affirmation of women's value and giftedness.

As Katie began to articulate her own feelings and thoughts, she spoke on behalf of a generation of women who had virtually no public voice within the church. Ironically, this also meant that Katie often walked alone in the face of the continuing silence. Yet she courageously persevered because of her unwillingness to give up on the church. Katie's voice continues to call the church to recognize the vast reservoir of gifts God has given to his people.

• • •

Endnotes

1. Katie tells her own story about her involvement with the women's movement in her recent autobiography. See Katie Funk Wiebe, *You Never Gave Me a Name: One Mennonite Woman's Story* (Telford: DreamSeeker Books, 2009), 195-225.
2. Katie Funk Wiebe, "Color Me a Person," *Mennonite Brethren Herald*, December 28, 1973, 2.
3. Katie Funk Wiebe, *Alone: A Search for Joy* (Winnipeg: Kindred Press, 1987), 198.
4. Wiebe, *You Never Gave Me a Name*, 25-26.
5. *Ibid.*, 73-74.
6. *Ibid.*, 73.
7. Wiebe, *Alone*, 199.
8. Wiebe, *Alone*, 205; Wiebe, *You Never Gave Me a Name*, 72.
9. Wiebe, *Alone*, 201.
10. Katie Wiebe, "The Work of Women," Letters to the Editor, *The Canadian Mennonite*, April 12, 1957, 2, 6.
11. See Walter Wiebe's acknowledgement of Katie's involvement in "How It Came About," *Youth Worker Program Helps: Volume One* (Winnipeg: Youth Committee of the Canadian Conference of the Mennonite Brethren Church of North America, 1960), 6.
12. See *Youth Worker*, September 1957, 2.
13. Katie Wiebe to Orlando Harms, September 5, 1960.
14. Katie Wiebe, Women and the Church, *The Christian Leader*, January 9, 1962, 21.
15. Wiebe, *Alone*, 200.
16. Wiebe, *You Never Gave Me a Name*, 96.
17. Katie Funk Wiebe, *Bless Me Too, My Father* (Scottdale: Herald Press, 1988), 62.
18. Wiebe, *Alone*, 41.
19. *Ibid.*, 58, 63, 76, 207.
20. For example, see Katie Wiebe, Women and the Church, *The Christian Leader*, January 23, 1962, 21; Katie Wiebe, Women and the Church, *The Christian Leader*, March 20, 1962, 21; and Katie Wiebe, Women and the Church, *The Christian Leader*, April 3, 1962, 21. For Katie's emphasis on reading, see also, Katie Funk Wiebe, "A Pilgrimage in Books," *Christian Living*, April 1962, 19; Katie Funk Wiebe, "Let's Return to Good Reading," *The Christian Leader*, March 2, 1965, 4-6; Katie Funk Wiebe, "Are You a Reading Woman?" *Gospel Herald*, April 6, 1965, 293-294; Katie Funk Wiebe, "Let's Think Right About Reading," *The Christian*

Leader, February 15, 1966, 4-5, 9; and Katie Funk Wiebe, "Books for the Marketplace," *The Christian Leader*, February 14, 1967, 3-5.

21. Katie Funk Wiebe, "Missing: An Adequate Theology," Women and the Church, *The Christian Leader*, August 2, 1966, 21; Katie Funk Wiebe, "Throw a Dishrag at the Devil," Women and the Church, *The Christian Leader*, May 26, 1964, 21; and Katie Funk Wiebe, "For Better Program Planning," Women and the Church, *The Christian Leader*, June 7, 1966, 21. For examples of women as models, see Katie Wiebe, Women and the Church, *The Christian Leader*, April 17, 1962, 21; and Katie Wiebe, Women and the Church, *The Christian Leader*, May 29, 1962, 21.

22. For studies of women's organizations in the United States, see Valerie G. Rempel, "Early Missionary Society Activity Among U.S. Mennonite Brethren Women," *Direction* 24, no. 2 (1995): 36-46; and Valerie G. Rempel, "'She Hath Done What She Could': The Development of the Women's Missionary Services in the Mennonite Brethren Churches of the United States," in *Bridging Troubled Waters: Mennonite Brethren at Mid-Century*, ed. Paul Toews (Winnipeg: Kindred Productions, 1995), 149-164. For studies of Canadian women's organizations, see Gloria Neufeld Redekop, *The Work of Their Hands: Mennonite Women's Societies in Canada* (Waterloo: Wilfrid Laurier University Press, 1996) and Gloria Neufeld Redekop, "Canadian Mennonite Women's Societies: More than Meets the Eye," in *Bridging Troubled Waters: Mennonite Brethren at Mid-Century*, ed. Paul Toews (Winnipeg: Kindred Productions, 1995), 165-174.

23. Katie Wiebe, Women and the Church, *The Christian Leader*, February 6, 1962, 21; Katie Wiebe, Women and the Church, *The Christian Leader*, May 15, 1962, 21; Katie Wiebe, Women and the Church, *The Christian Leader*, November 26, 1963, 21; and Katie Funk Wiebe, "A New Emphasis in Women's Work," Women and the Church, *The Christian Leader*, April 14, 1964, 21. See also, Katie Funk Wiebe, "The Place of Women in the Work of the Church," *The Canadian Mennonite*, March 1, 1963, 5 and Katie Funk Wiebe, "Can Our Women's Organizations be Revitalized?" *Mennonite Brethren Herald*, March 6, 1970, 21-23.

24. See Katie Wiebe, Women and the Church, *The Christian Leader*, August 21, 1962, 21; Katie Wiebe, Women and the Church, *The Christian Leader*, September 4, 1962, 21; Katie Funk Wiebe, "One of the First Impressions: Mennonites Don't Dress Alike," *The Canadian Mennonite*, August 17, 1962, 7; Katie Funk Wiebe, "The Place of Women in the Work of the Church," *The Canadian Mennonite*, September 7, 1962, 7; and Katie Funk Wiebe, "Women's Activities Around the World," *The Canadian Mennonite*, August 24, 1962, 7.

25. Wiebe, Women and the Church, September 4, 1962, 21.

26. Katie Wiebe, Women and the Church, *The Christian Leader*, September 3, 1963, 21; and Katie Funk Wiebe, "Why Were They There?" Women and the Church, *The Christian Leader*, December 20, 1966, 29.

27. See Harold Jantz, "Editorial: Barrier Fallen," *Mennonite Brethren Herald*, July 26, 1968, 3.

28. Wiebe, Women and the Church, September 4, 1962, 21 and Katie Funk Wiebe, "A Problem Without a Name," Women and the Church, *The Christian Leader*, April 13, 1965, 25.

29. Katie Funk Wiebe, "The Image is Wrong," Women and the Church, *The Christian Leader*, March 1, 1966, 21.
30. John H. Redekop, "Women—Second Class Christians," Personal Opinion, *Mennonite Brethren Herald*, June 24, 1966, 2. For Katie's response, see Katie Funk Wiebe, "No Second-Class Citizens Here," Wayside Inn, *Mennonite Brethren Herald*, July 22, 1966, 20.
31. Betty Friedan, *The Feminine Mystique* (New York: Dell Publishing, 1963).
32. Wiebe, "A Problem Without a Name," 25. For a review of Friedan's book, see Katie Funk Wiebe, "*The Feminine Mystique* (1)," *The Canadian Mennonite*, March 29, 1966. 52; and Katie Funk Wiebe, "*The Feminine Mystique* (2)," *The Canadian Mennonite*, April 5, 1966, 10.
33. Katie Wiebe, "Accepting the Message of the Family Years," *The Christian Leader*, April 30, 1965, 5.
34. Wiebe, *Alone*, 59, 76, 206. See also Wiebe, "Color Me a Person," 2-5, 7.
35. Wiebe, *Alone*, 206.
36. Katie Funk Wiebe, "Courting Women for Church Work." Viewpoint, *The Christian Leader*, March 28, 1967, 21. See also Katie Funk Wiebe, "A Voice for the Layman," Viewpoint, *The Christian Leader*, April 25, 1967, 21.
37. Wiebe, "Courting Women for Church Work," 21.
38. Katie Funk Wiebe, "Continuing Education for Women," Viewpoint, *The Christian Leader*, November 7, 1967, 29.
39. *Ibid*.
40. Katie Funk Wiebe, "Let's Involve Women," Viewpoint, *The Christian Leader*, September 10, 1968, 21.
41. See Katie Funk Wiebe, "To Conference, To Conference…," Viewpoint, *The Christian Leader*, December 15, 1970, 19; and Katie Funk Wiebe, "Members One of Another," Viewpoint, *The Christian Leader*, November 14, 1972, 19.
42. Katie Funk Wiebe, "In Search of Candor," Viewpoint, *The Christian Leader*, October 5, 1971, 23.
43. Katie Funk Wiebe, "The Ministry: Cleaning Up the Image," Viewpoint, *The Christian Leader*, March 24, 1970, 19.
44. Katie Funk Wiebe, "I Am Confused," Viewpoint, *The Christian Leader*, February 10, 1970, 19.
45. Waldo Wiebe to Art Fleming, August 30, 1971. See also Minutes, Southern District Committee of Reference and Counsel, September 9-10, 1971, 2; and Minutes, U.S. Conference Board of Reference and Counsel, December 13-14, 1971, 5.
46. Katie Funk Wiebe, "The Woman Question," Viewpoint, *The Christian Leader*, April 3, 1973, 19.
47. Katie Funk Wiebe, "At the Convention," *The Christian Leader*, November 27, 1973, 19.
48. See Herbert J. Brandt, "Man and Woman under the Lordship of Christ," *Yearbook of the Canadian Conference of Mennonite Brethren Churches: 63rd Convention* (Vancouver: Christian Press, 1974), 12-22; and David Ewert, "The Christian Woman in the Church and the Conference," *Yearbook of the Canadian Conference of Mennonite Brethren Churches: 63rd Convention* (Vancouver: Christian Press, 1974), 30-43.

49. See Elfrieda Duersken, "Response to the Paper by H. Brandt: 'Man and Woman under the Lordship of Christ,'" *Yearbook of the Canadian Conference of Mennonite Brethren Churches: 63rd Convention* (Vancouver: Christian Press, 1974), 24-26; and Esther Wiens, "Response to the Paper by D. Ewert: 'The Christian Woman in the Church and the Conference,'" *Yearbook of the Canadian Conference of Mennonite Brethren Churches: 63rd Convention* (Vancouver: Christian Press, 1974), 44-47.
50. Rachel D. Swartzendruber, "Discovering Voices Among Peculiar Quietness: An Analysis of U.S. Mennonite Women's Rhetoric in the Church Press 1963-1977" (M.C. Thesis, Wichita State University, 2006), 49. See Katie Funk Wiebe, "Liberation—For Men and Women," Viewpoint, *The Christian Leader*, November 3, 1970, 19; Katie Funk Wiebe, "Liberation—For Men and Women," *Gospel Herald*, December 8, 1970, 1011; and Katie Funk Wiebe, "Liberation for Men and Women," *The Canadian Mennonite*, November 20, 1970, 7.
51. See Wiebe, "I Am Confused," 19; and Katie Funk Wiebe, "On the Total Integration of Women." *The Canadian Mennonite*, February 13, 1970, 6, 8.
52. See Katie Funk Wiebe, "Where We're At...In Our Attitude Toward Women," *The Canadian Mennonite*, February 19, 1971, 9, 29; and Katie Funk Wiebe, "Women's Freedom, the Church's Necessity," *Direction* 1, no.3 (July 1972): 82-84.
53. Wiebe, "Where We're At," 9.
54. *Ibid.*, 29.
55. Wiebe, "Liberation—For Men and Women," Viewpoint, 19. Katie's apprehension with the "feminist" label continues to be evident in 1975. See Katie Funk Wiebe, "Another Kind of Feminism," Viewpoint, *The Christian Leader*, December 23, 1975, 11.
56. *Ibid.*
57. *Ibid.*
58. Wiebe, "Color Me a Person," 2. This article was eventually revised as the Epilogue in Wiebe, *Alone*, 271-290.
59. *Ibid.*
60. *Ibid.*, 2, 5.
61. Dave Wootton and Cathy Wootton, "Go to Scripture," *Mennonite Brethren Herald*, March 8, 1974, 12-13.
62. Katie Funk Wiebe, "Can We Hear the Prophets?" *The Christian Leader*, March 30, 1976, 19.
63. *Ibid.*
64. Wiebe, *You Never Gave Me a Name*, 203.
65. Katie Funk Wiebe, "A Giant Leap for Mankind," Viewpoint, *The Christian Leader*, June 26, 1973, 19. See also Katie Funk Wiebe, "A Giant Leap for Mankind," Family in the Seventies, *Mennonite Brethren Herald*, October 5, 1973, 27.
66. Wiebe, "Another Kind of Feminism," 11. See also Katie Funk Wiebe, "Another Kind of Feminism," *Mennonite Brethren Herald*, January 9, 1976, 32.
67. Wiebe, *You Never Gave Me a Name*, 202.
68. William Keeney to Katie Funk Wiebe, April 7, 1975.

69. Wiebe, *You Never Gave Me a Name*, 203. See "Members of the Task Force/ Committee on Women's Concerns," *MCC Committee on Women's Concerns Report*, July-August, 1983, 7.
70. See Minutes, Southern District Faith and Life Commission, February 8-9, 1974, 1. The following women participated in this meeting: Geraldine Penner, Kay Toews, Mildred Vogt, Katie Funk Wiebe, and Marie Wiens.
71. Minutes, Southern District Women's Missionary Service Executive Board, August 27, 1974, 2.
72. It should be noted that a fall retreat was held prior to the annual convention where Katie Funk Wiebe spoke on "The Role of Women in the Church, Home and Community." See *Yearbook: 65th Session Southern District Conference of the Mennonite Brethren Churches*, 18. The Faith and Life Commission did receive some feedback expressing concern about women discussing this topic, but the Commission noted that they were the ones who suggested this in the first place. See Minutes, Southern District Faith and Life Commission, November 9, 1974, 2.
73. Katie Funk Wiebe, "Freedom for All," Viewpoint, *The Christian Leader*, February 18, 1975, 19.
74. *Ibid.*
75. Katie Funk Wiebe, "Voices of Liberation" (paper presented at Symposium: Women and the Church, Fresno, CA, May 6-7, 1976), 4.
76. *Ibid.*, 28.
77. See John Klassen, "MCC News Release," August 31, 1978.
78. Katie Funk Wiebe, "Jesus and Women" (paper presented at Biblical Perspectives on Women in the Church, Clearbrook, B.C., November 18, 1978), 8-18.
79. Katie Funk Wiebe, "The Church's Response to Changing Roles for Men and Women" (paper presented at Biblical Perspectives on Women in the Church, Clearbrook, B.C., November 18, 1978), 5-17.
80. *Ibid.*, 3.
81. David Ewert to John A. Toews, December 8, 1978. See also John A. Toews to David Ewert, December 12, 1978; and Minutes, General Conference Board of Reference and Counsel, April 23, 1979, 1-4.
82. Katie Funk Wiebe to Henry H. Dick, November 14, 1979, 1.
83. *Ibid.*, 2.
84. David Ewert, "The 'Place' of the Woman in the Church" (paper presented at Current Issues in Church Leadership, General Conference Board of Reference and Counsel Study Conference, Clearbrook, B.C., May 8-10, 1980), 1-22.
85. "Resolution on the Place of the Woman in the Church," *Yearbook: 55th Session General Conference of Mennonite Brethren Churches*, August 7-11, 1981, 46-47.
86. Katie Funk Wiebe, "One Out of Twelve," Viewpoint, *The Christian Leader*, January 1, 1973, 19. See also Katie Funk Wiebe, "Come Higher Friends," Viewpoint, *The Christian Leader*, January 22, 1974, 19: Katie Funk Wiebe, "Mennonite Brethren Women: Images and Realities of the Early Years," *Mennonite Life* 36, no.3 (September 1981): 22-28; and Katie Funk Wiebe, "Woman's View," Viewpoint, *The Christian Leader*, July 12, 1983, 17. See also Katie Funk Wiebe, *Have Cart, Will Travel* (Hillsboro: North American

Conference of Mennonite Brethren Churches; Board of Christian Literature, 1974; Paulina Foote, *God's Hand Over My Nineteen Years in China* (Hillsboro, M.B. Publishing House, 1962); Katie Funk Wiebe, *Our Lamps Were Lit: An Informal History of the Bethel Deaconess Hospital School of Nursing* (Newton: Bethel Hospital School of Nursing; Alumnae Association, 1978); and Katie Funk Wiebe, ed., *Women among the Brethren: The Story of Fifteen Mennonite Brethren and Krimmer Mennonite Brethren Women* (Hillsboro: General Conference of the North American Mennonite Brethren Churches; Board of Christian Literature, 1979).
87. Clarence Hiebert and Edmund Janzen, "The Ministry of Women in our Churches," 1985.
88. Katie Funk Wiebe to Edmund Janzen and Clarence Hiebert, April 24, 1986.
89. Minutes, General Conference Board of Reference and Counsel, May 1-3, 1986, 6. For Katie's influence see Clarence Hiebert and Edmund Janzen to Katie Wiebe, May 19, 1986; and Herb Brandt to Katie Funk Wiebe, July 10, 1986. Other members of the Task Force included: Ray Bystrom, Waldo Hiebert, Lorina Marsh, John E. Toews, and Esther Wiens.
90. Katie Funk Wiebe, "Report to Task Force on Role of Women," February 28, 1987.
91. See "Resolution on Women in Ministry," *Yearbook: 57th Session General Conference of Mennonite Brethren Churches of North America* (August 7-11, 1987): 46-47.
92. *Ibid.*, 72.
93. "Love in the Church," *Yearbook: 57th Session General Conference of Mennonite Brethren Churches of North America* (August 7-11, 1987), 70.
94. See Minutes, General Conference Board of Reference and Counsel, September 28, 1990, 2; and Minutes, General Conference Board of Reference and Counsel, April 1-2, 1991, 2.
95. John E. Toews, Valerie Rempel, and Katie Funk Wiebe, eds., *Your Daughters Shall Prophesy: Women in Ministry in the Church* (Winnipeg: Kindred Press, 1992).
96. Katie Funk Wiebe, "Women in the Mennonite Brethren Church," in *Your Daughters Shall Prophesy*, edited by John E. Toews, Valerie Rempel, and Katie Funk Wiebe (Winnipeg: Kindred Press, 1992), 174. For an earlier version of the paper see Wiebe, "Mennonite Brethren Women: Images and Realities of the Early Years."
97. Katie Funk Wiebe, "Katie Funk Wiebe reflects on the conference: 'In a Mennonite Voice: Women Doing Theology,' held at Conrad Grebel College, April 30-May 2, 1992," *Conrad Grebel Review* 10, no.2 (Spring 1992): 210.
98. *Ibid.*, 211.
99. *Ibid.*, 213.
100. Katie Funk Wiebe, "A Pastoral Letter to Mennonite Brethren Women," *Sophia*, Winter 1994, 10-11. See "Women in Leadership," *Yearbook: 59th Session General Conference of Mennonite Brethren Churches* (July 7-11, 1993), 33-35.
101. *Ibid.*
102. *Ibid.*, 11.

103. Wiebe, *Bless Me Too, My Father*, 238.
104. *Ibid.*, 228.
105. Wiebe, "Jesus and Women," 9.

The Image is Wrong

Katie Funk Wiebe

It saddens me that the church is so little concerned or even aware of the many problems facing women today caused by the revolution in their work and living habits. The church is, however, openly concerned about the lack of personnel to fill the many vacancies in church, missions, welfare, and other fields. I think these two matters are more closely related than is immediately apparent.

We live in an age when the image of women as presented by all types of media is simply wrong. Women are held to an image which pictures them as merely an accessory to men or a decorative addition to the home, passive, dependent, conformist, incapable of critical thought or contribution to society, gaily content in a world of sex, babies, and kitchen.

Women are not really expected to have an interest in the world of ideas, politics, social problems, art, science, literature and the like. As a result intelligence, individuality, education, or even a life of service have become problems to some women. To avoid inner tensions it has become easy to make house, husband, and children an excuse to live comfortably and free of responsibility to other people.

Strangely enough, the church seems to uphold this image because there is a hint of something biblical in a passive, conformist image which stresses that a woman's main function in life is limited to sex.

Yet I find it difficult to believe that the Apostle Paul was speaking of a submission which had nothing to submit or a silence which was empty. Our present image of women does not fit women like Mary, Martha, Priscilla, Eunice, Lois, and others. Mothers who have no growing concern for other people's needs will not encourage daughters to become missionaries. Girls which are chained to an image which excludes the world of ideas from their lives will not find it easy to live as successful individuals.

The grave sin of this age is that we are sacrificing our girls to this image of emptiness—the cult of the flesh. To rescue them from it the church will have to stress the biblical image of women, an image which shows that women have many roles in life to fill.

These include not only wife, and mother, but also citizen, friend, neighbor, worker in the labor force, creator of the beautiful or cultural, and also servant in the church. It will have to teach more openly that a woman can serve as an individual without losing her femininity.

Margaret Mead, anthropologist, is concerned about the lack of involvement on the part of women in the problems of our day. According to her women have become as cave women again whose main ambition seems to be to get and to hold a man, to produce or adopt children who are there only to bring joy and pleasure to the parents. Any work which is done, even outside the home, holds no attraction in itself, but is subservient to the home.

She feels that women have forgotten that there are other homes, other children, other women who need love, understanding and healing. Women must find the new frontiers of service of this age.

Other voices besides Margaret Mead are speaking out in a concern about the changing role of women and how it affects them as well as society. The Carnegie Corporation reporting for 1960 stated that the greatest waste of human resources in the United States today is the under-utilization of intelligent women. Has the church really no need for such women?

The Department of Labor is concerned about women as they relate to the labor force. Mrs. Mary Dublin Keyserling, economist for the U. S. Women's Bureau, stated in McCalls Magazine last month that she wished vocational guidance counselors would make girls face the changing times more realistically by impressing them with the trends concerning women's place in the national labor force.

What concerns her is that so many girls now fail to prepare themselves for jobs which equal their talents, or fail to prepare at all for life after the children have left home. Such women drift into marriage, and through the childbearing years. And uncommitted living does not produce workers for the church.

The church will also need to think about these problems more deeply and to speak about them. It will have to help women break the prevailing image of a false femininity. It will have to help our younger women choose to be wives and mothers with greater sureness and confidence that this is of God. It will have to try to close the gap between what women of the church are capable of doing and what there is available to do. And it will also have to guide them in the terrible pressures of this age to take up remunerative work as the only alternative for a fulfilled life.

This guidance and encouragement, however, will have to come from our leaders, our pastors, and our teachers. It is not just a task for the sewing circle.

Katie Funk Wiebe, "The Image is Wrong," Women and the Church, *The Christian Leader*, March 1, 1966, 21.

Freedom for All

Katie Funk Wiebe

One of the subjects I hesitate most to write about is the role of women in the church. I have been misunderstood too often. Now and then some reader, usually a woman, dashes off a letter to me in which she rubs my soul over her washboard until I feel frazzled. That hurts.

So I write today with the awareness that my words will be interpreted not by my study and thinking, but by the reader's views and experience with the subject. I tread over this ground gently, feeling my footing word by word.

As the woman's movement in society develops and begins to infiltrate the church, the battle lines are being drawn more distinctly, which is unfortunate. Anyone who speaks for the freedom of persons, men and women, is immediately dubbed a Woman's Libber, and the tone is often demeaning, for Women's Lib seems to denote something crude and coarse. Yet the other side tends to label anyone who speaks against the movement as a male chauvinist pig. So the name-calling is more or less equal.

Some people see only those aspects of the women's movement they disagree with and therefore throw it all out. They see the movement of women into the ordained ministry, their greater participation in athletics and politics, the increasing incidence of crimes of violence by women, and the growing alcoholism and psychiatric problems among them, frequently attributed in part to the confusion of roles, as well as the abortion issue.

So, somehow, women have to be turned to their former traditional roles to get rid of these problems. Though the Women's Liberation movement decried a woman packaging herself as a sex object to attract and hold her man, now numerous Christian femininity seminars stress these goals as a Christian virtue. Family and youth seminars are teaching the theme of male authority as the answer to society's problems.

Some of this is only a natural reaction to the entire movement. But what concerns me more is that some who are most opposed to the women's movement seem to feel so little of the hurt which women in the church express because of their limited role.

As one gentleman wrote in another Mennonite periodical, "Let Jesus fill the vacancy where women want liberation." His words remind me too much of the Christian slaveowners in an earlier era who promoted slavery on the grounds it was unbiblical for an inferior race to want to be free. God had ordained it so. The slaves should be satisfied with their lot.

This year has been declared by the United Nations as International Women's Year to promote equality of rights and opportunities for men and women and to ensure the full participation of women in all aspects of their lives. I believe it also gives the church an opportunity to look at a matter which has grown too large for it to shrug off as insignificant. The truths have become too big.

Here is what I would like to see happen in this International Women's Year:

1. The development of an aggressive program of education in churches and church-related schools of biblical, Anabaptist, and historical materials on women. We need to know what true liberation in Christ means for both men and women so we don't keep hurting each other through ignorance. We need to move beyond proof-texting and not be afraid of what we will discover.

2. A readiness to accept the gifts of all members, both men and women, even if they don't fit the traditional sex roles.

I pray the church may become more open in recognizing that all people are individuals with various gifts and abilities not determined by sex, race, and social class.

3. An emphasis on the strengthening of the home, badly battered in this last decade by changing life-styles. The role of mothers needs more recognition and support, and fathers need encouragement to accept their role and responsibility in family training.

4. A greater readiness to lend a loving, listening ear to one another. In the past years I have heard too many jibes aimed at women who dared to question the traditional stance of the church. Christ never responded like this. He treated women seriously. I think we need unlimited liability for one another's hurts, seeking to help the one who feels oppressed instead of adding to her pain with a joke about Women's Lib, an organization many of these women do not see themselves a part of.

5. The deliberate decision to include more women in decision-making roles in the church. Women will need much encouragement to move away from the coffee-pouring, flower-arranging, minute-keeping roles, for many lack confidence in themselves, and therefore, lack the stature, status and feeling they can be as effective as men in these tasks. They feel their opinions are not as valuable and therefore pull back.

Some of my friends suggest that we may just have "to let nature take its course" in the whole matter. Such an answer is discouraging because in the meantime I see the church wasting much talent because of its rigid sex stereotyping. Although some people hesitate to question tradition because it seems to be criticizing the Scriptures, I believe the greater sin is not to question the past if individuals, particularly women, are limited in their service for God, and in some cases must move out of the church to find their place.

Katie Funk Wiebe, "Freedom for All," Viewpoint, *The Christian Leader*, February 18, 1975, 19.

Who Should Be Ordained?

Katie Funk Wiebe

The issue of women's ordination for the chaplaincy didn't make it to the floor at the recent convention of the General Conference of Mennonite Brethren Churches. Time ran out to discuss this sensitive issue.

My feelings are mixed about the matter. I might have voted against a motion to ordain women for any function—at least until the matter of ordination for men is reconsidered. The meaning of ordination, any kind of ordination, has become muddied in recent years. Technically, Mennonite Brethren see it as recognition of "a gift bestowed by the Lord" (*We Recommend*, p. 309). In actuality, it means other things.

The meaning of ordination as a recognition of gifts has refused to stay within its prescribed boundaries. Societal pressures direct its meaning to areas more concerned with status and authority. Ordination is becoming the official sign separating the clergy from the laity, even though all believers are laity, all are priests in the kingdom of God.

Therefore, the meaning of ordination needs clarification before it is applied to women. Is ordination the recognition of spiritual gifts or does it give official permission to preach, teach, preside at the Lord's Supper and other ordinances? Is it an initiation into the ranks of the clergy? Can ordination ever be undone? When one's pastoral ministry is completed, should it continue to be used for tax benefits?

People assume that 1 Timothy 4:14 and 2 Timothy 1:6, which speak of the laying on of hands, are the biblical basis for ordination. Yet a closer study of these passages does not support that view. Young Timothy was not installed into an office and given a title. In Acts 9:17, the laying on of hands on the Apostle Paul restored his sight and filled him with the Holy Spirit. In Acts 13:3, Barnabas and Saul were already in ministry when hands were laid on them. Jesus laid hands on no disciples to usher them into ministry.

Some modern scholars see ordination as having to do primarily with church polity rather than theology. Other people fear a loss of public status and power for the ordained clergy if women are ordained, for as women move into more church work, position and influence must be shared.

Historian Martin Marty writes that the continuation of ordination from the Catholic tradition during the Reformation prevented the laity from emerging as a powerful body. The new Protestants did not claim ordination was a sacrament, but they kept on ordaining without knowing why. Through ordination the church could control who became clergy.

Ruth A. Tucker concludes in her study of ordination (*Daughters of the Church*) that it would appear that while arguments concerning women's ordination (whether pro or con) may be meaningful with regard to denominational polity, no Bible passage can be used to build an argument for ordination to clerical office as usually conceived today.

Tucker quotes a Catholic scholar as saying that "almost every issue related to the subject remains unsolved." She cites another scholar who argues there is no evidence to support those views that presume modern ordination corresponds with early ordination ceremonies.

But the issue of women's ordination to the chaplaincy deserves a churchly hearing. Those opposing it say that women should not be ordained because traditionally women have never been ordained for pastoral ministries, which would include the chaplaincy. Priests of any kind should be male. Others oppose it because ordained women would strengthen the growing hierarchical structures in the church.

Support for women's ordination for the chaplaincy comes from those who hold that any woman or man who completes the qualifications for a profession, such as the chaplaincy, medicine, and law, should be adequately credentialed to pursue that career. The highest credentialing a denomination offers is required by some states for licensing chaplains. Gender should not be a determining factor.

Mennonite Brethren precedent for women's ordination offers support as well. We ordained women for special ministries in the past. Before 1957, when commissioning for women was introduced, more than 80 single and married women had been ordained for missionary service. The Krimmer Mennonite Brethren Church, who joined the Mennonite Brethren in 1960, also ordained women for deaconess ministries.

Another strong supporting argument is that women, like men, feel called to special ministries and receive gifts of the Spirit for such ministries. In Acts 2 the Spirit was poured on both men and women.

I would like to see us agree that all people who have received the gifts of the Spirit should be blessed and freed to serve. Furthermore, ordination and receiving the blessing of a congregation through the laying on of hands should be separated, for ordination is more related to church polity than to biblical practice. Yet I am aware that to change our thinking on this matter will be difficult.

Katie Funk Wiebe, "Who Should Be Ordained?" Viewpoint, *The Christian Leader*, November 6, 1990, 15.

114 | The Voice of a Writer

Chapter 6

Katie's Viewpoint

Wally Kroeker

Katie the Columnist

Any editor who has had to push the rock of Sisyphus up the hill every two weeks will readily grasp the value of a columnist whose copy was always on time and on target. That was my experience with Katie Funk Wiebe in the decade I edited *The Christian Leader*.

It was my good fortune to "inherit" her as a regular columnist when I came to the *Leader* (then a biweekly) in 1975. She had already been writing a column for more than a dozen years, originally called "Women in the Church" but later renamed "Viewpoint." During my time she would submit, regular as clockwork, another 200 columns plus feature articles. It was a comfort to know that amid the relentless press of a biweekly deadline I could count on at least one editorial item that could dependably go to the typesetter (remember them?) virtually as written.

Katie was already a seasoned professional by then. She had long before written articles for *The Youth Worker*, a Canadian MB Conference publication edited by her husband, Walter, and, in one of the peculiarities of the time, had signed his byline.[1] She had been not only his secretary and researcher but also his ghost writer.

Katie got a chance to write under her own name when Orlando Harms, manager of the Mennonite Brethren Publishing House in Hillsboro, Kansas, and my predecessor as editor of the *Leader*, invited Katie to become a free-lance columnist (but sent the invitation to her husband, not her).[2] Katie graciously accepted, and her first "Women in the Church" column appeared in January 1962 under the byline Mrs. Katie Wiebe. The focus was to be her "concerns and joys about the church, especially as they related to women."[3]

A year later Katie joined the Publishing House staff as an editorial assistant. However, the scope of the job (writing obituaries and church tidbits for the *Leader* and proofreading commercial print jobs) was tedious and held limited prospect of a serious editorial future.

The sluggishness of the Publishing House to enlarge Katie's job worked to my future benefit. In 1966 she was invited to teach Freshman English to a large incoming class at Tabor College. She had no degree but she'd been a student of writing for years. Orlando Harms allowed her to teach the course during her lunch hour, three days a week.[4] She did well, and the next year Tabor offered her a full-time job in publicity, with latitude to get formal training. Katie eventually earned two degrees in English and would spend 24 years at Tabor, all the while producing her *Leader* column on the side.

Her new role in academe brought fresh synergies. Tabor College, as the oldest Mennonite Brethren institution (founded in 1908), still harbored a sense of being the keeper of the Mennonite Brethren soul. In the 1970s it was enjoying the exuberance and tensions of Anabaptist "restoration" and Katie Funk Wiebe was a part of it. Tabor was intellectually fertile and home to some top Mennonite minds. "Today," she writes, "I value the opportunities to grow intellectually at Tabor even more than the opportunity to teach."[5] And that growth was shared, in biweekly increments, with the readers of her column.

A Pastoral Voice

When I breezed into Hillsboro in 1975, I did not know I was moving into the job that had been offered to her late husband, Walter, many years earlier (he had declined), and which Katie deserved more than I did. The MB mindset was being jostled and tested on many fronts. The American bicentennial of 1976 and its attendant festivities made some wonder if civil religion had overtaken the Mennonite Brethren. Other flashpoints were abortion and the proposed Equal Rights Amendment (ERA), both of which drew polarizing comment in the *Leader*.

Katie observed, and chronicled, not only the growing voice of women but also myriad other issues buffeting the Mennonite

Brethren world, always in down-to-earth language accessible to readers from Yale, South Dakota, to Reedley, California. If you wanted an entry point into new debates about, say, pop psychology or existentialism, you could count on her to explain a complicated issue and lay out implications for you and your denomination.

She did so on a blizzard of topics: racism, healing of memories, the new morality, artists in society, failure, parenting styles, the good life (crimped in those days by a fuel shortage), and the military draft (including women), which the U.S. government was considering resuming. She tackled evangelism, Bible study, sexist language, individualism, missions, "churchspeak," and all the latest bromides that flowed from those keen to shed their Anabaptist identity in an effort to seem more inviting to the unchurched.

For three decades hers was the most consistent pastoral voice heard by U.S. Mennonite Brethren. Regular readers would, over time, receive a robust mini-course in spiritual formation, servanthood, church polity, modern media, pastoral theology, Mennonite literature, and more.

Katie knew how to capture human interest and render thoughts in vivid images. "Does servanthood," she mused, "mean the employer sharpens the pencils and empties the wastebaskets?"[6] A column on the proliferation of new translations of Scripture began, "One day I quit...I quit reading the Bible—for a time—to clear the air."[7] Who would find spiritual uplift in the mundane task of parking a car?[8] Or theological lessons in cleaning out a closet?[9] Katie could.

Pomposity and pious inconsistency could test her patience. A column on treating people like litter observed, "most people would give a hardened murderer at least a chance to hear the gospel, but would feel uncomfortable if a professed homosexual came to church."[10]

One day she was selected for a survey of television habits. She later noted, "most of us eat more, pray less and watch more television than we'd like to admit," adding that "anytime we laugh at the sexual innuendoes of the TV talk show host or enjoy the adulterous relationships of soap opera stars, we give them a vote even though we may not be filling out a survey card."[11]

In a column urging Christians to read she lamented that "I know people who thank God for the Bible but whose Bibles are almost as new as the day they bought them 30 to 40 years ago."[12]

Katie herself read hungrily, not only new material but also treasured old chestnuts like A. W. Tozer, G. Campbell Morgan, and Oswald Chambers (whom she quoted often enough so you knew she had immersed herself in his *My Utmost for His Highest*, said to be the best-selling devotional book of all time). She introduced her audience to writers like Frederick Buechner and Martin Marty who were gaining an audience. She quoted Jacques Ellul and servant leadership guru Robert Greenleaf long before they became trendy.

Many topics remain hauntingly current. A Christmas column during the "other" Iranian crisis of 1979, when "words and bombs are piling up," waded into geopolitical tensions that readers may have pondered but lacked the words and nerve to ask, "Did Christ's coming change anything?" With gut-wrenching questions hanging in the air she looked into the eyes of her new grandson and remembered that Christ came into the world to share our humanity and pain. How current it all seems, 30 years later, with Iran firmly back on the world's radar.[13]

Major Themes

During my decade at the *Leader* I presided over some 200 of her columns (only a third of the total she produced). How do I now draw a thematic net around her free-range mind? At the risk of oversimplifying, I offer this attempt.

Soul care - Any regular reader of "Viewpoint" knew the inner life was important to Katie Funk Wiebe. One year she added eight to ten new books on prayer to her library.[14] She valued the deep streams that had nourished generations before her. While eager to recast enduring truths for a new day, she wasn't about to jettison that which had stood the test of time.

What contemplative virtues were being gulped up by the chaos of the day, she wondered frequently. "We don't need to get sucked into the frantic drive of modern life," she wrote, noting that "the early farmer-preachers of the Mennonite church often expressed profound thoughts because they had time to meditate all week while plowing or seeding."[15]

Had we preserved the husks of old flasks but let the precious wine dribble through our fingers? What had we lost when we moved beyond the "Aha" stories of our spiritual journey to higher intellectual levels, creedal statements, and scholarly analyses? "We defended fiercely what we believed, down to the fine points, even if we didn't always know why."[16] What were we taking from the past—the fire, or the ashes?

Did the current generation have something fresh to add to the narrative of history, or was it passing on "an empty bucket to their children instead of showing them where the well was." Better to nurture anew rather than trying to live off the "spiritual capital" of forebears, she wrote.[17]

And how, in this bewildering era, did a new Christian learn to pray? Was it easier in our society to find a guru to teach Transcendental Meditation than someone who can teach about prayer?[18]

We are Family - The "rearview mirror" of history was critical, whether it was Anabaptist origins, the Mennonite Brethren journey, or personal family history. It was important to know where we came from—spiritually and culturally. Katie was pro-family, and big on celebrating roots and leaning on one another.

One trip into the past spoke endearingly of the McLaughlin Buick, rumble seats and relatives who looked like Kojak and Edith Bunker. Her past—and ours—was important: "It has been a part in making us what we are."[19]

But this was more than nostalgia. While she could personally reach back to the Depression and "recall clearly the hoboes attached to the top of freight cars like barnacles to a ship as the trains moved past our home," she didn't stay there but segued to the confusing options that plagued young people now.[20]

Reunions underlined the value of mutual support, another frequent theme. She wrote: "One older woman, well over 80, still with her husband in their own home, feeling the walls of life slowly closing in upon her and her own vigor to keep them at a distance declining, once told me, 'Sometimes we two just stand here and hang on to one another.'" Reunions—of either the family or conference kind—meant reuniting "to hang on to one another for a few moments before the tempo of life picks up again. They say, 'We are family. We belong together.'"[21]

The Dust of Change - Katie reached out to those who felt tossed by the swirling pace of changing values, offering reassurance that they were not alone. Like the bewildered senior who felt blindsided by all that was going on in theology and society: "Was the Bible she had believed in for decades leaky? Was her value system outmoded?" Katie asked. "A person has to run very fast to keep up with the swift changes moving through society."[22]

Beyond comfort, however, were sober warnings to leaders. One lesson of history was that "we don't learn easily from experience on ways to handle change."[23]

The Castaways - What if, Katie once mused, a publisher put out a magazine exclusively for the poor and the hungry, the kinds of people you'd find in slums and refugee camps. What kind of "good news" would it contain?[24]

Impoverished and defeated people of all kinds were never far from Katie's compass. "Some days I step into my door shaking and angry," she wrote, "wanting to shout and rail at the mountains of suffering I have become aware of during the day."[25]

People who felt like social litter could find solace in Katie's columns, not only the poor, oppressed and people quarantined by gender or race, but also those "normal" people who for one reason or another felt left out or disillusioned with the church. She was alert to anything that made people feel apart, whether it was an inability to pray, or new marginalizing disorders like anorexia nervosa or agoraphobia, which then were unfamiliar to many readers.

Hospitality of Words - "I nearly rushed past. But then I stopped to say hello. Small, frail, silent, she sat alone at the end of a row of chairs," began a column on Christian hospitality.[26] It was so like Katie to locate and care for those who had been overlooked, bypassed and neglected, either psychologically or ecclesiastically, and let them know that they counted.

In the midst of our daily rush, the spiritual discipline of hospitality was more needed than ever. And Katie practiced it in print. Her ministry was a hospitality of words.

Offering a warm hearth did not mean automatic approval of every whim, however. There was plenty that Katie didn't like, and she wasn't hesitant to say so. She didn't like, for example, empty sermons piled high with fluffy meringue but no substance.

But at heart she was a reconciler, trying to keep us talking together. Everyone was welcome to join her conversation. She was always widening her embrace, even to "the other women's movement," where more traditional women came together to sew and pray for missions. She searched for common ground between them and the new women's movement which she was increasingly seen to embody.[27]

Women in the Church - One of the hotter firestorms Katie ignited during my tenure was on abortion. Disclaiming that she opposed abortion on demand and as a method of birth control, she laid out in only a few hundred words an impressive array of implications and issues deserving further reflection.[28] Those for whom the issue was etched in black marker recoiled at any hint of pencil or pastel. "I am indeed indignant," exclaimed one.[29] "I am so shocked that I am shaking," continued another.[30]

One missive, signed by 15 women from Fairview, Oklahoma, said, "We do not want others to operate under the misconception that Wiebe is speaking on behalf of all Mennonite women."[31] Katie would later note that the column on abortion sparked the most mail of her career, "but still I don't regret writing it."[32]

Another hot column was on the proposed Equal Rights Amendment (ERA), in which Katie detected merit that eluded those with deeper political fault lines.[33] It too generated emotional opposition, particularly from women.

The fact that both of these issues involved women helped feed a perception of Katie Funk Wiebe as the leading feminist in the Mennonite Brethren Conference. While she did maintain steady pressure against a male-dominated hierarchy, a tally of her "Viewpoint" columns indicates considerable restraint. But that didn't stop a small group of critics from seeing her mainly as a feminist lightning rod.

A woman who was troubled by what she saw as a rising tide of feminism took the editors to task, noting "with some interest the recent bowing to the ladies in filling church offices and in the content of *The Christian Leader*." The writer suggested changing the name of the denomination to "Mennonite Sistren."[34]

Those on the other side of the issue were equally vocal. One woman wrote that she wasn't looking for any office or position in the church or conference but was simply "tired of being unnoticed and unneeded except for food preparation and embroidery."[35]

Another woman commented after reading a feature report on the Alberta Mennonite Brethren Conference, "Do we have churches there or monastic orders? We saw 13 pictures of men's faces and heard only men's voices. Is that really all there is?"[36] Katie responded by challenging men and women to "welcome one another more readily into one another's public and private lives."[37]

Peacemaker - In the testy decade of 1975-85 the Mennonite Brethren center of gravity on issues like eschatology, hermeneutics and the role of women in ministry seemed to be shifting. The United States Conference was grappling with eroding financial support that impacted its colleges and publications. There were intramural tensions over Mennonite ethnicity, church growth strategies, and whether Mennonite Brethren should be defined as evangelical, Anabaptist, or both.

The 1980s brought with it the restlessness of the emerging "Me Decade," the beginning of the "culture wars," and the polarizing growth of the Moral Majority. When a Mennonite Brethren pastor attended one of Jerry Falwell's "I Love America" rallies he was troubled by what he regarded as misleading use of Scripture and mean-spirited denunciations of ideological foes.[38] When he wrote about it in the *Leader* he prompted perhaps the biggest conflagration of letters in the magazine's history.

Katie had not been involved in this particular episode, but the tone of the unhappy letters was familiar, and she sought to pour reconciling balm on roiling waters. She may not have liked the spirit that animated the outbursts but it was not her nature to write anyone off, either. If there was common ground to be found, Katie would plot its coordinates.

She wanted to help people "think Christianly." And that meant, among other things, a different intellectual approach. It was so easy, in times of national and ecclesiastical stress, to use "lean not on your own understanding" as an excuse to dismiss intellectual rigor, as if, "matters of faith do nicely, perhaps even better, without deep thought." Without ever mentioning it, alert readers could not miss the point of a subsequent column that mentioned neither Jerry Falwell nor the Moral Majority. "The strong meat of the Word is needed at a time such as this when truth has no clean cutting edge," she wrote. What was needed was more discernment in the church "for I can't see blind faith leading us through the maze of civil religion and hit lists of people and books. Today's issues require a spirit of discernment strengthened by love in the power of the Spirit of Christ."[39]

Katie's Task

That love was perhaps the dominant cross-cutting theme for Katie. In marking the 20th anniversary of her column she wrote that she saw her task as "to keep making the truth of God's love great with as much wonder as I can find words to express it."[40]

But it wasn't the drippy, sentimental love of greeting cards. It was a mature full-throated love that meant looking honestly at life and faith, confronting its challenges with passion and integrity, and pressing on with the guidance of a God-point-of-view. Her tone was, "let us hear each other, reason together, not delude each other, and move together toward more robust discipleship."

Katie described her role as

> to offer another point of view about issues in the church that may have been overlooked...
> I think of myself as someone trading feelings with you about matters which concern us both...So in my column I try to articulate

the puzzlements, joys and hurts about Christ and the church you may be trying to express. As I write, I see ordinary people who, like myself, are at times elated, perplexed, concerned or assured about Christ's church. As they page through the *Leader*, they are looking for a brief word from someone to assure them their feelings are shared.[41]

In her recent autobiography Katie reviews the struggles to find her voice as a writer in a male-dominated enterprise where virtually everything was produced by men, no matter how meagerly written. "No woman served as editor of a major church organ, only children's publications," she writes.[42] It is a tribute to her pioneering influence that today both *The Christian Leader* and the *Mennonite Brethren Herald* are edited by women.[43]

"For thirty years and more *The Christian Leader* editors gave me the rare privilege of speaking to the entire constituency as a columnist about my relationship with it.... For thirty years and more I could think in public."[44]

"As I clarified an issue for myself, I helped the fog to lift in others. That column became a journal of my life and concerns. In it I can trace my interests, ups and downs, periods of growth and stagnation. Grappling with a problem in my own life by putting it into words helped me find myself. I am grateful I had the opportunity to write this column for thirty years. It taught me the discipline of the deadline, the joy of creating with words, and especially the stewardship of ideas and words."[45]

In Appreciation

Editors can't always divine whether a particular column will be a towering home run or a feeble grounder. One column that didn't especially grab me spoke profoundly to a reader who had just experienced two of the worst weeks of her life. The woman wrote, "I wondered aloud, 'How did she know?' It's not often that a piece of writing hits you right between the eyes. Her column did…I am amazed at the way God uses words and wish this letter could be instead a hug for this sister who spoke at just the right time."[46]

A former Tabor colleague wrote, "I continue to be amazed at her ability to highlight significant issues with sensitivity, clarity and intellectual sharpness. While she continues to maintain a balanced perspective on issues it is clear that she remains deeply concerned about Christian response in the face of significant human injustice...."[47]

"The thought-provoking 'Viewpoint' is usually the first section we hit," said one reader, echoing many others. "We appreciate Katie Funk Wiebe's stirring up our faith and connecting it to all sorts of situations that we as Christians should relate to."[48]

A district minister wrote, "my mind was triggered with new ideas, thoughts, concepts. I simply call it inspiration!"[49]

I had the privilege of carrying Katie's column for a third of its 30-year run. For all that time, she relentlessly encouraged the church while also trying to hold it to account. If the Mennonite Brethren Church has become more accepting, energetic and expansive, it is due in no small measure to the persistent voice of Katie Funk Wiebe.

She defined reality for us.

And helped keep us honest.

• • •

Endnotes

1. Katie Funk Wiebe, *You Never Gave Me a Name: One Mennonite Woman's Story* (Telford: DreamSeeker Books, 2009), 76.
2. *Ibid.*, 96.
3. *Ibid.*, 112.
4. *Ibid.*, 121.
5. *Ibid.*, 133.
6. Katie Funk Wiebe, "Wheels and Pyramids," Viewpoint, *The Christian Leader*, February 14, 1978, 19.
7. Katie Funk Wiebe, "The Proof-text Game," Viewpoint, *The Christian Leader*, October 23, 1979, 17.
8. Katie Funk Wiebe, "Lessons in Parking," Viewpoint, *The Christian Leader*, January 13, 1981, 16.
9. Katie Funk Wiebe, "Cleaning the Closet," Viewpoint, *The Christian Leader*, July 24, 1984, 18.
10. Katie Funk Wiebe, "No Littering Allowed," Viewpoint, *The Christian Leader*, April 11, 1978, 17.

11. Katie Funk Wiebe, "I Eye the Monster," Viewpoint, *The Christian Leader*, July 29, 1980, 20.
12. Katie Funk Wiebe, "What's Your Reason?" Viewpoint, *The Christian Leader*, January 1, 1980, 19.
13. Katie Funk Wiebe, "Season of Courage," Viewpoint, *The Christian Leader*, December 18, 1979, 18.
14. Katie Funk Wiebe, "The Way It's Always Been Done," Viewpoint, *The Christian Leader*, December 4, 1979, 19.
15. Katie Funk Wiebe, "Undoing Pagan Influences," Viewpoint, *The Christian Leader*, August 29, 1978, 19.
16. Katie Funk Wiebe, "Tell Me the Old, Old Story," Viewpoint, *The Christian Leader*, May 19, 1981, 17.
17. Katie Funk Wiebe, "The Story of Generations," Viewpoint, *The Christian Leader*, August 26, 1980, 20.
18. Wiebe, "Undoing Pagan Influences," 19.
19. Katie Funk Wiebe, "Family Power," Viewpoint, *The Christian Leader*, January 16, 1979, 19.
20. Katie Funk Wiebe, "Moving Down the Fast Lane," Viewpoint, *The Christian Leader*, October 9, 1979, 17.
21. Katie Funk Wiebe, "Reunions: An Undeserved Place," Viewpoint, *The Christian Leader*, September 6, 1983, 19.
22. Katie Funk Wiebe, "Changing Values," Viewpoint, *The Christian Leader*, May 23, 1978, 19.
23. Katie Funk Wiebe, "Lesson from History," Viewpoint, *The Christian Leader*, September 9, 1980, 20.
24. Katie Funk Wiebe, "What Kind of Good News?" Viewpoint, *The Christian Leader*, March 28, 1978, 23.
25. Katie Funk Wiebe, "A Modern Psalm," Viewpoint, *The Christian Leader*, October 7, 1980, 17.
26. Katie Funk Wiebe, "The Gift of Presence," Viewpoint, *The Christian Leader*, June 2, 1981, 20.
27. Katie Funk Wiebe, "The Other Women's Movement," Viewpoint, *The Christian Leader*, May 5, 1981, 19.
28. Katie Funk Wiebe, "Convenience…or Murder?" Viewpoint, *The Christian Leader*, March 11, 1980, 20.
29. Mrs. Jake Steffen, "Situation Ethics?" What Readers Say, *The Christian Leader*, May 20, 1980, 13.
30. Mrs. Everett Dirks, "Shocked and Shaking," What Readers Say, *The Christian Leader*, June 3, 1980, 14.
31. Debby Ratzlaff, et al., "Taking Life is Love?" What Readers Say, *The Christian Leader*, July 15, 1980, 10-11.
32. Katie Funk Wiebe, "Two Decades of Deadlines," Viewpoint, *The Christian Leader*, January 26, 1982, 15.
33. Katie Funk Wiebe, "Of Law and Love," Viewpoint, *The Christian Leader*, August 12, 1980, 11.
34. Pauline M. Colahan, "Brethren and Sistren?" What Readers Say, *The Christian Leader*, December 4, 1979, 17.
35. Ruby J. Wiebe, "Unnoticed and Unneeded," What Readers Say, *The Christian Leader*, October 10, 1978, 25.

36. Frances Hiebert, "Monastic Albertans?" What Readers Say, *The Christian Leader*, July 12, 1983, 12.
37. Katie Funk Wiebe, "Woman's View," Viewpoint, *The Christian Leader*, July 12, 1983, 17.
38. Phil Esau, "A Subtle Deception," Forum, *The Christian Leader*, May 19, 1981, 10-11.
39. Katie Funk Wiebe, "The Christian Intellectual," Viewpoint, *The Christian Leader*, June 30, 1981, 19.
40. Wiebe, "Two Decades of Deadlines," 15.
41. Katie Funk Wiebe, "Columnist: Offering Another Point of View," *The Christian Leader*, February 28, 1978, 5.
42. Wiebe, *You Never Gave Me a Name*, 161.
43. Connie Faber is editor of *The Christian Leader* and Laura Kalmar is editor of the *Mennonite Brethren Herald*.
44. Wiebe, *You Never Gave Me a Name*, 264.
45. *Ibid.*, 172.
46. Pat Quigley, "Productive Pain," What Readers Say, *The Christian Leader*, February 26, 1980, 7.
47 John Bower, "Kudos for Katie," What Readers Say, *The Christian Leader*, September 23, 1980, 11.
48 Charles and Sharon Jones, "Stirred-up Faith," What Readers Say, *The Christian Leader*, May 4, 1982, 11.
49 Art Flaming, "Inspiration!" What Readers Say, *The Christian Leader*, January 25, 1983, 12.

Why I Write This Column

Katie Funk Wiebe

Within a few weeks one person asked me what it felt like to be a leftist, another accused me of being a feminist, and a third wondered, albeit while smiling why I wasn't being tried for heresy. A fourth person asked why I didn't take a broadside to some of the problems instead of dabbing at them with a flyswatter, and a number of
others wrote that I had put into words just what they were thinking.

Such an array of responses caused me to think through my reasons for writing this column which appears in *The Christian Leader* and *Canadian Mennonite*. The answer isn't simple, when I think of the deadlines which swing around with hammer-blow regularity, and the number of hours which can move around the clock before I have a column which satisfies me.

The main reason I write is not to make you come around to my viewpoint, but to cause you to think about the issue discussed. Your recent letters have encouraged me to believe that this happens. Thanks.

Yet I realize that in writing anything I have two myths to overcome: first, that God expects very little of a woman, particularly a Mennonite woman, except to sew and cook; and secondly, that evangelical Christianity is really not a thinking person's religion.

Somewhere we have perpetuated the myth that trust requires little thought and that God is more on the side of those who do not think seriously than of those who do—despite the fact that the Apostles Paul and John were intellectuals. Because I am an evangelical Christian woman in the Mennonite church, I have much to write about.

I firmly believe that as Christ-followers in an era of quick and sometimes violent change, we need to share our concerns and questions more openly, and also to be more generous with our praise.

I cherish this opportunity to share with you my vision of life—sometimes blurred by personal circumstances, other times a little clearer. Yet each time I sit down before my typewriter, I face the question of honesty. How much should one write about the contradictions one sees between theory and practice and the way we pretend that all is well? How generous can we afford to be in our praise of new trends?

What it amounts to is that I am asking you to question the lightness of your own thinking, even as I question mine about the place of the church in today's society and similar issues. We may have thought about them in one way previously. Dare we face them now? Dare we not face them?

There is nothing like living with a family of teen-agers or working in a college setting with young people continually jabbing one's mental ribs to make one rethink many of the questions about the faith, church and society.

I found that if I wanted to preserve my integrity, I had to answer these questions, but not with religious catchall phrases like "Let go and let God." If I did, I could bow out of life as a contributing person. Some readers have sensed that my viewpoints have changed on certain issues. I make no apologies for this. Change is necessary in this era.

To change one's attitude can be a difficult and painful procedure because it means honestly facing what is inside one. To change means being willing to follow new light without guilt about what others will say. To change means being willing to admit that even God doesn't always hold us to His original instructions.

I often think of Abraham, the man whom God asked to sacrifice his son. Abraham was convinced God wanted him to commit this act. Yet at the critical moment a ram appeared in the thicket and a voice told him to kill it instead of the boy. And Abraham changed his actions to suit the change in instructions.

Yet hadn't God told Abraham to sacrifice his son? Maybe the voice was that of the devil in disguise and not an angel's? Why didn't he stick to his original convictions? Oswald Chambers says Abraham didn't make a fetish of being consistent to his convictions instead of being inconsistent to God. This is a truth I try to write about: faithfulness to God is more important than faithfulness to tradition.

But I write mostly in the hope that you will come away from these few minutes with me with the stronger
assurance that even in a very troubled world the God-directed spirit will find a way. I believe this not because Christianity can be reduced to a formula or a system or even the Four Spiritual Laws but because God has promised to "dwell with him who is of a contrite and humble spirit."

Katie Funk Wiebe, "Why I Write This Column," Viewpoint, *The Christian Leader*, April 21, 1970, 23.

Convenience...Or Murder?

Katie Funk Wiebe

This is not the first word written about abortion—nor will it be the last. Before the debate about abortion is settled in Congress and in individual minds, thousands of words will be written, shouted and whispered. I hope a few will also be prayed.

I find abortion on demand an extreme position that is unacceptable. But I also believe that to hold that all abortion is murder is a trap the church should avoid. It reminds me of the attempts of some religious leaders of an earlier day to deny women in childbirth any kind of anesthetic on the grounds that it was God's will for a woman to suffer while giving birth. It was her punishment as the result of the fall. With that kind of reasoning every tractor, combine, lathe or saw a man uses to earn a living would also be sin!

We should decry the widespread abortion practices for the sake of personal and social convenience of the women—and also the men involved. Some men are more eager that their wives or girl friends get an abortion than the women themselves. To use abortion as a form of birth control is wrong.

The issue of abortion is without ready-made answers, yet I find that when it is discussed quietly among women it sometimes gets a different hearing than when discussed openly by theologians. I am troubled by our inconsistency in attitudes toward the matter. Some people argue against all abortion because they insist the women involved should suffer the consequences of their actions. Their concern seems to be more that the woman be punished by going through the pregnancy than that the child be born into a situation of love and that the others involved be redeemed for Christ.

One church crisis counselor writes that after years of counseling women with unwanted pregnancies he believes the church has pronounced the verdict "murder" without hearing all the evidence. He learned that the woman searching for an abortion cannot be stereotyped. She is not usually young, unmarried and promiscuous. She may be white or black, married or single, supported by her husband or boyfriend or deserted by him. She is generally 18 to 24, working or wanting to finish her education so that she can become self-supporting. She is often an active church woman.

Our attitudes toward the fetus are also inconsistent. A child born full-term or nearly so, if stillborn, is considered enough of a person to be given at least a small burial. Likewise the premature infant. But if a miscarriage takes place at six months or less, the hospital officials dispose of the fetus in some other way. If the miscarriage takes place even earlier, the woman may simply flush it down the toilet not always sure she was pregnant. If these fetuses were all considered as persons, shouldn't they be given a name, their premature death announced in the congregation, and be properly buried? How many parents plan to meet an involuntarily aborted fetus in heaven some day? Our present practices seem to affirm that a fetus is not considered true humanity until it reaches nearly full term, but our words say something else.

We're inconsistent also in the way we think of abortion either as all right or all wrong, and yet leave loopholes for some. The rich, even the Christian rich, will always find ways of getting therapeutic abortions if the mother's life is at stake, if she is an older woman facing an unwanted pregnancy, or if genetic counseling has determined the child will be deformed.

Yet the poor woman who has conceived a child out of rape or incest is expected to bear the child with the glib assurance that "the Lord will provide." Admittedly, the Lord has provided for many women raped during war and revolution when demonic forces broke through all moral and social restraints, and sin and evil controlled the land. Yet what anguish and agony must have accompanied each such pregnancy and birth. I find it hard to accept that God expects a young girl of 13 or 14 raped by her father to bear the burden simply because he has promised to be with people in trouble.

We also tend to confuse morality and legality. Though the government may make abortion an option at government expense for all women who desire it, this decision does not mean that Christians need to accept the morality of the position. What society condones is not always absolute truth. The government is not deciding truth, and its position need not be the position of the Christian.

The whole matter is at best a muddy slough. The issue seems to be to decide whether the fetus is a human being or a potential human being. Wholesale abortion at will is assuredly a slaughter of the innocent and we should oppose it. But to move to an extreme position which gives no room for exceptions is legalistic and unloving.

It is one thing to face such grave issues theoretically—another to face them in real life with a friend or relative. Someone has suggested that if the age group which decides matters such as conscription and war went to the front lines of battle, we would have fewer wars. It might also be that if the persons deciding such matters as abortion bore the children, the matter might have a different outcome also.

Katie Funk Wiebe, "Convenience…or Murder?" Viewpoint, *The Christian Leader*, March 11, 1980, 20.

Chapter 7

A Woman among the Brethren

Harold Jantz

There is something wonderfully ironic about the fact that the quiet-spoken, mild-mannered woman and author, who claimed she had "never" been given a name, has become perhaps the most widely known Mennonite woman in the Americas. Katie Funk Wiebe grew up in Mennonite Brethren settings at a time when women of the church were just beginning to assume visible leadership roles. But they were also increasingly being told that some positions in the church and some roles within society and the home were out of bounds to them. It wasn't always thus.

Even when some roles were firmly cast, Mennonite Brethren women could make their opinions known and men could yield to their persuasion. Few now know that in the first years that Mennonite Brethren gathered on the Canadian prairies as many as a thousand people met under a tent to worship and sing, listen to heartfelt preaching, and welcome brother and sister missionaries home from places half a world away. Women were there in numbers almost as great as the men. In the report of one of those years—1922—the annual yearbook relates that the audience listened raptly as Anna Thiessen told about her work as a city mission worker in Winnipeg. When the board of mission overseers told the convention that because of shortfalls in giving they might need to end Anna's assignment, the women protested. They might not have had official delegate status, but they made their opposition known and they said they would see to it that the money came in for her support. When the women were asked to indicate by a show of hands whether they wanted to help gather the needed funds, a "large number" raised their hands. That seems to have shamed the men, because a number of them, too, then indicated their willingness to lend support. As a result, the convention reappointed her to the mission assignment.[1] The following year's annual conference yearbook listed each individual woman and group who sent in money, down to the last 50 cents.[2]

The story is important because it indicates quite clearly that women were both present and could be heard if the issue had sufficiently captured their attention. In time, that sort of participation changed as Mennonite Brethren became increasingly acculturated to North American society and influenced by the debate in evangelical circles about public and family roles for women and men. But in the early years, women were expected to participate in the work of the church, especially in the area of missions.

The question about ordination of women to ministry had already been raised in Russia during the months of intense evangelistic activity by a largely Mennonite Brethren tent mission corps that formed immediately after the Bolshevik revolution. That heroic group had equal numbers of women and men. One of the women, Katharina Enns, was ordained by a Russian evangelical group after reaching the U.S. some years later.[3]

Among the scores of early Mennonite Brethren single and married women missionaries sent to China, India and Africa from America, the 1954 missionary album names 84 who were ordained.[4] In spite of longstanding practice, some church leaders grew uncomfortable with it and in 1957 a decision was made to commission women, rather than ordain them.[5]

In the decades that followed that decision, Katie Funk Wiebe became a catalyst in the ferment that eventually led to a new conversation and much different ways of seeing men and women's roles in the church. Her patient but persistent voice helped frame the debate about women's involvement in the church for a new generation of Mennonite Brethren men and women. It was especially Katie's willingness to temper her arguments to the mood of the church amidst the societal shifts of the era that brought greater and greater numbers to see the inevitability of the changes for which she was advocating.

A Woman Among the Brethren | 135

Reading Katie's Story

Katie's story can be read in a number of ways. She can be read as a child of sturdy and resilient immigrant Mennonite stock who arrived in Canada with the 1920s wave of refugees from the Soviet Union. She must be read as a youngster growing up in the largely Doukhobour community of Blaine Lake, outside but close to the Mennonite Brethren church community of her parents, in a family that knew how to live their faith within that "outside" setting. She certainly must be read as a very bright student—a Governor General Award-winning student—able to associate easily with others and eager to welcome challenges. She was not a retiring person. She knew her own mind. She was also an attractive young woman, confident, able to lead, yet willing to engage with others and suppress her interests for the sake of those close to her or within the wider community (often the church).

Katie's decision to enroll at the Mennonite Brethren Bible College (MBBC) placed her at the center of church thought and action—certainly in terms of the Canadian church—during the 1940s and 1950s. Although the piety she encountered there was quite different from the settings in which she had grown up, she found MBBC invigorating. There was also the added benefit of her work as secretary to President J.B. Toews, where, as she writes, she "could breathe the same theological air the respected 'JB' breathed."[6] To be able to interact with men of the stature of Toews, Abraham Unruh, and others brought many rewards. Henry H. Dick of Reedley, California, who knew Katie as a fellow student in those days, remembers that "in our conversations we knew we were hearing and responding to a thinking single woman. Easy answers were out of order."

Marriage to a tall, impoverished, and studious young man named Walter Wiebe introduced her to an entirely new life and any reading of her own accounts clearly establishes that while in some ways they were true soulmates, in other ways marriage represented a huge subjection of her interests to his. Graduation from Bible college, where the two met, soon led Walter to work as a teacher in the church. It led Katie to a heavy load of homemaking and the care of four children who arrived within a relatively short span. The rewards were few, particularly in view of the scant visibility for someone who was soon sharing writing and editorial responsibilities with her husband in the newly created conference periodical, *The Youth Worker*.

It is hard not to detect in Katie's writings an undercurrent of resentment toward the relentless focus on studies that dominated Walter's life. An incident in a class we shared as students at Waterloo Lutheran College (now Wilfrid Laurier University), remains clear in my mind and reveals the passion he had for his studies. Walter sat about a third of the way from the front of the class and the subject of the lecture must have engrossed him totally. He began responding in half audible tones in such a way that before long the teacher was speaking only to him. The rest of us might as well have been absent.

Walter remained a student—alongside his teaching stints—virtually to the end of his life. Katie, meanwhile, had to insure that all was well at home and find outlets for herself by inviting others in with whom she could engage in stimulating conversation. She did that exceedingly well. Once, someone gave the Wiebes a large, beautiful ham because of their limited circumstances. What did they do? They invited another young couple "to share their good fortune at a lovely supper," an act described by the recipient "as typically Katie and Walter." [7]

When the family's journey brought them to Hillsboro, Kansas, and death took Walter from the family scant weeks later, Katie faced a huge role reversal. Now she would need to be both father and mother to her children. She would need to earn the family's support, provide the family's face to the community, and be the children's advocate. She soon found, however, that she could only speak in her own voice. It turned out to be a powerful voice.

If we believe in Providence, we can believe that God brought her to the Publishing House, opened opportunities for her to write for The Christian Leader, and led her to a teaching position at Tabor College. Hillsboro provided perhaps as supportive a setting for her gifts to be put to generous use as any setting might have been. One does not have to agree with all she wrote or did to recognize the powerful voice she came to have through the writing and speaking she did from her platform in Hillsboro.

Giving Voice to the Culture

Katie started writing for *The Christian Leader* in 1962 in a column entitled "Women and the Church." It broke ground in its clear assumption that women have a role in the church, not merely in the home. In the early years Katie dealt mainly with safe subjects and treated issues that women might have expected to read there. But underneath, much more was churning for Katie. She has recently written that as she was cleaning out files, she came across a never-published piece from the 1960s entitled "An Immodest Proposal." It invited women to become an "official cheering section" at conferences since they could not be there as delegates. That way they could "serve coffee during the sessions in attractive uniforms, take telephone messages, pin identification badges on male delegates with a gleaming smile; hand out aspirins, ballots, and official documents; count ballots; even sing a few entertaining songs now and then."[8] It was too cutting and Katie never submitted it.

"Women and the Church" soon became "Viewpoint." Lynn Jost, a former colleague at Tabor College, has noted that "Viewpoint" "communicated that women can be thoughtful and provoked others to think. [Katie] encouraged women and girls to believe that women could contribute to MB theology and life." It was a significant contribution.

Part of what set Katie apart from many who were writing for the church at that time was her openness to and interaction with the larger culture. Katie developed the practice of reading widely and clipping much. Sometimes items she read or saved provided help she could share with women's groups who came to her for advice; often it was simply to enrich her own resources. Other times, the books and articles she read provided subject matter for her column.

In numerous places Katie has written about the profound impact Betty Friedan's book, *The Feminine Mystique*, had on her. In 1966 she reviewed it for the *Canadian Mennonite* at the request of editor Frank Epp.[9] It made a huge impression on Katie. Here was the culture facing the church head on. She says, "I couldn't believe other women thought the way I did, hundreds of them, maybe even thousands. I wasn't alone in my feelings about being set aside when it came to use of gifts."[10] In

Friedan's world, the goal and language were about self-actualization; in the church the language revolved around gifts. But it meant much the same thing. Much later in 1978, Katie said,

> Men didn't understand or believe the book. Some women didn't either. Yet for many women readers then, as now, the pain the author describes was real as hunger, for the women suffered an emptiness not satisfied by waxing well-polished furniture, cleaning, shopping, chauffeuring children, and watching television. And there seemed little freedom and encouragement to do anything else…The essential question…which emerged later, was, "Why don't I have the same opportunities for development that my husband has? Why don't I have the opportunity to use my mind and other gifts?"[11]

No Mennonite Brethren woman has reflected that concern more effectively than Katie Funk Wiebe. Few, if any, in the wider Mennonite world did it with greater effect than she. In fact, the first article to make "a blatant plea for Mennonites to consider ideas coming out of the feminist movement" was written by Katie and appeared in the *Gospel Herald*, the (Old) Mennonite Church magazine, in 1970.[12] Repeatedly, Katie provided the best example of writing that offered a "facilitating tone" in its support of the progression of women's role.[13]

Reflecting the Pain and Hope

Though her influence was felt far beyond the Mennonite Brethren, it was within her own church community that she ultimately realized her greatest rewards and often experienced her most painful rebuffs. Katie became widely known both in the U.S. and Canada for her regular appearances as a columnist in *The Christian Leader* and the relatively frequent reprints in the *Mennonite Brethren Herald*. She quickly acquired the reputation as the voice for change for women in the Mennonite Brethren church and it was Katie who was asked to speak or write when the role of women became the subject of discussion. Some cheered her on; others strongly criticized her.

A Woman Among the Brethren | 139

Here is Katie in 1972 in *Direction*, the periodical of Mennonite Brethren educational institutions:

> Women in the Mennonite churches will not always sit outside the inner circle of church life. The gap between what they can do and what they are allowed to do will disappear. The church will not always be afraid to give women the opportunity to develop full use of their talents of love, concern, intellect, [and] spiritual and special skills. They will not always be considered second class citizens in the kingdom of God. I rejoice.[14]

Her voice was prophetic. At the 1974 centennial of the coming of Mennonites to Kansas, she observed that it was becoming "increasingly clear that many individuals are examining truth in terms of personal value, rather than in terms of institutional loyalty."[15] The meaning for culture watchers was clear.

When Katie was asked to be one of the key presenters at the 1976 Mennonite Brethren symposium, "Women and the Church" she seized the opportunity. Her paper was entitled, "Voices of Liberation." If Mennonite Brethren women ever wanted a voice for change, this was it. She began by citing Betty Friedan's writings and while she acknowledged "extremists and radicals" in the movement, she clearly identified with women who "She began by citing Betty Friedan's writings and while she acknowledged "extremists and radicals" in the movement, she clearly identified with the psychologist who had written, "[Women] want freedom to have both marriage and a career. They want access to leadership positions and equal opportunity and equal pay for the kinds of jobs held by men. Women want to contribute to the level of their actual abilities, not just what's dictated by the traditional social roles."[16] She told her listeners that she sensed "the church was standing by and waiting for the whole hysteria to end. Church leaders seemed convinced this was not a spiritual issue, for Bible teaching seemed clear on the role and position of women. It consisted of three dimensions—obedience, submissiveness and silence."[17] She went on to describe the growing volume of discontent within both wider evangelical church circles and among Mennonite

Brethren: women want "to be considered full-fledged members of the human race, equal…yet not the same as men…Allowed to have their own identity."[18]

Some of her words will have sounded outrageously unfair to church leaders of the time, even if she felt them to be true, but her own experience had brought new perspective. "When my husband died…I found that without a husband I had no identity at all in a male-dominated church. I was a nobody in the eyes of some people," she said.[19] She urged the church to find ways to encourage women to develop their skills and gifts for use everywhere in the church, and described how the feminist movement was pushing for a release from "the bondage of sexist language," and the transformation of structures "that alienate and oppress men and women in all levels of life."[20] This involved not only the church, but also the "structure of marriage." She questioned the traditional roles of men and women in marriage. No one had ever confronted Mennonite Brethren on this issue so strongly.

In the fall of 1978, a MCC-sponsored symposium on women in the church, held in British Columbia, heard Katie speak twice. While she continued to speak strongly for full acceptance of the gifts of women, the tone of the addresses clearly took a more conciliatory bent. In one she very effectively described five aspects of Jesus' treatment of women. In the other she began by a relating a chance meeting of four women in the Wichita airport. All of the women were coming home from church-related meetings and all were waiting to be picked up by husbands or others—a reversal of what might have been the case a decade earlier.[21] She went on to say,

> Nearly everyone today has an answer to the problem of changing roles [of men and women]. Some of these answers are inadequate and dangerous; for example, those provided by radical feminists which state that men are the enemy, marriage and family are outmoded and unnecessary, that monogamous marriage is impossible in our fast-paced age, or that male-female differences are only physical, and

that independence and fulfillment are life's highest goals. We cannot accept such answers."[22] She added, "We've all become so preoccupied with individual rights, some of us—male and female—seem to be unable to realize that the most important principle is to submit totally to God, from which all other acts of submission and authority must be derived."[23] These were bridging statements. They helped ease some of the tensions her more feminist arguments generated.

As Elmer Martens has noted, Katie's "persistent urgings, through periodical columns and lectures, on women's equality with men in leadership...served to keep the issue of women's role in ministry from sliding into a minor agenda item." Gradually, the church moved forward, though change did not come quickly. In 1972, Frank C. Peters, who at various times was a college and university president, conference moderator, Bible college teacher and pastor, voiced the willingness of some to recognize the participation of women in congregational and conference meetings. Still, he was hesitant about them speaking publicly or assigning committee positions to them.[24]

David Ewert, one of the church's most influential biblical scholars, proposed a two-dimensional response: on the one hand, opening doors for the involvement of women in the church while at the same counseling caution, a stance that came to characterize the Mennonite Brethren approach. In 1974, when few women were attending conferences and none were on conference boards, he observed that "there is no indication anywhere that the gifts of grace are given to men in greater measure than to women."[25] Congregations who recognized those gifts, he stated, "might elect" women to provincial and national conference and these should "feel free" to make their contributions as any other delegate and also "participate on conference boards." But certain strictures, he argued, should remain, citing ordination to "the preaching ministry and pastoral leadership."[26] His directives led directly to an attempt to get women onto Canadian Conference boards the following year and then to General Conference boards.

When the General Conference floor was opened to women in 1987, it was Katie who was asked to address convention delegates. Her presentation was carefully termed a "devotional," recalled one delegate, though he noted that if a man were to have given it, it would have been a "sermon." [27] Another delegate still recalls it as "more inspiring than any other at the whole convention."[28] When the resolution on Women in Ministry Leadership came to the Canadian Conference in 2006, its language for supporting women in ministry echoed much that had been said and written in the decades that had gone before, some very like the language Katie herself had used. Women were asked "to minister as gifted, called and affirmed." It supported ordination of women in churches who had discerned the freedom to do so. But it also recognized a "diversity of convictions" and "several interpretive frameworks" through which churches or individuals had come to their conclusions about women in ministry. It then built the argument for the ministry of women from the practice and teaching of Jesus and Paul. In a cautionary passage, it stated that there might be times where "women's freedom" could "impede" the gospel and other times where "denying that freedom" could also impede the gospel. Both situations should be respected. Thus, at least in the Canadian case, Mennonite Brethren continued to embrace both freedom and caution.[29] The outcome, nonetheless, was support for women in leadership.

Voices of Affirmation

Very few appear prepared to argue with Katie today, and many strongly affirm the role she has played. It is clear that Katie indeed "paved the way for women to participate effectively in broader church-based and related ministry."[30] Luetta Reimer, a former professor at Fresno Pacific University, observed that "Katie has probably encouraged far more women than she will ever know. Through her column in *The Christian Leader* it was wonderful to discover a woman who could write with honesty and candor about all sorts of issues, including some that might traditionally have been off-limits."

Poet Jean Janzen has termed Katie "a blessed irritant" among Mennonite Brethren. "Even though she got a better hearing in the Mennonite Church USA, she continued to speak up about what it means to be a Christian woman in the last decades of the 20th century," says Janzen. "Her heart of sympathy for widows and singles was transparent and her encouragement of young women priceless." One of those young women is now a faculty member at Columbia Bible College. Janet Boldt took classes with Katie at Tabor College and was a roommate of Christine, Katie's daughter. Katie "stood tall, was committed to excellence and required excellence of her students," Janet recalls. She helped me understand that "I was responsible...to God for my life, all of it, and therefore to deny part of it, particularly my intellect, as our culture pressures women to do, was to deny the way God had made me and therefore to deny myself."

Time after time, Katie is cited as a role model in the way she conducted herself "despite misunderstanding and criticism and at times, exclusion from leadership positions."[31] Gay Lynn Voth, another former Tabor College student and later a faculty member at Columbia Bible College, applauds Katie for not "abandoning life in the denomination for another where she might have fitted in more comfortably...She serves as a model for not giving up, but remaining faithful." As writer and historian Helen Rose Pauls put it, Katie "encouraged women to 'go for it,' take advantage of the many opportunities open to them and not wallow in 'poor me' attitudes."

Mary Anne Isaak, a pastor in Clovis, California, notes that "doors opened for me because others had been knocking on them over a long period of time. I am keenly aware that my role on the pastoral team in an MB church has been made possible by people like Katie Funk Wiebe."

Katie influenced men, as well. Nick Rempel has been a pastor, conference leader and Tabor College board member. He recalls an occasion when he was asked to lead a discussion group on women in ministry and Katie happened to be in the group. As he called the group to order he saw Katie and another woman leader in the back weeping. "It was a sobering moment for me," Rempel says, for it conveyed to him "their perception that we weren't listening or hearing them." Former MCC International executive director, Ron Mathies, calls Katie "a breath of fresh air. In personal conversation, in her writing and speaking, she always had new ideas, or old ideas re-worked into new frameworks. She listened carefully, empathized graciously and encouraged generously." Katie's book, *Who are the Mennonite Brethren?* became required reading for many would-be pastors during the 1990s.[32] She was "a pacifistic Christian feminist," says Walter Unger, longtime president of Columbia Bible College. She was "a gentle prod in the long process among Mennonite Brethren toward more fully liberating women."

Time and again, leaders throughout the North American Mennonite Brethren church note the significant role Katie has played in the church. She was a "tireless advocate for women among the brethren," recalls former Southern District Minister, Roland Reimer. Her ideas were "insightful and corrective," though they caused "dissonance" among "the brethren [and] sisters" at times. In a similar fashion, Ed Boldt of Kitchener, a longtime friend, calls Katie's contribution "distinctive," even if it sometimes involved "controversial" views. She had "a quiet, insistent voice for women, for openness when we were closed," notes former seminary professor and pastor Loyal Martin.

Elfrieda Schroeder of Winnipeg, a former missionary to Congo and language teacher, says Katie pushed "us to admit our weaknesses and do something about them, but never without also pointing to our strengths and our heritage as MBs. Her numerous books on all aspects of life, but especially on social justice issues attest to this." Katie provided "readable historical and theological material," notes former Conference moderator Edmund Janzen, and modeled "with substantive scholarship that women can and do contribute much to the conceptual thought life of the church."

Peggy Goertzen, Director of the Center for Mennonite Brethren Studies at Tabor College, describes Katie in biblical terms. She was "a voice crying in the wilderness, a pioneer clearing the way within the Mennonite Brethren Church" who validated women within the community. Another prolific Mennonite Brethren columnist and author, John H. Redekop, terms Katie a "pioneer," and "a leader among women." Katie "focused on key issues, including the place of women in the church, but did so without rejecting the church. In fact, her writings built up the church by affirming women's contributions in the church," says Redekop. "She earned her right to be heard and her opinions respected," wrote Henry H. Dick, a former Conference moderator and pastor. "I think she got the MB leaders' attention as they noticed that other Christian groups accepted and used her gifts."

Katie "seemed to be able to be provocative and loyal, conservative and radical, feminist but not strident, all at the same time and without confusion," notes pastor and author Dan Unrau. She was "like a fussy housekeeper who was forever drawing attention to the cobwebs in the corners and the dust on the furniture," recalls Menno Martens, "thanks to her and others, the place is starting to look more tidy."

Bless You, Katie!

Katie Funk Wiebe's life journey has not been easy. It has brought pain into her life and sometimes made other lives a little less comfortable, as well. She might have found a warmer reception in other circles, especially in Mennonite settings outside the Mennonite Brethren conference, but she chose to stay and in staying, she helped bring about many of the changes for which she advocated. She is a gift to the church.

• • •

Endnotes

1. *Year Book of the Northern District Conference of the Mennonite Brethren Church of North America* (Hillsboro: Mennonite Brethren Publishing House, 1922), 35-36.
2. *Year Book of the Northern District Conference of the Mennonite Brethren Church of North America* (Hillsboro: Mennonite Brethren Publishing House, 1923), 26-28.
3. A copy of the ordination certificate is in the author's possession.
4. Katie Funk Wiebe, "'The Understanding of Woman's Place among Mennonite Brethren in Canada: A Question of Biblical Interpretation': Katie Funk Wiebe responds to Gloria Neufeld Redekop," *Conrad Grebel Review* 9, no.1 (Winter 1991): 76-78. See *Missionary Album of Missionaries Serving under the Board of Foreign Missions, Mennonite Brethren Conference* (Hillsboro: Board of Foreign Missions, 1954).
5. See *Year Book of the 47th General Conference of the Mennonite Brethren Church of North America* (Hillsboro: Mennonite Brethren Publishing House, 1957), 106.

6. Katie Funk Wiebe, *You Never Gave Me a Name: One Mennonite Woman's Story* (Telford: DreamSeeker Books, 2009), 23.
7. Ed Boldt to Harold Jantz. All letters to Harold Jantz are in the possession of the author.
8. Wiebe, *You Never Gave Me a Name*, 221.
9. See Katie Funk Wiebe, "*The Feminine Mystique* [1]," *The Canadian Mennonite*, March 29, 1966. 52; and Katie Funk Wiebe, "*The Feminine Mystique* [2]," *The Canadian Mennonite*, April 5, 1966, 10.
10. Wiebe, *You Never Gave Me a Name*, 199.
11. Katie Funk Wiebe, "Jesus and Women" (paper presented at Biblical Perspectives on Women in the Church, Clearbrook, B.C., November 18, 1978), 3.
12. Rachel D. Swartzendruber, "Discovering Voices Among Peculiar Quietness: An Analysis of U.S. Mennonite Women's Rhetoric in the Church Press 1963-1977" (M.C. Thesis, Wichita State University, 2006), 49. See also Katie Funk Wiebe, "Liberation—For Men and Women," *Gospel Herald*, December 8, 1970, 1011. This article was originally published in *The Christian Leader*. See Katie Funk Wiebe, "Liberation—For Men and Women," Viewpoint, *The Christian Leader*, November 3, 1970, 19.
13. Swartzendruber, "Discovering Voices Among Peculiar Quietness," 50.
14. Katie Funk Wiebe, "Women's Freedom, the Church's Necessity," *Direction* 1, no.3 (July 1972): 82. This article was originally published in *The Canadian Mennonite*. See Katie Funk Wiebe, "Where We're At…In Our Attitude Toward Women," *The Canadian Mennonite*, February 19, 1971, 9, 29.
15. Katie Funk Wiebe, "The 1974 Centennial: A Moment of Grace for Mennonite Brethren," *Direction* 3, no.2 (July 1974): 202.
16. Katie Funk Wiebe, "Voices of Liberation" (paper presented at Symposium: Women and the Church, Fresno, CA, May 6-7, 1976), 3.
17. *Ibid.*, 4.
18. *Ibid.*, 6, 8.
19. *Ibid.*, 9.
20. *Ibid.*
21. Katie Funk Wiebe, "The Church's Response to Changing Roles for Men and Women" (paper presented at Biblical Perspectives on Women in the Church, Clearbrook, B.C., November 18, 1978), 1.
22. *Ibid.*, 2.
23. *Ibid.*, 12.
24. See Frank C. Peters, "The Place of Women in the Life of the Church" (paper presented to the Ontario Board of Spiritual and Social Concerns, 1972, CMBS (Winnipeg), Papers and Essays, Box 8, Folder Mb; and Frank C. Peters, "The Place of the Sister in the Life of the Church" (paper presented to the Canadian Conference Board of Spiritual and Social Concerns, 1973, CMBS (Winnipeg), Papers and Essays, Box 8, Folder Mb.
25. David Ewert, "The Christian Woman in the Church and the Conference," in *Roles and Resources* (Addresses and Responses at the 1974 Faith and Life Convention of the Canadian Mennonite Brethren Churches, Vancouver, July 7-9, 1974), 29.
26. *Ibid.*, 34.

27. Menno Martens to Harold Jantz.
28. Loyal Martin to Harold Jantz.
29. "Women in Ministry Leadership," *Gathering 2006: Yearbook* (Canadian Conference of Mennonite Brethren Churches, July 6-8, 2006), 52-53.
30. Ed Boschman to Harold Jantz.
31. Janet Boldt to Harold Jantz.
32. See Katie Funk Wiebe, *Who Are the Mennonite Brethren?* (Hillsboro: Kindred Press, 1984).

If You're A Mennonite

Katie Funk Wiebe

"If you're a Mennonite, why don't you wear black stockings and an apron?" questioned a third grader of our daughter shortly after we moved into a community where many of the "plain folk" lived.

When a perplexed daughter reported the conversation at the dinner table, we enjoyed a chuckle over the incident as we explained the misunderstanding. Our daughter didn't know about these other Mennonites, even as that little girl didn't know about us.

"The third grader had learned to know the Amish and the Old Order Mennonites in the area. Black stockings, beards, bonnets and buggies aren't easily overlooked. And so to this little girl to be a Mennonite meant just one thing: to be different in appearance, to wear odd garb and to reveal odd attitudes.

My mind traveled back some 25 years to the day I had mentioned in school that I was a Mennonite. Our family was the only Mennonite family in the community. My statement had little effect on my classmates because outwardly, we were all the same. I myself did not know what it meant to be a Mennonite. I knew it only as the name of the church we attended in summer when roads permitted.

Today I am a member of the Mennonite Brethren Church. I became a member by choice after having stood at a distance for some time. When the opportunity was mine to accept or reject the church, I chose to fellowship with other Christians in a Mennonite Brethren church.

Through the years my attitudes to the church have varied. For a while I wore the name "Mennonite" like a coat that prickles and I tried to shed it at every opportunity. I considered joining a church with more "status." I was almost ashamed of our lowly origins as a minority group, and I felt it would be rather nice to belong to one of the big-name churches—churches which had esteem and popularity and had shed all narrow-minded traditionalism. How humiliating to be grouped by the press with minority groups in disrepute like the stripping Sons of Freedom, a radical sect of the peace-loving Doukhobors.

For a time as a member of a group of zealous students we considered seriously whether we shouldn't remove the word "Mennonite" from the official name of the church. As young gallants for the church, we were positive that the name was the high wall keeping people from Christ. We complained vigorously that the church wasn't doing enough for the cause of Christ and the reason was that we were termed Mennonites. A new label would turn us all into super-spiritual on-fire-for-the-Lord soul winners and the people would flock to our church.

Now I am a little older and I hope also a little wiser. I have found a quiet but confident loyalty to the church of my choice. I believe God has a task for the Mennonite Brethren Church and for each person in it willing to work.

I recognize that the church has many failings. I know we have not always met all problems on the growing edge of the church. I know there are mediocre Mennonite Brethren. But then no church I could run to is perfect; other churches have their "miniature Methodists, puny Presbyterians, bantam Baptists and pygmy Pentecostals." And if we are a powerless church, it is because of this very subnormal Christian living. According to Tozer, "Increased numbers of demi-Christians is not enough. We must have a better kind of Christian soon or within another half century we may have no true Christianity at all."

Any changes which must take place in the church must be made by the Spirit of God in the hearts of men. Changing the name won't be enough. You can't turn a crabapple into a Jonathan apple by giving it a new name. True love will win others regardless of the denominational tag that love wears. In the early days of our church in Russia the membership grew from 18 members to 600 in 12 years at a time when it wasn't popular to be a Mennonite Brethren. Spiritual hunger was met by true evangelical fervor and the church added to itself.

But if our church has weaknesses, I am thankful it also has strengths. I know I need not be apologetic of those aspects of our faith which God has visibly approved. Of course, it is important that we do not gloss over the weaknesses and gloat over our strengths. What our church needs most is loyal members who face the true situation and then work toward making it such a place of true fellowship and worship that God will be honored. The church needs our support, not our criticism.

I rarely pass a church building without pausing to read the name. As we traveled this summer on our vacation we often slowed down in passing an unusual church to read the name. What a disappointment to see a large, beautiful edifice but without any identification except a few words such as Mount Hope Church. But what a joy to find churches who declared freely who they were, revealing their loyalty to Christ and to their denomination.

Perhaps the greatest thrill came as we passed a number of Mennonite Brethren churches and could say that this was the group we had identified ourselves with and to whom God had also given a share in the work of witnessing of His love to mankind. This was my church. I needed it and it needed me.

Katie Funk Wiebe, "If You're a Mennonite," Women and the Church, *The Christian Leader*, November 10, 1964, 21.

Who Decides?

Katie Funk Wiebe

I hear people saying vehemently in response to some issue, "But my Bible says..." To me it sounds as if they have a Bible, and I have a Bible, and you have a Bible, and each Bible says a different thing.

The problem is that we're all intent on making sure that what we think the Bible says about the issue, whatever it may be, from evolution to abortion to child conversion comes out on top because it's our view.

Who decides issues not directly spoken to in Scripture? The answer, of course, is that we all do. Bible scholars and church leaders work at it, but so should you and I. As C. J. Dyck writes in *An Introduction to Mennonite History*, the Anabaptists accepted that the Scriptures were to be interpreted in the gathered congregation. "They believed that when Christians gather, the Word is preached, some listen, some prophesy, others weigh what is said, and then the Holy Spirit... will lead them to be of one mind."

Error in interpreting the Bible is lessened if the interpretation is hammered out within the community of faith in prayer and humility rather than by individuals. There is a grave danger of belief becoming hazardous to the faith life when there is no discerning community to provide the checks and balances to an interpretation.

For this reason I believe that adult Bible study is probably one of the most important activities in a congregation, but it can only be done as a body if all members of the body are there to do it.

There is only one Bible, our Bible, the Word of God given to all. To incarnate that Word in daily life is a task for all of us together—in small groups, in congregations, in denominations. All are ways of together finding out what God is saying to us today about his Word and the world.

And that process will gradually slip from us by default because such joint activity requires work—unless we grab it by the collar and restore it to its rightful place in our midst. Otherwise we'll be accepting those people who pronounce loudly, "My Bible says..." as the truth-givers.

While God assuredly speaks to the individual, interpretation of difficult passages should be tested by the community of faith, not accepted because someone has a good public relations office and a large publications budget.

Other believers should have a chance to say to us and we to them, "This statement you're making about the way God guides, or some other matter, is a truth for all of us." Each of us should also have the chance to say to the other person, "Though God doesn't seem to be speaking to me in that way, I'll go along with you until more of us come to a different understanding."

This means that some issues troubling society generally should trouble us more than they do. They should be on the study agenda of Bible study groups and congregations. Yet current issues like abortion, nuclear armaments, even homosexuality have never been spoken to in some congregations, for the curriculum doesn't make room for anything but the scheduled topic.

To be concerned only with honing the propositions of doctrine to razor-like clarity at top levels of leadership and then handing them down produces many words, but no living Word. The process of interpretation must be brought into the life of every believer in the church.

That, however, takes attention to detail, to organizing, and so forth, and that seems like inefficient time consumption. On the other hand, unless congregations are dealing with issues at the cutting edge of society, they slip back into comfortable contentment of the status quo.

I think a congregation should always be wrestling with some vital aspect of Scripture, adding to its knowledge and understanding of what the passage says. A congregation should always be theologizing.

Theologizing is an invitation for God to enter our lives with his truth and to direct our thinking through his Spirit, and lead us to greater certainty about him. Theologizing always develops out of personal struggle, like a butterfly bursting its bonds for the freedom of beauty. What was once thoroughly systematized and securely nailed to the wall like Luther's theses needs to be gone over again and again and re-appropriated.

This process does not duplicate the democratic method of majority rule. It is the way of allowing the Spirit to work through each member. It's our Bible only if we all work at its interpretation in the gathered community of the church.

Katie Funk Wiebe, "Who Decides?" Viewpoint, *The Christian Leader*, October 16, 1984, 17.

Chapter 8

An Intellectual High

Don Isaac

Katie holds a letter in her hand and chuckles. "I love this one," she says as she picks up up a letter from a former male student. We're sitting in the dining room of her 3rd floor apartment overlooking the stately early residential section of Wichita, Kansas. On the table are several three-inch-thick binders, full of letters and documents from her 24 years of employment at Tabor College. "Listen to this," she says. "You know what I told my friend? If you were my age, I'd be chasing you around like crazy…that's what I told him first semester…and I still mean it." She chuckles again and then says "but here's what he meant." "I don't know why I'm writing this…only to say you meant something to me…and it's important I start telling people that you have been very understanding and patient with me."[1]

Katie is serene now; reflective, content, at peace with herself, and confident—confidence much lacking when she accepted Wes Prieb's invitation to teach a section of Freshman English at Tabor in the fall of 1966.

The Early Work Years

When Katie, Walter and the four children left Kitchener, Ontario in the summer of 1962 for Hillsboro, Kansas, almost everything they owned and valued came with them in their Chevy. Only a few boxes and some furniture had been shipped by van to the rented house on West Grand. Walter's death, barely two months later, left Katie and the children in a new country without the comfort and close support of family and in a part-time job that could not support them.

Orlando Harms, editor of *The Christian Leader*, had written to Walter asking if Katie would write a regular women's column. Although piqued that he had not written directly to her, she had accepted the invitation. When Katie was offered full-time work at the Mennonite Brethren Publishing House, located in Hillsboro, she took it and hoped that it might broaden her role as a writer and spokesperson for the role of women in the church. She began writing for other periodicals and accepted a few speaking engagements but she was disappointed in her responsibilities at work, where she spent hours each day proofreading print jobs and occasionally writing obituaries and church news. She felt she was working for bread money; an identity crisis common to many people then and now.

Katie yearned for ways to learn more about writing, hoping to find a mentor to walk beside her, evaluate her work, and give advice. She found none. It would be some time before she discovered encouragers in older women who had also experienced the pain of restricted service: Hannah Willems, Esther Ebel, Viola Wiebe, all from Hillsboro, and later, Elizabeth Hiebert in Wichita.[2]

The Tabor Opportunity

In the fall of 1966, barely weeks before school began, Wes Prieb, acting dean at Tabor College, asked Katie to teach a Freshman English class. She did not have a bachelor's degree and had never taught school. Her college experience involved two years as a student at Mennonite Brethren Bible College in Winnipeg, Canada; different culturally and academically from Tabor. Yet the opportunity was intriguing. Here was a chance to work and live in the academic world where she could both teach and learn. She accepted, after assuring Orlando Harms that she would only be gone over the lunch hour.

Katie knew she could write but the idea of teaching others to write was fraught with fears and questions. Could she be the same person before her students as she was perceived to be in her columns—especially to young people learning noun/pronoun agreement? Her insecurity led her to write out her notes in detail for each class. It was an ambitious year, one she would find exciting, frustrating, and scary, but it gave her valuable experience and a glimmer of hope for a new future.

The following spring Katie was offered a full-time position as publicity director, editor of the *Tabor College Alumni Magazine*, advisor to the *Tabor College View*, and teacher of several sections of Freshman English Composition. Her beginning salary of $5,783 was the highest she or Walter had ever received.[3] Joanna had just turned 18 and would enter Tabor that fall. Susan, 15, would follow soon and Tabor offered substantial tuition discounts for faculty children. She would be home for the summer. The decision to join the faculty made sense.

Preparation for a New Vocation

While the decision to teach was partly pragmatic it was, more deeply, an opportunity to peel back the curtains before the world of ideas. Katie's need to write out every word before her students soon faded, replaced with more free-flowing conversation about literature, grammar, and prose. She enjoyed reading student papers, though grading often consumed her evening hours at home. Still, she knew she was not prepared academically to take on the full mantle of a professor. She went to work and quickly finished her B.A. at Tabor and almost immediately began her M.A. Degree in English at Wichita State University. For several summers she left Hillsboro at 6:30 in the morning, the children still asleep, to attend classes at Wichita State and returned at 1:30 p.m. after a fifty-cent lunch at McDonald's.[4] Katie was determined to finish the degree, write the monthly columns and articles, teach classes full-time and raise her family. She was an early supermom without the SUV or soccer kids.

A Perspective on College Life

Katie's tenure at Tabor began at the end of a decade of massive cultural change and the college was not immune to its effect on students or college politics. Dress codes and men's hairstyles were quickly moving from conservative to chic radical. Long hair and short dresses became common. Recruitment of athletes for new sports brought in an increasing number of men (mostly) and women who had no acquaintance with Anabaptist theology or Mennonite culture. The new diversity was welcomed but it required a new openness to dialogue by faculty used to the shorthand of Mennonite language. Drinking increased as did the pressure for dancing on or off campus. The sexual revolution, so much in the national news, seemed largely to bypass Tabor and Katie never brought into the classroom her personal feelings about the women's movement. "I had enough to do," she said, "just to master the material."[5] A peace club on campus had a short life, but its purpose was different than the student protests against the Viet Nam War that were so much in the news.

A new experiment in the yearly schedule carved out the month of January for intensive courses. It was called interterm and offered classes not taught during the regular semesters. Some students left for trips to Europe, Africa, or New York. Those on campus enjoyed the almost daily convocations featuring nationally known speakers addressing topics such as Christians and change, Vietnam, racial discrimination, abortion, pacifism, new morality, existentialism, and others. Katie has termed this heady diet of interterm speakers during the 1970s her "intellectual high." These times expanded her horizons, sharpened her mind, and whet her appetite for more of the same. "Some evenings," she said, "I could hardly contain myself because of all the new ideas I had fallen heir to that day. Today I value the opportunities to grow intellectually at Tabor even more than the opportunities to teach."[6]

Classroom Issues

Katie, used to the rigor of the British educational system used in Canada, discovered that many students were unprepared for serious academic work. She resisted the pressure to compromise her standards by giving easier assignments to her students or to grant extra time to athletes. She was dismayed to learn that some coaches asked faculty to change grades so a player could remain eligible. Eventually, she reluctantly modified her grading scale for all students; joining a growing nationwide practice of grade inflation.

Katie soon found that her grading standards earned her a reputation for discrimination against athletes. More than one mentioned in an evaluation that she hated athletes and automatically gave them lower grades than non-athletes. Katie replied to her critics (and occasionally an administrator) that since she almost never attended athletic events and paid little attention to campus social posturing, she rarely ever knew who was an athlete in her class. But the stigma dogged her throughout her teaching years.

Katie was particularly hurt when an influential student in her class, an athlete, burst into her office after the second meeting of the semester, and accused her quite strongly of teaching trash. He objected to the books and stories with some four-letter words that were required reading for the course—though he admitted having not yet read them. He dropped the course but not before exerting enough pressure on the College President and Dean that Katie felt her job was in jeopardy. Katie was shaken by the inability of this student to study significant literature for the lessons inherent and his inability to get beyond language he found objectionable.

She was also troubled by the apparent uneasiness of the college administrators to represent Tabor as an evangelical Christian liberal arts college. During Roy Just's presidential term, Tabor increasingly broadened its curriculum, hiring a new generation of young Anabaptist-minded scholars to help shape the identity of the College. Many Mennonite Brethren churches supported this trend, but it was not without some discomfort on campus. The "liberal" part of the college description was too easily identified with cultural permissiveness in society.

These early years at Tabor were formative for Katie as she worked at balancing her identity as a writer and teacher, her role as a faculty and church member, and her personal growth with her responsibility to a wider audience that was often conflicted about women's issues. She was increasingly sought after as a writer and speaker and she began to travel widely. The writing and speaking were symbiotic with teaching. The discipline of writing helped her teach students to write, and she brought back from her presentations at meetings and conferences stories to enhance the understanding of literature.

Faculty Evaluations

Katie had now been at Tabor ten years, spanning the most dynamic, life-changing events of her career. She had been widowed, found full-time work, learned how to teach, parented her children through school, finished two degrees, and published hundreds of articles.

In spite of these accomplishments, Katie often felt uncertain about her place at the College. She had been through several years with a few students and administrators who questioned her very spiritual core and level of teaching competence. In Katie's first major faculty evaluation in 1976 she was praised by both peers and students for her knowledge of materials, ability to transmit them, concern for student growth, and for helping students learn even when they were psychologically conditioned against the material. "In the area of technical competence, you are one of the better professors on campus, and we affirm and support you for this."[7] But the report also indicated that some students felt put down, discouraged, and overworked. Some saw Katie as a perfectionist and unwilling to consider their circumstances; too pessimistic, discriminating against athletes; and for a few colleagues, too focused on her feminist agenda.

Katie felt unsupported by administration and feared the evaluation would be used against her. She needed a friend who could understand her plight and her history. John E. Toews, chair of the Humanities Division and biblical scholar, suggested she might benefit from a change of pace that the "tightness" of Hillsboro represented for her. She listened carefully as he advised a time for reflection about her personality development and style.[8] Katie applied for a sabbatical the following year, listing her goals as developing (1) relationships with students and faculty, (2) public speaking skills, (3) theological questions and personal spiritual life, (4) committee skills, (5) writing skills, and (6) greater knowledge of her teaching field. Katie writes that at the end of that sabbatical year, "I returned to Tabor with a much freer spirit and stronger sense of my own worth as an individual and as a teacher and writer."[9]

Katie, the Emerging Feminist

Katie's experiences in dealing with a masculine world prior to Tabor had initially led her to be reserved and cautious as she observed college life. Her experiences with students only reinforced that tendency. There is little evidence that Katie used her teaching platform to promote a feminist agenda in her classes or to slant the curriculum she taught. Her binder, full of letters from students, does not contain any acknowledgment or criticism of such an agenda, but it does contain many, many complements for her caring attitude and her attention to detail regarding course content. She was content to focus on grammar, literature and poetry and to help students discover the beauty and truths within.

Yet her regular *Christian Leader* columns and articles coupled with the daily experience of being one of only a few women on the faculty sharpened her sensitivity to female roles in the college and church. She had reviewed *The Feminine Mystique* by Betty Friedan in 1966, one of the early books in the emerging feminist movement in America, and had been profoundly shaken by the book.[10] Now she found friendship and support from Clarence Hiebert, Tabor Bible teacher, who supported her misgivings about gender issues, and became for Katie and other women a long-time encourager and door opener.

When men and women on the faculty pushed for change in the masculine language of several required general education course titles, such as "Man and Values," by recommending more neutral titles such as "Human Values," it opened the door for a wider discussion of gender issues among faculty. In 1983 Katie was elected to the Faculty Advisory Committee, which undertook for the first time a thorough review of sexism on campus. The committee sent to the administration a multi-page document pointing out progress in acknowledging and elevating the role of women on campus but also listing a number of areas with continuing needs. The response was an affirmation of the work of the committee and a commitment to pursue its recommendations to appoint more women in faculty, administrative, and board positions; to reduce the use of masculine language across campus; to invite more women speakers; to give equal salaries to men and women in equal positions;

and to more generally commit to be more sensitive to gender issues. While administrators were not unaware of these needs, the 1984 Faculty Advisory Committee position paper on sexism and the response from administrators seemed to signal a significant commitment to become more inclusive and sensitive to these issues. Katie's role in helping to craft the document was another milestone in the development of her feminist voice, and a significant move for Tabor toward gender equality.[11]

Students Remember Katie

Institutional memories are fleeting, often obscured by actions that tell us little about the persons who walked the halls. One finds Katie's name sprinkled in committee or faculty minutes and occasionally, in the archives, letters to administrators or other faculty. She deeply cared about Tabor College and often expressed her feelings verbally to those she trusted, such as the interdisciplinary group of faculty who usually met informally toward the end of the day in the cafeteria. Here they shared and discussed student-stories, theological issues, and social or cultural issues in the dorms or on the playing field. She enjoyed this time of open conversation, laughter, arguments and the occasional lamenting over some issue. But Katie's legacy is most clearly enshrined with her students.

The letters in her binder reflect the diversity of students whose lives she touched. A student wrote of a class taken in the '70s in which he submitted an assignment written by another person. Now twenty years later the student asked for forgiveness and blessed Katie for the class.[12] Many students wrote letters after leaving Tabor to thank Katie for her continued communication with them; in many cases birthday cards or notes of comfort over some need. Those who went into teaching often wrote to thank her for the rigor of her classes in English.

Katie wrote back to a student, "You ask whether you can write. You do have the potential—it comes through in your writing. You seem to enjoy using language to make it work for you; that much is clear. But whether you can write is something only you can decide. Many people want to have written; too few actually want to write."[13]

A student who had dropped Katie's class and then dropped out of college wrote, "I thank you for all I learned in your class and for the instructor that you were. I appreciate your true concern for the students, their learning, preparedness for life, as well as their spiritual walk. I apologize for not being the student I should have been." Katie replied, "I pray that you may be able to return some day and salvage the year that the 'locust ate.'"[14]

A student teaching in South America wrote, "You have been an encouragement to me that I as a woman can work in the church if I feel God calling me to that. You touch my life through *The Christian Leader* and I thank you for being an encouragement in my life at Tabor."[15]

Another wrote, "I want to thank you for teaching me to be a better writer, to organize my thoughts, to organize my time, to weigh the situation before judging, to be responsible for my work, to appreciate a good piece of writing, and to be proud of my Mennonite background. I've always enjoyed listening to you pray—your prayers humble humanity and uplift God. Thanks for being my teacher at Tabor."[16]

After leaving Tabor a student wrote, "My first few years at Tabor I heard how tough you were, so I set my schedule so I wouldn't have your class, but after I took your literature class I noticed I made a big mistake by trying to find an easy English class. I wish I would have taken both my English classes from you; you really made me see the light."[17]

Reflections

When Katie retired from Tabor in 1990 she had completed two academic degrees, was chair of the English Department and the Faculty Personnel Committee, had taken two sabbaticals, participated on numerous committees, served as the faulty representative both to the Board of Directors and the Administrative Committee. She was awarded Professor Emeritus status and later on the Distinguished Alumni Award.[18] The lunch hour job had turned into a successful academic career.

Now in the comfort of her apartment, with more time to read and reflect, Katie relaxes and talks easily about the good and bad times at Tabor. Her deadlines are fewer and further apart. She's not focused on accomplishment now. She's done that, and done it well. Her written record continues to win acclaim and her binder of letters from past students or readers continues to grow. She is justly proud of being named one of the most influential Mennonites of the 20th Century by *The Mennonite*. Though her teaching home was at Tabor she was welcomed into the wider circle of Mennonite churches and institutions as a perceptive voice of prophecy calling for greater opportunities of service for women. That this voice was not as well accepted among the Mennonite Brethren disappointed her but did not deter her love for and service in the church.

In 2005 former student Sharon Warkentin Short interviewed Katie for a Ph.D. project. In response to her question about advice for a woman starting out in a higher education career, Katie replied that the academic world is intellectually invigorating but still contains subtle challenges of gender discrimination for women. Katie reflected on her own experiences at Tabor by quoting from her book *Bless me too, My Father*:

> I gradually became aware that as I moved about I carried with me the intense fear of being considered a fraud, of moving away from realty to words that were not true for me. Then one day I read in the newspaper that this feeling is common to women moving into new areas of work and thought in this age. It's called the impostor syndrome. Women can't quite accept they have the authority to do what they are doing because they have never been officially blessed for the task. They can't bless themselves because they see themselves as trespassers in uncharted territory. It helped to know that I was not alone in this feeling and that it was another form of false guilt women carry unnecessarily.[19]

Katie found her voice and her confidence at Tabor College. She left behind an enduring example of excellence in teaching, thorough preparation, significant feedback on assignments, an open office door for personal or class questions, and an ability and nerve to ask difficult questions when needed. She left in the hearts and minds of countless students a deep appreciation, not only for good writing and literature, but also as Miriam Hershberger said in her course evaluation she submitted about Katie, "a helpful counselor in my spiritual life and career decisions."[20]

• • •

Endnotes

1. Letter to Katie, 1972. All letters are part of Katie Funk Wiebe's personal files.
2. Katie Funk Wiebe email to Don Isaac, July 16, 2009.
3. Katie Funk Wiebe email to Don Isaac, July 13, 2009.
4. Katie Funk Wiebe, *You Never Gave Me a Name: One Mennonite Woman's Story* (Telford: DreamSeeker Books, 2009), 140.
5. Katie Funk Wiebe email to Don Isaac, July 16, 2009.
6. Wiebe, *You Never Gave Me a Name*, 133.
7. Cal Redekop to Katie Funk Wiebe, December 10, 1976.
8. John E. Toews memo to Faculty Personnel Committee, December 7, 1976.
9. Katie Funk Wiebe memo to Evaluation Committee, November 11, 1980.
10. Wiebe, *You Never Gave Me a Name*, 120.
11. Faculty Advisory Committee Report, Sexism on Campus, Tabor College, May 7, 1984.
12. Letter to Katie Funk Wiebe, May 1, 1992.
13. Letter to Katie Funk Wiebe, September 29, 1981.
14. Katie Funk Wiebe letter, December 31, 1984.
15. Letter to Katie Funk Wiebe, April 25, 1988.
16. Letter to Katie Funk Wiebe, Spring 1989.
17. Letter to Katie Funk Wiebe, n.d.
18. Wiebe, *You Never Gave Me a Name*, 124.
19. Katie Funk Wiebe to Sharon Warkentin, December 17, 2005. See Katie Funk Wiebe, *Bless Me Too, My Father* (Scottdale: Herald Press, 1988).
20. Letter to Katie Funk Wiebe, November 8, 1976.

The Conflict of Peace

Katie Funk Wiebe

Recently I attended a Colloquium (fancy name for conference) on Peace Studies in Mennonite Colleges and Seminaries at Elkhart, Indiana. I went with some hesitation.

Earlier I had glanced over some of the statements on the position of the Mennonite Brethren Church on peace and nonresistance. There seemed to be wholehearted endorsement of the position, yet I was aware that within the church some individuals have moved away from it.

Despite the growing popularity of the peace position with young people, for some others to opt for peace is to move in the direction of the loss of religious freedom to the communists and the downfall of the United States as a great nation. To keep the peace the country must stay at war.

I also realized that some churches, in a desire to identify more closely with the mainstream of American evangelicalism, have dropped the emphasis on nonresistance. They have outgrown what they consider to be an ethnic distinction.

Furthermore, I was fully aware that for many people the word "peace" has become a dirty word—not entirely without cause—synonymous with the great mass of underwashed, oversexed young people who flaunt the peace symbol and engage in spasmodic protests against the Establishment. Peace has a negative image because these people have made it mostly a protest movement with social justice the only important detail. A personal ethic is foreign to them. They are ready to accept a standard of values as it concerns corporate groups, but not for their own personal lives. That's their business.

Perhaps a lesser reason I was hesitant to attend was that I knew I was trespassing into traditional male territory. As I looked over a statement on these concerns prepared in 1955 by representatives of all the major Mennonite groups, I couldn't find one woman's name. Because the issues of peace have always been so closely related to war and conscription, conflict resolution has often been viewed as irrelevant to women. At least the women think so. I had many reasons to stay home, but I went nevertheless.

I came to some personal conclusions about peace and violence, not necessarily the conclusions of the other participants, which made my attendance worthwhile apart from the objective of the conference as related to college curricula.

I realized anew that it is a false belief that violence of any kind will cease by itself. Violence begets more violence. To condone one kind of violence is to condone all kinds. Because the amount of violence in a country may increase noticeably over a period of time due to various factors, so the concerted efforts of people within that society can work toward lessening the violence.

Our media today capitalize on violence. As one historian wrote, "A happy country has no history." A peaceful nation has no news. Our newspapers daily highlight the nation's violence because it is more interesting than news about peace. Headlines draw attention to war, murder, burglary, rape, and arson.

Repeatedly Americans are urged to find ways to protect themselves against attack by using Mace, karate, judo—all violence of a lesser kind. The media give their readers and listeners little encouragement to find out how love can work redemptively to bring about reconciliation either between individuals or nations. It is therefore up to the church to lead the way in directing people to peace.

I sensed that Christians quickly tend to polarize into two groups—those for evangelism and those for peace with the unspoken assumption that one must take sides. Inadvertently both groups steer the other away by not stressing that both are taught in the Scriptures. The issue is not peace or evangelism. It is impossible to make either one the expression of the highest virtue the way some groups focus on healing or tongues-speaking.

Peace without a foundation in the Word of God becomes a humanistic expression of man's concern for man—useful to a degree but a movement that tends to find its powers wane as the difficulties increase. Evangelism which excludes reconciliation and justice becomes an empty farce because it forgets that though a man may have a ticket to heaven, he still has quite a bit of traveling to do down here.

The peace movement which is only a big "No"—a negative protest of all governments and authorities—without accepting the responsibility of bearing the burdens of those against whom the injustices have been committed is as empty as the evangelical who saves a man's soul but forgets that man is a whole person with a body that gets tired and hungry. The newer terminology of "peace," "conflict resolution," draws attention to more positive concerns than did the older terms such as "nonresistance," "nonviolence," and "nonconformity."

The question came up at the conference whether it is naive and idealistic to study peace. Is it an idiosyncrasy of Mennonite groups? Is it our gimmick like the horse and buggy and dress of the Amish? If it is, I discovered that the Catholics in their search for renewal want this gimmick also, for to be a believer is to be a disciple of peace. I left the conference convinced that as long as the concept of peace as it relates to discipleship remains with the male sector of the church and is concerned only with war, it will remain a gimmick. If it is allowed to permeate the life of all believers in all areas of life, it be comes a way of life.

Katie Funk Wiebe, "The Conflict of Peace," Viewpoint, *The Christian Leader*, June 27, 1972, 19.

Tipping over the Tub

Katie Funk Wiebe

"What do you think of all this?" the man waiting by the church floor asked me. The question surprised me. I didn't know him and he didn't know me. What difference did it make to him what I thought of the Wichita Churches United for Peacemaking conference we were both attending? "Your comment at the apartheid workshop made me think you were informed about all this," he said. Again, a reference to "all this." "All this" included addresses on aspects of Christian peacemaking, including the spiritual basis for getting involved in nuclear arms control and the politics of prayer; workshops on prayer, apartheid, colonialism, world hunger, the sanctuary movement, Star Wars and environmental stewardship.

I told him briefly that I had come to learn. That I was a member of a historic peace church in which some members were not fully convinced of this position. That 1 was working my way through the nuclear arms issue and other matters. That I recognized that often prejudice is rooted in our theology. The man, a lawyer, admitted to a similar pilgrimage—he also was working his way through "all this."

I think someone needs to ask us occasionally what we think of "all this." Nuclear war is terrifying to contemplate. I'll admit I wasn't at the conference to learn how to demonstrate. I wasn't there to go over the biblical basis for nonresistant love. I had gone to find out whether, like the people in Nazi Germany, I am being blind to something so huge I can't see it for looking at it.

Jim Douglass, organizer of Ground Zero Center for Nonviolent Action, one of the key speakers, reiterated, "One must see evil to respond to it. We have to see the crisis to be open to it." He mentioned that a relative of one of the more than nine hundred persons who drank the fatal poison in the Jonestown massacre several years ago had asked, "Why didn't someone tip over the tub of cyanide-laced Kool-Aid?" That simple act might have saved hundreds of lives.

Why didn't someone reach out and dump the tub?

Possibly, and probably, because that someone had never even tipped over a thimbleful before.

Like many of us?

Yes, I think so. We tell ourselves that when the crisis comes, when people's lives are seriously threatened by sin and evil, we will rush heroically into the turmoil, and with great spiritual strength, push over tub after tub, freeing people from sin's domination. We think sin will invade our lives and nation like an army. But Satan doesn't work that way. Sin moves into our lives slowly, gently, easily, until we're so used to it, we feel comfortable with all aspects of it, big and small. When the tub of poison is finally sitting in front of us, we don't recognize it for what it is and we're gripped by a paralysis of will. Instead of action, we're ready with alibis. Who hasn't heard these before?

- What will people think if I should speak out loudly against what I consider a serious wrong in our society at this moment? To speak out might harm the business prospects of this community.

- It's the job of politicians to set things straight and to make rules for people to live by, not my responsibility.

- Pastors should lead out against sin and evil and show the rest of us the way. Ordinary people shouldn't be expected to take a stand.

- It's the job of men, not women and young people, to settle serious issues. They're the ones who should start tipping the tub.

- Nonresistant love isn't part of my theology just now. I believe Christ calls us to evangelism and missions, not to fighting evil in systems and structures. These nonresisters don't talk my language.

- I simply don't do peace (or tip tubs—or wash windows).

Douglass's point was that the tub of cyanide is sitting in front of us now in the form of the massive stockpiling of nuclear arms. His method of tipping the tub is not through hostile demonstrations, but by learning to know the enemy, and then establishing community with them and other concerned Christians.

He used the story of the Good Samaritan, a person despised by the Jews because of his cultural background, who rescued the man in the ditch. Jesus's use of the term "Good Samaritan" will have been as revolting to the Jews then as a parable of a Good Communist might be today.

We cannot change evil or injustice from the outside, Douglass said. People whose livelihood is dependent on the arms-buildup economy feel judged when pacifists demonstrate around them. So he and others are attempting to make friends with the members of the Trident nuclear submarine base near Seattle, Wash., by living next door to it.

"Unless we recognize the presence of God in the people who oppose us, we have no business being involved in non-resistant efforts."

Christians in Europe after World War 2 asked themselves why they had been blind to the growing evil in their nation. I think I went to the conference in the hope I need never share the Germans's hindsight.

Katie Funk Wiebe, "Tipping over the Tub," Viewpoint, *The Christian Leader*, December 10, 1985, 13.

Chapter 9

Lifting the Fog

Marlene Epp

Katie is among the best storytellers that I know. She herself says that "stories, like cream, have a way of coming to the top," and references the two kinds of cream in her childhood—the actual cream used by her mother for baking, and the cream that was her father's daily fare of storytelling.[1] Her stories often go straight to the heart of an issue, using images and anecdotes that illustrate and critique a question or event in ways that remain embedded in one's imagination. Katie's storytelling has been at the center of a transformation in how we think historically about Mennonites, and consequently, how we think about the present and future. Her historical research and writing has offered models for doing personal and family history, for regarding women's place in the past, and for rethinking church and denominational history.

For me, as another historian, a few of Katie's stories stand out. One of these, recounted in several of her publications, tells of her husband Walter's ordination to the ministry in 1953.[2] As his wife, she had also knelt before the presiding minister who laid his hand on her head while he prayed. Later, she discovered that his sweaty palm had left an imprint on her new black, velvet hat. The "permanent indentations" became for her a "mark of ordination" even while she had made no promises nor received a specific blessing for her new role as minister's wife. I first heard this story in 1998 when Katie gave the keynote address at a conference on gender in Mennonite history with the provocative title, "Me Tarzan, Son of Menno—You Jane, Mennonite Mama"![3] (When I, as one of the conference-organizers, first heard this title, my jaw dropped since I could imagine neither a Tarzan nor a Jane in Mennonite history.) This story was about her own personal history, carrying with it for Katie a mixed sense of pride and hurt—pride over her new status as a minister's wife, and hurt over both the ruin of her hat and her exclusion from the official ritual. Yet it was also a wider story, one that spoke volumes about women's sidelined place in church and community.

The story of the black velvet hat typifies Katie's way of doing history—using a story, often a personal one, to reveal how an individual experience reflects societal norms, beliefs, and patterns. Indeed, she said herself that "stories explain the truths of life better than many long sermons."[4] Katie's talent for combining colorful anecdote with incisive critique makes her eminently readable as a historian. She entertains even while she analyzes. As a historian, Katie's contribution has extended from the personal to the familial, to the gendered, and beyond that to a new way of thinking about the history of her religious community. As an advocate in her own era for a changed understanding of women's roles in church and society, and also within marriage and family, she knew that historical awareness of female presence and activity could help to make a case for that change.

Mooring Oneself with Personal Memoir

Many readers have been drawn to Katie Funk Wiebe through her personal life-writing. The book that chronicled her experience of losing her husband and living most of her life as a widow was (and continues to be) extremely popular; Katie's self-revelation has become a model for others.[5] It is her memoirs, however, that are among her most delightful and insightful pieces of writing (at least according to this historian who loves good memoirs). Storytelling, Katie writes, is about "harvesting one's life," a "creative process" that "nurtures the imagination."[6] And she has a great gift for bringing in the harvest.

Katie's personal life story, like everyone's, is built upon the accumulated life stories of many ancestors and more immediate family members. She was drawn to think historically about her own life, in part because of the letters received from relatives living in the Soviet Union in the 1920s and '30s—letters that told of unimaginable hardships, loss, and disappeared relatives. Her curiosity was piqued when she read, in a footnote in the family genealogy, that a female ancestor had the power of witchcraft.[7] In an effort to learn about these people so far away yet so close to her, she developed an interest in genealogy and eagerly imbibed the many family stories told in her childhood home. Finding clues to the saga of her maternal family's disappearance during the Bolshevik Revolution was as exciting as meeting her *Tante* Truda, her mother's younger sister, separated from the family for 57 years.

Continuing her quest, Katie traveled in 1989 to present day Ukraine where she visited ancestral places and spaces and met more relatives. She continued gathering genealogical data, translating letters, and finding missing links in family stories. She then wrote a number of family histories, mainly for family themselves because she "wanted them to know where they came from."[8] In exploring her personal and ancestral Mennonite past, Katie says she found the "source of my greatest riches as a writer."[9] And indeed, her writing about herself and her family and the place that the personal past has in a wider community and global story, is among Katie's best writing.

But well before she had published her own memoirs, Katie encouraged others to explore their own histories by writing a "how to" book about life writing, titled *Good Times With Old Times*.[10] In this guide, she emphasized the importance of knowing one's history, not in order to be nostalgic about the better times in the past, but to provide a mooring for living in the present and preparing for the future.[11] Using her own family as an example, she proposed that her children and grandchildren needed to know about the wars, migrations, famines, losses, and other hardships faced by their ancestors in order to grasp the strength of the human spirit in times of adversity and develop pride in that. Well before scholarly historians were considering individual and collective memory as something to be analyzed and interpreted for how it functioned in creating historical understanding, Katie acknowledged that her father's memories of the past, as revealed in storytelling, could differ from the memories that Katie would eventually hold about those same stories. As well, she astutely differentiated between autobiography—a more "controlled" form of writing that aims at completeness—and memoir, which she describes as a "series of portraits" that selects, emphasizes and interprets the events of one's life.[12]

In that guide to writing memoirs, Katie offered as example many stories from her own growing up years in Saskatchewan, material that would find its way into her 1997 memoir, *The Storekeeper's Daughter*.[13] This wonderful book tells gripping, delightful, and profound stories about being a child of immigrants, about living within yet on the edges of Mennonite Brethren church life, about surviving the Depression on the Canadian prairies, and about growing from girl to woman. Being a gifted creative writer, as much as a historian, the memoir reads like a novel, full of descriptive stories that Katie offers to readers as "a gift."[14]

Katie describes her most recent memoir (2009) as a "life review."[15] In it, she brings together many of the stories, anecdotes, and analyses that appeared in previous books, articles, and columns. The title, *You Never Gave Me a Name*, is a theme that had surfaced a number of times already in reflections about her life. The phrase was about her given name—was it Kate, Kay, Katya, Katherine?—yet also about other labels that gave her identity, such as German, Mennonite, Russian, and Dutch. In this memoir, Katie's own life story is a stark reflection of the status of women within Mennonite churches—and indeed within mid-twentieth century western society—during an era that predated second wave feminism. Her continual inward and outer struggles against gender expectations are revealed, as well as her continual successes in her chosen vocation, even while obstacles constantly faced her. Katie's autobiographical and memoir writing has entertained, inspired, and provided a model for doing personal history; she found her own name in writing about her life.

Giving Mennonite Women a Past

Not only did Katie Funk Wiebe give herself a name, but her wider and perhaps greatest contribution historically, was in giving names to countless Mennonite women, past and present. Katie's appreciation for biblical history, world history, and Mennonite history was often the foundation for her critique of women's place in the contemporary Mennonite and wider world. In the stories she told about her ancestors in Russia, she quite often illuminated patterns of power and gender that went well beyond "family history" to societal and communal history.

In her efforts to uncover the "underside" of women in Mennonite Brethren history, Katie observed that women were often hidden because their names were absent from the historical record. She noted the amusing example of Mennonite cookbooks in which recipes were attributed to the contributor's husband; as in a recipe for *Zwieback* authored by Mrs. Jacob Steingart. Or the irony exhibited in a roster of 60th wedding anniversary couples listed by only the men's names. She also bemoaned the difficulty in doing research when "men had control of the public record" and, as a result, archives and historical libraries neither gathered nor organized their materials with an interest in "powerless persons" such as women.[16] In this, she echoed the arguments made by a new cohort of women's historians influenced by second wave feminism in the 1970s and onwards. But she went beyond suggesting that historians try harder to incorporate women into "men's zone of power" (though this needed to be done as well) to encouraging an altered view of the past that raised up family relationships, childbirth and childrearing, and domestic labor as equally worthy of the historian's pen. Such an approach meant a shift in thinking about what constituted an historical source, to include cookbooks and quilts, for instance, along with institutional minutes.

She also put forward controversial factors that she felt contributed to the subordination of women in Mennonite communities: these included the fact that women were so often the "social conservators" of Mennonite culture, especially with regard to clothing and hairstyles that reinforced "submission, purity, and piety"; and the prohibitions against birth control that limited female reproductive rights and thus women's role in society and church.[17] Some of her convictions about women's right to use birth control came from her own experience, but it also emerged as she read Mennonite family histories and genealogies that were replete with stories about very large families and numerous mothers who died in childbirth or from the negative health consequences of repeated pregnancies.[18] As other North American feminists were rallying women with the slogan "the personal is political," Katie astutely observed that the Mennonite church in Russia and North America had a vested interest in maintaining women's primary role as reproducers. After all, large families meant consistent growth in biological church membership, while smaller families might lead to shrinking churches.[19]

Katie's writing about women was and is unique because she managed to combine the sometimes dichotomous approaches of celebrating women's creativity and fundamental contribution in their traditional spheres while also pointing out that women were barred from using their gifts in other spheres. Women's historians might describe this as the "victimization" versus "agency" approach. Katie's gift with using words allowed for this type of analysis, as evidenced in this description of her mother: "A woman's place was at home kneading soft dough with strong hands; with stripping milk from soft, warm udders; with serving *Prips* and *Schinkefleisch* to tired men when they came home from the fields; with cradling children into quietness; with loving deeply without spoken words; with praying silently, head bowed."[20] Here, Katie speaks almost reverentially about female domestic activity, and so emphasizes its importance, yet subtly reminds the reader of female silence and submission.

Her desire to give women a past and to provide role models for young Mennonite women was behind Katie's acceptance of an assignment to edit a collection of biographies of Mennonite Brethren women that appeared in 1979.[21] Playfully titled *Women Among the Brethren*, the book was the second of several biographical collections of Mennonite "women worthies" that were published in the midst of an exploding interest in "herstory."[22] Obviously inspired by the women's liberation movement, Katie's project was nevertheless cautioned to "stay away from feminist issues," though, by bringing visibility to the lives of fifteen women from the Mennonite Brethren past, the book was indeed a feminist contribution. Katie was also a forerunner in rethinking the terms of reference that often prioritized male experience in historical writing. For instance, she described the women profiled in the book as "leaders in the art of living and loving," thus demonstrating that leadership was not only about preaching, teaching, and administering.[23]

Katie's own contributions to the collection include an essay about Efrosinia Morozowa, a hardly-known Russian woman who was among the first to be baptized into the newly formed

(1860) Mennonite Brethren church in Russia and who reportedly evangelized on behalf of the breakaway movement.[24] She also wrote about Elizabeth Unruh Schultz, whose life was the quintessential immigrant story of the early 20th century, and Anna Falk Loewen, who was forced from her home in Ukraine in 1943 and was among the thousands of Mennonites, mainly women and children, who came to Canada as refugees after the Second World War.[25] All of these women were leaders in their own right.

The publication of *Women Among the Brethren* not only allowed women to see themselves in the past, but prodded the larger Mennonite community to consider its history in a more gender-balanced way. Earlier projects of writing about women had begun to do this: these include Katie's biography of long-time Mennonite Brethren missionary in China, Pauline Foote, and her history of the Bethel Deaconess Hospital School of Nursing in Kansas.[26]

Transforming Church History

Katie's search for women led her to give voice to another profoundly descriptive image: she described the way in which women appeared (or not) in Mennonite history was through "low-lying fog."[27] I used this image in my own book on Mennonite women, because it so vividly described the research process of squinting one's eyes to find a female presence in so many of the historical writings on Mennonites—Mennonite Brethren and otherwise.[28] Katie was among the first to recognize—and state publicly—that just because women were not easily visible in accepted and official stories of her denomination did not mean they were "just spectators."[29] And many of her writings demonstrated this. In a 1981 article, later published in the book, *Your Daughters Shall Prophesy*, she pointed out that the 18 male signatures on the founding document of the Mennonite Brethren church really represented 36 names, since the men as household "heads" were also signing for their wives.[30] Yet a founding myth evolved that had 18 men as founders of the new breakaway church. But as she continually put forward, women were very much there, as "advisors and secretaries to church-leader husbands," offering hospitality, serving as missionaries and in mission societies, and caring for the sick and hungry.[31] Katie boldly chastised historians for "shov[ing women] to the edge of the story of the founding of the MB church, making them invisible."[33]

Linking past and present, as she always did, Katie emphasized that for future generations of women to obtain equality in the church, they needed to identify with the crucial functions that women undertook in the past. And consequently, the history of the church needed to be rewritten. Her advocacy for "giving women a past" can be found in her critiques of the two series—one American, one Canadian—of survey histories of Mennonites in North America. About *Mennonites in American Society, 1930-1970*, she observed that women's voices "almost disappear[ed] at a time when they were beginning to have a voice in affairs."[34] About *Mennonites in Canada, 1939-1970*, she noted the challenge of including women's stories when the focus was on spheres of activity "from which they were actually systematically excluded"; such an approach comes across as "pinned on, incomplete [and] contrived," she said.[35] Arguing for new ways of doing history, she observed that women would be hard to find "if their accomplishments are evaluated only by the trappings and appearance of traditional power."[36] While women of necessity wrote their histories with reference to gender, men could seemingly write history and leave women out altogether, oblivious to the fact that their history was also deeply gendered in that it universalized male experience. In these survey histories, she observed, women were mainly seen through "a low-lying fog."

She was not only critical of women's absence from the historical record, but she observed that the Mennonite Brethren (and we can extend this to other Mennonites) carried an "ambivalent theology" that did not reflect women's experience. As examples, she referred to the manner in which the core Mennonite doctrine of nonresistance had little to say to women when it focused mainly on male dilemmas of wartime conscription; or to the mixed messages given to female overseas missionaries who were ordained for service yet prohibited from "preaching."[37] This ambivalence was of course also about the denominational name that remains gender-exclusive, a topic that Katie is somewhat less direct in addressing.

In writing about the history of her denomination, Katie did not hesitate to expose the absurdities (seen as such today) of certain church leaders. For example, about well-known Mennonite Brethren preacher H.H. Janzen, she questioned his statement that women who taught in the church were "most dangerous" because they were "more open to emotional influences" and emotions had no part in biblical teaching.[38] And when F.C. Peters—Mennonite Brethren preacher and university professor—called for an end to the discussion about women's issues in 1975, Katie commented, "He dismissed the matter as if women were children who could be sent out to play with a giant-sized bottle of detergent and a washing machine."[39] Katie was not afraid to critique the past.

Although Katie Funk Wiebe is most often described as a "writer" rather than an "historian," the fact that she is gifted at both tasks is what makes her collection of work so thoroughly engaging and accessible. As a Mennonite woman herself, she understands the linkages between her personal story, her gendered past, and the history of her church. At all of these levels, she was, and is, a leader in burning off the fog that hides historical knowledge.

• • •

Endnotes

1. Katie Funk Wiebe, *You Never Gave Me a Name: One Mennonite Woman's Story* (Telford: DreamSeeker Books, 2009), 276.
2. *Ibid.*, 68-69.
3. See Katie Funk Wiebe, "Me Tarzan, Son of Menno—You Jane, Mennonite Mama," *Journal of Mennonite Studies* 17 (1999): 9-21.
4. Katie Funk Wiebe, *Good Times With Old Times: How to Write Your Memoirs* (Scottdale: Herald Press, 1979), 71.
5. Katie F. Wiebe, *Alone: A Widow's Search for Joy* (Wheaton: Tyndale House Publishers, 1976).
6. Wiebe, *You Never Gave Me a Name,* 252.
7. *Ibid.*, 248-249.
8. *Ibid.*, 252.
9. *Ibid.*

10. For a revised edition see, Katie Funk Wiebe, *How to Write Your Personal or Family History: If You Don't Do It, Who Will?* (Intercourse: Good Books, 2009).
11. Wiebe, *Good Times With Old Times*, 24.
12. *Ibid.*, 38-39.
13. Katie Funk Wiebe, *The Storekeeper's Daughter: A Memoir* (Scottdale: Herald Press, 1997).
14. *Ibid.*, 10.
15. Wiebe, *You Never Gave Me a Name*, 247.
16. Wiebe, "Me Tarzan, Son of Menno—You Jane, Mennonite Mama," 13.
17. Wiebe, *You Never Gave Me a Name*, 219.
18. *Ibid.*, 58.
19. Wiebe, "Me Tarzan, Son of Menno—You Jane, Mennonite Mama," 18.
20. Wiebe, *You Never Gave Me a Name*, 164.
21. Katie Funk Wiebe, ed., *Women Among the Brethren: Stories of 15 Mennonite Brethren and Krimmer Mennonite Brethren Women* (Hillsboro: General Conference of Mennonite Brethren Churches, 1979).
22. For other biographical collections, see Mary Lou Cummings, ed., *Full Circle: Stories of Mennonite Women* (Newton: Faith and Life Press, 1978); Elaine Sommers Rich, *Mennonite Women: A Story of God's Faithfulness, 1683-1983* (Scottdale: Herald Press, 1983); and Ruth Unruh, ed., *Encircled: Stories of Mennonite Women* (Newton: Faith and Life Press, 1986).
23. Wiebe, *Women Among the Brethren*, x.
24. Katie Funk Wiebe, "The Russian Sister: Efrosinia Morozowa (C. 1850-?)," in *Women Among the Brethren: The Story of Fifteen Mennonite Brethren and Krimmer Mennonite Brethren Women*, ed. Katie Funk Wiebe (Hillsboro: General Conference of the North American Mennonite Brethren Churches; Board of Christian Literature, 1979), 1-15.
25. Katie Funk Wiebe, "In Journeyings Often: Elizabeth Unruh Schultz (1866-1943), " in *Women Among the Brethren: The Story of Fifteen Mennonite Brethren and Krimmer Mennonite Brethren Women*, ed.Katie Funk Wiebe (Hillsboro: General Conference of the North American Mennonite Brethren Churches; Board of Christian Literature, 1979), 55-70; and Katie Funk Wiebe, trans., "A Flight in Winter: Anna Falk Loewen (1902-)," in *Women Among the Brethren: The Story of Fifteen Mennonite Brethren and Krimmer Mennonite Brethren Women*, ed. Katie Funk Wiebe (Hillsboro: General Conference of the North American Mennonite Brethren Churches; Board of Christian Literature, 1979), 149-167.
26. Katie Funk Wiebe, *Have Cart, Will Travel* (Hillsboro: Board of Christian Literature, General Conference of the Mennonite Brethren Church of North America, 1974); Katie Funk Wiebe, *Our Lamps Were Lit: An Informal History of the Bethel Deaconess Hospital School of Nursing* (North Newton: Bethel Deaconess Hospital School of Nursing Alumnae Association, 1978).
27. Wiebe, "Me Tarzan, Son of Menno—You Jane, Mennonite Mama," 10.
28. Marlene Epp, *Mennonite Women in Canada: A History* (Winnipeg: University of Manitoba Press, 2008), 3.
29. Wiebe, *You Never Gave Me a Name*, 207.

30. See Katie Funk Wiebe, "Mennonite Brethren Women: Images and Realities of the Early Years," *Mennonite Life* 36, no.3 (September 1981): 22-28; and Katie Funk Wiebe, "Women in the Mennonite Brethren Church," in *Your Daughters Shall Prophesy: Women in Ministry in the* Church eds. John E. Toews, Valerie Rempel and Katie Funk Wiebe (Winnipeg: Kindred Press, 1992), 173-189. For another version of this article see Katie Funk Wiebe, "Mennonite Brethren Women: Images and Realities of the Early Years," *Direction* 24, no.2 (Fall 1995): 23-35.
31. Wiebe, *You Never Gave Me a Name*, 206.
32. *Ibid.*, 207.
33. Wiebe, "Me Tarzan, Son of Menno—You Jane, Mennonite Mama," 15. See Paul Toews, *Mennonites in American Society, 1930-1970: Modernity and the Persistence of Religious Community*, vol. 4 of *The Mennonite Experience in America* (Scottdale: Herald Press, 1996).
34. *Ibid.* See T.D. Regehr, *Mennonites in Canada, 1939-1970: A People Transformed*, vol. 3 of *Mennonites in Canada* (Toronto: University of Toronto Press, 1996).
35. Wiebe, *You Never Gave Me a Name*, 218.
36. Wiebe, "Women in the Mennonite Brethren Church," 175-177.
37. Wiebe, "Me Tarzan, Son of Menno—You Jane, Mennonite Mama," 17.
38. Wiebe, *You Never Gave Me a Name*, 202.

Come Higher Friends

Katie Funk Wiebe

The year 1974 marks the centennial for thousands of Mennonites of the arrival of their forefathers in America. Both in the United States and Canada, much machinery has been set in motion to make new contact with the past and to learn from it. The search for the past naturally also includes a search for the great among our forebears—those who moved to the front by courageous word and act.

And so our history includes men like Menno Simons and Ulrich Zwingli and Conrad Grebel; but also people like David Toews, C. F. Klassen, B. B. Janz, P. C. Hiebert, H. S. Bender and John F. Funk. These men should rightfully be honored for their contribution to God and man.

However, as I read Mennonite history books, it has always concerned me how few laymen, particularly women, are mentioned as having performed any distinctive service to either church or community outside the Anabaptist period. Some men are occasionally singled out, but women become part of the general mass of humanity which has no defining characteristics.

I realize, however, that this is not the true situation, nor is this omission from history always intentional. Our cultural heritage has reinforced the idea that greatness belongs to officialdom. An official church position seems to be deeded to get recognition, which is not entirely scriptural nor a true picture. Both laymen and laywomen have always moved out of their routine to serve God in specific ways.

I think back to the Apostle Paul, who, in writing to the Roman church, greeted nearly thirty people by name, not all preachers. About seven of these are women. I doubt that he carried Mennonite blood in his veins, for no Mennonite minister I know would have learned to know so many women on a first-name basis so soon.

During Anabaptist times laymen, including women, were numerous among the martyrs for their faith. Their names appear frequently in history: Anna Roggens was drowned as was Anna Buckhorst. Anna Cantiana was burned at the stake. Ursula Helriglin was imprisoned in St. Petersburg at the age of 17 and not released for five years.

The list goes on—this one was drowned, the next one burned. Anneken Hendriks was severely tortured to force her to give the names of other Mennonites. When she would not, she was tied to a ladder, her mouth filled with gunpowder and thrown into the flames. She was 53 years of age and could neither read nor write.

Yet as one studies Mennonite history of the period closer to our own, the names of women are missing almost entirely from the rosters of the great. Yet greatness is not measured by prominence, by ability, by position, by superior talents in preaching, art, music, politics, but by character. Jesus said, "Whosoever will be great among you, let him be your servant."

And there have been hundreds of thousands of unknown servants of God among the Mennonites in past history, both men and women, whose names will never be indexed in a history book. This centennial year, let us think of them also and pause to give thanks for their unknown contribution. God works through individuals, all kinds. The history of the church is the story of how individuals have let their influence be used for God.

For example, I think that women who were involved in some unofficial type of people-caring ministry in pioneer days should be added to the historical record. I think of a Mrs. Aganetha Barkman Reimer of the former Kleine Gemeinde who was of great service to the community of Steinbach, Manitoba, during her lifetime as a midwife.

Because the village had no medical help, the minister encouraged Mrs. Reimer, a young mother with more than half a dozen children, to take a midwife course in a distant city. In more than forty years of practice, she delivered about 700 babies. In difficult cases, she knelt before the patient's bed and prayed. When someone died, she was the undertaker. Her services were always free and she always found time for others in her devotion to God. Her story can doubtless be duplicated in many communities. But these stories are unrecorded.

We need to remember also those who spent their lives teaching in the early schools, helping the poor, working in orphanages, taking in strangers, before this type of work was taken over by institutions and motels. The names of hundreds of people will never be known who have encouraged and witnessed through a word or a letter, prayed silently, donated time and money, loved the unlovely, worked for justice. Yet they are also great.

Jesus told a parable about a feast at which the guests rushed to find the best seats. Sometimes the guest of honor was pushed to the bottom of the table in the scramble. Then the host had to restore the proper order and say to the one who should be sitting in the seat of honor, "Come higher, my friend. You belong here beside me."

To the many unknown "greats" of the past centuries who may have been pushed out of history books, out of memory, out of sight, let us say in this year of remembering, "Come higher, friends. You belong up here."

Katie Funk Wiebe, "Come Higher Friends," Viewpoint, *The Christian Leader*, January 22, 1974, 19.

Chapter 10

Stories Into Books

Peggy Goertzen

A perception often exists among writers and non-writers alike that those who write "well" or "brilliantly" have a magical, mysterious element to their writing, a "gift" that might be regarded as supernatural or divine. Katie Funk Wiebe has sometimes referred to her own "calling," but it is a calling born out of hard work, often tedious, tiresome, and painstaking. "Write, keep on writing, write about what you know. Write and the inspiration will come," she would say.[1] Katie followed her own advice. She put stories on paper and then turned them into books. More importantly, Katie put her own story on paper.

Katie's books sold widely and have been recognized with several awards. She has been described in promotional literature as "a Mennonite writer of distinction." At writers' conferences Katie is hailed as "a well known Mennonite writer," although this is difficult to define. Is Mennonite literature material written by a professing Mennonite, for a Mennonite audience, written from a Mennonite perspective, or containing Mennonite themes? Yet Katie's writing has appealed to a much broader audience than the Mennonite community. What has made Katie's writing distinctive and well-known in the realm of Mennonite literature and within the wider field of Christian writing?

Writing Other People's Stories

Katie began by writing historical accounts of Mennonite people and programs. Her first book, *Have Cart, Will Travel*, fleshed out the story of Paulina Foote, a Mennonite Brethren missionary to China.[2] Foote's ministry to preach and serve overseas was sanctioned by the rigidly conservative elder, Johann

Foth of the Ebenfeld Church, in his ordination message for her at Bessie, Oklahoma. It did not escape Katie that missionary Foote was a woman with an inner calling to serve Christ, a woman who served with the blessing of male leadership.

The Day of Disaster, a widely distributed paperback, chronicled the story of Mennonite Disaster Service (MDS) for their twenty-fifth anniversary.[3] Katie researched MDS files, MDS workers' unpublished notes, and interviewed numerous individuals who participated in the program. The story, well told with much detail and personal testimonies, was not considered historical enough by some yet the inclusion of personal stories from MDS workers facilitated the communication of the faith component, the spiritual dimension which is at the heart of MDS. With her Mennonite upbringing and its emphasis on mercy, compassion, and relief work, Katie was able to give an account of the efforts of Mennonite Disaster Service that reflected the core values she shared with MDS. The success of the book proved her approach. By February 1977 the book had sold 9,000 copies and a third reprint of 12,500 copies was ordered.

A similar phenomenon occurred with the writing of *Our Lamps Were Lit*, which Katie described as an "informal history" of the Bethel Deaconess movement in Newton, Kansas.[4] She included the personal stories of the sisters in the deaconess movement, which effectively communicated the core faith at the center of life and service of these women and this institution. Yet again, some wished for a more complete scholarly history.[5]

Other popular histories followed. *Women Among the Brethren*, a collection of fifteen stories of Mennonite women, was edited by Katie and offered what she described as "a valuable contribution to Mennonite literature and to literature about women" in its depictions of the values and judgments women lived by."[6]

The vehicle Katie used to depict these values and judgments was storytelling. It was a style of writing that increasingly came to characterize her work and she employed it well. Don Ratzlaff, former editor of *The Christian Leader*, now editor of the *Hillsboro Free Press*, notes that Katie "knows the power of a story. Just as Jesus told parables, she can tell a story and let it stand for itself."[7] She "made biographical writing an art," said James Juhnke, professor emeritus at Bethel College.[8]

Writing Her Own Story

Increasingly, Katie found that the most powerful story she could tell was her own. No one can argue with one's personal journey and the situations, struggles, and perspectives that are uniquely one's own. Katie learned to use stories from her life to illustrate or highlight an emphasis, a point, a reality, or a truth. She had a gift for "clearly defining her own personal feelings," and for selecting just the right story or anecdote and then expanding it in a larger context.[9] In the process she raised many questions, and dared to leave the clarity of a black-and-white world by moving into the ambiguity of a gray landscape. In her advanced composition classes at Tabor College, Katie was known to say, "If you have no questions about life, everything is solved with pat answers, clichéd slogans, you're not a writer."[10] In writers' workshops, Katie counseled, "Don't be afraid of not knowing. Welcome not understanding, having problems, being bewildered, and being forced to change."[11]

Katie's first autobiographical book, *Alone: A Widow's Search for Joy*, was written fourteen years after the death of her husband.[12] With time and distance from the experience, Katie was able to lay some of those experiences before the reader with a genuineness born of detail and vulnerability: identity following the death of a spouse, subsequent relationship to the community and church, and the biblical background that grounded her reflections about God. She was "searching for strength and for an attitude which can accept a difficult situation." She was thankful to God that she was able to do it, "sometimes after a hard struggle, but the victory has come."[13]

Alone, published by Tyndale House, quickly moved beyond a Mennonite readership. *The Methodist Mirror*, a newsletter of the First United Methodist Church in Warren, Ohio, enthusiastically recommended *Alone* as a book offering encouragement and inspiration to the widowed, the unmarried, and divorced women.[14] Others echoed the recommendation. *Alone* has been reprinted in two British editions, two German editions, and in Finnish.[15]

From the beginning, Katie determined to write *Alone* "in narrative fashion, making it my personal story, like Catherine Marshall's *Beyond Ourselves*. [I thought] the tone should be understandable and inspirational."[16] She looked to Bible commentator William Barclay for inspiration as she admired his insistence on simplicity of language so that the content was understandable to the average reader.[17] She worked hard to make her own writing accessible, trying "to write so that ordinary people can understand."[18]

As Katie continued to write, several themes began to emerge. First, she explored the role of women in church and community with its attendant challenges and inequalities. Her search for identity was a theme she returned to frequently. It initially surfaced in *Alone,* as she faced the loss of a husband and found herself in the uncomfortable shoes of a widow. She explored this theme again in *Bless Me Too, My Father* and *You Never Gave Me a Name*, by examining her family origins, her early church experience, the shaping years of her experiences at Mennonite Brethren Bible College, and her marriage.

Additionally, Katie's writing frequently focuses on the issues of aging, especially in *Life After Fifty*, *Border Crossings*, *Prayers of an Omega*, *The Storekeeper's Daughter*, *Bridging the Generations*, and *Good Times with Old Times*. Rather than running from old age, Katie embraced the aging process with its challenges, its pains and promises, its inequalities. Katie writes that she cherishes "the opportunity to share my stumbling through life with others."[19] She wrote in her preface to *Bless Me Too, My Father*: "I see the need for a book like this to show middle-aged and older people that the perplexities and change they are going through is normal."[20]

Her approach resonated with readers. One retired Mennonite pastor from Kitchener, Ontario wrote concerning Katie's book *Border Crossing*: "This is not an objective analysis of the issues around aging. It is not a guidebook. It simply opens windows for the reader to see the thoughts, struggles and feelings of the author as she makes *her* crossing."[21] Katie's style "keeps your interest and attention. She tells it like it is, and makes herself vulnerable," noted another reader. Others have used words such as "challenging," "stimulating," "helpful," and "insightful," to describe their responses to her books.

After reading *Bless Me Too, My Father*, a reader from Kingston, Tennessee wrote, "It took me a long time to read the book, for every paragraph had so much meaning! I could relate from my earliest memories to the last sentence in the book." Another reader from Kansas wrote, "In many places and situations, I found identity in your experiences and in the way you dealt with them. It was good to travel with you through those experiences and I'm glad you dared to tell us about them."[22] Jane Vajnar, columnist for the *Hillsboro Star Journal*, wrote concerning the same book, "I found myself identifying strongly with many of Wiebe's ideas and experiences. In fact, much of the book's value to me lay in the revelation that this highly educated, articulate and successful woman has suffered the same insecurities and buffets to self-esteem as the rest of us."[23]

That validation of human experience, experience which often produces the sense of chaos and suffering in "circumstances which resembled the aftermath of a Kansas tornado," is clearly one of Katie's strength.[24] German theologian, Jürgen Moltmann, wrote in one of his sermons, "When other people look at us with friendly eyes, we come alive. When other people recognize us for the individuals we are, we become free. And when we feel accepted and affirmed, we are happy. For human beings depend on acceptance as birds depend on air, and fish the water. Acceptance is humanity's element."[25]

Katie's storytelling enables the reader to look at human experience—joy, triumph, loss, grief, rejection, betrayal—with "friendly eyes," eyes of acceptance and understanding. We are not strange and different; we are not the only ones going through these particular experiences. Scripture is indeed true; "the rain falls on the just and the unjust" (Matt. 5:45). There is not something wrong with us when we have lost a parent, a child, a spouse, a friend, a job, a home, or we feel depression or anxiety over the stresses in our lives. We are human. We are normal. Katie's "friendly eyes" enable her to articulate others' thoughts or feelings on this journey and to give "normalcy" and validation to the human experience.

This honesty and forthrightness in the telling of her story, the deviation from a totally "rosy path" mindset and "orthodox" perspective, gives permission to readers to question, evaluate, and analyze within a safe framework. As one reader from Kansas put it, "She is good at being prickly."[26] Another commented, "She is not afraid of taking on sensitive subjects."[27] Katie's stories sometimes leave us uncomfortable, which stimulates us to consider again viewpoints and perspectives previously unchallenged. A frequent reader's response to Katie was, "You always make me think." Rene Pauls concurs, "I love how she tackles the issues that she personally has and is wrestling with. Her conclusions aren't always easy to read but are valid as I think on them!"[28] As a result of her challenge, readers have been shaped and re-shaped, particularly with regard to the role of women in the church and to the value of widowed individuals and older adults.

Writing for Mennonites

From the beginning, Katie saw herself as an agent of change within the church, particularly among Mennonite Brethren but also within the larger Mennonite family. For Katie, writing was one way to address the challenges facing the church. Katie and her husband Walter had initially felt that God had called them into a literature ministry and that call did not diminish with Walter's death. Katie was concerned with how the church often used "muddled" communication resulting in a "contaminated" or "carbonated" gospel. Katie's suggestions for change included using a "less prosaic" approach, less "Mennonite tribal language," and more stories.[29] Her use of the term "prosaic" offered a subtle critique of communication that was frequently uninteresting, unimaginative, dull, boring, or commonplace. Katie advocated utilizing stories with inclusive language and creative thought-provoking dynamics. Her goal was the development and strengthening of a "practical theology" not only for the church, but for herself.

It is disappointing that Mennonite Brethren have been less welcoming of Katie's writings than the extended Mennonite family and even other denominations. As was often the case, "she was known more broadly than locally."[30] Perhaps skepticism regarding the spirituality of questioning the ways of God and the will of God influenced her reception among Mennonite Brethren. Katie acknowledges that religious journalism seems to question the immutability of God and his Word.[31] A strong conservative sense of adherence to the Truth of God, no matter what, does not leave room for any intellectual or rational critique. The unwillingness to explore different lines of thinking resulted in some resistance. One Kansas reader admitted, "Katie's opinions were not my opinions." Sometimes the reluctance was generational.

But many Mennonite Brethren women, newly widowed, or friends of the newly widowed, sought encouragement in the pages of Katie's book *Alone: A Widow's Search for Joy*. Some found immediate encouragement through the identification and validation of their experience while others were discouraged. One reader noted that initially, "The timing was not right for me to read her books. So I did not pursue them."[32] A number of years later, this same woman found much meaning and help in Katie's writing.

But Katie's approach to Bible study, where she uses several translations, a concordance, Bible dictionaries and handbooks, and a discerning community—"I sort, reject, synthesize"—has given her credibility.[33] Rene Pauls, a Kansas reader of Katie's books, commented, "For somebody like Katie to have gone through all that she has, to be a woman in a generation when it was not good to be a woman, to come forth, to be somebody, is a real source of encouragement."[34] That affirmation comes through from others, as well. A longtime Mennonite Brethren church member noted, "In the broader picture, she has done a lot for women in the MB Conference to help them to have a place in the church and to recognize women's gifts." [35]

The wider Mennonite world has also recognized Katie's contributions to women and to the church. Robert Kreider, Mennonite educator and historian, notes that he has "appreciated her inter-Mennonite appreciations and sensitivities. In a gentle way, she helped affirm the role of women."[36] Kathryn Rempel, a retired Mennonite pastor, wrote to Katie,

> My life has taken a different course than yours, and yet there are many points at which I identify with what you write....Your writing is helpful to me because you put yourself into your books...You offer to me who you are. Thank you...I affirm you for 'hanging in there' in the MB Church and pioneering the way for women in leadership and ministry.[37]

Paul Schrag, editor of the *Mennonite Weekly Review*, affirms Katie's most recent book *You Never Gave Me A Name* as

> courageous, skillfully combining her personal story with the larger picture of changing roles of women in society and church. I think it is important, with the potential to be eye-opening for a younger generation of people who don't realize how much things have changed in just a few decades. She is truly a prophetic voice, both by recounting the past and also by describing her vision for full equality of women in the church...she is a historian, storyteller and prophet—and all in a popular style that makes her information and wisdom accessible. That's a rare combination.[38]

Teaching Others to Write

Katie did not have the benefit of a tangible mentor, no female Mennonite writer. Instead, she looked to other established authors as her mentors and friends—William Barclay, A.W. Tozer, Marion Hillyard, F.B. Meyer, Oswald Chambers, and Hannah Whitall Smith.[39] She honed her own skills through practice and the study of others. As she put it, "books are my friends and I receive much joy and strength from them."[40] But Katie has not been slow to help other writers. One of Katie's significant contributions, in the words of Robert Kreider, "is her role in modeling and encouraging others in the calling of writing."[41]

Her reputation as a writer resulted in many invitations to speak at writers' conferences and to present writers' workshops.

She has spoken to religious journalists, Mennonite writers, Mennonite reporters, emerging writers on topics as varied as "Getting Started as a Writer," to "Writing Devotionals."[42] Still, "her strength is writing the biography, the memoir," as Tabor College professor, Deborah Penner, has commented. "That is her strongest suit."[43] Katie's expertise and credibility has given power to her instruction to others in writing their own memoirs. She has become "a model in helping others to find their story" through a very personal approach.[44] Katie herself notes that she has "told many writing workshop participants that the more personal the writing, the more universal."[45]

Over twenty years ago I attended one of Katie Funk Wiebe's writing workshops. Katie spent a good hour giving comprehensive instruction, guidance and "helpful hints" regarding the process of writing and how one goes about starting to write. The impressions in my mind were embodied in words like laborious, time-consuming, and tedious. At the close of the workshop, perhaps sensing our need for encouragement, Katie gave these words, "And why do we write? Because we can't keep from writing. We can't help it. We have no other option." This resonated with my spirit. Yes, we write because we cannot keep from writing, just as we sneeze, because we cannot keep from sneezing.[46] There was hope for me. There was hope for everyone sitting around that table.

Honoring a Lifetime of Writing

Katie's desire to express her life—"to give herself away"—on paper came with a cost, a price to pay. She was continually faced with challenges—parenting four children as a single woman, making an income, going back to school, managing a home, and working on a career—all as a widow. In some circles, she was misunderstood and misrepresented; in others, she was isolated in that she had crossed some unspoken boundaries regarding gender and age.

In 2000 Katie was chosen as one of twenty people "having had the most powerful influence on life and belief of the General Conference Mennonite Church and Mennonite Church in the 20th century."[47] As a prolific Mennonite Brethren writer and speaker, "she is well known in broader Mennonite circles as a pioneer and inspiration for women seeking greater roles in church leadership. She is also recognized for raising the credibility of Mennonite writing and in later years has given voice to widowhood."[48] Katie has commented that "it was a humbling experience to know that people have been reading my material more than I realize."[49]

What made Katie's writing distinctive in the Mennonite world? The very fact that her literature was able to go beyond the boundaries of Mennonitism, that her books were accepted and welcomed among Methodists, Nazarenes, and Baptists as well as Mennonites. Her books were not targeted to a narrow or exclusive audience but were universal in theme and presentation. This appeal to a broader Christian audience was recognized and applauded through the receipt of the Silver Angel Award for *Bless Me Too, My Father* and honorable mention for *Border Crossing*. Silver Angels are presented for excellence in religious and moral quality in television, radio, motion pictures, records, videos, and books.[50] Mary Dorr, the founder of the Angel Awards, aimed to showcase "non-toxic entertainment— media for all ages, the kind that raises our spirits and contributes to the meaningful and enlightening examination of our lives."[51] Tabor College administrators, faculty and staff honored Katie with a surprise reception, where she said, "I never expected to receive a Silver Angel Award. I'm gratified that my ideas have received this affirmation."[52] Stanley Clark, Tabor's academic dean at the time, wrote to Katie, "I just learned about your Silver Angel award, and wanted to join the chorus of applause you are receiving. You have brought great credit to us, by your successful writing career. *Thanks for all you are doing.*"[53]

Because Katie could not keep from writing, the Mennonite world is blessed with the writings of a devout follower of Christ who was not afraid to share her own journey or ask the hard questions and who in the process validated the experiences and perspectives of thousands of believers. As one admirer put it, "Katie is a treasure. It is time to celebrate this wonderful, gifted writer who has given so much to the Mennonite Brethren as well as to the greater Mennonite community in her books, articles and teachings. Her books are a 'must read' for in her writings we learn to know the real Katie."[54]

Stories Into Books | 195

• • •

Endnotes

1. Katie Funk Wiebe, speaking notes.
2. Katie Funk Wiebe, *Have Cart, Will Travel* (Hillsboro: North American Conference of Mennonite Brethren Churches; Board of Christian Literature, 1974). See also Paulina Foote, *God's Hand Over My Nineteen Years in China* (Hillsboro, M.B. Publishing House, 1962) and Katie Funk Wiebe, "Telling the Resurrection Story," *The Christian Leader*, March 31, 1987. 17.
3. Katie Funk Wiebe, *Day of Disaster: The Story of Modern-Day Samaritans* (Scottdale: Herald Press, 1976).
4. Katie Funk Wiebe, *Our Lamps Were Lit: An Informal History of the Bethel Deaconess Hospital School of Nursing* (Newton: Bethel Hospital School of Nursing; Alumnae Association, 1978).
5. James Juhnke, interview by Peggy Goertzen, September 7, 2009.
6. "Mennonite Women's Stories Told in Recently Published Paperback," *Hillsboro Star-Journal*, October 17, 1979, 4A.
7. Don Ratzlaff, interview by Peggy Goertzen, September 9, 2009.
8. Juhnke, interview.
9. Ben Wiens, interview by Peggy Goertzen, September 2009.
10. Katie Funk Wiebe, personal annotations in Maxine C. Hairston, *Successful Writing: A Rhetoric for Advanced Composition*, (New York: Norton Publishing, 1981), 14.
11. Katie Funk Wiebe, "Ten Points to Get Started as a Writer." Personal files.
12. Katie F. Wiebe, *Alone: A Widow's Search for Joy* (Wheaton: Tyndale House, 1976).
13. Katie Funk Wiebe to Victor Oliver, January 25, 1976.
14. *The Methodist Mirror*, First United Methodist Church newsletter, Warren Ohio, July 28,1978.
15. See Katie Funk Wiebe, *Alone: A Search for Joy* (Lakeland: Marshall, Morgan and Scott, 1976); Katie Funk Wiebe, *Auf einmal allein: Eine Frau sucht ihren Weg*. Translated by Friedhilde Horn (Witten: Bundes-Verlag, 1976); Katie Funk Wiebe, *Alone: Through Widowhood and Beyond—A Search for Joy* (London: Hodder and Stoughton, 1989); Katie Funk Wiebe, *Yksin* (Hämeenlinna: Päivä Osakeyhtiö, 1990); and Katie Funk Wiebe, *Und dann war ich allein: Wenn der Partner nicht mehr da ist*. Translated by B. Selchert (Giessen/Basel: Brunnen Verlag, 1991).
16. Katie Funk Wiebe to Victor Oliver, February 19, 1975.
17. Katie Funk Wiebe, interview by Peggy Goertzen, April 23, 2009.
18. Katie Funk Wiebe, interview by Peggy Goertzen, December 12, 2009.
19. Katie Funk Wiebe, *You Never Gave Me a Name: One Mennonite Woman's Story*, (Telford: DreamSeeker Books, 2009), 170.
20. Katie Funk Wiebe to Paul Schrock, January 30, 1987. Also Katie Funk Wiebe, *Bless Me Too, My Father* (Scottdale: Herald Press,1988), preface.
21. Katie Funk Wiebe, Personal files.
22. Comments collected personally from various readers.

23. Jane Vajnar, "Authors Grapple with Heritage," *Hillsboro Star Journal*, December 13, 1989, 2A.
24. Wiebe, *Alone*, p.27
25. Katie Funk Wiebe, "The Communication Challenge of the Church: External and Internal," n.d. Personal files.
26. Marilyn Bartel, interview by Peggy Goertzen, August 19, 2009.
27. Ratzlaff, interview.
28. Renee Pauls to Peggy Goertzen, September 13 2009.
29. Katie Funk Wiebe, notes from writer's workshop, n.d. Personal files.
30. Roland Reimer, interview by Peggy Goertzen, August 27, 2009.
31. Katie Funk Wiebe, notes from writer's workshop, n.d.
32. Rosella Martin, interview by Peggy Goertzen, August 21, 2009.
33. Katie Funk Wiebe, *Bless Me Too, My Father* (Scottdale: Herald Press, 1988).
34. Rene Pauls, interview by Peggy Goertzen, August 28, 2009.
35. Hilda Vogt, interview by Peggy Goertzen, August 2009.
36. Robert Kreider to Peggy Goertzen, September 10, 2009.
37. Kathryn Rempel to Katie Funk Wiebe, March 1989.
38. Paul Schrag to Peggy Goertzen, September 14, 2009.
39. Katie Funk Wiebe, interview by Peggy Goertzen, April 2009. See also Wiebe, *You Never Gave Me a Name*, 163, and Katie Funk Wiebe, *Second Thoughts* (Hillsboro, Kansas: Kindred Press, 1981), preface.
40. Katie Funk Wiebe to Lola M. Kyte, March 9, 1992.
41. Robert Kreider to Peggy Goertzen, September 11, 2009.
42. Mennonite Writer's Conference Program Agenda, Hesston, Kansas, September 1990. Personal files.
43. Deborah Penner, interview by Peggy Goertzen, August 31, 2009.
44. Deborah Penner, interview by Peggy Goertzen, September 2, 2009.
45. Wiebe, *You Never Gave Me a Name*, 170.
46. Katie Funk Wiebe, "Why Do You Sneeze?" Viewpoint, *The Christian Leader*, March 16, 1976, 21.
47. "20 for the 20th Century," *The Mennonite*, February 22, 2000, 4.
48. *Ibid*, 6.
49. Katie Funk Wiebe, interview by Peggy Goertzen, December 12, 2008.
50. Katie Funk Wiebe to Peggy Goertzen, January 7, 2009.
51. "Kudos" *The News*, Christian College Coalition for Enduring Values, May 1989, 2.
52. "Wiebe receives award," *Hillsboro Star Journal*, April 12, 1989, 7A.
53. Stanley Clark to Katie Funk Wiebe, April 11, 1989.
54. Lois Reimer to Peggy Goertzen, August 31, 2009.

Why Do You Sneeze?

Katie Funk Wiebe

She stood in front of me after our class reunion, waiting for an answer. Her dark hair was cleanly parted in the center and pulled back. Equally dark eyes, slightly troubled yet eager, turned to me from behind the large-rimmed glasses.

"Do you think I could be a writer?"

I paused to answer. Why should I encourage anyone to join me in the long, lonely hours at a typewriter, struggling to overcome the fear of the blank page before me? Should I tell her how often I have whittled at an idea that looked promising, only to find that instead of creating a graceful bird poised for flight, I had fashioned another lumbering ox which had to be permanently bedded down in the waste paper basket with others of his kind.

"Do you think I could be a writer?" The question came with greater firmness.

She knew she had talents in writing, yet as I returned her clear gaze, I wondered what she meant by writing.

Did she mean sifting through her vocabulary for the spectacular phrases which draw attention? Did she mean filling reams with sentimental goo? Did she see writing as emoting on paper about drifting over the great seas of loneliness or as unloading her generous feelings about God's nearness?

My answer comes late, Violet, but here it is.

Yes you can be a writer, if you know how to work hard. Someone once told me that writing is the art of applying the seat of the pants to the seat of the chair. He doubted whether there was any such thing as talent for writing—only pressure, which the individual has to apply himself.

The best writers are not the ones with the greatest talents. They are the ones who think of writing as Churchill did—like any other job—marching an army, for example. They do it because it's their job.

If you wait until the mood hits you or until you have caught up with other work, you will never write a word. You'll succeed if you can write for long stretches of time without one smidgen of inspiration, all the time feeling a terrible dryness; or if the weather is a balmy 85 degrees and the family is outside on the patio enjoying the first spring barbecue while you hang over your typewriter. If you can move writing out of the category of a hobby or something squeezed into spare time to top-ranking priority, you'll make it. Most writing is not mere accident or the result of high inspiration. Usually it comes by work—hard work and lots of it.

You can be a writer if you have a love for words, not just a flare for them. Consider each word a precious gift from God, given to you for a special purpose. Words can't do their work if they are tossed around like confetti. They must be selected with loving care.

I believe one of the worst diseases of modern society is jargon. Like huge warts, its ugliness protrudes everywhere, weighting meaning down to the ground instead of setting it free. In an age when phrases like "parameters" and "program expansion techniques" and "residential desirability scales" have tainted even religion, you can be a writer only if you make yourself the enemy of all that shrouds and buries the truth.

But you will need to consider other factors. As a writer you must be willing to be honest about yourself and your writing. Ken Macrorie in *Telling Writing* terms anything which is written to impress as "Engfish," because it reminds him of fish which have stood in the sun for several days. Both stink. You can be a writer if you are willing to let your writing force you to grow. "No one knows who he is until he has tried to put himself on paper. And no one knows what His world is until he has tried to describe it," writes Richard Sewall.

But even this is not enough. You can write only if you have conquered the fear of failing—and also of succeeding. Both fears can keep you from even trying.

Lastly, you can write if you do it not for the glamor, not for the kick of seeing yourself in print, but because you are convinced that writing is your assignment from God. When you get your commission from Him, you are not responsible for the outcome of your work, only for your faithfulness to the task.

Countless times as you write, even with this sense of calling, you will find yourself overwhelmed by the growing crime, violence, murder and corruption. The evidence will seem to abound that God's program for the salvation of the world is an illusion and that love and justice and forgiveness are dying out. But if you keep sending out the minority report that Christ's love is forever, you will become surer of yourself as a writer for you will find your writing and your faith in Christ as Lord of life are all of a piece.

Then if someone asks you why you write, you can respond with a question: "Why do you sneeze?" You have no other option.

Katie Funk Wiebe, "Why Do You Sneeze?" Viewpoint, *The Christian Leader*, March 16, 1976, 21.

Chapter 11

The World of Mennonite Writing

Daniel Hertzler

The latter half of the 20th century witnessed a flowering of Mennonite periodical publishing. All the Mennonite groups in the United States and Canada had official publications and there were also unofficial or quasi-official periodicals which had reasonable circulations. My concern is to show the kinds of work Katie Funk Wiebe did for Mennonite periodicals beginning with *Christian Living*, a monthly originally subtitled "A Magazine for Home and Community," of which I was editor from 1960 to 1973.[1] A review of the thirty-eight articles Katie Funk Wiebe published between 1962 and 1997 provides an idea of the kind of work she did for Mennonite periodicals. My intention in this chapter is to be illustrative rather than exhaustive.[2]

Christian Living

Katie's first article in *Christian Living* appeared in April, 1962.[3] Entitled "A Pilgrimage in Books," it illustrates one of the strengths of Katie's writing, namely that she was able and willing to put herself front and center and to tell it like it was. Getting this first article published involved an awkward exchange between writer and editors, which Katie described in a preface she wrote for my own memoir. Katie reminisced,

> I sent an article to *Christian Living* magazine. No answer. Months later came a check for five dollars and some tattered remains. Editor Hertzler had chopped out the few sections he wanted to use and returned the rest. *So this*

is the way editors work, I surmised. But my next articles were published whole and my relationship with Dan was always generous.[4]

I could seek to justify myself—a new writer we did not know, editors always too busy, article not really well written—but I do not recall these details.

I have reviewed those "few sections" to see what interested us enough to publish them. I found two personal anecdotes in this one page article plus a closing generalization. For one, Katie indicated that books had become important to her as soon as she could read. "I moved from a child's world of dreams into the world of books when I learned to spell out the words of 'Little Half Chick,' a story in our first grade reader. I have never left it."[5]

For another, she reported how she discovered a book that was to be important for her spiritual development. At the age of 20 in a state of personal uncertainty she discovered in a reading room the book, *My Utmost for His Highest*, by Oswald Chambers. "That day a weak, faltering faith received strengthening, and aimless feet were put on course. A life without ambition was given a goal. A rebellious spirit yielded to a Master."[6] She failed to get the title of the book or the name of the author but some years later she and her husband received a copy of the book as a wedding present. "I rejoiced as at the return of a long-lost friend. For many years now I have read in it with great inspiration and help."[7] This personal "here-I-am" kind of article was to become a staple of Katie's writing for periodicals.

Katie's second article in *Christian Living* is an example of another type, which was to become an illustration of her ability: an article based on journalistic research. "Stay Here and Open an Office," published in November 1962, is a personal profile of Dorothy Swartzentruber who, according to the article, once prayed that her life could be spent in some important work.[8] However, Katie "didn't find her in some distant mission school teaching native children, but in a rather ordinary looking office in the heart of Canada...directing the work of six women in assembling 4000 copies of a 16-page mimeographed booklet."[9] This article demonstrated that already Katie was able to research and write about another person or situation. I was to call upon her more than once for this kind of article.

So on the one hand, Katie shared her own experience. On the other, she researched and described the experiences of others. What becomes clear from a review of her articles is that her own perspective was significantly affected by the death of her husband in November 1962, leaving her with four small children. In March 1963 she published an article entitled "Living Apart for the Lord: To Stay-at-Home Wives," regarding busy husbands who were not always available to their families.[10] In a note about her as author, the editors mentioned that her husband died "last November 17." Having already written the article, Mrs. Wiebe added this comment: 'God in his infinite wisdom has caused this separation. Though a much harder one, I want to be ready to learn the deeper spiritual truths which God has for me.'"[11]

Widowhood was a theme to which she would return from time to time. Some of her early reflections included, "To Be a Widow" in July 1964 and "Parents Without Partners" in March 1966.[12] This second article began with a quote from her young son: "'I want you at home. I don't want to be baby-sitted.' I tried to erase these words and a vision of my little boy's tear-stained face from my mind as I drove away from the baby-sitter's home to go to work. But what could I do?"[13]

In December 1972 Katie dealt with the issue of sexism in "I Believe in Persons."[14] She described a number of situations when her functioning in the church was restricted because of her sex. But she observed that "some women enjoy their safe bondage to tradition and are slow to strike out in new frontiers of service."[15] Katie was not among them.

In 1983 Katie contributed two articles for a special issue on aging. In "Why Shouldn't I Look and Think my Age?" Katie concluded with the words, "I smile at the woman in the mirror. She smiles back. We like each other."[16]

A number of her articles went beyond her own experience and might be labeled "reflective wisdom." In January 1964 she published "Learn a Thing from Grandmothers" and in March 1965 we find "Parents Provide the Pattern," which she concludes with a personal anecdote.[17] In July 1982 there is

"Making the Most of a Vacation" where she observes that "leisure should include a goal of becoming more involved with the church at another level if the individual or the family is traveling away from home."[18]

In January, November, and December 1967 Katie published three didactic short stories. In "The Invitation" she wrote of the problem of a missionary on furlough trying to come up with something edifying to report to a women's group in the home country.[19] In "The Church that Ate for Profit" she reflected on the irony of holding a feast to raise money to feed the poor.[20] Finally, in "The Red Catalog Dress" she dealt with a dilemma of interpersonal relationships among preadolescent girls.[21] After these three stories she seems not to have published any more fiction in *Christian Living*.

However, she did undertake a review of three short stories, evidently on assignment from the editors. In 1967 *Christian Living* published three stories by Rudy Wiebe. It would appear that we saw these as more sophisticated fiction than our usual fare and so asked Katie to review them in October 1967. In "Rudy Wiebe and 'Man as He Is.'" she wrote, "In his three short stories...Wiebe has once again avoided the straight line formula which deposits the reader and the characters in blissful soul rest in the concluding paragraphs."[22] At the end she concluded that "good literature is always a wedge, prying us away from the narrow outlook to the vision of what God expects of us."[23]

In the 1970s Katie provided two extensive documentary articles as part of an eight-part series describing various Mennonite groups. The series began with Cornelius J. Dyck's article "Pilgrims and Servants: How North American Mennonites Respond to the World."[24] The two articles by Katie included, "Yonder Mennonite Who Is He?" in which she described the Church of God in Christ Mennonites.[25] Her second was "Sorting the Evangelical Mennonites" in 1973, which described four different Mennonite groups who included "Evangelical" in their names.[26] This series was supported by a grant from the Schowalter Foundation so that writers could be enabled to do to research. Katie took this seriously and provided extensive information gleaned from her research.

Katie's final article in *Christian Living* appeared in the Summer 1997 issue and was another personal statement. "A Name of My Own" was an excerpt reprinted from her book *The Storekeepers Daughter*.[27] She wrote, "I never liked my name when growing up...It was an immigrant name—something brought along from Russia."[28] So she made a pilgrimage to the town in Saskatchewan where she grew up and as a result "I embraced my roots...I left town bearing the name Katie proudly."[29]

So there she is. Take her or leave her. Katie has used her experience as the stuff for much of her writing, letting her sorrows and joys hang out and so enrich the lives of readers.

Gospel Herald

In 1973 I was transferred from the monthly *Christian Living* to the weekly *Gospel Herald*.[30] I was to find that Katie had been there before me. My predecessor, John Drescher, had already been publishing her articles. The first I found appeared on April 6, 1965 and was a typical Katie Wiebe broadside, "Are You a Reading Woman?"[31] In the article she told of a friend who confessed that "television had deprived her of the greatest heritage of the mind. She was a woman who didn't read."[32] The article ends with an exhortation, "Take up a book and read. Now is the time. Reading is for you."[33] A second article appeared on April 22, 1969. It was another trumpet sound, "A Call to Decency," where she inveighed against immodesty among women and observed that "one of the cruelest tyrants in a woman's life can be the decree of fashion."[34]

The pace picks up in 1970 with eight articles and a dozen in 1971. Through 1991 Katie's work is to be found in every yearly volume of the *Gospel Herald*. Katie simply chose to submit articles she thought were appropriate for a broader audience to other Mennonite publications. As an editor, I did not feel obligated to use the articles unless I needed them, but the record shows that I needed quite a few.

The topics she chose ranged widely from Christian doctrine and piety to family life, politics, and church architecture. I'm not aware that any *Gospel Herald* readers took strong exception to her writing but readers from another publication did object at times. In 1976 Katie published "Open Season on Writers" in the *Gospel Herald*, which had previously been written for *The Christian Leader*.[35] She begins, "Patty Hearst gets hate mail. So do I." The essay defended writing such as hers and closed with, "the church periodical that adds no new thinking cannot hope to hold thinking readership, for it is only as an individual faces new questions and issues of faith that growth takes place."[36]

In addition to opinion articles, Katie wrote several research based articles for the *Gospel Herald*. The first was "Measuring the Vision," in 1975.[37] This article was sponsored by *Meetinghouse*, an inter-Mennonite editor's group, and featured the sociological study of five Mennonite groups published in *Anabaptists Four Centuries Later*.[38] Katie provided a condensed and more popular version. She concluded, "The confidence of the five groups cannot now remain in statistics, tables and charts. They are not the reality of the Mennonites even as clothes and food and customs are not the reality of the Anabaptist vision. They are all illusory substitutes for the greater realities of faith, hope, love, and peace. These are not captured by figures. The goal still lies ahead."[39]

In 1977 Katie provided a series of five articles describing the work of five Mennonite Church program boards: Publishing House, Board of Missions, Mutual Aid, Board of Congregational Ministries, and the Board of Education.[40] With support again from the Schowalter Foundation, Katie visited the five institutions and sent questionnaires to board members and a random sample of *Gospel Herald* readers. Katie was a little disappointed with responses to the questionnaires. In a comment from her included in my editorial on March 29 she said, "I sensed from the way these came back that many have few distinct opinions about the Boards…Board members did better usually, but I sensed a lot of fuzziness about what is actually happening. And this despite strong affirmations of loyalty to the church."[41]

Festival Quarterly

For some 20 years, Katie compiled a humor column for *Festival Quarterly*, following the publication of an article on the lack of Mennonite humor.[42] Beginning in 1975 her column, "Reclassified," provided an opportunity for readers to submit humorous stories or jokes about Mennonites. In 1983 Katie described the material in the column as folklore rather than jokes. She wrote, "Folklore often begins with a true event, but it may not. However, it originates with the people and is dependent on them for distribution. If the grapevine won't accept it, it withers immediately."[43] Among the stories included we find the following: "While in Toronto, an Old Order Mennonite from Waterloo started to walk in the direction of the landmark King Edward Hotel. A taxi pulled up beside him and the driver asked, 'King Edward?' 'No, just Edward Martin from Waterloo,' he replied."[44]

Evidently readers generally took the humor as intended, but following one particular issue, several expressed disappointment and concern about the use of expletives, "We take strong offense at such low-class, off color humor."[45] In response to their letters, Katie apologized and acknowledged "that as a student and teacher of language, I am probably more aware that some people use expletives without a reference to any objective reality. They may not even know the meaning of the words they are using, but which are extremely offensive to others."[46]

Of course some of the stories are more durable than others. It seems that unintended meanings usually persevere as in the case of the following: "The executive secretary of the Women's Missionary Society stepped proudly to the convention podium, financial record in hand. After detailing the past year's record of generous giving, she declared, 'We ladies are really proud of our figures.'"[47]

Additional Mennonite Publications

Katie also wrote for young people. *With*, a Mennonite publication for young people carried "A Time to Tear Down, A Time to Build Up" in 1975, in which Katie described the context of the 16th century and the beginning of Anabaptism.[48] In 1976 she provided interviews with two Mennonite teenagers who said, "My parents were Mennonites—and they're Divorced"; a sensitive subject Katie was willing to take up.[49]

Katie would also write Bible lessons, an assignment generally reserved for pastors and seminary professors. For example, she wrote a quarter of thirteen lessons for *Adult Bible Study Guide* in 1983, entitled "Old Testament Personalities."⁵⁰ This provided her with an opportunity to comment on the ambiguities affecting persons who are called upon to be faithful while living in a less than supportive culture. The final lesson in the series covered Mordecai and Esther. Katie observed that "we all give our lives for something—for amassing wealth, for achieving a reputation, for pleasure, for gaining control—the list is endless. Esther's example urges us to examine what we are devoting our lives to."⁵¹

Katie's work continues into the present century. *DreamSeeker*, a quarterly on-line magazine, carried a classic Katie article in 2002 called, "Galloping, Naked, in the Night."⁵² She acknowledged that "I have known too much fear. I've been too hesitant at times to move ahead."⁵³ Even so, we remember her earlier reflection about hate mail. This article is an excerpt from the second edition of her book, *Border Crossing: A Spiritual Journey*, which was being published by DreamSeeker Books in 2003.⁵⁴

A second *DreamSeeker* entry from the same book is entitled "Who? Me? A Fundamentalist?" and appeared in 2006.⁵⁵ In this article she reflected on how she has rejected some fundamentalist teachings, which she at one time supported. Yet she has stayed with her church even though she would aspire to be in one where women's roles are not restricted. But "at this stage in my life I have a clearer understanding of the messages I received in my childhood. I've been able to move beyond some but to keep those that are nonnegotiable."⁵⁶ She is still Katie Funk Wiebe.

One more ongoing contribution to Mennonite periodicals may be noted. She has written and continues to write book reviews for the *Mennonite Weekly Review* (MWR). I contacted Paul Schrag, editor of *Mennonite Weekly Review* for his perspective on Katie as a book reviewer. He replied,

> For many years Katie Funk Wiebe has been one of the most frequent and incisive contributors to *Mennonite Weekly Review*'s "On My Desk" book review column. Her interests range across diverse genres, from fiction to

history, biography, current events and church issues. She doesn't shy away from challenging and controversial subjects. With a keen sense of writing for a popular audience, she plays a key role in bringing worthwhile books to the attention of *MWR*'s inter-Mennonite readership.[57]

In 1962 Katie began writing, "I moved from a child's world of dreams into the world of books...I have never left it."[58] With Katie Funk Wiebe, one thing never changes.

• • •

Endnotes

1. *Christian Living* began in 1954 as a merger of the *Christian Monitor* (1909) and the *Mennonite Community* (1947). It was to last until 2002.
2. Katie's bibliography in this volume will show the extent of her publications.
3. Katie Funk Wiebe, "A Pilgrimage in Books," *Christian Living*, April 1962, 19.
4. Katie Funk Wiebe, "Foreword," in *A Little Left of Center: An Editor Reflects on His Mennonite Experience*, Daniel Hertzler (Telford: Pandora Press, 2000), 9.
5. Wiebe, "A Pilgrimage in Books," 19.
6. *Ibid.*
7. *Ibid.*
8. Katie Funk Wiebe, "'Stay Here and Open an Office,'" *Christian Living*, November 1962, 28-29.
9. *Ibid.*, 28.
10. Katie Funk Wiebe, "Living Apart for the Lord," *Christian Living*, March 1963, 22-24.
11. Daniel Hertzler and Loren Lind, "Among Those Present," *Christian Living*, March, 1963, 1.
12. See Katie Funk Wiebe, "To Be a Widow," *Christian Living*, July 1964, 12-13; and Katie Funk Wiebe, "Parents Without Partners," *Christian Living*, March 1966, 8-10.
13. Wiebe, "Parents Without Partners," 8.
14. Katie Funk Wiebe, "I Believe in Persons," *Christian Living*, December 1972, 20-23.
15. *Ibid.*, 23.
16. Katie Funk Wiebe, "Why Shouldn't I Look and Think my Age?" *Christian Living*, March/April, 1983, 19. See also Katie Funk Wiebe, "Plant More Tomatoes than You'll Need," *Christian Living*, March/April, 1983, 40-42.

17. Katie Funk Wiebe, "Learning a Thing from Grandmother," *Christian Living*, January 1964, 32-34; and Katie Funk Wiebe, "Parents Provide the Pattern," *Christian Living*, March 1965, 24-26.
18. Katie Funk Wiebe, "Making the Most of Vacations," *Christian Living*, July 1982, 19.
19. Katie Funk Wiebe, "The Invitation," *Christian Living*, January 1967, 6-8.
20. Katie Funk Wiebe, "The Church that Ate for Profit," *Christian Living*, November 1967, 26-28.
21. Katie Funk Wiebe, "The Red Catalog Dress," *Christian Living*, December 1967, 12-14.
22. Katie Funk Wiebe, "Rudy Wiebe and 'Man as He Is,'" *Christian Living*, October 1967, 30.
23. *Ibid.*, 32.
24. Cornelius J. Dyck, "Pilgrims and Servants: How North American Mennonites Respond to the World," *Christian Living*, November 1969, 20-23.
25. Katie Funk Wiebe, "Yonder Mennonite: Who Is He? A Portrait of the Church of God in Christ Mennonite (Holdeman)," *Christian Living*, February 1970, 2-9.
26. Katie Funk Wiebe, "Sorting the Evangelical Mennonites," *Christian Living*, March 1973, 8-14.
27. See Katie Funk Wiebe, *The Storekeeper's Daughter: A Memoir* (Scottdale: Herald Press, 1997).
28. Katie Funk Wiebe, "A Name of My Own," *Christian Living*, Summer 1997, 5.
29. *Ibid.*, 7.
30. The *Gospel Herald* was established in 1908 as the successor to *Gospel Witness* (1905) and *Herald of Truth* (1864).
31. Katie Funk Wiebe, "Are You a Reading Woman?" *Gospel Herald*, April 6, 1965, 293-294.
32. *Ibid.*, 293.
33. *Ibid.*, 294.
34. Katie Funk Wiebe, "A Call to Decency," *Gospel Herald*, April 22, 1969, 369.
35. Katie Funk Wiebe, "Open Season on Writers," *Gospel Herald*, January 6, 1976, 6. See also Katie Funk Wiebe, "Open Season on Writers," Viewpoint, *The Christian Leader*, November 11, 1975, 7.
36. *Ibid.*
37. Katie Funk Wiebe, "Measuring a Vision," *Gospel Herald*, May 13, 1975, 358-361.
38. J. Howard Kauffman and Leland Harder, *Anabaptists Four Centuries Later: A Profile of Five Mennonite and Brethren in Christ Denominations* (Scottdale: Herald Press, 1975).
39. Wiebe, "Measuring a Vision," 361.
40. Katie Funk Wiebe, "What Is The Mennonite Church?" *Gospel Herald*, March 29, 1977, 265-269; Katie Funk Wiebe, "The Agenda of the People," *Gospel Herald*, April 12, 1977, 305-309; Katie Funk Wiebe, "An Insurance Company That Writes Love Into Its Contracts," *Gospel Herald*, April 26, 1977, 345-349; Katie Funk Wiebe, "BCM—Board of

Congregational Ministries," *Gospel Herald*, May 10, 1977, 382-385; and Katie Funk Wiebe, "Forming a People of God," *Gospel Herald*, May 31, 1977, 442-445.
41. Daniel Hertzler, "The State of the Boards," Editorial, *Gospel Herald*, March 29, 1977, 280.
42. Katie Funk Wiebe, "Why Mennonites Can't Laugh at Themselves," *Festival Quarterly*, Summer 1974, 5, 22.
43. Katie Funk Wiebe, "Finding Our Own Folklore," Reclassified, *Festival Quarterly*, August, September, October 1983, 31.
44 Katie Funk Wiebe, "The Ubiquitous MCC Quilt," Reclassified, *Festival Quarterly*, Summer 1987, 38.
45. Henry and Susan Bergmann, Letters, *Festival Quarterly*, May, June, July 1983, 35. See also Winston O. Weaver, Letters, *Festival Quarterly*, May, June, July 1983, 35. For the column causing concern, see Katie Funk Wiebe, "More Foibles," Reclassified, *Festival Quarterly*, November, December 1982, January 1983, 34.
46. Katie Funk Wiebe, "Katie Funk Wiebe Responds," Letters, *Festival Quarterly*, May, June, July 1983, 35.
47. Katie Funk Wiebe, "Yea, Mennonites, Still the Best?" Reclassified, *Festival Quarterly*, November, December 1983, January 1984, 34.
48. Katie Funk Wiebe, "A Time to Tear Down, A Time to Build Up," *With*, October 1975, 2-8.
49. Katie Funk Wiebe, "My Parents Are Mennonites—and They're Divorced," *With*, July/August 1976, 38-45.
50. Katie Funk Wiebe, "Old Testament Personalities: Lessons 1-13," *Adult Bible Study Guide*, ed. Laurence Martin, (Scottdale: Mennonite Publishing House, 1983), 2-79.
51. *Ibid.*, 79.
52. Katie Funk Wiebe, "Galloping, Naked, in the Night," *DreamSeeker Magazine*, Summer 2002, 16-23.
53. *Ibid.*, 21.
54. Katie Funk Wiebe, *Border Crossing: A Spiritual Journey*, rev. ed. (Telford: DreamSeeker Books, 2003).
55. Katie Funk Wiebe, "Who? Me? A Fundamentalist?" *DreamSeeker Magazine*, Autumn 2006, 24-29.
56. *Ibid.*, 29.
57. Paul Schrag to Daniel Hertzler, 2009.
58. Wiebe, "A Pilgrimage in Books," 19.

Open Season on Writers

Katie Funk Wiebe

Patty Hearst gets hate mail. So do I. Occasionally. Not in huge quantities like she does, nor for the same reasons.

It came as a mild surprise to me a few years ago that to write publicly made me a wide open target for readers to take pot shots at. Some hit fairly; I appreciate well thought through criticism. It is helpful. But others punch well below the belt with each word wrapped in barbed wire—in the name of Christ. Those letters are harder to accept and understand.

The pattern of such letters becomes familiar. How can you be a Christian? How can you write such stuff as a woman? How can you be a Mennonite? One reader suggested I change my name and leave the Mennonites for the "English" world.

In one mail I have experienced the frustration of getting both a complimentary and a chastising letter for the same article. Obviously what one reader considers a mild statement, the other sees as something worthy of the rack. Some read their own attitudes into articles, often assuming that if I am for one thing, I must be against another. If I am for single women, I must be against marriage; if I am for women, I must be against men; if I am for another denomination, I must be against Mennonites.

Any editor of a religious publication who has published controversial materiel knows the line of attack.

Step One: Name calling. People who feel threatened are often first to resort to negative labels (liberal, racist, fundamentalist, social gospeler, women's libber, etc.) to wall off the persons they can't agree with.

Step Two: "Take me off your mailing list."

Step Three: "If you publish some more stories like that one, I won't donate another cent to missions or your institution."

Step Four: (With verbal club held high) "If you don't quit printing such stuff, I'll go to the president, chairman, board" (the old equivalent of "I'll tell Mama on you").

Final step: "We're now attending a church where the whole Word of God is preached."

As I tell my journalism students, if you can't stand the heat, get out of the kitchen. The bigger question is whether there needs to be so much heat.

Can members of the family of God discuss controversial issues without getting quite so angry? Have we moved so far apart that anyone who speaks from a different viewpoint threatens our peace of mind? Would it help to have a Jack Anderson writing in our midst to keep us all humble and aware of our failures, problems, and so forth?

To publish or not to publish controversy has valid arguments on both sides. The supporters of the more conservative view state that too much openness in church periodicals about the unsuccessful aspects of the Christian witness hurts the cause of Christ. Ordinary laymen cannot accept imperfection in their spiritual leaders nor digest many new ideas. In the process of getting a new issue out on the table, more people are hurt than helped. Contributions fall off, loyalty weakens, and the entire effort sags. Weaker members must be supported.

On the other hand, say the supporters of the opposing view, to maintain a credible church press, it must report more than the good and large things about the church and its activities. Otherwise we create a fuzzy image of the church, one which shows it as a group of happy, tax-exempt tourists who have had their request for clear weather all the way to the Pearly Gates guaranteed.

Spokesmen for this side insist the religious press should not cater to human weakness, but should reckon on the grace and wisdom of God to help believers handle all kinds of material. By factual and consistent reporting of controversial and unpleasant topics, the religious press can help readers develop powers of judgment beyond measuring spirituality by counting the numbers of times Christ is mentioned or Scripture verses are quoted.

They hold that unless more openness occurs in the religious press, the credibility gap and the cynicism which has developed with regard to the secular press will be transferred to the church papers. When the time comes that a church member reads all is well but hears by rumor all is not well, his confidence in the ability of God's children to communicate will suffer.

Furthermore, the church periodical that adds no new thinking cannot hope to hold the thinking readership, for it is only as an individual faces new questions and issues of the faith that growth takes place.

The experience of being controversial and of getting even a few poison pen letters has been invaluable. I recognize that controversy will always take on a personal note in a small denomination. I sense the need to be even clearer and more concerned about transmitting the mind and love of Christ. I realize writers need to be more sensitive to the unsophisticated reader who cannot handle irony and humor.

But I also understand anew that to refuse to give room to controversial issues does not mean they cease to exist. Nor to present them that one loves Christ and the church any less. The mission of Christian journalism must always be to crusade for change but also to strengthen the church.

Katie Funk Wiebe, "Open Season on Writers," Viewpoint, *The Christian Leader*, November 11, 1975, 7.

Why Mennonites Can't Laugh at Themselves

Katie Funk Wiebe

I wish I could say that humor, like new life in spring, is bursting out all over the Mennonite horizon. But it isn't. All I see is a few green shoots piercing the soil. But those few blades are good news.

I have a friend who gently chides the Mennonites for being a grim, humorless bunch of people who have never learned to laugh at themselves. When I reflect upon Mennonite publications generally, I have to agree. Humor is not our specialty.

Unlike the Jews, whose buffeting by life's harsh experiences has enabled them to laugh at themselves, their overanxious mamas, their gefilte fish, and their bar mitzvahs, the Mennonites seem to have inherited a dour outlook on life.

How can it be otherwise? queries my friend. You are so dead serious, he says, and so dead certain you are right about everything related to your theology, your institutions, and even your leaders, you see nothing presumptuous about having achieved superstatus with God.

And I add in a little whisper: and sometimes we see nothing incongruous about speculating that if God hadn't spotted faithful Abram in Ur of the Chaldees, He would surely have waited a little while longer until Menno arrived on the scene, and then sent him and his followers on the journey in quest of the Promised Land. And without doubt, they wouldn't have spent forty years in the wilderness either.

Basically, a sense of humor stems from a humble approach to life which sees the incongruities which exist between the ideal and the actual. The humble man can laugh at himself because he recognizes that human nature is flawed, that Christianity is seldom found pure, and that he is sometimes mistaken. True humor merely cuts through pretenses and reveals a person as he is—a human creature in need of the grace of God. And it is always done with kindness.

On the other hand, the humorless person is usually super-loyal to his gold-star ideas. If faced with a different viewpoint, he sets himself up as a protector of the status quo. His loins are girt about with strong opinions, he is protected by the breastplate of self-righteousness, the shield of dogma, and the helmet of self-sufficiency. His sword is a ready tongue. To twit a weakness is a sure indication one is making light of sacred elements or moving toward foolish jesting, or at the very least, yielding to the enemy.

Recently I've enjoyed hearing the sound of good laughter as the Low-German culture is being revived in connection with the Kansas centennial celebrations. Its down-to-earth expressions and customs contrast sharply with our present attempts at sophistication. As I listen I ask whether this interest is actually the beginning of a new interest in humor, or whether we are still laughing at someone else—the people we were and never really liked to be—bumbling immigrants who stumbled to awareness.

Regardless, this interest is a step in the right direction. We may yet catch up to the Jews. But we need a touch of humor in other areas as well.

How about a Mennonite Art Buchwald? He could move into the politics of Mennonite gatherings of all kinds. "The Adventures of Kornelius at the Conference," bumping into delegates with his overstuffed briefcase, looking for a private room to hold a secret session for his seating committee, might teach us more about ourselves than we want to know. After reading such a column for a while, it might become clearer that we have not yet apprehended, but are still reaching.

If we couldn't dig up a Buchwald, perhaps the gift might be stirred up in a Charles M. Schulz to produce a comic strip about Charlie Schmidt and his dog, Schnappy. Like his predecessor, Schnappy might from time to time imitate Wilhelm Yoder, ace conscientious objector, or perhaps even a Joe "Menno" Cool, stalking the church-related college campus.

We need a Mennonite Erma Bombeck to pull humorously the facade of perfection from homemaking and to show parents that though this task may be both frustrating and rewarding, it is best accomplished basted with a few dollops of humor. It's okay to let others know that sometimes our *zwieback* are tough, our shoofly pie is runny, and our children forget to change their socks. And a mother need not consider herself a permanent failure if she feels like hiding in the dryer for a few moments of privacy.

Or lacking any of these, perhaps "Life in these Mennonited States" might encourage the humble approach, as gleaned from church bulletins and elsewhere:

"A chicken supper will be held on June 28 to raise money for MCC Pakistan famine. $2.50 for all you can eat."

"The church family will meet at 6:00 p.m. for a time of prayer and evaluation of the evaluation meetings held recently."

"General sinning begins at 7:00 p.m."

"April 30—National Day of Fasting and Prayer'— 6:30 p.m., supper meeting at Betty's Cafe of local MDS."

The Volkswagen people used to run a series of ads which poked fun at their own product and made life more enjoyable for everyone. Perhaps if we could learn how to josh the Mennonites and their foibles, we could make life more enjoyable for the Baptists, and the Presbyterians, and even the Pentecostals, as well as ourselves.

And someday, who knows, God might lead us all to that Promised Land.

Katie Funk Wiebe, "Why Mennonites Can't Laugh at Themselves," *Festival Quarterly*, Summer 1974, 5, 22. Reprinted from *Festival Quarterly*. © by Good Books (www.GoodBooks.com). Used by permission. All rights reserved.

Chapter 12

Aging with Spirit

Delores Friesen

At 85, Katie Funk Wiebe is still vibrant, determined, and sharp. She makes tea for my husband and me, then sits for a bit; only to get up and return with her arms full of files of speeches and articles on aging. Inspired in part by the early death of her daughter Christine, who longed for "white hair and old age," Katie has produced over one hundred speeches, articles, book reviews, chapters, and books on the topic of aging with spirit. She tells us story after story of opportunities and events where she was given the chance to talk to older persons at retreats, churches, educational institutions, and community gatherings. She is passionate, witty, and articulate. If she has a bully pulpit, perhaps this is it.

This stage of Katie's career began with an invitation from the Mennonite Health Association (MHA). They asked her to come to a conference on aging at Messiah College in June 1992, and subsequently to edit and be the core writer for *Life After 50: A Positive Look at Aging in the Faith Community*.[1] The book is not a "how-to-grow-old-gracefully" book; instead, it offers a challenge to "achieve meaning, maintain hope, and continue to serve through being and doing as long as possible and solely through being as the years advance."[2] Katie's message is clear; the final years of life are to be used for growth, service, and investment in the lives of others.

Beginnings

One of the earliest harbingers of this emphasis in Katie's life and work was her 1979 volume on writing memoirs, *Good Times with Old Times*, which has remained in print for the last three decades. She calls this kind of writing, "harvesting life," and encourages her readers to look for the patterns and themes in their lives. She believes, along with Frederick Buechner, that "it is through our stories about people we have met along the way that God makes himself known to each of us personally and powerfully. To lose track of our stories is to become impoverished both spiritually and humanly."[3]

Her first classes of older adults affirmed Katie's gifts of practicality, encouragement, and clear, forthright thinking and speaking. Her book, *Life after 50*, makes it clear that Katie was writing and speaking first and foremost to aging persons themselves, not to those who would plan programming for them. Her primary purpose was to help her audiences find meaning and purpose for their lives. Aging was to be seen as a process that involved "both challenge and grace…regardless of circumstances."[4] She continues to work tirelessly to overturn and critique stereotypes of older adults as "sick, poor, senile, and unproductive," or alternatively, "rich, indifferent to society's needs and hedonistic."[5] Katie defines her audience as members of a faith community who are interested in planning for a meaningful life and service as older adults, or those who are relating to older persons, whether these are parents, relatives, or friends.[6]

Several themes emerge time and again in her writings on aging and are represented in her 1994 book, *Prayers of an Omega: Facing the Transitions of Aging*.[7] The *Omega* prayers are grouped into five divisions that encompass not only Katie's prayer life, but serve as a window to the themes of her work on aging.

Transition into the Land of the Older Adult

As she tells it, Katie herself transitioned into the land of the older adult through her disgust and anger at receiving an envelope of coupons from an advertising agency for her 65th birthday.

> The brown paper envelope said that the coupons had been selected specially for me: coupons for a laxative, arthritis pain medicine, denture adhesive, undergarments designed for leakage control, bran flakes, a specially

designed chair for people with back problems, door chimes to extend the sound of the doorbell, magnifier for reading, card shuffler, side-cutting nail clipper, night driving glasses, specially designed slippers for people with feet that change size during the day, hearing aids. I felt like a deflated tire. Was this what lay ahead for me? Growing older was scary.[8]

Twenty years later, as we sit in her living room, that very envelope with its yellowed and faded coupons, falls out of one of her bulging folders on aging and it still raises her ire—she feels strongly that there has to be more for those who enter the aging years.

Katie got to work, unpacking, deflating, and deconstructing the myths that have developed about older people. They are not disengaged from life, inflexible, or grumpy, she argued, nor are they all serene and joyous. They are not senile, deficient in intellectual capacity, asexual, or homogenous. Katie studied the demographics, musing about what it is like to be part of a society where at age 85, there are 257 women to every 100 men and where people live many more years than their parents and grandparents did decades ago. She read writers like Rabbi Abram Heschel, Henri Nouwen, Elbert Cole, Elizabeth O'Connor, and Elise Boulding, sociologists and theologians mainly, and began to articulate the meaning and value of wisdom, continuity, telling one's story, and becoming involved in life in new ways.

Katie believes that the goal for an aging society is "to add meaning to life." "Life is a gift, we need to see ourselves as growing people, always pursuing the wonder of the day, taking care of what is happening inside of us."[9] With her amazing penchant for getting to the heart of the matter and keeping things straightforward and clear, Katie decided she would not introduce herself as a "retired teacher," but would always introduce herself by what was happening in her life in the present, not the past.

Family Life

Family life took on new layers of involvement and understanding as she began to write more explicitly about her growing up years in Canada. Her immigrant parents had a well defined faith, spoke German and Russian, followed strict gender roles, and maintained a set routine of work and worship. She often alludes to her parents' aging and retirement processes in her own writing and speaking. Her father's life had been so defined by work, that when he aged, all he wanted to do was "rest." Katie saw his withdrawal from active life and was determined to avoid making the same choice.

Her mother, on the other hand, showed her how to live with change and generously gave away nearly everything she owned. She had a rich intellectual and spiritual life and marveled at the changes she had seen and experienced. When she was nearly 90, she shared with Katie that sometimes, when it felt like life was closing in on them, she and Katie's father had just "stood and hung on to one another."[10] According to Katie, "that's the essence of family celebration. We come together to hang on to one another for a little while before the tempo of life picks up again or a change takes place."[11] Katie recognized that our parents are within us, "close to our bone, for better or for worse."[12] She continues to exercise the strengths passed on to her and seeks to exorcise the constraints, "especially worrying about what people will think of me if I depart from traditional ways."[13]

Katie's four children all helped her "choose a fuller life" and contributed to her emphasis on cross-generational interaction that both blesses and guides young people and strengthens and deepens their elders. Working together helps everyone mature and grow. Her message is clear: know yourself, know where you came from, who your elders are, what they stood for, and where they came from; and know what you believe and who you believe in. Tell your story, your family's story, and your faith story in order to pass on the wisdom gained across the years and generations. Understand your past, but invest in the future.

Facing Changes

Among the changes that older adults face, the one that seems to trouble Katie the most is the 2000 discretionary hours of time available every year. She laments that many volunteer jobs simply involve activities such as filing and sorting, things which do not challenge older adults to grow or to utilize their expertise and wisdom. As a man told her one evening after she spoke on aging, "I have a thousand horsepower engine inside me, but am being asked to do one hundred horsepower jobs."[14] She quotes Paul Tournier, who says "choosing becomes the supreme vocation of old age" and presses older adults to become wisdom people and vision builders, who develop spiritual strength and stamina.[15]

Katie asks older adults to simplify and re-anchor their faith, reinvent themselves, and learn as much as they can about aging, especially as it relates to the inner life. She reminds people that discipleship does not end at age 65—as followers of Jesus, everyone is called to live a life of service and ministry. Instead of succumbing to society's emphasis on physical well-being and financial security, she calls on the church to counter the pull towards independence with God's call to depend on God and on one another.

As a creative writer, Katie has thought long and hard about the role of creativity and aging. She defines creativity as "a process of discovery about life, a willingness to tolerate ambiguity, and a willingness to fail."[16] It is particularly important to be creative in later life so that one can love life despite its diminishments. One must be prepared to risk and not be afraid of failure. Unlike most other approaches to aging, Katie spends very little time discussing the diminishments of hearing loss, failing eyesight, bodily aches, pains, and disabilities. Instead she focuses on taking both what disturbs and exalts you, internally and externally and wrestling with it, reforming it, until somehow you have altered both it and yourself.[17] Katie encourages her readers and listeners to "look for another, better way by listening to one's own inner dialogue, writing down the questions about what is happening in your life, facing the discontent in your life—nudges, questions, problems, tensions. What is stirring inside you? What do you dream about? What gives you joy?"[18]

Katie addresses the theme of accepting change and making something out of one's life in all of her books, but she has little patience for those who bind themselves and others in the past.

She sees change as a good thing, something to be embraced, a place to use imagination, the courage of faith, and disciplined action. One has to be willing to fail and come back the next day and try again. One also has to be willing to be misunderstood, and be willing to free others to fail and try again! Katie identifies fear as a demanding chain and asks us to suspend premature judgment and exercise faith; otherwise fear can keep us from never moving ahead.[19]

Challenged by Trials

In *Prayers of an Omega*, several prayers deal with loss, grief, death, and pain. It is terrain she knows well, having experienced the untimely deaths of her husband and daughter. In conversation with Katie, she repeatedly wondered aloud why and how this book became so popular, especially with nursing home chaplains. It is no surprise that these prayers are works of art, capturing experiences and feelings of loss, grief, and faith. One of my personal favorites is titled "I Sure Liked to Drive my Car." When I read this aloud recently to seminary students enrolled in an Aging and Long Term Care class, there were very few dry eyes in the classroom:

> Lord, this morning I turned in my license to drive…But I miss the feel of a ring of hard keys in my pocket. I reach for them, just to give them a caress. But they're not there. I want to go out and start the car. For no reason. Then I remember. The car is gone. I will never back it out of the garage onto the road again. I will never again experience the power of the engine with me at the wheel… Reach out your hand, my Lord, and place it here in the warm hollow of my hand where I used to hold the keys.[20]

These prayer poems were inspired by the Psalms, and like their earlier counterparts, they "tell it like it is"—they lament, but they also ring with faith in a good God. Unlike her other writing, these have a poetic feel and a touch of emotion that goes far deeper than her own story, to something more universal—the transitions of aging and the power of faith.

> Am I afraid to die? Shall I be afraid when the time comes? It will come, I know. At twilight, light loses and darkness wins. Yet night is the promise of day even as death is the promise of life and love and the joy of your nearness, heavenly Father. I don't want to go just yet, Lord. But when I hear you knocking, I'll be ready, for I trust your mercy. Amen."[21]

Katie's ability to enter the life, gender, emotion, and situation of another is uncommon, and this group of persons training to become pastors and counselors recognized through Katie's words what they need to do to accept their own mortality and journey with others who are facing grief, loss, pain, and death. This is part of Katie's legacy—she doesn't try to explain or pontificate, or quote statistics or tell us how to minister to others or how to prepare for our own death. She just enters fully into her own life, and the lives of those with whom she interacts and puts into words what we are feeling and needing.

Looking to the Next Generation

The last theme, handing the work of the kingdom over to the next generation, also grows out of her own personal experience of not having this kind of mentorship available for herself. Certain doors, jobs, opportunities were closed to her simply because she was a woman, or a widow. She says, "I lacked strong women-teacher-intellectual models. I needed someone to encourage, to stroke, to coach, to support my dreams and help me put them into effect. I needed someone to create space for me to develop my goals, and particularly, to give moral support in times of stress."[22]

Now she challenges older adults to use their freedom to develop their gifts and their experience of coping and surviving in order to mentor and support those younger than themselves. She wants her writing and speaking to help older adults once again dream dreams about the kingdom and fulfill God's plan for their lives in making those visions of God's kingdom come true.[23] Some of the specific spiritual needs she identifies include: prioritizing your life, nurturing the inner life, maintaining faith, hope, joy and creativity, finding forgiveness, letting go of grudges and bitterness, becoming more aware of God's active presence, and enabling grace in every stage in life.

She chides older adults for feeling that they have nothing to talk about or to share with younger persons. Instead she says,

> Tell others the way you have come—share the grace, mercies, blessings of God, moments of insight…Tell about God of the gaps—and the ordinary times when God was there… Tell your story. Tell stories of God's grace and you will be blessed and you will bless others…The great miracles of God are never headlined in newspapers…One of the best ways to build a bridge for the young coming after you is by sharing your personal story of a blessing.[24]

Katie goes on to describe blessings as: "forgiving the one who hurt us, remaining faithful to a spouse when tempted to have an affair, standing by children who mess up their lives, courage when life is against you, working for justice in an unjust world, living in unity in a congregation…freedom from competition, the need to acquire, the pressure to conform, freedom from childhood illusions, and freedom to pursue new goals and dreams."[25] All of these are ways to hand on the work of the Kingdom to the next generation.

Katie believes that knowing God—his grace and salvation—is the meaning of life and that since God is always waiting ahead, none of us needs to be hampered by the stage of life we are in. God cannot be kept captive by any one age group![26] She argues that older adults can decide what kind of older person they will be. "We need to show young people that old age is not all frightening or sad, or ugly or nonproductive—or even dull. They need to see wisdom, experience, joy in life, steadiness of faith."[27] "Her wonderful metaphors and words help individuals and institutions relish the role of handing the work of the kingdom over to the next generation instead of holding on and being fearful of changes. As she puts it, "An authentic story makes it impossible to pass off a string of words as the essence of the redeemed life. Above all, it passes on to one's children not an empty bucket, but shows them where to find the well."[28]

Challenges for the Church

Katie continues to call the church to a greater faithfulness regarding how it values and utilizes older adults. She feels that the church keeps asking the wrong questions. One of the major deficiencies she sees is that the church focuses on the weaknesses of old age instead of asking, "Is that all there is to life when one is older?" She calls on the church to put content into aging, to go beyond caring for physical and financial needs to see the needs of spirit and emotion, to stimulate older adults in mind, spirit, and body so that they see themselves as growing people, always open, always pursuing the wonder of the day; people who live in anticipation of what the day will bring instead of expecting emptiness.[29]

She also challenges the church to develop new thinking, rituals, and symbols that go beyond social events and visitation during crises. She chides the church for thinking that older adults have little to offer, and wonders aloud several times in our afternoon of conversation about why the church spends so much on youth ministries and youth pastors, but rarely budgets or gives attention to senior adult ministries. When there are pastoral services to seniors, it is nearly always visitation and pastoral care for the frail, ill, and dying; not visionary engagement with the many older adults who have discretionary energy, time, income, and skills to be employed in the service of God.

Furthermore, she argues passionately for Christian education and sermons that will challenge the mature adult to understand and delve into theological questions, biblical studies, and commitments that go beyond a Sunday school faith. Instead of "a lot of nice little devotionals," Katie makes a plea for direct teaching about older adult spirituality, temptations, and struggles of faith.[30]

She has sought to bridge this gap in several educational pieces designed for use in the church. *Bridging the Generations*, commissioned by Faith and Life Press, includes study guide questions and activities at the end of each chapter, plus sidebars of illustrative materials for teachers and group facilitators.[31] This book picks up many of the themes that she has written about on aging, especially breaking down stereotypes, mentoring younger people, and the need for intergenerational programming in the church.

Another small monograph, *Older Adults and Faith: Making New Maps*, is part of the Faith Development Series again published by Faith and Life Press.[32] Katie addresses factors that affect spiritual vitality in older adults, what the Bible teaches about old age, theological and Anabaptist principles that should direct the church's thinking about aging, and how the faith community can make a difference to the person facing the end of life. Katie views this last booklet as a distillation of all of her other writing and speaking on aging. Indeed, both are excellent Christian education pieces that will continue to be used for years to come.

Lasting Contributions and Legacy

Katie's writings on aging seem to be directed mostly to older adults who have good health, leisure time, and adequate resources. There's not much on wandering in the desert or the dark night of the soul, and little mention of depression, dementia, or end of life decisions. There is also little acknowledgement of what happens to older adults who no longer have the physical and mental strength to care for themselves or to do meaningful work. But conceivably this would have distracted from her central message on aging which we all need to hear; a clear call for faithfulness and a life of service invested for the good of others.

Perhaps her most important legacy is that she seems to know us better than we know ourselves. She is not given to flowery prose or tears; she builds her case, illustrates it, shares her passion and her own commitment, and then expects her readers and those who listen to her speak to do the same. She creates a metaphor, paints a word picture, tells a story, describes a universal experience, and articulates the thoughts and feelings that would otherwise remain unspoken. She tells us that we can't retire from the journey, or plunge in the "sea of God's grace and then bask lazily on the shore thereafter."[33] We may start off with naiveté, and may experience struggles, confusion, and disillusionment along the way, but the aging journey is one where we experience the grace of God as never before as we transition from an emphasis on "doing" to "being."[34] Relationships and stories become central to our lives and our legacies, and they sustain us along the journey. As Katie says it, "the land of the aging may look like deep water...but deep water and drowning are not the same thing. The water may get deeper...but going in beyond my depth means trusting more."[35]

• • •

Endnotes

1. Katie Funk Wiebe, ed., *Life after 50: A Positive Look at Aging in the Faith Community* (Newton: Faith and Life Press, 1983).
2. *Ibid.*, ii.
3. Katie Funk Wiebe, *You Never Gave Me a Name: One Mennonite Woman's Journey* (Telford: DreamSeeker Books, 2009), 247.
4. Wiebe, *Life after 50*, viii.
5. *Ibid.*
6. *Ibid.*, ix.
7. Katie Funk Wiebe, *Prayers of an Omega: Facing the Transitions of Aging* (Scottdale: Herald Press, 1994).
8. Wiebe, "Senior Friends Talk" (lecture, March 21, 2002). Notes from Katie's personal files.
9. *Ibid.*
10. Katie Funk Wiebe, *Bless Me Too, My Father* (Scottdale: Herald Press, 1988), 258.
11. *Ibid.*
12. Katie Funk Wiebe, *Border Crossing: A Spiritual Journey*, rev. ed. (Telford: Pandora Press, 2002), 116.
13. *Ibid.*
14. Wiebe, *You Never Gave Me a Name*, 235.
15. Katie Funk Wiebe, "Retirement and Me" (presentation at Hesston Mennonite Church, Hesston, KS, 1990), 1.
16. Katie Funk Wiebe, "Late Life Creativity—Chore or Challenge?" (presentation at East Wichita Shepherd's Center, n.d.), 1.
17. *Ibid.* In another earlier manuscript, "Creativity: Chore or Challenge?" given at Salem, Oregon, October 19, 1986, Wiebe has a longer statement enclosed in quotation marks, but with no source given: "Creativity to me is taking what both disturbs and exalts you, internally and externally, and wrestling with it, reforming it, until somehow you have altered both it and

yourself. It is the refusal to accept, at a gut level, what other people say about what's important to you. It also means working long enough and hard enough that you can reproduce for others what you have learned to do, think and feel in your own struggle." It is not clear whether this is her own definition, or something she gleaned from her extensive reading. This particular manuscript from her personal files is only three pages long, and has almost more handwritten notes than typescript, but it seems to form the basis and foundation of many later speeches and presentations on writing, creativity and older adult years: chore or challenge.

18. *Ibid.*
19. *Ibid.*, 3.
20. Wiebe, *Prayers of an Omega*, 57-58.
21. *Ibid.*, 96-97.
22. Wiebe, *Bless Me Too, My Father*, 219.
23. Katie Funk Wiebe (speech given at Faith and Life Press, Anaheim, CA, February 13, 1993); and Katie Funk Wiebe (speech given at Bethel Enrichment Series, April 14, 1993). She also quotes Elbert Cole in this speech and has obviously been influenced by his writings and work. Although the exact source is not documented, she attributes the following to Cole: "Everything we do for young people we need to do for the older adult...We must see ourselves not just as people being maintained but as God's people with a vision of God's life for us and in turn become contributors of life."
24. Katie Funk Wiebe, "Blessings at Any Age" (speech given in at least four locations: McPherson First Baptist Church, Laurelville, PA, Kidron, Ohio, United Methodist Women of Berne, Kansas.)
25. *Ibid.*, 5.
26. *Ibid.*
27. Katie Funk Wiebe, "Aging with Meaning and Hope in the Faith Community." Presentation notes from Wiebe's personal files; no date, and no location given.
28. Wiebe, *Bless Me Too, My Father*, 238.
29. Katie Funk Wiebe. Speech given at a Faith and Life Press event, Anaheim, CA, February 13, 1993; and Katie Funk Wiebe, Bethel Enrichment Series, Bethel College, North Newton, KS, April 14, 1993.
30. Wiebe, Katie Funk, "Retirement and Me," presentation given at Hesston Mennonite Church, 1990, 3.
31. Katie Funk Wiebe, *Bridging the Generations* (Scottdale: Herald Press, 2001).
32. Katie Funk Wiebe, *Older Adults and Faith: Making New Maps* (Newton: Faith and Life Press, 1995). See also Katie Funk Wiebe, *Older Adults and Faith: Their Spiritual Development and Relationship to the Church* (Newton: Faith and Life, 1995).
33. Wiebe, *You Never Gave Me a Name*, 269.
34. *Ibid.*, 268-278. Katie attributes these views on the journey of faith to Paul Ricoeur.
35. *Ibid.*, 207.

Time for Purple with Red

Katie Funk Wiebe

I thought I'd slip past my 65th birthday without much ado. I was mistaken. This milestone became more than a little glitch in the road.

Daughter Joanna sent a specially designed card: "This is to certify that Katie Wiebe, having achieved sufficient experience and savoir-faire, is now authorized to engage in spontaneous and outrageous behavior, including staying up past her bedtime, roaming the world, talking to strangers, and, of course, wearing purple whenever the mood strikes her."

She hadn't forgotten that I had once written that people would know I was old when I wore purple with a red hat. Enclosed with her card was an outrageously beautiful purple and red silk scarf.

The other children had a special party with video camera to catch pearls of wisdom falling from my newly aged tongue. "Tell us stories we've never heard before," said son James.

Every medical insurance program somehow learned about this birthday and offered a still better deal in supplemental insurance.

A cousin sent me a certificate of membership in a family club he has started, giving me junior status in the land of the family's aging.

Obviously I've arrived someplace. But where am I?

Elders in a previous generation were the transmitters of tradition to the upcoming generation. Today with all the new technology appearing on the market, the older generation's experience is often obsolete. Our children have to teach us to operate modern equipment.

Mothers used to teach daughters to cook "out of their head." Whereas mothers owned one or, at the most, two well-worn cookbooks, daughters today have shelves of them. I ask my daughters how to make new dishes like macaroni salad and "party" mashed potatoes.

Even being guardians of values and providing continuity to a society is difficult for elders because the generations live so widely separated. And who cares about the older generation's thoughts about values? Their values are much too tied to avoiding gossip.

Sixty-five feels comfortable right now. I like wearing low-heeled shoes and feeling free to ask for decaffeinated coffee. But I wonder about 75 and 85.

Growing up is scary. An adolescent moving into adulthood has to find him or herself. Today the cartoon strip "For Better or Worse" shows the teenager who's been having hormone attacks telling his friends that he's been feeling weird lately.

He says, "My voice cracks a lot, and I get sort of, you know, depressed. My knees ache, I'm always hungry, and my skin is starting to look like someone with cleats ran over it. And all the time our parents keep saying, 'Enjoy being a teenager...these are the best years of your life!'"

Moving into old age is also scary. One's hearing decreases. Small-type reading is set aside for later—probably never. Knees ache, waistline changes, skin looks like a slowly deflating balloon. Stairs one once ran up now are life-threatening. Memory loss is embarrassing. Sometimes I get sort of, you know, lonely. And my children say, "Enjoy being an elder!"

Statistics continue to point to the fact that before long about 50 percent of society will be over the age of 50. Congregations will have an even higher percentage. What influence can such a large body of stable, sensible and experienced people have on society? What role should this large body have in the church?

Several decades ago observers were noting the tremendous waste of resources in church and society because women's gifts were not being used. Is the church once again going to be blind to the possibilities of this growing segment within the body of believers? These are the people with more flexible time (although most retirees would say they are busier than ever), more discretionary income, and more valuable experience and wisdom to share with others. Yet programming frequently continues as if the majority of the congregation is below 50.

Among the recent mail I received was an invitation from a retirement center touting all that it does for its residents to enrich their lives. I felt a strange emptiness as I read through this glossy four-color brochure. Then I figured it out. This center said much about what it did to provide food, lodging, exercise, and entertainment. It said little about how it encouraged residents to keep moving toward service ministries.

As I look ahead to the next decade, my greatest concern is not how I will entertain myself, but whether I will find opportunities to remain active in ministry. Will the church encourage me to keep reaching out?

Admittedly the time will come when some elderly will have to learn appropriate dependence as the generations exchange roles and children take over the care of aging parents.

Yet only the elderly can assure those younger than themselves whether the faith life can endure. Only they can share the purple and red glories of this age. And I worry because wearing purple with a red hat requires practice. And I don't see enough practicing.

Katie Funk Wiebe, "Time for Purple with Red," Viewpoint, *The Christian Leader*, October 10, 1989, 15.

After 30 Years, It's Time for a Change

Katie Funk Wiebe

Thirty years ago, when I began this column for *The Christian Leader*, I had a desire to write and I thought I had something to say to the church I loved. Yet I needed an audience.

Editor Orlando Harms first gave me that audience, a very special gift to a writer, for without an audience a writer is impotent. Editors Wally Kroeker and Don Ratzlaff kept giving me that gift. I thank each one for their confidence and encouragement when I wanted to quit.

My first years were anxious ones. I wrote each column weeks before it was due. I was fearful my small supply of words, that most precious of all commodities to a writer, would run out before the deadline, that most terrifying of all taskmasters, arrived.

For 30 years I have had the privilege of thinking out loud and sharing my life with you. I will miss that regular audience. I thank each reader who responded. A small note or a long letter often caused my heart to dance cartwheels with joy.

I began as a writer for Mennonite Brethren women. In the early years, I often bemoaned the absence of a mentor and strong female intellectual role models. When my life changed because of my husband's death, and the need to find remunerative work to support my four children, and eventually a career, I moved to a broader audience. The particular joy in column writing is that you don't have to run on the same track as everyone else.

People called me a writer long before I called myself a writer. As long as I only dabbled in writing, I could reject its disciplines when less demanding activities called. Elizabeth O'Connor taught me the necessity of answering God's call by naming one's gift and accepting that that act will put us into tension with things as they are. I found that to be true.

When I accepted God's call, the way opened to writing books, articles, curriculum, devotional material and speaking engagements. Writing became a blessed burden.

Over the years I received opportunities among other religious bodies, particularly the Mennonite Church. Herald Press and Tyndale House published my first books for the trade market. Slowly, I overcame my inbred fears of other Mennonites so that today I often think of myself as an inter-Mennonite.

I have watched Mennonite journalism mature from a mere infant to a sophisticated adult. Years ago, I expected great hosts of young Mennonite Brethren writers to clamor to be let into the profession. I was disappointed. For some reason, we do not produce and nurture writers, poets, artists, composers. But that's grist for a column that may never be written.

We also are not developing articulate members concerned about theological issues. Too few readers write reflective letters to the editor that objectively probe and analyze topics other than abortion and nonresistance. We may be becoming more Catholic than we care to admit if we allow our ministers to tell us what to think, rather than working through an issue ourselves.

As I read 30 years of columns, I see myself having evolved spiritually, theologically and intellectually. I hope that continues. I soon rejected religious platitudes in the face of personal challenges to my faith. Clichés work only when life moves smoothly. I winnowed out the chaff and clung to the fundamentals.

As I felt my own pain and that of other women because of the church's disregard for the treasures buried in its own pews—the gifts of its women—I felt compelled to speak out. These gifts lay deeply unused under a pile of proof texts and cultural conditioning. Many still do. But change is slowly coming to our congregations. For that I am grateful.

I moved from the traditionalist position—that the main role for women is a supportive and sacrificial one—to what I believe is a more correct biblical view: that God sees men and women as equals in sin, salvation and service. Today I am more convinced than I was in the early 1960s of the need to speak to the demeaning of women in society. The high incidence of violent rape is one constant reminder of this devaluation.

What else have I written about these 30 years? Any topic that intrigued me, one of which was the role of language in thought and behavior. I love words and how they function. They are God's gift to us.

I note that I have written little about missions and evangelism, the kingpins of Mennonite Brethren faith and polity. Though it was a major topic of my writing when I was young, I think I unconsciously felt that certain aspects of our corporate life are off-limits to lay writers.

The process of change continues. As I grow older, I sense that the growing body of older adults, a new phenomenon, is considered a problem, like women were. Yet in these older adults lies another large unmined treasure-trove of gifts. The young-old can either be challenged to new forms of service or be sucked into senior leisure lifestyles.

It's been a good 30 years. I will often wish for the opportunity to write another column, but other pursuits beckon. Thanks for reading more than 700 columns and about 525,000 words. My word supply never ran out.

Katie Funk Wiebe, "After 30 Years, It's Time for a Change," Viewpoint, *The Christian Leader*, December 31, 1991, 9.

Chapter 13

Yielding and Reaching

Valerie G. Rempel and Lorraine Dick

Katie Funk Wiebe was a restless young woman looking for something to read when she picked up a copy of *My Utmost for His Highest* and read these words from 1 Peter 1:16: "Ye shall be holy; for I am holy." The words "leaped from the page to arrest me," she would write later. "That day a weak, faltering faith received strengthening, and aimless feet were put on a course."[1]

Katie's "aimless" feet eventually found their way into what she described as the "shoes of a writer."[2] However, they were not just any writer's shoes. These were shoes specially fitted for service to the church. In them, Katie has been able to share her reflections on the nature of God and God's purposes in the world in a way that invites her audience to join her on a pilgrimage of faith. As she puts it, "I desperately want people to understand the connection between God's word and daily life."[3]

In choosing to write for the church, Katie allows readers to share in her faith journey. Her writing reflects a deep spirituality that has been shaped by her study of the Bible, the devotional and theological writings of other Christians, and her own experiences. It is what Martin Rovers and Lucie Kocum have described as a holistic spirituality, one that "gives meaning, stability, and purpose to life."[4] It is expressed in her faith in God, her understanding of the Christian life, and her commitment to the church as a community of faith.[5]

Faith in God

Katie's confession of faith is clearly anchored in the Christian tradition. She writes, "I have a basic faith in God and his Son Jesus Christ, which is sometimes quite simple—a sense of the existence of God in a dimension beyond the material world. I believe in sin and evil. I believe in God's grace, love, and forgiveness."[6]

Katie's initial faith experiences grew out of her family setting and her varied church experiences. There were, of course, questions and tensions that emerged in that setting. Her parents' faith was sure and their commitment to church fellowship was strong, but as has been noted elsewhere it was a commitment expressed in multiple communities—the local Russian Baptist congregation, the Mennonite Brethren church across the river and, for the children, the United Church of Canada in town. In her Mennonite setting she "was introduced to Christian Endeavor, revival meetings, church discipline, German Golden Texts, green curtains for dividers strung on wires, riverside baptisms, kneeling for prayer, and missionary conferences held in huge tents."[7] The "powerful voices" that called her to a particular expression of faith in this community were challenged by the equaling appealing voices calling her to the world of imagination.[8]

For a time, Katie tried to ignore both sets of voices. She chose to enroll at a technical college as preparation for a business career and has confessed that she "found it wise not to read seriously of the life of discipleship, [as] it might implicate my life."[9] Her encounter with the devotional writings of Oswald Chambers changed that. Chambers, a young Scottish minister, had run the Bible Training College in London before leaving to serve as YMCA chaplain in Egypt during World War I. After his early death, his widow edited and published the collection of meditations titled *My Utmost for His Highest*. It has become a classic of devotional literature and Katie has frequently acknowledged its central place on her reading shelf along with other devotional writers such as A.W. Tozer and Hannah Whitall Smith.

Chambers' theology was strongly shaped by Wesleyan holiness with its stress on the necessity of entire sanctification.[10] The call to be holy was more than simply a call to govern one's life and behavior. Chambers understood holiness to be the central purpose of life, something to be intensely craved. "Holiness means unsullied walking with the feet, unsullied talking with the tongue, unsullied thinking with the mind—every detail of the life under the scrutiny of God. Holiness is not only what God gives me, but what I manifest that God has given me."[11]

Katie's own life and writing reflects this kind of an orientation toward God. She writes of the Christian life as something to grasp and cherish. "[Christ] intended his followers to make life itself their vocation while on this earth. Eternal life does not begin in heaven, but here, in time, when the new birth takes place...When a person gives this redeemed life over to God, God gives back to that person his or her true self to serve him."[12]

What becomes especially noteworthy in Katie's understanding of the Christian life is that this call to follow Jesus does not lead to a total denial of the self. Instead, the self finds true identity in following Christ. In yielding to Christ one finds freedom to serve, using the gifts and talents God gives each individual for service to the church and the world.

This quest for identity has been a theme throughout Katie's life. Her own growing realization that identity must be rooted in Christ came in the months and years following widowhood. She has put it like this:

> I had discovered that full identity is possible in Christ Jesus and that the teaching of the Bible granted me the right to unique personhood. My long and difficult pilgrimage did not end with widowhood. I learned that I needed a central core of strength not provided by the culture (with its emphasis on sex and vacuity for women) nor by the church (with its emphasis on woman's limitations), nor by the demands of being a woman (wife, mother, and widow later on). The strength came only as I regarded myself the way God sees me: a person whose faith is in the atoning work of Christ on the cross.[13]

For Katie, this redeemed life is something that moves toward newness. Faith should never be static—it is something that can grow and change throughout life. Again and again through her writings we are confronted with her example of choosing to say "yes" to the claims that Jesus Christ set before her. She understands that "the Christian life is a meaningful relationship between a personal God and the person who chooses to follow him...The life of faith is an intelligent relationship with God based on trust and an understanding of his Word."[14] There is always a reaching towards God and a willingness to use all capacities in service to God.

This is an important distinction in Katie's understanding of the Christian life. Her Mennonite community gave her the concept of *Gelassenheit*, a German word that, in the Anabaptist tradition, speaks of a willingness to submit all aspects of the self to God. Katie affirms this concept but critiques what some have done with it, especially when it suggests the suppression of individuality. There is, indeed, a death to self that is called for in Scripture, but it is balanced by the invitation to fullness of life.[15] This theme is repeated throughout Katie's writing as she speaks of answering this call in her own life and challenges others—no matter what their age—to live and serve God fully.

Katie is also firmly committed to God's Word as the central way to know God and to nurture one's faith in God. Katie frequently encourages people to pick up the Bible and read for themselves: "The Word of God must be closer to us than a book lying on a shelf. The truths of the Word cannot magically leap from its unopened pages to find a hiding place in our lives. Faith in Christ is nurtured through knowledge of Him gained in study, meditation and prayer."[16] As she has found strength and help in the Bible, she has challenged men and women to do the same. Katie simply calls all Christians to be theologians, wisely observing that "theology is the task of every believer, male or female...because we live according to our theology."[17] For Katie, "the task of theology is to root believers firmly in the Christian life by thinking through God's word for their own lives as it relates to their particular context."[18]

The Christian Life

Katie's invitation for all believers to see themselves as theologians grows out of her own awareness of how our view of God shapes our behavior. She also understands how our experiences shape our view of God. As a storyteller, Katie has frequently taken her life experiences, her reading, and the translations from her inner soul to let us see how she is making meaning in her own life.

Katie has written eloquently of the early years of marriage and motherhood, and the tension of that period. It was a time of trying to conform to what was expected of her in these roles. She describes it in this way: "I couldn't grasp that the spirit, the mind, the imagination, the inner life, must also be satisfied or its hunger pains can lead to another kind of death. The worst aspect of this turmoil was that I didn't dare discuss my confusion with anyone—not even with myself. To do so would reveal a liberal, and worse still, an unspiritual attitude toward life."[19] It is easy to hear the echoes of the voices of her youth—those voices that so often seemed in opposition in their call to very particular forms of godliness versus the life of the imagination. It was a critical turning point in Katie's life when she began to bring those voices together; to realize the gift of an imagination in service to the church. Spirituality turned out to be much more than conformity to a set of cultural expectations. True spirituality was expressed in the totality of one's life and work and being. It meant seeing oneself as a unique being created by God and then offering that life up to God.

At the heart of Katie's spirituality, then, is a profound commitment to the life of discipleship. It is expressed in her commitment to the study of God's Word and life lived by the strength of the Holy Spirit.[20] It is also expressed in a willingness to embrace as God-given the gifts of imagination and creativity. As Katie puts it, "there is a mystery and beauty to godliness. And the writer who uses her imagination allows the mystery of God to remain without feeling compelled to push everything into formulas and boxes."[21] Rather than a life of rules and restrictions, the Christian life becomes "a series of choices and commitments directed by God's compelling love."[22]

These choices and commitments have been profoundly tested through her experience of loss. Early widowhood, singleness, and the death of her daughter Christine, have pushed Katie to probe Scripture and the Christian tradition for answers. Where did she fit in the world of couples? How did she fit into the work world or into church? And most importantly, how was she to understand the work and presence of God in the midst of such profound loss?

Katie has been quick to point out that easy Christian platitudes provide insufficient answers to these questions. Death confronts us with the problem of meaning in suffering and challenges God's goodness. Suffering changes us. She writes, "Suffering draws us closer to God or it embitters. A person can't remain the same…A person can't be bitter about life and full of joy simultaneously…But bitterness doesn't come from death or loss; it is born in our hearts."[23]

Here again, Katie articulates the possibility of choice. In her own life she has chosen to affirm God's goodness and provision even in the midst of sorrow, finding that the pathway of acceptance is the way that leads to God. This is not a blind fatalism but an acknowledgement of God's hand in one's life, that even painful circumstances can be used by God for God's glory. "What has happened, has happened. You do not know why. You cannot change the situation, but in faith you will accept it, knowing that God permitted it."[24] This form of yielding to God is not without pain but it does come with an assurance that God is still present even in the midst of pain.

For Katie, healing comes through acceptance and through accepting, one comes to know God as the divine comforter. In 1964 she wrote, "The acceptance of the loss of a loved one is more than a passive acknowledgement of the fact that the person is gone. It is a deliberate choosing before God of the way that is now before you as your way. This yielding of your will to God in complete submission is the way of victory and the pathway to service and blessing."[25]

It is not surprising that the question of suffering as it relates to God's will has shaped Katie's understanding of God. Katie routinely resists seeing God as some sort of divine ATM, dispensing blessings after the insertion of prayer. "Believe in

God because God is God and not a blessing machine," she writes. "Faith means trusting in both favorable and unfavorable circumstances."[26] Even when God seems absent, waiting for God to act is, Katie writes, "an indication of hope."[27] It is God who gives grace in the midst of pain and suffering. It is God who will bring peace and comfort.

Katie's own experience of loss has made her sensible of the different kinds of losses people sustain. Yes, there are the obvious losses of spouses and family members, but she is quick to point out the losses that come with aging as people leave jobs that formed identity, illness that brings restrictions, or loneliness when people find themselves moved to the fringes of church and social life. Here again, Katie speaks to the goodness of God as sustainer and provider and calls for older adults to be models in their continued striving for maturity in Christ.[28]

This call to look forward is a deliberate perspective that has profoundly shaped Katie's life and comes through time after time in her writing. Spiritual lessons can still be learned, Katie insists, and offers lessons from her own life. "Today you taught this old dog a new trick…I was a believer in Christ. I knew and cherished your forgiveness of my sins. But I couldn't forgive her for what she had done to me. And I never saw my hardness as sin. Today I learned that an older person like myself can forgive someone even for something that happened long ago but left a bad and lingering memory."[29] This confession, in the form of a prayer, is drawn from Katie's own experience. It is the kind of vulnerability that demonstrates Katie's willingness to share of herself, which serves as a model for the Christian community.

While Katie's life has been shaped by sorrow, she has refused to let the experience of loss define her. Katie has determinedly looked forward and she speaks confidently of being able to celebrate God's mercy and goodness once again.[30] Still, she acknowledges that there is a cost to following Jesus. She has written, "The life of faith has many joys. One of the greatest is to know you are living in God's will. But there is also a price to pay. It is full and complete obedience to God. You must be willing to let Him rule your life. And such a step may bring about many changes in your life, particularly with regard to things—for the life of faith is opposed to the life lived for things."[31] Katie rejects "the whole health, wealth, prosperity theology" that is often so attractive, choosing instead to follow the God who is revealed in "words, deeds, prayer, and his still, small voice."[32]

The Community of Faith.
Katie became a member of the Mennonite Brethren church by choice after she "had stood at a distance for some time."[33] She has stayed because she values "MB biblicism and open spirituality."[34] That commitment to the church reflects her understanding of its central place in the life of a Christian. Katie never advocates a lone ranger approach to spirituality. "Spiritual individualism and independence," she has written, "threatens our accountability to one another, our unity and our very life as a body of believers."[35] The Christian life is nurtured in community.

That commitment has not meant an unquestioning acceptance of all church practices. Her writing reflects much thought over what the church is and what it is meant to be. She understands that theologies "have fads or trends," and those who interpret Scripture may be guided as much by cultural patterns as by the good news itself.[36] She has warned of the danger of simply choosing a lens by which to interpret Scripture and then using it to privilege certain truths over others. Katie has been especially critical of groups who interpret Scripture in ways that justify oppression or prop up the powerful, and she has pushed Christians to ask whether the church is holding onto traditions that no longer serve God's purpose for it.[37] Her exploration of issues related to aging has shaped her call for the church to resist pushing older adults aside as if they no longer have gifts for ministry and service.

Katie's desire for the church to seek truth in Scripture, to study and pray together, reflects her own practices and commitments to Scripture. That practice stood her in good stead when she began to wrestle with the way the church treated women. She read the Bible with new interest as she struggled to understand "what kind of sieve" should be used to separate texts that applied to women from texts that applied only to men.[38] "What was at heart of the contradiction between faith and enforced submission of women? Was the contradiction in God and the Bible? Or in women and men who claimed to be Christian, yet opposed the full development of women in church and society," she asked.[39] Katie grieved the church's unwillingness to bless women for ministry, for being reluctant to recognize God's calling and gifting even as she accepted God's call on her life. Yet even when powerful church leaders resisted the inclusion of women in public ministries, Katie chose to stay.

Katie's appreciation for the open spirituality of the Mennonite Brethren tradition has not blinded her to what she views as a contemporary push toward performance in worship services. Her own inclination is toward the transcendence of God and she shows little patience for worship practices that seem trivial or that leave little room for "wonder and mystery" in worship.[40] She mourns the passing of the rich tradition of church and mission festivals that has often been replaced by a focus on secular holidays such as Mother's Day or Valentine's Day. Still, she recognizes that the church and the Christian tradition are always clothed in a cultural context. The challenge is to sort out what is gospel and what is culture. She calls the church to lead, indeed to be at the "cutting edge of society…fighting sin where it is virile" and speaking for "truth and righteousness."[41] This is a call for the church to live out its commitment to the Christian life in a way that acknowledges that the "fully committed life in Christ is risky and dangerous."[42] She challenges the church at large to reach towards the fulfillment of its mission.

While Katie has chosen to stay a member of a Mennonite Brethren church, she has also found meaning and spiritual nurture in other faith communities. In recent years, Katie has deliberately widened her church experiences because she "did not want to die without having experienced worship with other Christians."[43] The benefit has been a wider vision of the mission of the church and the way that God is at work in various settings.

Conclusion

In her book of prayers, Katie describes the "law of old age" as "yielding and reaching."[44] It is a phrase that nicely captures her understanding of the need for grace in accommodating the realities of an aging body while still exploring the possibilities of mind and spirit. It is also a phrase that seems to capture the heart of Katie's spirituality. It is expressed in her desire to yield herself to God while always reaching for a deeper relationship with God. She calls the church to do the same, to live under the lordship of Christ while reaching toward the fulfillment of the church's mission in the world.

Spiritual writing is always about calling us to a deeper relationship with God. It is writing that catches our imagination and pushes us to consider new ways of thinking about or living out the Christian life. In reading Katie's words we encounter someone who is, as Wes Prieb puts it, "'doing theology,' seeking to understand and explain God's relationship with his children. Her practical theology emerges from real human experience and is never static. She has had the freedom to change her views during a lifelong process of making new discoveries on the trail."[45]

Katie's recent autobiography makes that same point. She writes that over the course of her life she has learned "that faith is a journey with God, not just an initial turning to him and then a long slow slide into home base. Faith is not a quick plunge into the sea of God's grace followed by basking lazily on the shore thereafter. Faith is a process of continual growth from the first simple reaching out to God…to becoming more Christ-like with advancement in years."[46]

Katie is never content to stand still and she invites us to join her in looking forward to what God has in store for us.

• • •

Endnotes

1. Katie Funk Wiebe, "A Pilgrimage in Books," *Christian Living*, April 1962, 19.

2. Katie Funk Wiebe, "How I Received the Shoes of a Communicator," *The Christian Leader*, April 24, 1990, 14-15.
3. *Ibid.*, 15.
4. Martin Rovers and Lucie Kocum, "Development of a Holistic Model of Spirituality," *Journal of Spirituality in Mental Health* 12, no. 1 (January 2010): 17.
5. *Ibid.*, 17. Rovers and Kocum suggest that spirituality has three dimensions expressed as "faith in the presence of God/transcendent, hope and meaning and purpose in life, and love expressed with family and community."
6. Katie Funk Wiebe, *Bless Me Too, My Father: Living by Choice, Not by Default* (Scottdale: Herald Press, 1988), 220.
7. Wiebe, "How I Received the Shoes," 14.
8. *Ibid.*
9. *Ibid.*
10. J.I. Packer, "Supernaturalizing the Natural," review of *Oswald Chambers: Abandoned to God*, by David McCasland. *Christianity Today*, October 4, 1993, 36.
11. Oswald Chambers, *The Golden Book of Oswald Chambers: My Utmost For His Highest; Selections for the Year* (New York: Dodd, Mead & Co., 1935), 245.
12. See Katie Funk Wiebe, *Second Thoughts* (Hillsboro: Kindred Press, 1981), 20-21.
13. Katie Funk Wiebe, *Alone: A Search for Joy* (Winnipeg: Kindred Press, 1987), 51-52.
14. *Ibid.*, 10.
15. *Ibid.*, 20.
16. Katie Wiebe, Women and the Church, *The Christian Leader*, January 23, 1962, 21.
17. Katie Funk Wiebe, "Growing with the Seasons of Life," *Direction* 24, no.2 (Fall 1995): 79.
18. *Ibid.*
19. Katie Funk Wiebe, *You Never Gave Me a Name: One Mennonite Woman's Story* (Telford: DreamSeeker Books, 2009), 73-74.
20. Wiebe, *Bless Me Too, My Father*, 34.
21. Wiebe, *You Never Gave Me a Name*, 171.
22. Wiebe, *Bless Me Too, My Father*, 130.
23. Wiebe, *Alone*, 43.
24. Katie Funk Wiebe, "When You Sorrow," Women and the Church, *The Christian Leader* September 15, 1964, 21.
25. *Ibid.*
26. Wiebe, *You Never Gave Me a Name*, 272.
27. Wiebe, *Bless Me Too, My Father*, 119.
28. Katie Funk Wiebe, *Prayers of an Omega: Facing the Transitions of Aging* (Scottdale: Herald Press, 1994), 21.
29. *Ibid.*, 29.
30. Wiebe, *Alone*, 13.
31. Katie Wiebe, Women and the Church, *The Christian Leader*, March 6, 1962, 21.
32. Wiebe, *You Never Gave Me a Name*, 272.

33. Katie Funk Wiebe, "If You're a Mennonite," Women and the Church, *The Christian Leader* November 10, 1964, 21.
34. Wiebe, *You Never Gave Me a Name*, 265.
35. Katie Funk Wiebe, "Dressed in Doubleknit," Viewpoint, *The Christian Leader* March 5, 1985, 17.
36. Wiebe, *You Never Gave Me a Name*, 273.
37. Katie Funk Wiebe, "Honky Hermeneutics," Viewpoint, *The Christian Leader* September 26, 1976, 19.
38. Wiebe, *Bless Me Too, My Father*, 228.
39. *Ibid.*, 229.
40. Wiebe, *You Never Gave Me a Name*, 267.
41. Wiebe, *Second Thoughts*, 88.
42. Wiebe, *You Never Gave Me a Name*, 267.
43. *Ibid.*, 264.
44. Wiebe, *Prayers of an Omega*, 19.
45. Wesley J. Prieb, "Katie, A Writer in Pilgrimage," *Direction* 24, no. 2 (Fall 1995): 84.
46. Wiebe, *You Never Gave Me a Name*, 269.

Sorting Prayer Thoughts

Katie Funk Wiebe

As the New Year begins I find myself no longer making resolutions like I used to in youth. Instead I sort through my beliefs to identify what to take with me into the coming year and what to leave behind. I strain to rid myself of cultural additives. They slip into spiritual food as much as into the processed foods we buy over the counter.

I ask myself what I believe about God and Jesus Christ, his Son. Is my concept of the church the same? of evangelism and missions? of social action? of worship and the disciplines of the inner life?

Prayer remains a difficult assignment for me, and I believe also for many other computer-age Christians. Although I sense a groundswell movement toward a more reflective life, it isn't a mass migration as yet.

As people enter this New Year, characterized by political, economic and social restlessness, they recognize that life is more than eating and drinking. They know that life will require more than a full billfold, a full tank of gas and a full stomach—but they still hope these will do.

Prayer is not a priority for the secularized Christian who considers all of life a prayer and explains it shouldn't be isolated as a separate activity. I accept that premise, but I also believe it must be more.

I recall the speaker some 30 years ago who told about the time her butter dish was empty and there was no money to buy more. She placed her hands over the dish and prayed, expecting God to fill the dish, so she and her husband could butter their bread. Instead, they ate many meals without butter.

When we think of prayer as primarily petition, we run into problems because experiences of unanswered prayer and Christ's words about answered prayer don't match. I admit to such thoughts during the past year.

So the sorting continues. Why do I keep on praying prayers of petition, even though I know some starving people have prayed for food and received it and others have prayed and died of starvation; some have prayed for safekeeping on a journey and arrived safely and others have prayed and been injured? Habit? Ignorance? Blind faith?

Not at all.

Years ago I learned a list of explanations for why God doesn't answer prayer (perhaps it's unfortunate some Bible teachers go to such pains to emphasize these): You're not praying in the will of God. You're asking amiss. God's answer is "No." You don't have enough faith. Sin in your life makes it impossible for God to answer your prayer. His answer is "Wait." You didn't wrestle with God—you weren't persistent enough. You can't expect him to do a miracle for each person.

All these reasons have some truth to them, but prayer which is an attempt to test God's power, to manipulate him to a showdown, is not prayer, but a duel, a kind of bargaining or badgering to prove to ourselves God is on our side. Prayer to get a miracle isn't the reason I keep on praying.

I move to other areas of the subject. It has become clear in the last years that I can't use prayer as a device to protect my children from the difficulties and problems which are simply the result of being human. I can't use prayer as an attempt to make life easier for them than it has been for me. I can't use prayer to force my ideas of what they should do in life on them as God's will for their lives. Children must be free to choose. Prayer was never intended to be perennial training wheels. Yet parents should never stop praying for their children. It's somewhat paradoxical.

I've learned also I can't use prayer as a substitute for obedience to his Word. It's easier to pray for the Laotian refugees in our community than to help them learn to speak English. It's easier to pray for the lonely than to take time to visit them. It's easier to pray for mission endeavors than to take time to study about them and become involved. It's easier to talk about social justice than become part of the answer. The balance between the inner life and the outer life always requires fine tuning.

I find my thinking about prayer for the will of God has also changed, a matter which has been one of life's great agonies, because for a long time I had the idea the will of God was like a railroad track—fixed and inflexible. Elton Trueblood, in *A Place to Stand*, has helpful words on this subject. He says that because we are persons and God is a Person, the will of God isn't predetermined like a mechanical device. We have choices, and if our goal is to honor Christ with our whole being, that choice is his will. Our commitment to honoring God in the decision we make thoughtfully and prayerfully is more important than agonizing day after day about it.

So I keep sorting. I don't expect God to function like my private errand boy or personal genie, meeting my every momentary need. But that doesn't keep me from praying about personal and material needs. Sudden news of difficulty in the family circle or among friends sends me rushing before God with only one request, "God, make it different, less hurting." I think he understands.

Then what about prayer for the New Year? I can point to answers to prayer. I can point to unanswered prayer. But that is not the issue. I affirm again prayer must be part of the Christian life. It can't be left out without denying the reality of God. It is an affirmation of faith in God as Creator and Lord. To pray is to make myself open to his working in my life and in the lives of those I pray for. So the process of sorting has resulted in a resolution anyway—to keep talking with God about anything that concerns us.

Katie Funk Wiebe, "Sorting Prayer Thoughts," Viewpoint, *The Christian Leader*, December 30, 1980, 16.

I've Changed My Mind

Katie Funk Wiebe

I celebrate two birthdays each year—one on the day I always thought was my natal day and the other on the date which appears on my birth certificate. Such extended celebrating gives much time for reflection about the passing years, especially about change. Here are some things I find I've changed my mind about:

(1) Old dogs *can* learn new tricks. Much folk wisdom used to be passed on to us children via proverbs and witty sayings. Some, like "A stitch in time saves nine," I still believe. Others I reject vigorously, like the idea that old dogs can't learn new tricks.

I've met many "old dogs" who are learning new concepts, new attitudes and new skills with each passing birthday. They enroll in continuing education classes and enjoy them. Last year I joined a woodworking course at the local high school. Though I may never again guide a radial saw through a board, I now have conquered my fear of power tools by learning to use them under guided instruction.

The proof of my skills stands in my office in the form of a walnut-stained, probably too solid, bookshelf, on which hammerhead marks and drips of glue mysteriously appeared after it was completed. But it is a recognizable bookshelf.

Old dogs can learn to build, to draw, to paint, to write, to teach, to lead, to speak—even to change their minds about long-held ideas. These "early-borns," as one older friend calls his peers, may have arthritis in their bones, but they don't have to have it in their attitudes—unless they want to.

(2) We Christians dearly love to line up ideas and concepts, like millennialism, into neat packages of belief, so that we can recall them more easily or put them on display for friends, or even hand them out to non-Christians in pamphlet form. We enjoy building systems of thought. We like establishing programs of activity. We believe God works through systems and programs.

Some of us get upset when the generation below us urges us to fight sin and evil in the systems and structures of society. I've often heard people say with great emphasis that sin resides in persons, not in systems. We must work to convert the person, not the system or structure.

I no longer believe that evil resides only in individuals. Like goodness and truth, it resides also in social systems developed by human beings. When Christ spoke against the Pharisees, he was speaking against the evil in the religious structures and systems of his day. When he spoke to the woman at the well, he was addressing her as an individual. He worked both fronts.

(3) At an earlier age I didn't believe there was such a thing as exclusive language. I've changed my mind. I believe sexist language in an aware society excludes.

I heard a sermon which began with the reading of a Scripture passage beginning with "Brothers." Throughout his comments the minister used the generic "man" to refer to both sexes. All his pronouns were masculine. All his illustrations dealt with males of various ages and occupations and their emotions and responses to life. In his meditation no women or girls had interesting, challenging or enlightening experiences worth repeating in public. He never said, "I heard this story about a young girl who. . . ."

His application was to "go preach the Word," a specific activity traditionally reserved only for a small part of most congregations, sometimes only for one person.

I am convinced that Christians who speak of wanting to draw others into the kingdom of God should show their concern by adapting their language to their audience. Maybe if 65 to 70 percent of a congregation is female, a minister should try using only female pronouns some Sunday!

(4) I believe there is a middle-age crisis which varies from person to person. For some people life moves along without interruption from the last heart breaking adolescent crush to the rocking chair stage. For others, middle age is a heaving ocean of emotion related to job change, physical health, thoughts about success or failure, or even something as expected as the children leaving home.

Suddenly I've discovered that the house seems 20 feet longer with no child to send to answer the front doorbell, and the grocery store and post office are at least twice as far away when I have to go. I feel as lost and displaced at times as an adolescent entering the adult world.

(5) Though you may have wished all your life for a larger house, a bigger fridge and more storage space, what you need most in the second half-century is not more rooms, more freezer space or a bigger garage, but only more friends.

(6) The hardest things in life, even as one grows older, are not doing your daily exercises, paying the taxes and eating less but continuing to learn to say you're sorry, forgiving the person who

has hurt you and relinquishing power voluntarily so others will get the opportunity to exercise their gifts.

Number seven is still in the embryo stage. It has to do with accepting the ambiguities of life as well as the certitudes of God's grace and truth. I don't think the one excludes the other.

Katie Funk Wiebe, "I've Changed My Mind," Viewpoint, *The Christian Leader*, September 25, 1979, 20.

A Comprehensive Bibliography of the Writings and Oral Presentations of Katie Funk Wiebe

Compiled by
David Giesbrecht, Doug Heidebrecht, and Susan Huebert

An initial compilation of Katie Funk Wiebe's bibliography was completed by David Giesbrecht for the Fall 1995 issue of *Direction* (pages 88-97), which was dedicated in honor of Katie. Since then Katie has continued to write.

As part of this present volume we wish to recognize the tremendous gift of Katie's writing by providing the opportunity to explore her work through this bibliography. While we have found the description "comprehensive" to be elusive, the richness of Katie's life of writing makes it a worthy aspiration.

We have included in this bibliography a complete list of Katie's columns, "Women and the Church" and "Viewpoint," published in *The Christian Leader*. She often sent these columns to other magazines, where many were reprinted, sometimes under different titles. Katie's breadth of reading is reflected in her numerous book reviews.

The bibliography is organized chronologically and then in categories under each year. The list of items in each category is again arranged chronologically.

1952-1961

Edited Works
Youth Worker. Walter Wiebe, co-editor, Canadian Conference of Mennonite Brethren Churches; Youth Committee, 1952-1961.
Youth Worker Program Helps. Walter Wiebe, co-editor, 1958-1961.

Articles and Columns
"Project for Mother's Day." *The Youth Worker*, March-April, 1953, 7.
"If Christ Had Not Come!" *The Youth Worker*, November-December, 1956, 9-12.

"An Area of Neglect: Our Young Married People." *The Youth Worker*, March-April, 1957, 3-4.
"The Work of Women." Letters to the Editor, *The Canadian Mennonite*, April 12, 1957, 2, 6.
"Sask. Mennonite Brethren Plan New Mission Work." *The Canadian Mennonite*, June 14, 1957, 4.
"Bethany Institute Family Commemorates Thirty Years." *The Canadian Mennonite*, August 23, 1957, 7.
"Why He Came..." *The Youth Worker*, November 1958, 7-10
"The Life and Work of Dr. K.L. Schellenberg"(with Walter Wiebe). *Youth Worker Program Helps*. Topic V, 1959, 20-27.
"A Tract Never Dies." *The Youth Worker*, March 1959, 12-14.
"Contents: One Speaker." *The Youth Worker*, January 1960, 5-6.
"What is the Place of Drama in Our Churches?" *The Youth Worker*, February 1960, 2-5.
"The Story of Religious Drama." *The Youth Worker*, February 1960, 6-7.
"If Christ Had Not Come!" *Youth Worker Program Helps, Volume 1*, edited by Walter and Katie Wiebe, 135-139. Winnipeg: Canadian Conference of Mennonite Brethren Churches; Youth Committee, 1960.
"Planning for Youth Sunday." *Youth Worker Program Helps*, Topic V, 1960, 22-34.
"Does Christian Stewardship Tolerate Commercialism with the Church or Its Auxiliary Organizations?" *Youth Worker Program Helps*. Topic II, 1960, 8-12.
"The Christ-centered Life." *Youth Worker Program Helps*, Topic VI, 1960, 35-41.
"What Does Baptism Mean to Me?" *Youth Worker Program Helps*. Topic I, 1960, 1-7.
"Does Christian Stewardship Tolerate Commercialism within the Church or its Auxiliary Organizations?" *Youth Worker Program Helps*, 1960, 8-12.
Youth Worker Program Helps, Volume 1 (with Walter Wiebe). Winnipeg: Canadian Conference of Mennonite Brethren Churches; Youth Committee, 1960.
"After High School, What?" *Youth Worker Program Helps*, Topic X, 1961, 61-67.
"Bound to be Read." *Youth Worker Program Helps*, Topic VII, 1961, 42-47.
"The Youth Workers' Conference." *The Youth Worker*, January 1961, 4-7.
"Your Place in the Church's Christian Literature Program" (with Walter Wiebe). *Youth Worker Program Helps*. Topic II, 1961, 7-18.
"Make Ready." *Youth Worker Program Helps*, Topic IV, 1961, 25-33.
"Operation Hat." *The Evangelical Christian*, September 1961, 25-27.
"Record Attendance at Ontario Women's Rally." *The Canadian Mennonite*, June 30, 1961, 1, 10.
"Your Place in the Church's Christian Literature Program" (with Walter Wiebe). *Youth Worker Program Helps*, 1961, 7-18.

Comprehensive Bibliography | 257

Book Reviews

Review of *Effective Readings for Special Days and Occasions* by Laura S. Emerson. *Gospel Banner*, July 13, 1961.

Review of *Mother-Daughter Banquets* by Grace Ramquist. *Gospel Banner*, July 13, 1961.

Review of *Devotional Programs for Women's Groups No. 3.* by Lora Lee Parrott. *Gospel Banner*, July 13, 1961.

Review of *God Blessed Me with a Heart Attack* by Richard G. Dunwoody. *Gospel Banner*, November 9, 1961.

Review of *Devotional Programs for Adult Groups* by Leslie Parrott. *Gospel Banner*, November 16, 1961.

Review of *The Billy Sunday Story* by Lee Thomas. *Gospel Banner*, November 23, 1961.

Review of *Out of My Life* by Raymond V. Edman. *Gospel Banner*, November 23, 1961.

Review of *Light from Heaven* by Christmas Carol Kauffman. *Gospel Banner*, November 30.1961.

Review of *Unlikely Saints of the Bible* by William C. Fletcher. *Gospel Banner*, November 30, 1961.

Review of *How Can These Things Be? And Other Messages* by Bill H. Lewis. *Gospel Banner*, December 7, 1961.

Review of *Say "Yes" to Life!* by Anna B. Mow. *Gospel Banner*, December 14, 1961.

1962

Articles and Columns

"Come, Ye Thankful People, Come." *Youth Worker Program Helps*. Topic I, 1962, 1-8

"Where Do You Think You are Going?" *Youth Worker Program Helps*. Topic IV, 1962, 23-29.

"Be Thou Faithful Unto Death." *Youth Worker Program Helps*. Topic IX, 1962, 65-73.

"Church Secretarial Services for K-W Ministers." *The Canadian Mennonite*, March 23, 1962, 5.

"A Pilgrimage in Books." *Christian Living*, April 1962, 19.

"Kitchener Christian Writers Meet." *The Canadian Mennonite*, June 15, 1962, 5.

"Interview with a High School Guidance Teacher." *The Canadian Mennonite*, July 27, 1962, 1, 8.

"One of the First Impressions: Mennonites Don't Dress Alike." *The Canadian Mennonite*, August 17, 1962, 7.

"Women's Activities Around the World." *The Canadian Mennonite*, August 24, 1962, 7.

"The Place of Women in the Work of the Church." *The Canadian Mennonite*, September 7, 1962, 7.

"'Stay Here and Open an Office.'" *Christian Living*, November 1962, 28-29.

Women and the Church
Women and the Church, *The Christian Leader*, January 9, 1962, 21.
Women and the Church, *The Christian Leader*, January 23, 1962, 21.
Women and the Church, *The Christian Leader*, February 6, 1962, 21.
Women and the Church, *The Christian Leader*, February 20, 1962, 21.
Women and the Church, *The Christian Leader*, March 6, 1962, 21.
Women and the Church, *The Christian Leader*, March 20, 1962, 21.
Women and the Church, *The Christian Leader*, April 3, 1962, 21.
Women and the Church, *The Christian Leader*, April 17, 1962, 21.
Women and the Church, *The Christian Leader*, May 1, 1962, 21.
Women and the Church, *The Christian Leader*, May 15, 1962, 21.
Women and the Church, *The Christian Leader*, May 29, 1962, 21.
Women and the Church, *The Christian Leader*, June 12, 1962, 21.
Women and the Church, *The Christian Leader*, June 26, 1962, 21.
Women and the Church, *The Christian Leader*, July 10, 1962, 21.
Women and the Church, *The Christian Leader*, July 24, 1962, 21.
Women and the Church, *The Christian Leader*, August 7, 1962, 21.
Women and the Church, *The Christian Leader*, August 21, 1962, 21.
Women and the Church, *The Christian Leader*, September 4, 1962, 21.
Women and the Church, *The Christian Leader*, September 18, 1962, 21.
Women and the Church, *The Christian Leader*, October 4, 1962, 21.
Women and the Church, *The Christian Leader*, October 16, 1962, 21.
Women and the Church, *The Christian Leader*, October 30, 1962, 29.
Women and the Church, *The Christian Leader*, November 13, 1962, 24.
Women and the Church, *The Christian Leader*, November 27, 1962, 21.
Women and the Church, *The Christian Leader*, December 11, 1962, 21.
Women and the Church, *The Christian Leader*, December 25, 1962, 21.

Book Reviews
Review of *They Sang Through the Crisis* by John Malcus Ellison. *Gospel Banner*, March 15, 1962.

Review of *Beloved World* by Eugenia Price. *Gospel Banner*, March 22, 1962.

Review of *The Book of Mormon—True or False?* by Arthur Budvarson. *Gospel Banner*, March 22, 1962.

Review of *The Life of God in the Soul of Man* by Henry Scougal. *Gospel Banner*, April 5, 1962.

Review of *Science Returns to God* by James H. Jauncey. *Gospel Banner*, April 19, 1962.

Review of *Faith's Unclaimed Inheritance* by Frank Houghton. *Gospel Banner*, April 26, 1962.
Review of *The Children's Simplified New Testament* by Olaf M. Norlie. *Gospel Banner*, April 26, 1962.
Review of *Every Day with Jesus* by Mendell Taylor. *Gospel Banner*, May 3, 1962.
Review of *God's Methods for Holy Living* by Donald Grey Barnhouse. *Gospel Banner*, May 3, 1962.
Review of *Women Who Made Bible History* by Harold J. Ockenga. *Gospel Banner*, June 14, 1962.
Review of *The Maze of Mormonism* by Walter R. Martin. *Gospel Banner*, June 28, 1962.
Review of *Let There Be Music* by Lorie C. Gooding. *Gospel Banner*, October 4, 1962.
Review of *Total Prayer for Total Living* by Thomas A. Carruth. *Gospel Banner*, October 11, 1962.
Review of *Buckwheat Summer* by Ruth Unrau. *Gospel Banner*, October 18, 1962.
Review of *My Favorite Picture Stories from the Bible* by Dena Dorfker. *Gospel Banner*, October 18, 1962.
Review of *Pages from God's Case-book* by John Hercus. *Gospel Banner*, October 18, 1962.
Review of *The Theology of Jehovah's Witnesses* by George D. McKinney, George D. *Gospel Banner*, November 1, 1962, 14.
Review of *When John Wesley was a Boy* by Helen B. Walters. *The Christian Leader*, November 13, 1962, 24.
Review of *Cuba's Miracle Lad* by Don W. Hillis. *The Christian Leader*, November 13, 1962, 24.
Review of *Buckwheat Summer* by Ruth Unrau. *The Christian Leader*, November 27, 1962, 21.
Review of *The Crying Heart* by Clara Bernice Miller. *The Christian Leader*, December 11, 1962, 21.

1963

Articles and Columns
"Living Apart for the Lord." *Christian Living*, March 1963, 22-24.
"The Place of Women in the Work of the Church." *The Canadian Mennonite*, March 1, 1963, 5.
"Accepting the Message of the Family Years." *The Christian Leader*, April 30, 1963, 3-5.
"Christ and My Life's Work." *Youth Worker*, July/December 1963, 56-63.

Women and the Church
Women and the Church, *The Christian Leader*, January 8, 1963, 21.
Women and the Church, *The Christian Leader*, January 22, 1963, 21.
Women and the Church, *The Christian Leader*, February 5, 1963, 29.
Women and the Church, *The Christian Leader*, February 19, 1963, 21.
Women and the Church, *The Christian Leader*, March 5, 1963, 21.
Women and the Church, *The Christian Leader*, March 19, 1963, 21.
Women and the Church, *The Christian Leader*, April 2, 1963, 29.
Women and the Church, *The Christian Leader*, April 16, 1963, 21.
Women and the Church, *The Christian Leader*, May 14, 1963, 21.
Women and the Church, *The Christian Leader*, May 28, 1963, 25.
Women and the Church, *The Christian Leader*, June 11, 1963, 21.
Women and the Church, *The Christian Leader*, June 25, 1963, 21.
Women and the Church, *The Christian Leader*, July 9, 1963, 21.
Women and the Church, *The Christian Leader*, July 23, 1963, 21.
Women and the Church, *The Christian Leader*, August 6, 1963, 21.
Women and the Church, *The Christian Leader*, August 20, 1963, 21.
Women and the Church, *The Christian Leader*, September 3, 1963, 21.
Women and the Church, *The Christian Leader*, September 17, 1963, 21.
Women and the Church, *The Christian Leader*, October 1, 1963, 25.
Women and the Church, *The Christian Leader*, October 15, 1963, 21.
Women and the Church, *The Christian Leader*, October 29, 1963, 25.
Women and the Church, *The Christian Leader*, November 12, 1963, 21.
Women and the Church, *The Christian Leader*, November 26, 1963, 21.
Women and the Church, *The Christian Leader*, December 10, 1963, 21.
Women and the Church, *The Christian Leader*, December 24, 1963, 21.

Book Reviews
Review of *Beyond the Middle Years* by Grace V. Watkins. *The Christian Leader*, January 8, 1963, 21.
Review of *Success in Money Matters* by Harold F. Linaman. *The Christian Leader*, February 5, 1963, 29.
Review of *If You Ask Me* by Mary Hope. *The Christian Leader*, June 11, 1963, 21.
Review of *Growing Stead* by Verna J. Joiner. *The Christian Leader*, June 25, 1963, 21.
Review of *Homemade Happiness* by Wayne Dehoney. *The Christian Leader*, July 9, 1963, 21.
Review of *Food-n-Fun Craft* by Eleanor L. Doan and Gladys McElory. *The Christian Leader*, July 23, 1963, 21.
Review of *Search to Belong* by Christmas Carol Kauffman. *The Christian Leader*, August 6, 1963, 21.

Review of *What Did Tommy Say* by Louise Price Bell. *The Christian Leader*, August 20, 1963, 21.
Review of *First Steps for Little Feet* by Charles Foster. *The Christian Leader*, August 20, 1963, 21.
Review of *Christian Family Living*. *The Christian Leader*, September 17, 1963, 21.
Review of *The Christian Family and Home* by Alexander C. DeJong. *The Christian Leader*, September 17, 1963, 21.
Review of *A Woman's World* by Clyde M. Narramore. *The Christian Leader*, October 15, 1963, 21.
Review of *Mama was a Missionary* by Charles Ludwig. *The Christian Leader*, October 29, 1963, 25.
Review of *But Not Forsaken* by Helen Good Brenneman. *The Christian Leader*, December 24, 1963, 21.

1964

Articles and Columns
"Learning a Thing from Grandmother." *Christian Living*, January 1964, 32-34.
"How Can We Discover and Develop Christian Writers." *The Christian Leader*, February 2, 1964, 6-7, 20-21.
"Congo in Crisis." *The Christian Leader*, March 3, 1964, 6-7.
"A Pig for a Pig." *Christian Living*, May 1964, 11-12.
"What Is a Christian Writer?" *The Christian Leader*, May 26, 1964, 16-17.
"Recruiting Christian Writers." *The Christian Leader*, June 9, 1964, 20-21.
"To Be a Widow." *Christian Living*, July 1964, 12-13.
"Let's Commemorate His Birth" (with Walter Wiebe). *Youth Worker*, July/December 1964, 54-64.
"Your Church and You" (with Walter Wiebe). *Youth Worker*, July/December 1964, 40-53.

Women and the Church
Women and the Church, *The Christian Leader*, January 7, 1964, 21.
Women and the Church, *The Christian Leader*, January 21, 1964, 21.
"You Can Be a Literature Evangelist." Women and the Church, *The Christian Leader*, February 18, 1964, 29.
"Read to Grow." Women and the Church, *The Christian Leader*, March 31, 1964, 29.
"A New Emphasis in Women's Work." Women and the Church, *The Christian Leader*, April 14, 1964, 21.
"Mothers Have a Redeemer God." Women and the Church, *The Christian Leader*, April 28, 1964, 21.

"A Deeper Concept of Missions Needed." Women and the Church, *The Christian Leader*, May 12, 1964, 21.
"Throw a Dishrag at the Devil." Women and the Church, *The Christian Leader*, May 26, 1964, 21.
"For Women Only." Women and the Church, *The Christian Leader*, June 9, 1964, 25.
"Not Substitute Living." Women and the Church, *The Christian Leader*, June 23, 1964, 21.
"The Right to Pray." Women and the Church, *The Christian Leader*, August 4, 1964, 21.
"When They Move." Women and the Church, *The Christian Leader*, August 18, 1964, 21.
"When You Sorrow." Women and the Church, *The Christian Leader*, September 15, 1964, 21.
"Mediocrity or Mission?" Women and the Church, *The Christian Leader*, September 29, 1964, 21.
"When Are We Old?" Women and the Church, *The Christian Leader*, October 13, 1964, 21.
"A Pattern for Peace." Women and the Church, *The Christian Leader*, October 27, 1964, 25.
"If You're a Mennonite." Women and the Church, *The Christian Leader*, November 10, 1964, 21.
"Perhaps Even Menno Simons." Women and the Church, *The Christian Leader*, November 24, 1964, 21.
"Waiting for Christmas." Women and the Church, *The Christian Leader*, December 8, 1964, 25.
"Love at the Bottom of the Stairs." Women and the Church, *The Christian Leader*, December 22, 1964, 21.

Book Reviews
Review of *Right Side Up* by Betty Carlson. *The Christian Leader*, January 7, 1964, 21.
Review of *A Guidebook for Teens* by Warren Wiersbe. *The Christian Leader*, January 21, 1964, 21.
Review of *Literature Evangelism* by George Verwer. *The Christian Leader*, February 18, 1964, 29.
Review of *Growing with Your Children* by Ray F. Koonce. *The Christian Leader*, March 3, 1964, 21.
Review of *C. T. Studd, Cricketer, Pioneer* by Norman J. Grubb. *The Christian Leader*, March 3, 1964, 13.
Review of *The Spirit of Holiness* by Everett Lewis Cattell. *The Christian Leader*, March 17, 1964, 21.

Review of *Points for Parents* by Martin P. Simon. *The Christian Leader*, March 31, 1964, 29.
Review of *Hidden Rainbow* by Christmas Carol Kauffman. *The Christian Leader*, April 14, 1964, 21.
Review of *For One Moment* by Christmas Carol Kauffman. *The Christian Leader*, April 14, 1964, 21.
Review of *The Pastor's Wife and the Church* by Dorothy Harrison Pentecost. *The Christian Leader*, April 28, 1964, 21.
Review of *Come to My Party* by Margaret Epp. *The Christian Leader*, May 26, 1964, 21.
Review of *Larry and Kathy* by Esther Eby Glass. *The Christian Leader*, June 8, 1964, 25.
Review of *That Wheel in Your Hands* by Lawrence P. Fitzgerald. *The Christian Leader*, August 4, 1964, 21.
Review of *Manual for GMSA Leaders* by Winifred Erb Paul. *The Christian Leader*, September 29, 1964, 21.
Review of *God's Will and Your Life* by T.R. Matson. *The Christian Leader*, October 13, 1964, 21.
Review of *They Met God* edited by J.C. Wenger. *The Christian Leader*, October 27, 1964, 25.
Review of *Prairie Pals* by Alice Deckert. *The Christian Leader*, December 8, 1964, 25.

1965

Articles and Columns
"Increasing the Family Fortune: A Study in Christian Family Worship." *Youth Worker*, January/June 1965, 46-55.
"Parents Provide the Pattern." *Christian Living*, March 1965, 24-26.
"Let's Return to Good Reading." *The Christian Leader*, March 2, 1965, 4-6.
"Are You a Reading Woman?" *Gospel Herald*, April 6, 1965, 293-294.
"Our Bible Campers." *Sunday School Banner*, July 18, 1965, 7-8.
"If You Would be a Comforter." *Christian Living*, October 1965, 27-28.
"Who Is a Missionary?" *Program Guide*. Southern District Mennonite Brethren Churches WMS, 1965-66, 25-37.

Women and the Church
"Wings for 1965." Women and the Church, *The Christian Leader*, January 5, 1965, 21.
"A Suggested Reading List for 1965." Women and the Church, *The Christian Leader*, January 19, 1965, 21.
"Are You a Youth Watcher?" Women and the Church, *The Christian Leader*, February 2, 1965, 25.

"How Prayer Built a Church." Women and the Church, *The Christian Leader*, February 16, 1965, 21.
"The Real Questions." Women and the Church, *The Christian Leader*, March 16, 1965, 21.
"Some Modern Anabaptists." Women and the Church, *The Christian Leader*, March 30, 1965, 21.
"A Problem Without a Name." Women and the Church, *The Christian Leader*, April 13, 1965, 25.
"A Ministry to Mothers." Women and the Church, *The Christian Leader*, April 27, 1965, 21.
"Literature Alone Can't Do It." Women and the Church, *The Christian Leader*, May 25, 1965, 21.
"A Useless Frill?" Women and the Church, *The Christian Leader*, June 8, 1965, 21.
"Have Car Will Travel." Women and the Church, *The Christian Leader*, June 22, 1965, 21.
"Safeguards for Your Child's Marriage." Women and the Church, *The Christian Leader*, July 6, 1965, 21.
"To Each Her Task." Women and the Church, *The Christian Leader*, July 20, 1965, 21.
"Woman to Woman." Women and the Church, *The Christian Leader*, August 3, 1965, 25.
"Ready for College?" Women and the Church, *The Christian Leader*, August 17, 1965, 21.
"We Can't Use Her—She's Working." Women and the Church, *The Christian Leader*, August 31, 1965, 21.
"The Traditional Place for Revival." Women and the Church, *The Christian Leader*, September 14, 1965, 21.
"Be It Ever So Humble." Women and the Church, *The Christian Leader*, September 28, 1965, 21.
"The Unforgettable Teacher." Women and the Church, *The Christian Leader*, October 12, 1965, 13.
"Service in an Era of Change." Women and the Church, *The Christian Leader*, October 26, 1965, 25.
"Another Book for Women." Women and the Church, *The Christian Leader*, November 9, 1965, 21.
"Thanksgiving—No Embarrassment." Women and the Church, *The Christian Leader*, November 23, 1965, 29.
"District WMS Conferences Held." Women and the Church, *The Christian Leader*, December 7, 1965, 25.
"Create Your Own Christmas Traditions." Women and the Church, *The Christian Leader*, December 21, 1965, 21.

Comprehensive Bibliography | 265

Book Reviews

Review of *Hellbent for Election* by P. Speshock. *The Christian Leader*, January 5, 1965, 21.

Review of *A Farthing in Her Hand* edited by Helen Alderfer. *The Christian Leader*, March 16, 1965, 21.

Review of *God Speaks to Women Today* by Eugenia Price. *The Christian Leader*, March 16, 1965, 21.

Review of *Tariri—My Story* as told to Ethiel Emily Wallis. *The Christian Leader*, September 17, 1965, 21.

Review of *God is for the Alcoholic* by Jerry G. Dunn. *The Christian Leader*, October 26, 1965, 25.

Review of *Sometimes I Feel Like a Blob* by Ethel Barrett. *The Christian Leader*, December 7, 1965, 25.

1966

Articles and Columns

"A Career at Church (The Challenge of Church Vocations)." *Youth Worker*, January/June 1966, 25-36.

"When a Family Moves South of the 49th." The Wayside Inn, *Mennonite Brethren Herald*, January 14, 1966, 17.

"Let's Think Right About Reading." *The Christian Leader*, February 15, 1966, 4-5, 9.

"Zwieback Hospitality—Obsolete?" The Wayside Inn, *Mennonite Brethren Herald*, February 25, 1966, 18.

"Parents Without Partners." *Christian Living*, March 1966, 8-10.

"Which Version?" The Wayside Inn, *Mennonite Brethren Herald*, April 8, 1966, 12.

"Women's Work in the Church." The Wayside Inn, *Mennonite Brethren Herald*, May 27, 1966, 16.

"Devotion or Commotion (Church Etiquette)." *Youth Worker*, July/December 1966, 14-17

"No Second-Class Citizens Here." The Wayside Inn, *Mennonite Brethren Herald*, July 22, 1966, 20.

"Thanksgiving—No Embarrassment." The Wayside Inn, *Mennonite Brethren Herald*, September 30, 1966, 17.

"Women—and 'Commission in Conflict.'" The Wayside Inn, *Mennonite Brethren Herald*, November 4, 1966, 17.

"The Red Catalog Dress." *Family Herald*, December 22, 1966, 22-23.

Women and the Church

"Our First Task is Enlargement." Women and the Church, *The Christian Leader*, January 4, 1966, 21.

"New Wineskins for Women's Work." Women and the Church, *The Christian Leader*, January 18, 1966, 21.
"Teaching to Choose." Women and the Church, *The Christian Leader*, February 1, 1966, 25.
"The Image is Wrong." Women and the Church, *The Christian Leader*, March 1, 1966, 21.
"Where Should We Fellowship?" Women and the Church, *The Christian Leader*, March 15, 1966, 21.
"My Comforters." Women and the Church, *The Christian Leader*, March 29, 1966, 21.
"That Blah Feeling." Women and the Church, *The Christian Leader*, April 12, 1966, 21.
"Needed: Better Mothers." Women and the Church, *The Christian Leader*, April 26, 1966, 25.
"Challenge or Chore?" Women and the Church, *The Christian Leader*, May 10, 1966, 21.
"A Plan and a Purpose." Women and the Church, *The Christian Leader*, May 24, 1966, 21.
"For Better Program Planning." Women and the Church, *The Christian Leader*, June 7, 1966, 21.
"Substitute, But Not a Cure." Women and the Church, *The Christian Leader*, July 5, 1966, 21.
"The Missionary Wife and Her Work." Women and the Church, *The Christian Leader*, July 19, 1966, 21.
"Missing: An Adequate Theology." Women and the Church, *The Christian Leader*, August 2, 1966, 21.
"An Overflowing Heart." Women and the Church, *The Christian Leader*, August 16, 1966, 21.
"No Back Door to Heaven." Women and the Church, *The Christian Leader*, August 30, 1966, 21.
"The Gift of Tears." Women and the Church, *The Christian Leader*, September 27, 1966, 21.
"Finding a New Pattern." Women and the Church, *The Christian Leader*, October 11, 1966, 25.
"Vietnam—Agony and Opportunity." Women and the Church, *The Christian Leader*, October 25, 1966, 21.
"A Timely Topic for Women." Women and the Church, *The Christian Leader*, November 22, 1966, 21.
"Why Were They There?" Women and the Church, *The Christian Leader*, December 20, 1966, 29.

Book Reviews

Review of *The Feminine Mystique* by Betty Friedan. *The Canadian Mennonite*, March 29, 1966. 52.

Review of *The Feminine Mystique* by Betty Friedan. *The Canadian Mennonite*, April 5, 1966, 10.

Review of *The Feminine Crisis in Christian Faith: The Bible's Challenge to Today's Woman* by Elizabeth Achtemeier. *The Canadian Mennonite*, November 1, 1966, 10.

Review of *No Graven Image* by Elisabeth Elliot. *WMSA Voice*, December 1966.

1967

Articles and Columns

"Mother, What Will It Be Like?" *Program Guide*. Southern District Mennonite Brethren Conference WMS, 1966-67.

"The Women's Class." The Wayside Inn, *Mennonite Brethren Herald*, January 6, 1967, 16.

"The Invitation." *Christian Living*, January 1967, 6-8.

"Books for the Marketplace." *The Christian Leader*, February 14, 1967, 3-5.

"March 25-27." *Worship Together*, edited by A.J. Klassen, 22-23. Board of Christian Education, Mennonite Brethren Church, Hillsboro, March-April, 1967.

"Christian Journalism for Today." *The Journal of Church and Society* 3, no.1 (Spring 1967): 23-31.

"Mennonites in an Artist's Eye." *The Mennonite*, September 5, 1967, 528-530.

"Rudy Wiebe and 'Man as He Is.'" *Christian Living*, October, 1967, 30-32.

"The Tyranny of Sex." The Wayside Inn, *Mennonite Brethren Herald*, October 20, 1967, 17.

"The Church that Ate for Profit." *Christian Living*, November 1967, 26-28.

"You'll Never Know Until You Try!" *Mennonite Brethren Herald*, November 10, 1967, 4-5.

"The Red Catalog Dress." *Christian Living*, December 1967, 12-14.

Women and the Church

"A Threefold Prayer." Women and the Church, *The Christian Leader*, January 3, 1967, 29.

"A Small or Large Organization?" Women and the Church, *The Christian Leader*, January 17, 1967, 21.

"The Creative Approach." Women and the Church, *The Christian Leader*, January 31, 1967, 21.

"Making the Adult Department Adult." Women and the Church, *The Christian Leader*, March 14, 1967, 21.

Viewpoint
"Courting Women for Church Work." Viewpoint, *The Christian Leader*, March 28, 1967, 21.
"The Silent Generation." Viewpoint, *The Christian Leader*, April 11, 1967, 21.
"A Voice for the Layman." Viewpoint, *The Christian Leader*, April 25, 1967, 21.
"Change Without Decay." Viewpoint, *The Christian Leader*, May 9, 1967, 21.
"A Game Christians Should Play." Viewpoint, *The Christian Leader*, May 23, 1967, 21.
"We Have Lost Our Heroes." Viewpoint, *The Christian Leader*, June 6, 1967, 21.
"Canada—Land of Hope." Viewpoint, *The Christian Leader*, June 20, 1967, 21.
"What Kind of Book?" Viewpoint, *The Christian Leader*, July 4, 1967, 21.
"Where We Don't Expect Change." Viewpoint, *The Christian Leader*, July 18, 1967, 21.
"Why We Can't Wait." Viewpoint, *The Christian Leader*, August 15, 1967, 21.
"Potato Thinking or Bridgebuilding." Viewpoint, *The Christian Leader*, August 29, 1967, 21.
"Can We Update Sacrifice?" Viewpoint, *The Christian Leader*, September 12, 1967, 21.
"God is for Real." Viewpoint, *The Christian Leader*, September 26, 1967, 21.
"A Heady Subject." Viewpoint, *The Christian Leader*, October 10, 1967, 21.
"Blue Ribbon Winners." Viewpoint, *The Christian Leader*, October 24, 1967, 21.
"Continuing Education for Women." Viewpoint, *The Christian Leader*, November 7, 1967, 29.
"A Second Look at Charlie Brown." Viewpoint, *The Christian Leader*, November 21, 1967, 21.
"A Glimpse of a New Wineskin." Viewpoint, *The Christian Leader*, December 3, 1967, 21.
"More Real Than Real." Viewpoint, *The Christian Leader*, December 19, 1967, 21.

1968

Articles and Columns
"Experiment in Christian Education." *Mennonite Brethren Herald*, March 8, 1968, 4-6.
"Who Am I a Neighbor To?" *Christian Living*, May 1968, 22-23.
"If You Would be a Comforter." *Mennonite Brethren Herald*, May 17, 1968, 6-7.
"A Parent Without a Partner." *Mennonite Brethren Herald*, October 4, 1968, 4-6, 26-27.
"Relationships Must Be Truthful." *The Canadian Mennonite*, October 8, 1968, 4.

Viewpoint

"Let's Begin at the Beginning." Viewpoint, *The Christian Leader*, January 2, 1968, 25.

"1,000 Hours of Television." Viewpoint, *The Christian Leader*, January 16, 1968, 21.

"The Battle Against Words." Viewpoint, *The Christian Leader*, January 30, 1968, 21.

"What's in Mennonite Humor?" Viewpoint, *The Christian Leader*, February 13, 1968, 25.

"'There is No Place to Go.'" Viewpoint, *The Christian Leader*, February 27, 1968, 29.

"Discuss or Perish." Viewpoint, *The Christian Leader*, March 12, 1968, 21.

"Being Born Again." Viewpoint, *The Christian Leader*, March 26, 1968, 21.

"The Chance of a Lifetime." Viewpoint, *The Christian Leader*, April 9, 1968, 21.

"Let's Take a Look at Ourselves." Viewpoint, *The Christian Leader*, April 23, 1968, 21.

"Of Retreats and Women." Viewpoint, *The Christian Leader*, May 7, 1968, 21.

"Too Late for the Ferry." Viewpoint, *The Christian Leader*, May 21, 1968, 21.

"The Fear of Old Age." Viewpoint, *The Christian Leader*, June 4, 1968, 21.

"A Summer Bookshelf." Viewpoint, *The Christian Leader*, June 18, 1968, 21.

"The Day I was a Number." Viewpoint, *The Christian Leader*, July 2, 1968, 21.

"The Rich and the Poor." Viewpoint, *The Christian Leader*, July 16, 1968, 21.

"The Pace is Too Slow." Viewpoint, *The Christian Leader*, July 30, 1968, 21.

"A Backlash to the Social Gospel." Viewpoint, *The Christian Leader*, August 13, 1968, 21.

"A Hard Pill to Swallow." Viewpoint, *The Christian Leader*, August 27, 1968, 21.

"Let's Involve Women." Viewpoint, *The Christian Leader*, September 10, 1968, 21.

"Lessons from the Past." Viewpoint, *The Christian Leader*, September 24, 1968, 21.

"Why Not Try a Second Career?" Viewpoint, *The Christian Leader*, October 8, 1968, 21.

"The Problem is Not New." Viewpoint, *The Christian Leader*, October 22, 1968, 21.

"The Tightrope Walker." Viewpoint, *The Christian Leader*, November 5, 1968, 21.

"Thanks for Everything." Viewpoint, *The Christian Leader*, November 19, 1968, 21.

"A Prayer We Don't Have to Pray." Viewpoint, *The Christian Leader*, December 3, 1968, 21.

"Perfume or Potatoes." Viewpoint, *The Christian Leader*, December 17, 1968, 21.

1969

Articles and Columns

"Unfinished Business." *Christian Living*, February 1969, 16-17, 38.
"A Student's Diary of Renewal." *The Canadian Mennonite*, February 18, 1969, 4.
"A Call to Decency." *Gospel Herald*, April 22, 1969, 369-370.
"The Fears of Old Age." *Railroad Evangelist*, March 1969, 5.
"The Shopping Trip." *Christian Living*, June 1969, 12-14.
"In Search of God." *The Canadian Mennonite*, September 19, 1969, 7.
"Bargain Basement Bibles." *The Canadian Mennonite*, October 17, 1969, 5.
"The Right Currency." *The Canadian Mennonite*, October 24, 1969, 4
"Just a Swallow Away." *The Canadian Mennonite*, November 7, 1969, 4.
"God Alive and Working in Hillsboro." *The Canadian Mennonite*, November 28, 1969, 5.
"A Baby or a Man?" *The Canadian* Mennonite, December 12, 1969, 6.
"Unfinished Business." The Wayside Inn, *Mennonite Brethren Herald*, December 26, 1969, 18-19.

Viewpoint

"What's in a Name?" Viewpoint, *The Christian Leader*, January 14, 1969, 21.
"A Vision of Glory" Viewpoint, *The Christian Leader*, January 28, 1969, 21.
"The Church at Home in a House." Viewpoint, *The Christian Leader*, February 11, 1969, 21.
"Thoughts About a Love Affair." Viewpoint, *The Christian Leader*, February 25, 1969, 19.
"About Basketball and Church Involvement." Viewpoint, *The Christian Leader*, March 11, 1969, 19.
"Modern Blindness." Viewpoint, *The Christian Leader*, March 25, 1969, 19.
"Toward Brotherhood." Viewpoint, *The Christian Leader*, April 8, 1969, 19.
"Doing One's Thing." Viewpoint, *The Christian Leader*, April 22, 1969, 19.
"We Need Our Young People." Viewpoint, *The Christian Leader*, May 6, 1969, 19.
"Space-age Parenthood." Viewpoint, *The Christian Leader*, May 20, 1969, 19.
"Women and the Church." Viewpoint, *The Christian Leader*, June 3, 1969, 23.
"At What Age Baptism?" Viewpoint, *The Christian Leader*, June 17, 1969, 19.
"The Revolution We Can Do Without." Viewpoint, *The Christian Leader*, July 1, 1969, 19.
"In Search of God." Viewpoint, *The Christian Leader*, July 15, 1969, 19.
"Mrs. Preacher." Viewpoint, *The Christian Leader*, July 29, 1969, 19.
"To Receive or to Use." Viewpoint, *The Christian Leader*, August 12, 1969, 19.
"The Prophets of Doom." Viewpoint, *The Christian Leader*, August 26, 1969, 19.
"Colored or Regular?" Viewpoint, *The Christian Leader*, September 9, 1969, 19.

"Communication by the Young." Viewpoint, *The Christian Leader*, September 23, 1969, 19.
"Bargain Basement Bibles." Viewpoint, *The Christian Leader*, October 7, 1969, 23.
"The Right Currency." Viewpoint, *The Christian Leader*, October 21, 1969, 19.
"Just a Swallow Away." Viewpoint, *The Christian Leader*, November 4, 1969, 23.
"God at Work in Hillsboro." Viewpoint, *The Christian Leader*, November 18, 1969, 19.
"A Baby or a Man?" Viewpoint, *The Christian Leader*, December 2, 1969, 19.
"Shoulder Tapping." Viewpoint, *The Christian Leader*, December 16, 1969, 19.
"So Easy to Forget." Viewpoint, *The Christian Leader*, December 30, 1969, 23.

Book Reviews
Review of *Who Shall Ascend* by Elisabeth Elliot. *The Canadian Mennonite*, May 16, 1969, 8.

Presentations
"Available to God." Tenth Annual Missionary Rally of Ontario MB Churches, St. Catharines, Ontario, April 22, 1969.

1970

Articles and Columns
"Of Young Men and the Cloth." *The Canadian Mennonite*, January 9, 1970, 6.
"So Easy to Forget." *The Canadian Mennonite*, January 16, 1970, 6.
"Prayer: Source of Anguish, Comfort." *The Canadian Mennonite*, January 23, 1970, 6, 10.
"Yonder Mennonite: Who Is He? A Portrait of the Church of God in Christ Mennonite (Holdeman)." *Christian Living*, February 1970, 2-9.
"Male Hair: The L-o-n-g and the Short of It." *The Canadian Mennonite*, February 6, 1970, 7.
"On the Total Integration of Women." *The Canadian Mennonite*, February 13, 1970, 6, 8.
"A New Definition of Fellowship: Modern Times have Just Begun." *The Canadian Mennonite*, February 27, 1970, 7, 11.
"Can Our Women's Organizations Be Revitalized?" *Mennonite Brethren Herald*, March 6, 1970, 21-23.
"Call to Worship: Great Reform Begins with the Inner Man." *The Canadian Mennonite*, March 13, 1970, 6.
"The Ministry: Cleaning Up the Image." *The Canadian Mennonite*, March 27, 1970, 7.
"The Witness of Maturity." *Christian Living*, April 1970, 14-17.

"Word and Reality: Never to be Confused." *The Canadian Mennonite*, April 10, 1970, 6.
"Memo from a Widow." *Mennonite Brethren Herald*, April 17, 1970, 5-7.
"Why KFW Writes This Column." *The Canadian Mennonite*, May 8, 1970, 6.
"Until We Have Voices." *The Canadian Mennonite*, May 29, 1970, 7.
"Elmer Gantry: The Revolt Against the Religion of the Village." *The Journal of Church and Society* 6, no.1 (Spring 1970): 54-64.
"Can We Make the Play Come True?" *The Canadian Mennonite*, June 5, 1970, 7.
"Fathers are Not Obsolete." *The Canadian Mennonite*, June 12, 1970, 7.
"Never Too Late for College." *Mennonite Brethren Herald*, June 12, 1970, 2-4.
"The Nebulous Authority of 'They.'" *The Canadian Mennonite*, June 19, 1970, 7.
"Can't Escape Politics." *The Canadian Mennonite*, July 3, 1970, 7.
"Sermons: The Sunday Morning Event." *The Canadian Mennonite*, July 17, 1970, 7.
"Education for Violence." *The Canadian Mennonite*, July 31, 1970, 7.
"Until We Have Voices." *Gospel Herald*, August 18, 1970, 682.
"Church Buildings: Centers of Salvation or Exclusive Sanctuaries?" *The Canadian Mennonite*, August 21, 1970, 7.
"We Can't Escape Politics." *Gospel Herald*, September 1, 1970, 723.
"Have You Grown Up?" *Mennonite Brethren Herald*, September 4, 1970, 2-5.
"Preparing Parents for College." *The Canadian Mennonite*, September 4, 1970, 7.
"When is the Church not a Cathedral?" *Gospel Herald*, September 15, 1970, 766.
"Status Quo or Ready to Go." *The Canadian Mennonite*, September 18, 1970, 6-7.
"Preparing Parents for College." *Gospel Herald*, October 6, 1970, 838.
"The Event on Sunday Morning." *Gospel Herald*, October 3, 1970, 862.
"We've Lost the Uneasy Feeling." *The Canadian Mennonite*, October 2, 1970, 6.
"Living by the Book." *The Canadian Mennonite*, October 16, 1970, 6.
"The Return of Christian Endeavor." *The Canadian Mennonite*, October 30, 1970, 6.
"Education for Violence." *Gospel Herald*, November 17, 1970, 973.
"Liberation for Men and Women." *The Canadian Mennonite*, November 20, 1970, 7.
"We've Lost the Uneasy Feeling." *Gospel Herald*, November 24, 1970, 992.
"Faith and Mutual Burden-Bearing." *The Canadian Mennonite*, November 27, 1970, 7.
"Widowhood Is Coming." *Christian Living*, December 1970, 12-15.
"Life is for Living: 'Christ Living in Me...Not in a Worm.'" *The Canadian Mennonite*, December 4, 1970, 6.
"Liberation—For Men and Women." *Gospel Herald*, December 8, 1970, 1011.
"To Conference to Conference: We Can't Live Without Them; We Can't Live With Them." *The Canadian Mennonite*, December 18, 1970, 6.

Viewpoint

"Is Prayer Valid for the Seventies?" Viewpoint, *The Christian Leader*, January 13, 1970, 19.

"The Long and Short of It." Viewpoint, *The Christian Leader*, January 27, 1970, 19.

"I Am Confused." Viewpoint, *The Christian Leader*, February 10, 1970, 19.

"Towards a New Definition of Fellowship." Viewpoint, *The Christian Leader*, February 24, 1970, 19.

"A Call to Worship." Viewpoint, *The Christian Leader*, March 10, 1970, 19.

"The Ministry: Cleaning Up the Image." Viewpoint, *The Christian Leader*, March 24, 1970, 19.

"The Thirteenth Floor Is Still There." Viewpoint, *The Christian Leader*, April 7, 1970, 19.

"Why I Write This Column." Viewpoint, *The Christian Leader*, April 21, 1970, 23.

"Can We Make the Play Come True?" Viewpoint, *The Christian Leader*, May 5, 1970, 19.

"Learning from the Dandelions." Viewpoint, *The Christian Leader*, May 19, 1970, 19.

"Until We Have Voices." Viewpoint, *The Christian Leader*, June 2, 1970, 19.

"Fathers are Not Obsolete." Viewpoint, *The Christian Leader*, June 16, 1970, 19.

"We Can't Escape Politics." Viewpoint, *The Christian Leader*, June 30, 1970, 19.

"The Event on Sunday Morning." Viewpoint, *The Christian Leader*, July 14, 1970, 19.

"Education for Violence." Viewpoint, *The Christian Leader*, July 28, 1970, 19.

"When Is a Church Not a Cathedral?" Viewpoint, *The Christian Leader*, August 11, 1970, 19.

"Preparing Parents for College." Viewpoint, *The Christian Leader*, August 25, 1970, 19.

"Status Quo or Ready to Go." Viewpoint, *The Christian Leader*, September 8, 1970, 19.

"We've Lost the Uneasy Feeling." Viewpoint, *The Christian Leader*, September 22, 1970, 19.

"Living by the Book." Viewpoint, *The Christian Leader*, October 6, 1970, 19.

"The Return of Christian Endeavor." Viewpoint, *The Christian Leader*, October 20, 1970, 19.

"Liberation—For Men and Women." Viewpoint, *The Christian Leader*, November 3, 1970, 19.

"Back to Puritan Thinking." Viewpoint, *The Christian Leader*, November 17, 1970, 19.

"Live is for Living." Viewpoint, *The Christian Leader*, December 1, 1970, 19.

"To Conference, To Conference..." Viewpoint, *The Christian Leader*, December 15, 1970, 19.
"Let's Forget About Being Nice." Viewpoint, *The Christian Leader*, December 29, 1970, 23.

1971

Articles and Columns
"Let's Forget About Being 'Nice' and See the People, See the Wonderful People." *The Canadian Mennonite*, January 1, 1971, 8.
"Common Folk Need Theology." *The Canadian Mennonite*, January 8, 1971, 6.
"Life is for Living." *Gospel Herald*, January 15, 1971, 14.
"Hoarding is the Game." *The Canadian Mennonite*, January 29, 1971, 6.
"The Luxury of Isolation." *The Canadian Mennonite*, February 5, 1971, 4.
"Where We're at...In Our Attitude Toward Women." *The Canadian Mennonite*, February 19, 1971, 9, 29.
"Widowhood Without Worry." *The Messenger*, March 1, 1971, 10-12.
"Needed—Strong Beliefs." *Gospel Herald*, April 20, 1971, 360.
"The Bread of Daily Life." *Gospel Herald*, June 1, 1971, 495.
"Fathers are Not Obsolete." *Gospel Herald*, June 15, 1971, 544.
"The Name of the Game." *Gospel Herald*, June 22, 1971, 560.
"The Luxury of Isolation." *Gospel Herald*, August 24, 1971, 696.
"The Swinging Christians." *Gospel Herald*, September 7, 1971, 737.
"The Case Against Obscenity." *Gospel Herald*, September 28, 1971, 804.
"Cheap at any Price." *Gospel Herald*, October 12, 1971, 850.
"Magic is not for Christians." *Gospel Herald*, October 19, 1971, 869.
"Women Alone in a Couples World." *Canadian Mennonite Reporter*, November 1, 1971, 5.
"The Battle of the Symbol." *Gospel Herald*, November 2, 1971, 910-911.
"Christmas Memories." *Gospel Herald*, December 21, 1971, 1051.
"A Call to Worship." *Wesleyan Advocate*, December 27, 1971, 5-6.

Viewpoint
"Theology for the Laity." Viewpoint, *The Christian Leader*, January 12, 1971, 19.
"The Name of the Game." Viewpoint, *The Christian Leader*, January 26, 1971, 19.
"The Luxury of Isolation." Viewpoint, *The Christian Leader*, February 9, 1971, 19.
"Can the Earth be Saved." Viewpoint, *The Christian Leader*, February 23, 1971, 23.
"The Battle of the Symbol." Viewpoint, *The Christian Leader*, March 9, 1971, 19.

"Work, Worship and Leisure." Viewpoint, *The Christian Leader*, March 23, 1971, 19.
"The Mass or the Individual?" Viewpoint, *The Christian Leader*, April 6, 1971, 19.
"They're Turning the World Upside Down." Viewpoint, *The Christian Leader*, April 20, 1971, 19.
"The Bread of Daily Life." Viewpoint, *The Christian Leader*, May 4, 1971, 19.
"Fish for My People." Viewpoint, *The Christian Leader*, May 18, 1971, 19.
"The Swinging Christians." Viewpoint, *The Christian Leader*, June 1, 1971, 19.
"Not for the Sake of the Record." Viewpoint, *The Christian Leader*, June 29, 1971, 19.
"We Need Our Young People." Viewpoint, *The Christian Leader*, July 13, 1971, 19.
"Cheap at Any Price." Viewpoint, *The Christian Leader*, July 27, 1971, 19.
"Magic Is Not for Christians." Viewpoint, *The Christian Leader*, August 10, 1971, 27.
"Flies, Worms, and Butterflies." Viewpoint, *The Christian Leader*, August 24, 1971, 27.
"The Case Against Obscenity." Viewpoint, *The Christian Leader*, September 7, 1971, 19.
"The Humble Approach." Viewpoint, *The Christian Leader*, September 21, 1971, 19.
"In Search of Candor." Viewpoint, *The Christian Leader*, October 5, 1971, 23.
"Why Not Write?" Viewpoint, *The Christian Leader*, October 19, 1971, 19.
"Women Alone In a Couples World." Viewpoint, *The Christian Leader*, November 2, 1971, 19.
"Use Your Common Sense?" Viewpoint, *The Christian Leader*, November 16, 1971, 23.
"What I Don't Want for Christmas." Viewpoint, *The Christian Leader*, November 30, 1971, 27.
"The Christmas of Yesterday." Viewpoint, *The Christian Leader*, December 14, 1971, 23.
"The Church's New Clothes." Viewpoint, *The Christian Leader*, December 28, 1971, 23.

1972

Articles and Columns
"Women Alone in a Couple's World." *Gospel Herald*, January 4, 1972, 11.
"Can the Earth be Saved?" *Gospel Herald*, January 25, 1972, 79.
"The Church's New Clothes." *Gospel Herald*, February 15, 1972, 150.
"Living by the Book." *Gospel Herald*, March 17, 1972, 218.

"Let Us Worship." *Gospel Herald*, April 25, 1972, 380.
"Leave Her Alone." *Gospel Herald*, May 9, 1972, 421.
"Discovering a Meaningful Life." *Rejoice!* June/July/August, 1972, 24-27.
"Finding God's Guidance." *Rejoice!* June/July/August, 1972, 28-31.
"Praising the Lord." *Rejoice!* June/July/August, 1972, 32-35.
"Confession and Forgiveness." *Rejoice!* June/July/August, 1972, 36-39.
"Deepening Our Relationship with God." *Rejoice!* June/July/August, 1972, 40-43.
"It's All in the Family." *Christian Living*, July 1972, 6-8, 31,
"Ken Walks Again." *Sharing*, July 1972, 2-3, 9-10.
"Women's Freedom, the Church's Necessity." *Direction* 1, no.3 (July 1972): 82-84.
"All in the Family." *The Christian Leader*, July 25, 1972, 6-7.
"Faith versus Common Sense." *Gospel Herald*, August 22, 1972, 656.
"All in the Family." *Mennonite Brethren Herald*, August 24, 1972, 6-7.
"Work, Worship, and Leisure." *Gospel Herald*, August 29, 1972, 676.
"Can A Widow Survive in Today's Church?" *Eternity*, September 1972, 20-21.
"Women Alone in a Couples' World." *Vital Christianity*, October 15, 1972, 9-11.
"Sharing the Suffering." *Gospel Herald*, October 24, 1972, 864.
"When God Does Not Heal." *Christian Living*, November 1972, 20-23.
"Evangelism of the Masses." *Gospel Herald*, November 7, 1972, 907-908.
"I Believe in Persons." *Christian Living*, December 1972, 20-23.
"What I Don't Want for Christmas." *Gospel Herald*, December 5, 1972, 986.
"When God Does Not Heal." *The Christian Leader*, December 12, 1972, 6-7.

Viewpoint

"Clear Only If Known." Viewpoint, *The Christian Leader*, January 11, 1972, 19.
"The Machine in Your Life." Viewpoint, *The Christian Leader*, January 25, 1972, 19.
"Too Many Babies." Viewpoint, *The Christian Leader*, February 8, 1972, 19.
"Bridging the Credibility Gap." Viewpoint, *The Christian Leader*, February 22, 1972, 19.
"Let Us Worship." Viewpoint, *The Christian Leader*, March 7, 1972, 19.
"Leave Her Alone." Viewpoint, *The Christian Leader*, March 21, 1972, 19.
"The List on the Bulletin Board." Viewpoint, *The Christian Leader*, April 4, 1972, 19.
"The Paper Mountain." Viewpoint, *The Christian Leader*, April 18, 1972, 19.
"Jobs Available Anytime." Viewpoint, *The Christian Leader*, May 2, 1972, 23.
"Sharing the Suffering." Viewpoint, *The Christian Leader*, May 16, 1972, 19.
"Black Like Me." Viewpoint, *The Christian Leader*, May 30, 1972, 19.
"The Language Event." Viewpoint, *The Christian Leader*, June 13, 1972, 19.
"The Conflict of Peace." Viewpoint, *The Christian Leader*, June 27, 1972, 19.

"The Opposition of the Scared." Viewpoint, *The Christian Leader*, July 11, 1972, 19.
"The Birthpangs of Love." Viewpoint, *The Christian Leader*, July 25, 1972, 23.
"Losing God Through Nature." Viewpoint, *The Christian Leader*, August 8, 1972, 19.
"The Search for Greatness." Viewpoint, *The Christian Leader*, August 22, 1972, 19.
"Looking for the Battle." Viewpoint, *The Christian Leader*, September 5, 1972, 19.
"Evangelism of the Masses." Viewpoint, *The Christian Leader*, September 19, 1972, 19.
"*Deus ex Machina*" Viewpoint, *The Christian Leader*, October 3, 1972, 19.
"What Shall We Do About the Devil." Viewpoint, *The Christian Leader*, October 17, 1972, 19.
"The Invisible Mennonite." Viewpoint, *The Christian Leader*, October 31, 1972, 19.
"Members of One Another." Viewpoint, *The Christian Leader*, November 14, 1972, 19.
"The Creative Approach." Viewpoint, *The Christian Leader*, November 28, 1972, 19.
"Needed: A Capacity for Outrage." Viewpoint, *The Christian Leader*, December 26, 1972, 23.

1973

Articles and Columns
"What Shall We Do About the Devil?." *Gospel Herald*, January 23, 1973, 76.
"Needed: A Capacity for Outrage." *Gospel Herald*, February 6, 1973, 115.
"Books: A Path Through the Woods." *The Christian Leader*, February 20, 1973, 4-5.
"When God Does Not Heal." *Evangelical Visitor*, February 25, 1973.
"Sorting the Evangelical Mennonites." *Christian Living*, March 1973, 8-14.
"The Invisible Mennonite." *Gospel Herald*, March 20, 1973, 255.
"Morals versus Lifestyle." *Gospel Herald*, March 27, 1973, 275.
"When God Does Not Heal." *Mennonite Brethren Herald*, April 20, 1973, 22-23.
"The Woman Question." The Wayside Inn, *Mennonite Brethren Herald*, May 4, 1973,
"The Other Side." *Gospel Herald*, August 7, 1973, 604.
"A Giant Leap for Mankind." Family in the Seventies, *Mennonite Brethren Herald*, October 5, 1973, 27.
"The Meeting Season." *Gospel Herald*, November 13, 1973, 866.
"Colour Me a Person." *Mennonite Brethren Herald*, December 28, 1973, 2-5, 7.

Viewpoint

"One Out of Twelve." Viewpoint, *The Christian Leader*, January 9, 1973, 19.
"A New Course of Study." Viewpoint, *The Christian Leader*, January 23, 1973, 19.
"The Twilight Zone." Viewpoint, *The Christian Leader*, February 6, 1973, 19.
"Morals Versus Life-style." Viewpoint, *The Christian Leader*, March 6, 1973, 19.
"Greasing the Carousel." Viewpoint, *The Christian Leader*, March 20, 1973, 19.
"The Woman Question." Viewpoint, *The Christian Leader*, April 3, 1973, 19.
"Toward Christian Community." Viewpoint, *The Christian Leader*, April 17, 1973, 19.
"Families in Trouble." Viewpoint, *The Christian Leader*, May 1, 1973, 19.
"In Search of a Heritage." Viewpoint, *The Christian Leader*, May 15, 1973, 19.
"The Sharing Game." Viewpoint, *The Christian Leader*, May 29, 1973, 19.
"Pushing God Through a Mailing Tube." Viewpoint, *The Christian Leader*, June 12, 1973, 19.
"A Giant Leap for Mankind." Viewpoint, *The Christian Leader*, June 26, 1973, 19.
"The Other Side." Viewpoint, *The Christian Leader*, July 10, 1973, 19.
"The Great Reversal." Viewpoint, *The Christian Leader*, July 24, 1973, 19.
"Taboo Religion." Viewpoint, *The Christian Leader*, August 7, 1973, 19.
"The Meeting Season." Viewpoint, *The Christian Leader*, August 21, 1973, 19.
"Changing the Labels." Viewpoint, *The Christian Leader*, September 4, 1973, 19.
"The Sexual Wilderness." Viewpoint, *The Christian Leader*, September 18, 1973, 19.
"Night and Day." Viewpoint, *The Christian Leader*, October 2, 1973, 19.
"Under the Sycamore Tree." Viewpoint, *The Christian Leader*, October 16, 1973, 19.
"Old Man, Old Woman." Viewpoint, *The Christian Leader*, October 30, 1973, 23.
"Let the Angel Out." Viewpoint, *The Christian Leader*, November 13, 1973, 19.
"At the Convention." Viewpoint, *The Christian Leader*, November 27, 1973, 19.
"Thoughts for Advent." Viewpoint, *The Christian Leader*, December 11, 1973, 27.
"Peace on Earth." Viewpoint, *The Christian Leader*, December 25, 1973, 19.

1974

Books

Have Cart, Will Travel. Hillsboro: North American Conference of Mennonite Brethren Churches; Board of Christian Literature, 1974.
Rooted Deep: Centennial Souvenir Booklet for Kansas Mennonite Churches. Co-edited with Maynard Shelly. Hillsboro: Tri-College Centennial Committee, 1974.

A Study Guide to The Freedom of Forgiveness by David Augsburger. Chicago: Moody, 1974.

Sections in Books
"Dedication." In *Manitoba Mennonite Memories, 1874-1974*. x-xii. Winnipeg: Mennonite Centennial Committee, 1974.

Articles and Columns
"Memo From a Widow." *Church Advocate*, 1974, 5-6, 8.
"Let the Angel Out." *Gospel Herald*, January 1, 1974, 10.
"Come Higher, Friends." *Gospel Herald*, February 12, 1974, 134.
"Let's Share." *Christian Reader*, February/March 1974.
"In the Name of Christ." *Gospel Herald*, April 9, 1974, 299.
"Can A Widow Survive in Today's Church?" *Power For Living*, May 19, 1974, 4-7.
"The Art of Shelving." *Gospel Herald*, June 4, 1974, 469.
"Can A Widow Survive in Today's Church?" *Today*, June 9, 1974, 1-4.
"Faith and Art: A Compatible Team." *Mennonite Brethren Herald*, June 28, 1974, 2-4, 30.
"God's Redeeming Grace." *Rejoice!* June/July/August 1974, 24-27.
"God's Eternal Purposes." *Rejoice!* June/July/August 1974, 28-31.
"Renewed in Mind and Spirit." *Rejoice!* June/July/August 1974, 32-35.
"Partnership in the Gospel." *Rejoice!* June/July/August 1974, 36-39.
"Why Mennonites Can't Laugh at Themselves." *Festival Quarterly*, Summer 1974, 5, 22.
"The 1974 Centennial: A Moment of Grace for Mennonite Brethren." *Direction* 3, no.2 (July 1974): 201-206.
"The Invisible Poor." *Gospel Herald*, July 2, 1974, 535.
"While Making Gravy." *Gospel Herald*, September 10, 1974, 686.
"Thanks, You Helped Me." *Mennonite Brethren Herald*, October 4, 1974, 25-27
"The P.R. Mentality." *Gospel Herald*, October 8, 1974, 761-762.
"Remembering the Forgotten: Who is the Greatest?" *Mennonite Reporter*, November 25, 1974, 7.
"Who Will Help Me Raise My Children?" *Christian Living*, December 1974, 30-33.
"The Fake Factor." *Gospel Herald*, December 24, 1974, 968.
"Living the Creative Way." *Mennonite Brethren Herald*, December 27, 1974, 2-4.
"When God Does Not Heal." *Standard*, December 29, 1974, 4-5.

Viewpoint
"Body-life—or a Cat." Viewpoint, *The Christian Leader*, January 8, 1974, 19.
"Come Higher Friends." Viewpoint, *The Christian Leader*, January 22, 1974, 19.

"In the Name of Christ." Viewpoint, *The Christian Leader*, February 5, 1974, 19.
"The Book You Never Read." Viewpoint, *The Christian Leader*, February 19, 1974, 19.
"The Rhetoric of Nicknames." Viewpoint, *The Christian Leader*, March 5, 1974, 19.
"That's What We're All About." Viewpoint, *The Christian Leader*, March 19, 1974, 19.
"A Man and a Cross." Viewpoint, *The Christian Leader*, April 2, 1974, 19.
"A Place to Stand." Viewpoint, *The Christian Leader*, April 16, 1974, 19.
"Going to the Movies." Viewpoint, *The Christian Leader*, April 30, 1974, 19.
"The Art of Shelving…" Viewpoint, *The Christian Leader*, May 14, 1974, 23.
"Words for the Graduate." Viewpoint, *The Christian Leader*, May 28, 1974, 19.
"The Invisible Poor." Viewpoint, *The Christian Leader*, June 11, 1974, 19.
"A Summertime Quiz." Viewpoint, *The Christian Leader*, July 9, 1974, 23.
"While Making Gravy." Viewpoint, *The Christian Leader*, July 23, 1974, 19.
"Six Marks on the Wall." Viewpoint, *The Christian Leader*, August 6, 1974, 19.
"Strength for September." Viewpoint, *The Christian Leader*, August 20, 1974, 23.
"The P.R. Mentality." Viewpoint, *The Christian Leader*, September 3, 1974, 19.
"Escaping Mass Blackmail." Viewpoint, *The Christian Leader*, September 17, 1974, 19.
"Does Someone Have to Pay?" Viewpoint, *The Christian Leader*, October 1, 1974, 19.
"The Fake Factor." Viewpoint, *The Christian Leader*, October 15, 1974, 27.
"The Hiding Place." Viewpoint, *The Christian Leader*, October 29, 1974, 19.
"Hunger for Hunger." Viewpoint, *The Christian Leader*, November 12, 1974, 19.
"Building Whose Kingdom?" Viewpoint, *The Christian Leader*, November 26, 1974, 19.
"Strengthening the Root." Viewpoint, *The Christian Leader*, December 10, 1974, 19.
"When Hunger Becomes Real." Viewpoint, *The Christian Leader*, December 24, 1974, 27.

Book Reviews
"The Temptations of Big Bear: A Review of Rudy Wiebe's New Novel." *The Mennonite*, March 5, 1974, 154-155.
Review of *The Great Reversal: Evangelism Versus Social Gospel* by David O. Moberg, *Direction* 3, no.1 (April 1974): 185-186.

Presentations
"Feature Writing." General Conference Mennonite Church Christian Writers Workshop,
North Newton, Kansas, June 30-July 3, 1974.

1975

Sections in Books

"When God Does Not Heal." In *Learning to Cope*, by Helen Good Brenneman, 59-67. Scottdale: Herald Press, 1975.

Articles and Columns

Reclassified, *Festival Quarterly*, Winter 1975, 14.
"Can A Widow Survive in Today's Church?" *Standard*, January 26, 1975, 2-3.
"Lost: One Heaven." *Gospel Herald*, February 25, 1975, 142.
"It's Time to Think." *Gospel Herald*, April 8, 1975, 272-273.
"Can A Widow Survive in Today's Church?" *Evangel*, April 17, 1975, 5-6.
Reclassified, *Festival Quarterly*, May/June/July 1975, 35.
"Church Member Profile: A Massive Effort to Measure a Vision." *Mennonite Reporter*, May 1975, 10-11.
"Measuring a Vision." *Gospel Herald*, May 13, 1975, 358-361.
"Measuring a Vision." *The Mennonite*, May 13, 1975, 300-302.
"On Black and White Mennonites." *Gospel Herald*, May 20, 1975, 386.
"Measuring a Vision." *The Christian Leader*, May 27, 1975, 2-5.
"Measuring a Vision." *Mennonite Brethren Herald*, June 27, 1975, 1-4.
Reclassified, *Festival Quarterly*, August/September/October 1975, 35.
"Colour Me a Person." *The Christian Home*, August, 1975, 28-32.
"Finding Self in Divine Encounter." *Rejoice!* September/October/November, 1975, 40-43.
"Struggling with Pride and Jealousy." *Rejoice!* September/October/November, 1975, 44-47.
"Finding Strength in Serving God." *Rejoice!* September/October/November, 1975, 48-51.
"Placing Others Before Self." *Rejoice!* September/October/November, 1975, 52-55.
"Becoming Reconciled." *Rejoice!* September/October/November, 1975, 56-59.
"At the Convention." The Last Word, *Mennonite Brethren Herald*, September 5, 1975, 32.
"Children of Cain." *Gospel Herald*, September 9, 1975, 634.
"A Pig for a Pig." *The Evangel*, September 14, 1975, 1-4.
"A Rare Work of Art." The Last Word, *Mennonite Brethren Herald*, September 19, 1975, 32.
"A Time to Tear Down, A Time to Build Up." *With*, October 1975, 2-8.
"Feeling Guilty." *Gospel Herald*, October 7, 1975, 714.
"Widows and Singles...Pushed Out of Noah's Ark." *The Mennonite*, October 7, 1975, 554-556.

"The Fall Season." The Last Word, *Mennonite Brethren Herald*, October 17, 1975, 32.
Reclassified, *Festival Quarterly*, November/December 1975, January 1996, 14.
"Write a Christmas Gift and Strengthen the Root System." *Mennonite Reporter*, November 10, 1975, 10.
"Widows and Singles...Pushed Out of Noah's Ark." *The Christian Leader*, November 11, 1975, 2-5.
"A Conversion to Violence." *Gospel Herald*, November 25, 1975, 849.

Viewpoint
"Sleeping in the Back Seat." Viewpoint, *The Christian Leader*, January 7, 1975, 19.
"The Hidden Persuaders." Viewpoint, *The Christian Leader*, January 21, 1975, 19.
"Lost: One Heaven." Viewpoint, *The Christian Leader*, February 4, 1975, 19.
"Freedom for All." Viewpoint, *The Christian Leader*, February 18, 1975, 19.
"Have You Heard the Call?" Viewpoint, *The Christian Leader*, March 4, 1975, 19.
"It's Time to Think." Viewpoint, *The Christian Leader*, March 18, 1975, 19.
"On Black and White Mennonites." Viewpoint, *The Christian Leader*, April 1, 1975, 19.
"The Fog Machine." Viewpoint, *The Christian Leader*, April 15, 1975, 19.
"The Cutting Edge." Viewpoint, *The Christian Leader*, April 29, 1975, 19.
"Language Pollution." Viewpoint, *The Christian Leader*, May 13, 1975, 19.
"Helping the Glue to Stick." Viewpoint, *The Christian Leader*, June 10, 1975, 23.
"To Pass the Peace." Viewpoint, *The Christian Leader*, July 8, 1975, 19.
"Guilt Junkies." Viewpoint, *The Christian Leader*, July 22, 1975, 19.
"Fifty-seven Varieties." Viewpoint, *The Christian Leader*, August 5, 1975, 19.
"Children of Cain." Viewpoint, *The Christian Leader*, August 19, 1975, 19.
"At the Convention." Viewpoint, *The Christian Leader*, September 2, 1975, 19.
"A Rare Work of Art." Viewpoint, *The Christian Leader*, September 16, 1975, 19.
"The Fall Season." Viewpoint, *The Christian Leader*, September 30, 1975, 19.
"Conversion to Violence." Viewpoint, *The Christian Leader*, October 14, 1975, 19.
"Steak Religion." Viewpoint, *The Christian Leader*, October 28, 1975, 19.
"Open Season on Writers." Viewpoint, *The Christian Leader*, November 11, 1975, 7.
"The Second Careerist." Viewpoint, *The Christian Leader*, November 25, 1975, 13.
"The Anti-commitment Spirit." Viewpoint, *The Christian Leader*, December 9, 1975, 19.
"Another Kind of Feminism." Viewpoint, *The Christian Leader*, December 23, 1975, 19.

1976

Books

Alone: A Widow's Search for Joy. Wheaton: Tyndale House, 1976.
Alone: A Search for Joy. Lakeland: Marshall, Morgan and Scott, 1976. (British edition)
Auf einmal allein: Eine Frau sucht ihren Weg. Translated by Friedhilde Horn. Witten: Bundes-Verlag, 1976. (German edition)
Day of Disaster: The Story of Modern-Day Samaritans. Scottdale: Herald Press, 1976.

Sections in Books

"Introduction." In *Black and Mennonite* by Hubert Brown, 9-11. Scottdale: Herald Press, 1976.

Articles and Columns

"I Dream of Me." *Christian Reader,* January/February 1976.
"Open Season on Writers." *Gospel Herald,* January 6, 1976, 6.
"Another Kind of Feminism." The Last Word, *Mennonite Brethren Herald,* January 9, 1975, 32.
"Another Kind of Feminism." *Gospel Herald,* January 20, 1976, 44.
Reclassified, *Festival Quarterly,* February/March/April 1976, 34.
"Waiting to Get on Board." *Christian Living,* February 1976, 10-14.
"Needed: A Capacity For Outrage." *The Evangel,* February 8, 1976, 1-2.
"Back to Basics." *Gospel Herald,* February 17, 1976, 123.
"The Anti-commitment Spirit." *Gospel Herald,* February 24, 1976, 154.
"How to be Bold." *Gospel Herald,* April 6, 1976, 289.
"A Pig for a Pig." *Vista For Adults,* April 11, 1976, 1-3.
Reclassified, *Festival Quarterly,* May/June/July 1976, 58.
"Can We Hear the Prophets?" *Gospel Herald,* May 11, 1976, 400.
"Helping the Glue to Stick." The Last Word, *Mennonite Brethren Herald,* June 11, 1975, 32.
"My Parents Are Mennonites—and They're Divorced." *With,* July/August 1976, 38-45.
"A Reading for Women." *MCC Peace Section: Task Force on Women in Church and Society,* July 1976, 7.
"What's This Battle About Headship and Submission." *Christian Living,* July 1976, 10-15
"What is a Vision?" *Gospel Herald,* July 6, 1976, 547.
"Clustering." The Last Word, *Mennonite Brethren Herald,* July 9, 1975, 32.
"A Pig for a Pig." *The Messenger,* August 4, 1976, 8-9.
"Clustering." *Gospel Herald,* August 10, 1976, 610.

"A Search for Renewal." The Last Word, *Mennonite Brethren Herald*, August 20, 1975, 32.
"Labor Day Reflections." *Vista For Adults*, September 5, 1976.
"The Hard Place." *Gospel Herald*, September 28, 1976, 747.
"Teach Me to Dance." The Last Word, *Mennonite Brethren Herald*, October 1, 1975, 32.
"A Search for Renewal." *Gospel Herald*, October 19, 1976, 803.
"'They' and 'Us.'" *Gospel Herald*, October 12, 1976, 775.
Reclassified, *Festival Quarterly*, November/December 1976, January 1977, 34-35.
"Money Talk." *Gospel Herald*, November 2, 1976, 841.
"What I Don't Want For Christmas." *Evangel*, November 7, 1976, 3-4.
"Turning Affliction into Victory." *The Christian Leader*, November 9, 1976, 2-4.
"A Piece of the Rock." *Gospel Herald*, November 23, 1976, 912.
"Bible, Coat and Purse." *Rejoice!* December 1976, January/February 1977, 1-3.
"Time for Living." *Gospel Herald*, December 7, 1976, 930-931.

Viewpoint
"What's Your Frame of Reference?" Viewpoint, *The Christian Leader*, January 6, 1976, 17.
"Back to Basics." Viewpoint, *The Christian Leader*, January 20, 1976, 19.
"You Wrote This One." Viewpoint, *The Christian Leader*, February 3, 1976, 19.
"How to Be Bold." Viewpoint, *The Christian Leader*, February 17, 1976, 19.
"Love in Overalls." Viewpoint, *The Christian Leader*, March 2, 1976, 19.
"Why Do You Sneeze?" Viewpoint, *The Christian Leader*, March 16, 1976, 21.
"Can We Hear the Prophets?" Viewpoint, *The Christian Leader*, March 30, 1976, 19.
"The Gospel and the Nation." Viewpoint, *The Christian Leader*, April 13, 1976, 19.
"Two Sides of a Counterfeit Coin." Viewpoint, *The Christian Leader*, April 27, 1976, 19.
"Of Computers and Visions." Viewpoint, *The Christian Leader*, May 1, 1976, 17.
"To Each a Gift." Viewpoint, *The Christian Leader*, May 25, 1976, 19.
"A Rock and A Hard Place." Viewpoint, *The Christian Leader*, June 8, 1976, 19.
"Clustering." Viewpoint, *The Christian Leader*, July 6, 1976, 19.
"'They' and 'Us.'" Viewpoint, *The Christian Leader*, July 20, 1976, 20.
"A Search for Renewal." Viewpoint, *The Christian Leader*, August 3, 1976, 19.
"Money Talk." Viewpoint, *The Christian Leader*, August 17, 1976, 19.
"Teach Me to Dance." Viewpoint, *The Christian Leader*, August 31, 1976, 19.
"The Glory Has Not Departed." Viewpoint, *The Christian Leader*, September 14, 1976, 23.
"Honky Hermeneutics." Viewpoint, *The Christian Leader*, September 28, 1976, 19.

"A Piece of the Rock." Viewpoint, *The Christian Leader*, October 12, 1976, 19.
"Time for the Living." Viewpoint, *The Christian Leader*, October 26, 1976, 19.
"The Hesitant Church." Viewpoint, *The Christian Leader*, November 23, 1976, 19.
"New Learnings About the Family." Viewpoint, *The Christian Leader*, December 7, 1976, 19.
"No Gift Exchange." Viewpoint, *The Christian Leader*, December 21, 1976, 27.

Book Reviews
Review of *How To Be Happy In No Man's Land* by Iverna Tompkins with Irene Harrell. *Provident Book Finder*, May-June 1976, 8-9.
Review of *Who Walk Alone* by Margaret Evening. *Provident Book Finder*, May-June 1976, 19.
Review of *Women Beyond Roleplay* by Elizabeth Skoglund. *The Christian Leader*, June 8, 1976, 15.
Review of *Celebrate Your Freedom* by Don Williams. *Provident Book Finder*, July-August 1976, 4.
Review of *Clusters—Lifestyle Alternatives for Families and Single People* by Paul Chapman, Editor. *Provident Book Finder*, July-August 1976, 4.
Review of *In My Father's House* by Corrie ten Boom. *Provident Book Finder*, July-August 1976, 8.
Review of *The Seeker* by William Alan Bales. *Provident Book Finder*, September-October 1976, 17.
Review of *The Survivor* by James Forman. *Provident Book Finder*, September-October 1976, 17.
Review of *A Woman Called Moses* by Marcy Heidish. *Provident Book Finder*, September-October 1976, 18.

Presentations
"Voices of Liberation." Anabaptist and Mennonite Brethren History and Practice Symposium on Women in the Church, Fresno, California, May 6-7, 1976.
"Writing, Widowhood and Humor." Dutch Family Festival Cultural Series, Intercourse, Pennsylvania, July 12, 1976.

1977

Sections in Books
"Can I Make It as Both Father and Mother?" In *For Families Only: Answering the Tough Questions Parents Ask*, edited by J. Allan Petersen, 196-202. Wheaton: Tyndale House, 1977.

"To the Unknown Great." In *Mennonite Memories: Settling in Western Canada*, 2nd ed., edited by Lawrence Klippenstein and Julius G. Toews, 312-315. Winnipeg: Centennial Publications, 1977.

Articles and Columns
"In Praise of Male Feminists." *Daughters of Sarah*, January 1977, 1-3.
"Widows and Singles...Pushed Out of Noah's Ark." *The Messenger*, January 1977
"The Call to Nobility." The Last Word, *Mennonite Brethren Herald*, January 7, 1977, 32.
"New Learnings about the Gospel." *Gospel Herald*, January 18, 1977, 46.
Reclassified, *Festival Quarterly*, February/March/April 1977, 34.
"A Woman MDSer in Every Car." *The Christian Leader*, February 1, 1977, 14-15.
"Making Peace with Violence." *Gospel Herald*, February 8, 1977, 114.
"Why Read Mennonite Literature?" *The Christian Leader*, February 15, 1977, 5-6.
"Widows and Singles...Pushed Out of Noah's Ark." *Sabbath Recorder*, March 1977, 9-10.
"Who Am I?" *Faith At Work*, March 1977, 30-31.
"Cause or Call?" *Gospel Herald*, March 1, 1977, 182.
"The Glory Has Not Departed." The Last Word, *Mennonite Brethren Herald*, March 4, 1977, 32.
"What Is The Mennonite Church?" *Gospel Herald*, March 29, 1977, 265-269.
"Hooked on Love—Aggie Klassen." *With*, April 1977. 6-10.
"To Arrange or Not to Arrange a Marriage." *Christian Living*, April 1977, 8-10.
"The Agenda of the People." *Gospel Herald*, April 12, 1977, 305-309.
"Making Peace with Violence." The Last Word, *Mennonite Brethren Herald*, April 15, 1977, 32.
"An Insurance Company That Writes Love Into Its Contracts." *Gospel Herald*, April 26, 1977, 345-349.
Reclassified, *Festival Quarterly*, May/June/July 1977, 42.
"It Can Happen Today." *Gospel Herald*, May 3, 1977, 363.
"BCM—Board of Congregational Ministries." *Gospel Herald*, May 10, 1977, 382-385.
"Forming a People of God." *Gospel Herald*, May 31, 1977, 442-445.
"Wives, Husbands and Work." The Last Word, *Mennonite Brethren Herald*, June 24, 1977, 40.
"The Insurance Firm that Writes Love into Its Contracts: Mennonite Mutual Aid." *The Christian Leader*, July 19, 1977, 17-19.
"Wives, Husbands, and Work." *Gospel Herald*, July 26, 1977, 567.
Reclassified, *Festival Quarterly*, August/September/October 1977, 34.

"Why Read Mennonite Literature?" *Mennonite Brethren Herald*, August 5, 1977, 7-8.
"Finding the Enemy." *Gospel Herald*, August 30, 1977, 653.
"Strengthening the Root System." Last Word, *Mennonite Brethren Herald*, September 2, 1977, 32.
"Ring Around the Heart." *Gospel Herald*, September 27, 1977, 720.
"Men's Missionary Squares." *Gospel Herald*, October 4, 1977, 742.
"No-Sweat Christianity." *Mennonite Brethren Herald*, October 28, 1977, 5.
Reclassified, *Festival Quarterly*, November/December 1977, January 1978, 34.
"The Pop Psychologists." *Gospel Herald*, November 8, 1977, 834.
"Til Death Do Us Part." *Mennonite Brethren Herald*, November 11, 1977, 24.
"What's a Neighbor For?" *Gospel Herald*, November 15, 1977, 859.
"Crossing the Line." *Gospel Herald*, December 6, 1977, 905.
"No Gift Exchange." *Gospel Herald*, December 13, 1977, 933.
"First All-India Conference Joins Women in Mutual Tasks." *Mennonite Reporter*, December 26, 14.

Viewpoint

"Needed: A New Nobility." Viewpoint, *The Christian Leader*, January 4, 1977, 19.
"Making Peace with Violence." Viewpoint, *The Christian Leader*, January 18, 1977, 17.
"Cause or Call?" Viewpoint, *The Christian Leader*, February 5, 1977, 19.
"Room for Grace." Viewpoint, *The Christian Leader*, March 1, 1977, 19.
"It Can Happen Today." Viewpoint, *The Christian Leader*, March 15, 1977, 14.
"Mini-Courses in Living." Viewpoint, *The Christian Leader*, March 29, 1977, 23.
"Wives, Husbands and Work." Viewpoint, *The Christian Leader*, April 12, 1977, 20.
"Footprints in the Sands of Time." Viewpoint, *The Christian Leader*, April 26, 1977, 19.
"With the Lord." Viewpoint, *The Christian Leader*, May 10, 1977, 20.
"Next in Line." Viewpoint, *The Christian Leader*, May 24, 1977, 19.
"Finding the Enemy." Viewpoint, *The Christian Leader*, June 7, 1977, 19.
"After Death and Divorce." Viewpoint, *The Christian Leader*, July 5, 1977, 21.
"Purr Words and Snarl Words." Viewpoint, *The Christian Leader*, July 19, 1977, 14.
"A Search for Renewal." Viewpoint, *The Christian Leader*, August 3, 1977, 19.
"On Artists and Millionaires." Viewpoint, *The Christian Leader*, August 16, 1977, 19.
"Crossing the Line." Viewpoint, *The Christian Leader*, August 30, 1977, 14.
"Men's Missionary Squares." Viewpoint, *The Christian Leader*, September 13, 1977, 19.

"The Pop Psychologists." Viewpoint, *The Christian Leader*, September 27, 1977, 24.
"What's a Neighbor For?" Viewpoint, *The Christian Leader*, October 11, 1977, 17.
"No-sweat Christianity." Viewpoint, *The Christian Leader*, October 25, 1977, 17.
"Battered Parents." Viewpoint, *The Christian Leader*, November 8, 1977, 17.
"Passage to India." Viewpoint, *The Christian Leader*, December 20, 1977, 9.

Book Reviews
Review of *'Twas Seeding Time* by John L. Ruth. *Provident Book Finder*, January-February 1977, 1.
Review of *The Mantle* by William H. Stephens. *Provident Book Finder*, January-February 1977, 9.
Review of *The Family Album* by Arthur and Nancy DeMoss. *Provident Book Finder*, January-February 1977, 21.
Review of *Oral—The Warm, Intimate Unauthorized Portrait of a Man of God* by Wayne A. Robinson. *Provident Book Finder*, March-April 1977, 10.
Review of *Tell It on the Mountain* by William R. Lasky. *Provident Book Finder*, March-April 1977, 17.
Review of *Are There Any Answers?* By Clark H. Pinnock. *Provident Book Finder*, March-April 1977, 20.
Review of *The Christian Mother* by Jacky Hertz. *Provident Book Finder*, May-June 1977, 3.
Review of *Community and Commitment* by John Driver. *Provident Book Finder*, May-June 1977, 3-4.
Review of *Sparrow on the Housetop* by Ruth Hunt. *Provident Book Finder*, May-June 1977, 12.
Review of *You and Your Aging Parent* by Barbara Silverstone & Helen Kandel Hyman. *Provident Book Finder*, May-June 1977, 18.
Review of *I'm Divorce—Are You Listening, Lord?* by Peggy S. Buck. *Provident Book Finder*, May-June 1977, 20.
Review of *Make Your Illness Count* by Vernon J. Bittner. *Provident Book Finder*, May-June 1977, 21.
Review of *The Names* by M. Scott Momaday. *Provident Book Finder*, May-June 1977, 21.
Review of *The New Community* by Elizabeth O'Connor. *Provident Book Finder*, July-August 1977, 9-10.
Review of *If You're There, Show Me* by Zola Levitt. *Provident Book Finder*, July-August 1977, 20.
Review of *In But Still Out* by Elizabeth Howell Verdesi. *Provident Book Finder*, July-August 1977, 26.

Review of *Ordinary People* by Judith Guest. *Provident Book Finder,* September-October 1977, 4.
Review of *A Quiet Revolution: The Christian Response to Human Need—A Strategy for Today* by John Perkins. *Provident Book Finder,* September-October 1977, 12.
Review of *The Secrets of Our Sexuality: Role Liberation for the Christian* by Gary R. Collins. *Provident Book Finder,* September-October 1977, 19.
Review of *Widows and Widowhood* by James A. Peterson & Michael L. Briley. *Provident Book Finder,* September-October 1977, 19.
Review of *Daily Thoughts for Disciples* by Oswald Chambers. *Provident Book Finder,* September-October 1977, 20.
Review of *Profiles: People Who Are Helping to Change the World* by Helen Kooiman Hosier. *Provident Book Finder,* September-October 1977, 21.

Presentations
"Who Will Mind Creative Writing?" Summer Workshop for Elementary Teachers, McPherson College, McPherson, Kansas, June 13-17, 1977.
"Women's Work in the Light of Our Heritage and Mission." All-India Mennonite Women's Conference, Dhamtari, India, November 1-6, 1977.

1978

Books
Our Lamps Were Lit: An Informal History of the Bethel Deaconess Hospital School of Nursing. Newton: Bethel Hospital School of Nursing; Alumnae Association, 1978.

Sections in Books
"The Barriers Are Not Real." In *The Ethnic American Woman: Problems, Protests, Lifestyle,* edited by Edith Blicksilver, 178-181. Dubuque: Kendall/Hunt, 1978.
"The Judgment of the People." In *The Way of the Cross and Resurrection: Meditations for the Lenton Season,* edited by John M. Drescher, 83-95. Scottdale: Herald Press, 1978.

Articles and Columns
"First Women's Conference Stresses Unity in Christ." *The Christian Leader,* January 3, 1978, 12-13.
"Have Cart, Will Travel." *The Christian Leader,* January 3, 1978, 6-7.
"Conference Unites Indian Women." *Mennonite Brethren Herald,* January 6, 1978, 10.
"Help for Battered Parents." The Last Word, *Mennonite Brethren Herald,* January 10, 1978, 32.
"Why Read Mennonite Literature?" *Gospel Herald,* January 17, 1978, 42-44.

"How Shall One Feed the Hungry? A Day in Calcutta." *Mennonite Reporter*, January 23, 1978, 10.
"Battered Parents." *Gospel Herald*, January 24, 1978, 61.
"Schools for Hungry Minds." *The Christian Leader*, January 31, 1978, 12-13.
Reclassified, *Festival Quarterly*, February/March/April 1978, 34.
"To Arrange or Not to Arrange." *Mennonite Brethren Herald*, February 3, 1978, 28-29.
"Schools for Hungry Minds: The Children of Calcutta." *Mennonite Reporter*, February 6, 1978, 9.
"Purr Words and Snarl Words." *Gospel Herald*, February 7, 1978, 117.
"Feeding the Hungry in Calcutta." *The Christian Leader*, February 14, 1978, 10-11.
"Columnist: Offering Another Point of View." *The Christian Leader*, February 28, 1978, 5.
"The Healing of Memories." *Gospel Herald*, February 28, 1978, 173.
"'Soyabeens! Soyabeens!'" *The Christian Leader*, February 28, 1978, 7.
"What to Expect When Worshipping in India." *Festival Quarterly*, Spring 1978, 21.
"'Soyabeans' Experiment Promotes Young Businessmen." *Mennonite Reporter*, March 6, 1978, 2.
"Nepal—Where Old Intersects New." *The Christian Leader*, March 14, 1978, 14.
"The Healing of Memories." The Last Word, *Mennonite Brethren Herald*, March 17, 1978, 36.
"Wheels and Pyramids." *Gospel Herald*, March 28, 1978, 258.
"Feeding the Hungry in Calcutta." *Mennonite Brethren Herald*, March 31, 1978, 14.
"Cows, Castes and Christian Callings." *With*, April 1978, 20-25.
"What Kind of Good News?" The Last Word, *Mennonite Brethren Herald*, April 14, 1978, 32.
"Old and New Intersect in Isolated Nepal." *Mennonite Reporter*, April 17, 1978, 15.
"What Kind of Good News." *Gospel Herald*, April 18, 1978, 315.
"Mennonite Humor—International." Reclassified, *Festival Quarterly*, May/June/July1978, 42.
"Sonam, You Have a Future." *With*, May 1978, 34-38.
"Sixty-five and Over." *Gospel Herald*, May 2, 1978, 357.
"Can You Tell the Difference?" The Last Word, *Mennonite Brethren Herald*, May 12, 1978, 36.
"Can You Tell the Difference?" *Gospel Herald*, May 23, 1978, 413.
"No Littering." *Gospel Herald*, May 30, 1978, 435.
"Spreading the Good News." *Rejoice!* June/July/August 1978, 8-11.
"Resolving the Conflict." *Rejoice!* June/July/August 1978, 12-15.

Comprehensive Bibliography | 291

"Responding to the Good News." *Rejoice!* June/July/August 1978, 16-19.
"Success and Persecution." *Rejoice!* June/July/August 1978, 20-23.
"Paul Ministers Through Letters." *Rejoice!* June/July/August 1978, 24-27.
"The Militarization of Women." *Gospel Herald*, June 6, 1978, 451.
"Time for the Living." *Mennonite Brethren Herald*, June 9, 1978, 28.
"The Para-Church Agencies and the Church in India." *Direction* 7, no.3 (July 1978):32-35.
"A Piece of Rock" The Last Word, *Mennonite Brethren Herald*, July 7, 1978, 32.
"Mennonites, Masqueraders, and Ministers." Reclassified, *Festival Quarterly*, August/September/October 1978, 38.
"The Unloved Cat." *Gospel Herald*, August 1, 1978, 579.
"Mennonites Like Me." *Gospel Herald*, August 22, 1978, 634.
"Undoing Pagan Influences." *Gospel Herald*, October 10, 1978, 772.
"What If...?" *Gospel Herald*, October 4, 1978, 825.
"Tanta Truda: My Aunt, an Umsiedler." *Mennonite Reporter*, October 30, 1978, 14.
"Flying High." *Gospel Herald*, November 14, 1978, 871.
"Arguments or Excuses?" *Gospel Herald*, November 14, 1978, 897.
"Newspaper Faith." *Gospel Herald*, November 21, 1978, 922.
"Urges Stronger Witness for Peace." *Mennonite Reporter*, December 25, 1978, 1.
"After Wichita, What is a Mennonite?" The Last Word, *Mennonite Brethren Herald*, September 15, 1978, 40.
"Undoing Pagan Influences." The Last Word, *Mennonite Brethren Herald*, October 31, 1978, 32.
"Family Reunion." Reclassified, *Festival Quarterly*, November/December 1978, January 1979, 50.
"Newspaper Faith." The Last Word, *Mennonite Brethren Herald*, November 10, 1978, 32.
"Cause or Call?" The Last Word, *Mennonite Brethren Herald*, December 22, 1978, 36.

Viewpoint

"Workers Together." Viewpoint, *The Christian Leader*, January 17, 1978, 15.
"Healing of Memories." Viewpoint, *The Christian Leader*, January 31, 1978, 15.
"Wheels and Pyramids." Viewpoint, *The Christian Leader*, February 14, 1978, 19.
"Sixty-five and Over." Viewpoint, *The Christian Leader*, February 24, 1978, 18.
"Who Are You Kidding?" Viewpoint, *The Christian Leader*, March 14, 1978, 20.
"What Kind of Good News?" Viewpoint, *The Christian Leader*, March 28, 1978, 23.
"No Littering Allowed." Viewpoint, *The Christian Leader*, April 11, 1978, 17.
"The Militarization of Women." Viewpoint, *The Christian Leader*, April 25, 1978, 10.

"Can You Tell the Difference?" Viewpoint, *The Christian Leader*, May 9, 1978, 17.
"Changing Values." Viewpoint, *The Christian Leader*, May 23, 1978, 19.
"Mennonites Like Me." Viewpoint, *The Christian Leader*, June 6, 1978, 18.
"Who's Right? Who's Wrong?" Viewpoint, *The Christian Leader*, July 4, 1978, 20.
"The Unloved Cat." Viewpoint, *The Christian Leader*, July 18, 1978, 19.
"My Aunt, an *Umsiedler*." Viewpoint, *The Christian Leader*, August 1, 1978, 19.
"After Wichita 1978, What is a Mennonite?" Viewpoint, *The Christian Leader*, August 15, 1978, 13-14.
"Undoing Pagan Influences." Viewpoint, *The Christian Leader*, August 29, 1978, 19.
"Flying High." Viewpoint, *The Christian Leader*, September 12, 1978, 18.
"What If...?" Viewpoint, *The Christian Leader*, September 26, 1978, 19.
"Arguments or Excuses?" Viewpoint, *The Christian Leader*, October 10, 1978, 23.
"Newspaper Faith." Viewpoint, *The Christian Leader*, October 24, 1978, 19.
"Who Are *The Mennonite* Brethren?" Viewpoint, *The Christian Leader*, November 7, 1978, 13.
"Men and Children." Viewpoint, *The Christian Leader*, November 21, 1978, 20.
"The Wife of the Servant of the Church." Viewpoint, *The Christian Leader*, December 5, 1978, 19.
"For All Committee Members." Viewpoint, *The Christian Leader*, December 19, 1978, 19.

Book Reviews

Review of *Not Dying: A Psychoanalyst's Memoir of His Wife's Death* by F. Robert Rodman. *Provident Book Finder*, January-February 1978, 11.
Review of *A Place Called Community* by Parker J. Palmer. *Provident Book Finder*, March-April 1978, 3.
Review of *Enough is Enough* by John V. Taylor. *Provident Book Finder*, March-April 1978, 6.
Review of *Quote Unquote* by Lloyd Cory. *Provident Book Finder*, March-April 1978, 17.
Review of *The Church and the Older Person* by Robert M. Gray & David O. Moberg. *Conversations on Growing Older* by C. Gilhuis Eerdmans. *In the Fullness of Time* by Avis D. Carlson. *Maggie Kuhn on Aging*, by Dieter Hessel, editor. *The Second Season* by Estelle Fuchs. *Survival Handbook for Children of Aging Parents* by Dr. Arthur N. Schwartz. *Why Survive?* By Robert N. Butler, M.D. *Provident Book Finder*, May-June 1978, 11-12.
Review of *I'm Eve: The Compelling story of the Internationally Famous Case of Multiple Personality* by Chris Costner Sizemore & Ellen Sain Pittillo. *Provident Book Finder*, May-June 1978, 20.

Review of *The Relational Revolution: An Invitation to Discover an Exciting Future for our Life Together* by Bruce Larson. *The Christian Leader*, May 9, 1978, 19.
Review of *A Russian Dance of Death: Revolution and Civil War in the Ukraine*, by Dietrich Neufeld. *Provident Book Finder*, July-August 1978, 10-11.
Review of *How Far, Felipe? An I Can Read History Book*, by Genevieve Gray. *Provident Book Finder*, September-October 1978, 22.
Review of *The Devil Did Not Make Me Do It* by Paul M. Miller. *Provident Book Finder*, November-December 1978, 41.
Review of *He Gave Us a Valley* by Helen Roseveare. *Provident Book Finder*, November-December 1978, 45.
Review of *Walking Through the Fire: A Hospital Journey* by Laurel Lee. *Provident Book Finder*, November-December 1978, 46.
Review of *In the Fullness of Time* by Avis D. Carlson. *Provident Book Finder*, November-December 1978, 46.
Review of *Psychology As Religion: The Cult of Self-Worship* by Paul. C. Vitz. *Provident Book Finder*, November-December 1978, 31-32.
Review of *The Devil Did Not Make Me Do It* by Paul M. Miller. *Provident Book Finder*, November-December 1978, 34.
Review of *Walking Through Fire* by Laurel Lee. *Provident Book Finder*, November-December 1978, 40.
Review of *With Courage to Spare* by John B. Toews. *Mennonite Reporter*, November 27, 1978, 9.

Presentations
"Am I My Mother's Keeper?" Virginia Mennonite Home Auxiliary, Harrisonburg, Virginia, February 10, 1978. Workshop leader, St. Davids Christian Writers' Conference, St. Davids, Pennsylvania, June 18-23, 1978.
"The Church's Response to Changing Roles for Men and Women." Biblical Perspectives on Women in the Church," Mennonite Central Committee British Columbia, Clearbrook, B.C., November 18, 1978.
"Jesus and Womanhood." Biblical Perspectives on Women in the Church, Mennonite Central Committee British Columbia. Clearbrook, B.C., November 18, 1978.

1979

Books
Good Times with Old Times: How to Write Your Memoirs. Scottdale: Herald Press, 1979.
Women among the Brethren: The Story of Fifteen Mennonite Brethren and Krimmer Mennonite Brethren Women. Editor. Hillsboro: General Conference of the North

American Mennonite Brethren Churches; Board of Christian Literature, 1979.

Sections in Books
"In Journeyings Often: Elizabeth Unruh Schultz (1866-1943)." In *Women among the Brethren: The Story of Fifteen Mennonite Brethren and Krimmer Mennonite Brethren Women*, edited by Katie Funk Wiebe, 55-70. Hillsboro: General Conference of the North American Mennonite Brethren Churches; Board of Christian Literature, 1979.
"Katie Funk Wiebe." In *Our Struggle to Serve*, edited by Virginia Hearn, 131-141. Waco: Word, 1979.
"The Russian Sister: Efrosinia Morozowa (C. 1850-?)." In *Women among the Brethren: The Story of Fifteen Mennonite Brethren and Krimmer Mennonite Brethren Women*, edited by Katie Funk Wiebe, 1-15. Hillsboro: General Conference of the North American Mennonite Brethren Churches; Board of Christian Literature, 1979.

Translations
"A Flight in Winter: Anna Falk Loewen (1902-)." In *Women among the Brethren: The Story of Fifteen Mennonite Brethren and Krimmer Mennonite Brethren Women*, edited by Katie Funk Wiebe, 149-167. Hillsboro: General Conference of the North American Mennonite Brethren Churches; Board of Christian Literature, 1979.

Articles and Columns
"The Wife of the Servants of the Church." *Gospel Herald*, January 2, 1979, 7.
"The Last of the Seventies." The Last Word, *Mennonite Brethren Herald*, January 5, 1979, 32.
"For All Committee Members." *Gospel Herald*, January 16, 1979, 35.
"Overheard at World Conference." Reclassified, *Festival Quarterly*, February/March/April 1979, 34.
"Finding the Enemy." The Last Word, *Mennonite Brethren Herald*, February 2, 1979, 40.
"The Year of the Child." The Last Word, *Mennonite Brethren Herald*, February 16, 1979, 36.
"How to Get Rid of the Theys." *Gospel Herald*, February 27, 1979, 182.
"The More Excellent Way." *Rejoice!* March/April/May 1979, 40-43.
"Gifts That Build the Church." *Rejoice!* March/April/May 1979, 44-47.
"God's Living Letters." *Rejoice!* March/April/May 1979, 48-51.
"The Ministry of Reconciliation." *Rejoice!* March/April/May 1979, 52-55.
"Giving that Glorifies God." *Rejoice!* March/April/May 1979, 56-59.
"The Year of the Child." *Gospel Herald*, March 13, 1979, 220.

"Pop Psychologists and the Religion of Self." The Last Word, *Mennonite Brethren Herald*, March 30, 1979, 32.
"DeYoderized (Wo)mennonites." Reclassified, *Festival Quarterly*, May/June/July 1979, 78.
"How to Get Rid of the Theys." *Quaker Life*, May 1979, 19-20.
"The More We Eat Together." *Gospel Herald*, May 1, 1979, 364.
"The Big 'X.'" The Last Word, *Mennonite Brethren Herald*, May 11, 1979, 32.
"The Big 'X.'" *Gospel Herald*, May 15, 1979, 399.
"That Church Press Release." The Last Word, *Mennonite Brethren Herald*, May 25, 1979, 36.
"When Did You See a Radical Christian?" *Gospel Herald*, June 26, 1979, 517.
"What Kind of Good News?" *Faith Today*, July/August 1979, 18.
"What Kind of Good News?" *The Messenger*, July 5, 1979, 16.
"Men and Children." *Gospel Herald*, July 24, 1979, 581.
"The Good Live Begins with…" The Last Word, *Mennonite Brethren Herald*, July 27, 1979, 32.
"Mennonite….Comedy." Reclassified, *Festival Quarterly*, August/September/October 1979, 34.
"What is Theology?" Editorial, *Mennonite Brethren Herald*, August 10, 1979, 12.
"The Good Life Begins…" *Gospel Herald*, August 14, 1979, 647.
"Caught in the Draft." *Gospel Herald*, August 21, 1979, 677.
"How Pleasant Valley Kept the Wolf Away." *Sharing*, Fall 1979, 10-13.
"Mentors." *Perspectives: The Tabor College Bulletin*, Fall 1979, 3-4.
"Sonam, You Have a Future." *Rejoice!* September/October/November 1979, 4-7.
"Who's Missing?" *Gospel Herald*, October 2, 1979, 783.
"The Review Mirror." *Gospel Herald*, October 23, 1979, 831.
"Moving Down the Fast Lane." The Last Word, *Mennonite Brethren Herald*, October 26, 1979, 40.
"Mennonite Innocents Abroad." Reclassified, *Festival Quarterly*, November/December 1979, January 1980, 34.
"Being a Thinking Thanker." *The Christian Leader*, November 20, 1979, 4-5.
"Thanksgiving and Mennonites." *The Mennonite*, November 20, 1979.
"Who Will Survive?" Translation, *Mennonite Brethren Herald*, November 23, 1979, 2-5.
"Season of Courage." *Gospel Herald*, December 25, 1979, 1030-1031.

Viewpoint

"The Last of the Seventies." Viewpoint, *The Christian Leader*, January 2, 1979, 15.
"Family Power." Viewpoint, *The Christian Leader*, January 16, 1979, 19.

"Getting Rid of the 'They's.'" Viewpoint, *The Christian Leader*, January 20, 1979, 25.
"The Year of the Child." Viewpoint, *The Christian Leader*, February 13, 1979, 23.
"A Three-cheer Event." Viewpoint, *The Christian Leader*, February 27, 1979, 19.
'The More We Eat Together." Viewpoint, *The Christian Leader*, March 13, 1979, 23.
"Sloppy Agape." Viewpoint, *The Christian Leader*, March 27, 1979, 27.
"The Big X." Viewpoint, *The Christian Leader*, April 10, 1979, 19.
"The Mennonite Lone Ranger." Viewpoint, *The Christian Leader*, April 24, 1979, 17.
"The Myths of Parenting." Viewpoint, *The Christian Leader*, May 8, 1979, 19.
"The Church Press Release." Viewpoint, *The Christian Leader*, May 22, 1979, 20.
"T-shirt, Bumper Sticker or...?" Viewpoint, *The Christian Leader*, June 5, 1979, 20.
"Caught in the Draft." Viewpoint, *The Christian Leader*, June 19, 1979, 19.
"The Good Life Begins with..." Viewpoint, *The Christian Leader*, July 17, 1979, 19.
"Stewardship—An Acquired Habit." Viewpoint, *The Christian Leader*, July 31, 1979, 19.
"What is Theology?" Viewpoint, *The Christian Leader*, August 14, 1979, 19.
"One of Our Members is Missing." Viewpoint, *The Christian Leader*, August 28, 1979, 19.
"The Rearview Mirror." Viewpoint, *The Christian Leader*, September 11, 1979, 19.
"I've Changed My Mind." Viewpoint, *The Christian Leader*, September 25, 1979, 20.
"Moving Down the Fast Lane." Viewpoint, *The Christian Leader*, October 9, 1979, 17.
"The Proof-text Game." Viewpoint, *The Christian Leader*, October 23, 1979, 17.
"Is Winning Everything?" Viewpoint, *The Christian Leader*, November 6, 1979, 19.
"The Way It's Always Been Done." Viewpoint, *The Christian Leader*, December 4, 1979, 19.
"Season of Courage." Viewpoint, *The Christian Leader*, December 18, 1979, 18.

Book Reviews

Review of *For the Love of My Daughter: A Mother's Bittersweet Story* by Mary Ellen Ton. *Provident Book Finder,* January-February 1979, 11.
Review of *The Last Word* by Jamie Buckingham. *Provident Book Finder,* January-February 1979, 21.
Review of *A Future with Hope* by Harvey Kline and Warren Eshbach. *Provident Book Finder,* March-April 1979, 5.

Review of *A Good Age* by Alex Comfort. *Provident Book Finder,* March-April 1979, 5.

Review of *Our Struggle to Serve* by Virginia Hearn. *Provident Book Finder,* March-April 1979, 8-9.

Review of *Coming Together* by Dave Jackson. *Provident Book Finder,* March-April 1979, 17-18.

Review of *The Gospel According to Pontius Pilate* by James R. Mills. *Provident Book Finder,* March-April 1979, 19.

Review of *Wisdom from Women of the Bible* by Edith Den. *Provident Book Finder,* March-April 1979, 20.

Review of *Me and My Family Tree* by Paul Showers. *Provident Book Finder,* March-April 1979, 22.

Review of *Karen! Karen!* by Karen Mains. *Provident Book Finder*, May-June 1979, 5-6.

Review of *Jesus and the Freed Woman* by Rachel Conrad Wahlberg. *Provident Book Finder*, May-June 1979, 29.

Review of *Woman in the World of Jesus* by Evelyn and Frank Stagg. *Provident Book Finder,* May-June 1979, 29.

Review of *Deaf Like Me* by Thomas S. Spradley & James P. Spradley. *Provident Book Finder*, July-August 1979, 8-9.

Review of *How Green is My Mountain* by Ruth Klaasen. *The Christian Leader*, August 28, 1979, 16.

Review of *Take Care: Translating Christ's Love into a Caring Ministry* by C.W. Brister. *Provident Book Finder*, September-October 1979, 3.

Review of *Feeling Good About Feeling Bad: A Look at Irrational Guilt* by Paul L. Warner. *Provident Book Finder*, September-October 1979, 9.

Review of *Herland* by Charlotte Perkins Gilman. *Provident Book Finder*, September-October 1979, 18.

Review of *Strangers in Exile* by Hans Harder. *Provident Book Finder*, September-October 1979, 19.

Review of *How Green Is My Mountain by* Ruth Klaasen. *Provident Book Finder*, September-October 1979, 19-20.

Review of *The Grandmother's Book* by Joan Lowery Nixon. *Provident Book Finder*, November-December 1979, 27.

Review of *Affliction* by Edith Schaeffer. *Provident Book Finder*, November-December 1979, 27.

Review of *Caught in the Crossfire* by Levi Keidel. *Provident Book Finder*, November-December 1979, 38.

Review of *Our Struggle to Serve* edited by Virginia Hearn. *Provident Book Finder*, November-December 1979, 38-39.

Review of *Take Care: Translating Christ's Love into a Caring Ministry* by C.W. Brister. *Provident Book Finder*, November-December 1979, 42.

Presentations

"Commissioned to Care." General Conference Mennonite Church Western District Women's Retreat, Camp Mennoscah, Kansas, September 8-9, 1979.

"Women of God Past and Present." Women's Day on Campus, Tabor College, Kansas, October 6, 1979. Keynote speaker and workshop leader, "Audience and Marketing," General Conference Mennonite Church, Canadian Mennonite Bible College, Winnipeg, Manitoba, November 23-29, 1979.

1980

Book Sections

"Mennonite Disaster Service (MDS)." In *Witness and Service in North America: Peace Witness, Mental Health and Voluntary Service*, edited by C. J. Dyck, 118-119. Scottdale: Herald Press, 1980.

Articles and Columns

"Passing Along the Faith." *Today's Christian Woman*, Winter 1980, 64-65, 116, 119.

"What's Your Reason?" The Last Word, *Mennonite Brethren Herald*, January 4, 1980, 32.

"Prayer, That Elusive Thing." *Gospel Herald*, January 8, 1980, 23.

"Who will Read and Who will Grow?" *Gospel Herald*, January 22, 1980, 55.

"Mennonite Mamas." Reclassified, *Festival Quarterly*, February/March/April, 1980, 34.

"The Breeze Before the Draft." *Gospel Herald*, February 12, 1980, 135.

"Safe Passage." *Gospel Herald*, March 18, 1980, 224-225.

"The Breeze Before the Draft." *Quaker Life*, April 1980.

"Convenience or Responsibility." *Gospel Herald*, April 8, 1980, 296-297.

"Why Can't Daddy Read?" *Christian Reader*, May/June 1980.

"Come, Anabaptist, Let's go Play!" Reclassified, *Festival Quarterly*, May/June/July, 1980, 42.

"Is Winning Everything?" *The Messenger*, May 9, 1980, 15.

"To Arm or Not to Arm" The Last Word, *Mennonite Brethren Herald*, May 9, 1980, 36.

"A Step Toward Self-Identity." *Gospel Herald*, May 20, 1980, 406-407.

"Old is Not Old." *Gospel Herald*, June 17, 1980, 494.

"Moving the Inner Baggage." *Gospel Herald*, July 22, 1980, 571.

"My Fill of Bread." *Gospel Herald*, July 29, 1980, 598.

"Where Do We Fit In?" *The Christian Leader*, July 29, 1980, 9.

"Why Would Anyone Want a Mennonite?" Reclassified, *Festival Quarterly*, August/September/October 1980, 44.

"One of Our Members is Missing" The Last Word, *Mennonite Brethren Herald*, August 8, 1980, 32.
"The Story of the Generations" The Last Word, *Mennonite Brethren Herald*, August 29, 1980, 32.
"God's Covenant with David." *Rejoice!* September/October/November 1980; 28-31.
"God's Covenant and Israel's Sin." *Rejoice!* September/October/November 1980; 32-35.
"God's Covenant and Jeremiah." *Rejoice!* September/October/November 1980; 36-39.
"God's Covenant and Ezra." *Rejoice!* September/October/November 1980; 40-43.
"Facing Down the One-eyed Monster." *Gospel Herald*, September 2, 1980, 693.
"Of Law and Love." *Gospel Herald*, October 7, 1980, 790.
"Can One Fail and Remain a 'Good' Mennonite?" *Festival Quarterly*, November/December 1980, January 1981, 12-13.
"Living Our Consciences!!" Reclassified, *Festival Quarterly*, November/December 1980, January 1981, 44.
"A Modern Psalm." *Gospel Herald*, November 18, 1980, 923.
"Swat Them With Me." *Gospel Herald*, November 11, 1980, 910.
"The Language of Faith." *Gospel Herald*, December 16, 1980, 1011.
"Power and the Gospel." *Gospel Herald*, December 30, 1980, 1045.

Viewpoint
"What's Your Reason?" Viewpoint, *The Christian Leader*, January 1, 1980, 19.
"Don't Waste the Pain!" Viewpoint, *The Christian Leader*, January 15, 1980, 17.
"Safe Passage." Viewpoint, *The Christian Leader*, January 29, 1980, 19.
"The Breeze Before the Draft." Viewpoint, *The Christian Leader*, February 12, 1980, 22.
"Up Close and Personal." Viewpoint, *The Christian Leader*, February 26, 1980, 20.
"Convenience...or Murder?" Viewpoint, *The Christian Leader*, March 11, 1980, 20.
"A Step to Self-Identity." Viewpoint, *The Christian Leader*, March 25, 1980, 19.
"To Arm or Not to Arm." Viewpoint, *The Christian Leader*, April 8, 1980, 19.
"Checkpoints of Commitment." Viewpoint, *The Christian Leader*, April 22, 1980, 18.
"Old is Not Old." Viewpoint, *The Christian Leader*, May 6, 1980, 18.
"The Hurt that is Not in the Head." Viewpoint, *The Christian Leader*, May 20, 1980, 20.
"Summer Camp Lessons." Viewpoint, *The Christian Leader*, June 3, 1980, 17.
"Moving the Inner Baggage." Viewpoint, *The Christian Leader*, June 17, 1980, 19.

"My Fill of Bread." Viewpoint, *The Christian Leader*, July 15, 1980, 11.
"I Eye the Monster." Viewpoint, *The Christian Leader*, July 29, 1980, 20.
"Of Law and Love." Viewpoint, *The Christian Leader*, August 12, 1980, 11.
"The Story of Generations." Viewpoint, *The Christian Leader*, August 26, 1980, 20.
"Lesson from History." Viewpoint, *The Christian Leader*, September 9, 1980, 20.
"A Search for Abigail." Viewpoint, *The Christian Leader*, September 23, 1980, 17.
"A Modern Psalm." Viewpoint, *The Christian Leader*, October 7, 1980, 17.
"Swat Them with Me." Viewpoint, *The Christian Leader*, October 21, 1980, 18.
"The Debt is Great." Viewpoint, *The Christian Leader*, November 4, 1980, 17.
"The Language of Faith." Viewpoint, *The Christian Leader*, November 18, 1980, 13.
"Power and the Gospel." Viewpoint, *The Christian Leader*, December 2, 1980, 19.
"A Christmas Manifesto." Viewpoint, *The Christian Leader*, December 16, 1980, 19.
"Sorting Prayer Thoughts." Viewpoint, *The Christian Leader*, December 30, 1980, 16.

Book Reviews

Review of *Christian Life Patterns: The Psychological Challenges of Religious Invitations Of Adult Life* by Evelyn Eaton Whitehead & James D. Whitehead. *Provident Book Finder*, January-February 1980, 7.
Review of *Valleys and Vistas* by David Bogard. *Provident Book Finder*, March-April 1980, 5.
Review of *Mending: The Pain and Healing of a Widow's First Year* by Dorothy Hsu. *Provident Book Finder*, March-April 1980, 6.
Review of *Call the Darkness Light* by Nancy Zaroulis. *Provident Book Finder*, March-April 1980, 20.
Review of *Lydia* by Lois Henderson. *Provident Book Finder*, March-April 1980, 20.
Review of *River of Glass* by Wilfred Martens. *Provident Book Finder*, March-April 1980, 20.
Review of *The Russian Empire: A Portrait in Photographs* by Chloe Obolensky. *Provident Book Finder*, March-April 1980, 23.
Review of *The Two of Them* by Aliki. *Provident Book Finder*, March-April 1980, 31.
Review of *Signs of Spring* by Laurel Lee. *Provident Book Finder*, May-June 1980, 26-27.
Review of *River of Glass* by Wilfred Martens. *Direction* 9, no.3 (July 1980): 40.
Review of *The Far-Off Hills: An American Widow Discovers Modern India* by Rita Anton. *Provident Book Finder*, July-August 1980, 11.
Review of *Triumphs of the Imagination* by Leland Ryken. *Provident Book Finder*, September-October 1980, 23.

Review of *The Siberian Seven* by John Pollock. *Provident Book Finder*, November-December 1980, 11.
Review of *Abigail* by Lois T. Henderson. *Provident Book Finder*, November-December 1980, 11.

Presentations
Workshop leader, Third Annual Writer's Conference, People's Place, Intercourse, Pennsylvania, January 18-19, 1980.
"Have You Got the Key?" Mennonite Brethren Workshop for Writers, Clearbrook, B.C., March 21-22, 1980.
"Getting the Right Start." Mennonite Brethren Workshop for Writers, Clearbrook, B.C., March 21-22, 1980.
"How to Write Your Memoirs at Any Age," Mennonite Brethren Workshop for Writers, Clearbrook, B.C., March 21-22, 1980.
"Contribution of the Past." Annual meeting of the Laurelville Church Centre, Laurelville, Pennsylvania, July 1980.

1981

Books
Second Thoughts. Hillsboro: Kindred Press, 1981.

Articles and Columns
"The New Year Too Will Need Prayer." The Last Word, *Mennonite Brethren Herald*, January 2, 1981, 32.
"Prayer: a Difficult Assignment." *Gospel Herald*, January 20, 1981, 36-37.
"Why *The Mennonites* Have a Double Set!" Reclassified, *Festival Quarterly*, February/March/April, 1981, 46.
"Out on the Street." *Gospel Herald*, February 17, 1981, 136.
"Here Is My Place." *The Christian Leader*, February 24, 1981, 2-4.
"Focus on Mentoring for and by Women." *MCC Peace Section Task Force on Women in Church and Society Report*, March-April 1981, 1-3.
"The Awakening." *Gospel Herald*, April 7, 1981, 263.
"Mennonite Women Seek Wholeness in Ministry." *The Christian Leader*, April 21, 1981, 18-19.
"Sharing Death." *Gospel Herald*, April 28, 1981, 338.
"Barriers That Are Not Real." *MCC Peace Section Task Force on Women in Church and Society Report*, May-June 1981, 9-10.
"Burkholder and Simons in Trouble." Reclassified, *Festival Quarterly*, May/June/July, 1981, 42.
"The Power and the Glory." *Christian Reader*, May/June 1981.
"Join Me On the Rack." *With*, June 1981, 4-7.

"These Too Belong to the Body." *Gospel Herald*, June 23, 1981, 497-499.
"Toward a Pause that Refreshes." *The Christian Leader*, June 30, 1981, 8-9.
"The Splendor of Growing Older." *Today's Christian Woman*, Summer 1981, 78-81.
"My Fill of Bread." *World Vision*, July 1981, 14.
"Thoughts for Beggars' Day." *Gospel Herald*, July 7, 1981, 535.
"The Mennonite Look and Label." Reclassified, *Festival Quarterly*, August/September/October 1981, 38.
"The Christian Thinker." *Gospel Herald*, August 4, 1981, 599.
"Is Winning Everything?" The Last Word, *Mennonite Brethren Herald*, August 7, 1981, 32.
"These, Too, Belong to the Body." *The Christian Leader*, August 11, 1981, 2-5.
"A Matter of Integrity." *Gospel Herald*, August 18, 1981, 630.
"A Sane Approach Deciding What to Read." *Today's Christian Woman*, Fall, 1981, 43.
"When Will I Ever Grow Up?" *Today's Christian Woman*, Fall 1981, 78-81.
"Mennonite Brethren Women: Images and Realities of the Early Years." *Mennonite Life* 36, no.3 (September 1981): 22-28.
"Why Is This Service Different?" *With*, October 1981, 14-16.
"Shouldn't I Know You?" Reclassified, *Festival Quarterly*, November/December 1981, January 1982, 32.
"The Moral Miracle." *Gospel Herald*, November 17, 1981, 851.
"I Ate My Way to Emptiness." *The Lutheran*, November 18, 1981, 15.
"Give the Ax to Secular Humanism." *Gospel Herald*, November 24, 1981, 878.

Viewpoint

"Lessons in Parking." Viewpoint, *The Christian Leader*, January 13, 1981, 16.
"Out on the Street." Viewpoint, *The Christian Leader*, January 27, 1981, 20.
"Plan A or Plan B." Viewpoint, *The Christian Leader*, February 10, 1981, 19.
"The Awakening." Viewpoint, *The Christian Leader*, February 24, 1981, 19.
"Sharing Death." Viewpoint, *The Christian Leader*, March 10, 1981, 15.
"Your Humble Servant." Viewpoint, *The Christian Leader*, March 24, 1981, 19.
"The State of Senility." Viewpoint, *The Christian Leader*, April 7, 1981, 19.
"The Other Women's Movement." Viewpoint, *The Christian Leader*, May 5, 1981, 19.
"Tell Me the Old, Old Story." Viewpoint, *The Christian Leader*, May 19, 1981, 17.
"The Gift of Presence." Viewpoint, *The Christian Leader*, June 2, 1981, 20.
"Thoughts for Beggars Day." Viewpoint, *The Christian Leader*, June 16, 1981, 19.
"The Christian Intellectual." Viewpoint, *The Christian Leader*, June 30, 1981, 19.
"A Matter of Integrity." Viewpoint, *The Christian Leader*, July 28, 1981, 17.
"A New Set of Elders." Viewpoint, *The Christian Leader*, August 11, 1981, 17.

"A Happiness Collection." Viewpoint, *The Christian Leader*, August 25, 1981, 19.
"The Enemy Within." Viewpoint, *The Christian Leader*, September 8, 1981, 19.
"Answers without Questions." Viewpoint, *The Christian Leader*, September 22, 1981, 19.
"The Moral Miracle." Viewpoint, *The Christian Leader*, October 6, 1981, 17.
"The Achievement of Death." Viewpoint, *The Christian Leader*, October 20, 1981, 19.
"Let's Celebrate." Viewpoint, *The Christian Leader*, November 3, 1981, 19.
"The Professional Christian." Viewpoint, *The Christian Leader*, November 17, 1981, 19.
"The Adult Learners." Viewpoint, *The Christian Leader*, December 1, 1981, 17.
"The Gift of a Story." Viewpoint, *The Christian Leader*, December 15, 1981, 13.
"Warped Wood." Viewpoint, *The Christian Leader*, December 29, 1981, 21.

Book Reviews
Review of *Living More with Less* by Doris Janzen Longacre. *The Christian Leader*, January 27, 1981, 13.
Review of *The Sweetheart of the Silent Majority* by Carol Felsenthal. *Today's Christian Woman*, Winter 1981-82, 119-120.
Review of *Beyond Loneliness,* by Elizabeth Skoglund. *Provident Book Finder*, January-February 1981, 5.
Review of *The Best of Elton Trueblood* edited by James R. Newby. *Provident Book Finder*, January-February 1981, 14.
Review of *The Battered Woman* by Lenore E. Walker. *Provident Book Finder*, January-February 1981, 20.
Review of *Death on an Island* by Gayle G. Roper , David C. Cook. *Provident Book Finder*, March-April 1981, 5.
Review of *Holy Company: Christian Heroes and Heroines* by Elliott Wright. *Provident Book Finder*, May-June 1981, 32.
Review of *Lincoln's Mothers: A Story of Nancy and Sally Lincoln* by Dorothy Clarke Wilson. *Provident Book Finder*, July-August 1981, 10.
Review of *Understanding Watchman Wee* by Dana Roberts and *Meet Brother Nee* by James Chen. *Provident Book Finder*, July-August 1981, 13.
Review of *Women, Change, and the Church* edited by Nancy Van Scoyoc and Ezra Earl Jones. *Provident Book Finder*, July-August 1981, 35.
Review of *The Treasury of Clean Jokes* by Tal D. Bonham. *Provident Book Finder*, September-October 1981, 3.
Review of *Writing That Works* by Kenneth Roman & Joel Raphaelson. *Provident Book Finder*, September-October 1981, 5.
Review of *A Woman's Quest for Serenity* by Gigi Tchividjian. Fleming H. Revell. *Provident Book Finder*, September-October 1981, 7.

Review of *The Sweetheart of the Silent Majority: Biography of Phyllis Schafly* by Carol Felsenthal. *Provident Book Finder*, September-October 1981, 8.
Review of *Winterflight: A Novel* by Joseph Bayly. *Provident Book Finder*, November-December 1981, 26.

Presentations
"Good Times with Old Times." Kansas Library Association, Wichita, Kansas, March 27, 1981.
"The Seasons of a Woman's Life." "What Early MB Women Teach Us About Life's Priorities," WMS of Ontario MB Churches, Vineland, Ontario, April 14, 1981.
"Mennonite Brethren Women: Images and Realities." The Mennonite Brethren Historical Society of the West Coast, Fresno, California, May 3, 1981.
"How We Welcome Secularism into Our Churches and Homes." Manitoba Sunday School Convention of Mennonite Churches, Assiniboine Camp, Manitoba, October 24, 1981.
"Making Adult Education Adult." Manitoba Sunday School Convention of Mennonite Churches, Morden, Manitoba, October 24-30, 1981.

1982

Articles and Columns
"Why Was It So Hard to Believe?" (with Christine R. Wiebe) *With*, January 1982, 32-37.
"The Professional Christian." The Last Word, *Mennonite Brethren Herald*, January 15, 1982, 32.
"The Professional Christian." *Gospel Herald*, January 19, 1982, 38.
"Looking Down the Edge." *Gospel Herald*, January 26, 1982, 54.
"'Business is Business.'" Reclassified, *Festival Quarterly*, February/March/April, 1982, 34.
"Where are the Heros?" *Gospel Herald*, March 2, 1982, 147.
"How to Start a Civil War." *Gospel Herald*, March 16, 1982, 179.
"The Battle for Better Health." *Gospel Herald*, April 13, 1982, 254.
"Preacher Season." Reclassified, *Festival Quarterly*, May/June/July, 1982, 34.
"Power for the People." *Gospel Herald*, May 25, 1982, 361.
"How Do Mennonites Spell Relief?" *With*, June 1982, 13-16.
"Mary: Woman Favored by God." *Rejoice!* June/July/August 1982, 8-11.
"Zaccheaus: Oppressor Liberated." *Rejoice!* June/July/August 1982, 12-15.
"Seekers of Power." *Rejoice!* June/July/August 1982, 16-19.
"Judas: A Friend Who Betrayed." *Rejoice!* June/July/August 1982, 20-23.
"No Longer a Widow." *Today's Christian Woman*, Summer 1982, 97-99.
"Making the Most of Vacations." *Christian Living*, July 1982, 16-19.

"*The Mennonite* Patina." Reclassified, *Festival Quarterly*, August/September/ October 1982, 34.
"The Mennonite Female Diakonate." *Gospel Herald*, August 24, 1982, 571.
"The Style of Low German Folklore." *Journal of the American Historical Society of Germans from Russia* 5, no.3 (Fall 1982): 45-52.
"What Do You Believe?" *Today's Christian Woman*, Fall 1982, 104-107.
"Special Interest Conventions." *Gospel Herald*, September 28, 1982, 656.
"Sometimes I Wonder" (with Christine R. Wiebe). *With*, October 1982, 17-19.
"Widowhood Twenty Years Later." *Gospel Herald*, October 26, 1982, 730.
"More Foibles." Reclassified, *Festival Quarterly*, November/December 1982, January 1983, 34.
"The Empty Center." *Gospel Herald*, November 2, 1982, 748.
"What I Don't Want For Christmas." *Live*, December 5, 1982, 3-4.
"No Longer a Sin." *Gospel Herald*, December 28, 1982, 890.

Viewpoint

"Two Decades of Deadlines." Viewpoint, *The Christian Leader*, January 26, 1982, 15.
"A Hen's Pace." Viewpoint, *The Christian Leader*, February 9, 1982, 21.
"How to Start a Civil War." Viewpoint, *The Christian Leader*, February 23, 1982, 19.
"Battling for Better Health." Viewpoint, *The Christian Leader*, March 9, 1982, 23.
"Servants of Healing." Viewpoint, *The Christian Leader*, March 23, 1982, 19.
"The Mennonite Female Diaconate." Viewpoint, *The Christian Leader*, April 6, 1982, 16.
"Another Kind of Divorce." Viewpoint, *The Christian Leader*, April 20, 1982, 16.
"People Power." Viewpoint, *The Christian Leader*, May 4, 1982, 20.
"Honoring Parents." Viewpoint, *The Christian Leader*, May 18, 1982, 17.
"A Summer Quiz." Viewpoint, *The Christian Leader*, June 1, 1982, 15.
"Choosing a Covering." Viewpoint, *The Christian Leader*, June 29, 1982, 19.
"Lord I'm Listening." Viewpoint, *The Christian Leader*, July 27, 1982, 19.
"Of Special Interests." Viewpoint, *The Christian Leader*, August 24, 1982, 15.
"The Empty Center." Viewpoint, *The Christian Leader*, September 7, 1982, 18.
"Come and Go." Viewpoint, *The Christian Leader*, September 21, 1982, 17.
"Twenty Years Later." Viewpoint, *The Christian Leader*, October 5, 1982, 19.
"To Burn a Book." Viewpoint, *The Christian Leader*, October 19, 1982, 18.
"For Adults Too." Viewpoint, *The Christian Leader*, November 2, 1982, 19.
"No Longer a Sin." Viewpoint, *The Christian Leader*, November 16, 1982, 13.
"A Language Lesson." Viewpoint, *The Christian Leader*, November 30, 1982, 20.
"Advent Miracles." Viewpoint, *The Christian Leader*, December 14, 1982, 17.
"Ethics of Violence." Viewpoint, *The Christian Leader*, December 28, 1982, 15.

Book Reviews

Review of *Strengthening the Adult Sunday School Class* by David Murray. *Provident Book Finder*, January-February 1982, 15.

Review of *Katie* by Margaret Graham. *Provident Book Finder*, January-February 1982, 20.

Review of *Practicing the Presence of the Spirit* by Myron S. Augsburger. *Provident Book Finder*, March-April 1982, 7.

Review of *The Earth Is One Body* by David Waltner-Toews. *Provident Book Finder*, March-April 1982, 11.

Review of *A Merry-Mouse Book of Favorite Poems* selected and illustrated by Priscilla Hillman. *Provident Book Finder*, March-April 1982, 12.

Review of *Christian Women at Work* by Patricia Ward & Martha Stout. *Provident Book Finder*, March-April 1982, 16

Review of *The Complete Woman: Living Beyond Total Womanhood* by Patricia Gundry. *Provident Book Finder*, May-June 1982, 8.

Review of *The Language of Canaan and the Grammar of Feminism* by Vernard Eller. *Festival Quarterly*, May/June/July, 1982, 24.

Review of *Living Without Salt* by Karin B. Baltzell & Terry M. Parsley. *Provident Book Finder*, July-August 1982, 14.

Review of *Letters to Barbara* by Glenn Meeter. *Provident Book Finder*, September-October 1982, 8.

Review of *My Family Tree Workbook: Genealogy for Beginners* by Rosemary A. Chorzempa. *Provident Book Finder*, September-October 1982, 25.

Review of *Prayers in Later Life* by Rita F. Snowden. *Provident Book Finder*, November-December 1982, 12.

Review of *Effective Body Building* by C. Peter Wagner. *Provident Book Finder*, November-December 1982, 21.

Presentations

"Servanthood and Creativity." Bible Conference of the Mennonite Church, Lombard, Illinois, March 19-20, 1982.

"Mennonite Humour." Sideboard, Elkart, Indiana, May 2, 1982.

"The Style of Low German Folklore." 13th International Convention, American Historical Society of Germans from Russia, Wichita, Kansas, August 3-8, 1982.

"The Style of Low German Folklore." Annual Convention of the American Historical Society of Germans from Russia, August 6, 1982.

"Teacher, How Many Words Do I Need For Tomorrow's Essay?" LARK Banquet for Hesston College, Hesston College, Kansas August 27, 1982.

"What Doth God Require of Your?" "Limiting God Through Immaturity," Pen-Mar WMSC Retreat, Hagerstown, Maryland, Fall, 1982.

"Making Christ Lord of a Caring Ministry." "Discipleship Begins Where You Are,"WMSC annual Inspirational Meeting, Mennonite Church of Normal, Illinois, October 2, 1982.

1983

Book Sections

"Alternative Systems of Health Care Available to the Consumer." In *Ethical and Stewardship Dimensions of Rising Health Care Costs*, 116-128. Goshen: Mennonite Mental Health Association; Mennonite Medical Association; Mennonite Mutual Aid, 1983.

"Old Testament Personalities: Lessons 1-13." *Adult Bible Study Guide*, edited by Laurence Martin, 2-79. Scottdale: Mennonite Publishing House, 1983.

Articles and Columns

"The Ethics of Violence." *Gospel Herald*, January 18, 1983, 35.
"The Giant Waiting at the Door." *The Christian Leader*, January 25, 1983, 6-8.
"Uh-Oh." Reclassified, *Festival Quarterly*, February/March/April, 1983, 34.
"Peacemaker Language." *Gospel Herald*, February 1, 1983, 75.
"Why Shouldn't I Look and Think my Age?" *Christian Living*, March/April, 1983, 17-19.
"Plant More Tomatoes than You'll Need." *Christian Living*, March/April, 1983, 40-42.
"In a Coupled Society." *Gospel Herald*, April 26, 1983, 291.
"Making Our Way..." Reclassified, *Festival Quarterly*, May/June/July, 1983, 25.
"Katie Funk Wiebe Responds." Letters, *Festival Quarterly*, May/June/July, 1983, 35.
"Why People Don't Read." *Gospel Herald*, June 21, 1983, 427.
"Ten Years Later: Katie Funk Wiebe." *MCC Committee on Women's Concerns Report*, July-August, 1983, 5-6.
"The Importance of the Private Sphere." *Mennonite Brethren Herald*, July 29, 1983, 32.
"Finding Our Own Folklore." Reclassified, *Festival Quarterly*, August/September/October 1983, 31.
"Low German: The Language of the True Believer!" *Festival Quarterly*, August/September/October 1983, 12-14.
"Choosing a Women's Organization." *Today's Christian Women*, Fall 1983, 94.
"Give Us the Dream." *Gospel Herald*, October 11, 1983, 699.
"Yea, Mennonites, Still the Best?" Reclassified, *Festival Quarterly*, November/December 1983, January 1984, 34.
"I Wish I Knew." *Gospel Herald*, November 1, 1983, 755.
"A Good Mennonite." *Mennonite Brethren Herald*, November 4, 1983, 36.

"Widowhood Is Not a Lifelong Sentence." *Christian Living*, December 1983, 8-10.
"Learning New Tricks." *Gospel Herald*, December 27, 1983, 895.

Viewpoint
"Peacekeeper Talk." Viewpoint, *The Christian Leader*, January 25, 1983, 20.
"The Real News." Viewpoint, *The Christian Leader*, February 22, 1983, 20.
"The Wondrous Cross." Viewpoint, *The Christian Leader*, March 8, 1983, 17.
"A Call for All." Viewpoint, *The Christian Leader*, March 22, 1983, 20.
"Crime of Violence." Viewpoint, *The Christian Leader*, April 5, 1983, 21.
"Secular Clergy." Viewpoint, *The Christian Leader*, April 26, 1983, 15.
"Are There Answers?" Viewpoint, *The Christian Leader*, May 17, 1983, 18.
"Minority Activity." Viewpoint, *The Christian Leader*, June 7, 1983, 18.
"Woman's View." Viewpoint, *The Christian Leader*, July 12, 1983, 17.
"Church at Risk." Viewpoint, *The Christian Leader*, August 16, 1983, 17.
"Reunions: An Undeserved Place." Viewpoint, *The Christian Leader*, September 6, 1983, 19.
"Give Us the Dream." Viewpoint, *The Christian Leader*, September 20, 1983, 19.
"A Good Mennonite." Viewpoint, *The Christian Leader*, October 4, 1983, 20.
"I Wish I Knew." Viewpoint, *The Christian Leader*, October 18, 1983, 18.
"The Little Engine that Could." Viewpoint, *The Christian Leader*, November 1, 1983, 20.
"Power Isn't Power." Viewpoint, *The Christian Leader*, November 15, 1983, 19.
"Another Guilt Trip." Viewpoint, *The Christian Leader*, November 29, 1983, 15.
"After *The Day After*." Viewpoint, *The Christian Leader*, December 13, 1983, 17.
"Holiday Cheer." Viewpoint, *The Christian Leader*, December 27, 1983, 13.

Book Reviews
Review of *Is the Bible Sexist?* by Donald G. Bloesch. *Provident Book Finder*, January-February 1983, 32.
Review of *Making Things Happen: Guide for Members of Volunteer Organizations* by Joan Wolfe. *Provident Book Finder*, March-April 1983, 4.
Review of *Space* by James A. Michener. *Provident Book Finder*, May-June 1983, 13.
Review of *Walking With Loneliness* by Paula Ripple. *Provident Book Finder*, May-June 1983, 16.
Review of *The Religion of Power* by Cheryl Forbes. *Provident Book Finder*, May-June 1983, 28.
Review of *The New Book of Christian Quotations* compiled by Tony Castle. *Provident Book Finder*, September-October 1983, 3.
Review of *Mennonite Women: A Story of God's Faithfulness* by Elaine Sommers Rich. *The Christian Leader*, October 4, 1983, 17.

Review of *The Language of Canaan and the Grammar of Feminism* by Vernard Eller. *The Other Side*, November 1983, 28, 30-31.
Review of *Is the Bible Sexist?* by Donald G. Bloesch. *The Other Side*, November 1983, 28, 30-31.
Review of *Reformation: A Picture Story of Martin Luther* by Dietrich Steinwede. *Provident Book Finder*, November-December 1983, 3.
Review of *Laughing Out Loud and Other Religious Experiences* by Tom Mullen. *Provident Book Finder*, November-December 1983, 7.

Presentations
Keynote speaker, Christian Writers' Conference, Steinbach Bible College, Steinbach, Manitoba, February 25-26, 1983.
"Alternative Health-Care Systems." Mennonite Health Association Subcommittee on Rising Health Care Costs, Laurelville Camp, Pennsylvania, July 1983.
"Nurturing into Body Life." Virginia Mennonite Conference. Harrisonburg, Virginia, July 15-16, 1983.

1984

Books
Who Are the Mennonite Brethren? Hillsboro: Kindred Press, 1984.

Articles and Columns
"Stories Pastors Tell." Reclassified, *Festival Quarterly*, Winter 1984, 42.
"The Mennonite Diaconte." *MCC Committee on Women's Concerns Report*, January-February 1984, 8-9.
"People of Promise." *Gospel Herald*, April 24, 1984, 287.
"Don't Give Me a J!" *Gospel Herald*, March 13, 1984, 183.
"Can 'Good' Mennonites Fail?" *Festival Quarterly*, Spring 1984, 12-13.
"Nothing is Forever." *Gospel Herald*, May 29, 1984, 379.
"Mennonites and the Wellness Revolution." *Gospel Herald*, June 12, 1984, 422.
"Mennonite Evaluation." Reclassified, *Festival Quarterly*, Summer 1984, 46.
"Achieving a New Identity: The Southern District Conference." *The Christian Leader*, July 24, 1984, 2-11.
"Achieving a New Identity: The Southern District Conference." *Mennonite Brethren Herald*, August 17, 1984, 2-7, 9-10.
"Planting in New Places." *Mennonite Brethren Herald*, August 17, 1984, 6.
"Ever Resourceful." Reclassified, *Festival Quarterly*, Fall 1984, 42.
"Ideas that Don't Fit." *Gospel Herald*, September 11, 1984, 639.
"The Big Birthday." *Gospel Herald*, October 9, 1984, 705.
"Keeping Peace in the Church." *Gospel Herald*, October 30, 1984, 751.

"Growth Beyond the Role." *Partnership Magazine*, November/December 1984, 26-29.
"How Many Words?" *Gospel Herald*, December 4, 1984, 847.

Viewpoint
"Awards Ceremony." Viewpoint, *The Christian Leader*, January 24, 1984, 19.
"Don't Give me a J!" Viewpoint, *The Christian Leader*, February 7, 1984, 10.
"Receiving a Face." Viewpoint, *The Christian Leader*, February 21, 1984, 20.
"No Room for Cricket." Viewpoint, *The Christian Leader*, March 6, 1984, 19.
"Words or Bologna?" Viewpoint, *The Christian Leader*, March 20, 1984, 15.
"People of Promise." Viewpoint, *The Christian Leader*, April 3, 1984, 19.
"What Helps?" Viewpoint, *The Christian Leader*, April 17, 1984, 17.
"The Golden Age of Faith." Viewpoint, *The Christian Leader*, May 1, 1984, 20.
"Mennonite Wellness." Viewpoint, *The Christian Leader*, May 15, 1984, 18.
"Teaching Leadership." Viewpoint, *The Christian Leader*, May 29, 1984, 18.
"The Dog, the Gate." Viewpoint, *The Christian Leader*, June 26, 1984, 19.
"Cleaning the Closet." Viewpoint, *The Christian Leader*, July 24, 1984, 18.
"On the Road." Viewpoint, *The Christian Leader*, August 21, 1984, 18.
"My Friend Job." Viewpoint, *The Christian Leader*, September 4, 1984, 20.
"The Big One." Viewpoint, *The Christian Leader*, September 18, 1984, 18.
"Keeping Peace in the Church." Viewpoint, *The Christian Leader*, October 2, 1984, 21.
"Who Decides?" Viewpoint, *The Christian Leader*, October 16, 1984, 17.
"How Many Words?" Viewpoint, *The Christian Leader*, October 30, 1984, 17.
"Substitute Faith." Viewpoint, *The Christian Leader*, November 13, 1984, 20.
"Peace Begins With..." Viewpoint, *The Christian Leader*, November 27, 1984, 17.
"Getting into the Pit." Viewpoint, *The Christian Leader*, December 11, 1984, 20.
"What's in a Name?" Viewpoint, *The Christian Leader*, December 25, 1984, 15.

Book Reviews
Review of *My Lovely Enemy* by Rudy Wiebe. *Conrad Grebel Review* 2, no.1 (Winter 1984): 75-80.
Review of *Servant Leadership* by Robert K. Greenleaf. *Provident Book Finder*, January-February 1984, 15.
Review of *The Night and Nothing* by Gale D. Webbe. *Provident Book Finder*, March-April 1984, 6.
Review of *Moody, The Biography* by John Pollock. *Provident Book Finder*, September-October 1984, 2.
Review of *Anabaptist Portraits* by John Allen Moore. *Provident Book Finder*, September-October 1984, 28-29.

Presentations

"How Christian Literature Works." Choice Books, Sarasota, Florida, February 1984.

Creative Writing Workshop Leader, Butler County Community College, Eldorado, Kansas, October 26-27, 1984.

1985

Book Sections

"Studies in Esther and Job." *The Adult Quarterly*, 51, no.4 (June/July/August), 1-40. Hillsboro: Mennonite Brethren General Conference Board of Christian Education, 1985.

"The Image of Women in Mennonite Literature." In *Visions and Realities: Essays and Creative Literature Dealing with Mennonite Issues*, edited by Harry Loewen and Al Reimer, 231-242. Winnipeg: Hyperion Press, 1985.

"Foreward." In *And Then There Were Three* by Sara Wenger Shenk, 9-12. Scottdale: Herald Press, 1985.

Articles and Columns

"Peace Begins with…" *Gospel Herald*, January 1, 1985, 5.
"Getting into the Pit." *Gospel Herald*, January 8, 1985, 19.
"Churchspeak." *Gospel Herald*, February 5, 1985, 91.
"The Information Age." *Gospel Herald*, February 26, 1985, 139.
"Growth Beyond the Role." *Minister's Supplement to Pentecostal Record*, March 1985, 2-4.
"Substitute Faith." *Gospel Herald*, March 19, 1985, 196.
"Books are to be Read." *Gospel Herald*, March 26, 1985, 216.
"The Other Cheek." Reclassified, *Festival Quarterly*, Spring 1985, 38.
"Double Knit for the Sake of the Gospel." *Gospel Herald*, April 23, 1985, 286.
"Record Breakers." *Gospel Herald*, April 30, 1985, 304.
"Record Breakers." *Mennonite Brethren Herald*, May 3, 1985, 7-8.
"Faith in the Midst of Despair." *Rejoice!* June/July/August 1985, 44-47.
"God Will Not Forsake His Own." *Rejoice!* June/July/August 1985, 48-51.
"Judgment, Repentance, and Hope." *Rejoice* June/July/August 1985, 52-55.
"Prepared for God's Return." *Rejoice!* June/July/August 1985, 56-59.
"The Season of Narcissi." *Gospel Herald*, June 25, 1985, 445.
"How Do Mennonites Spell Relief?" *With*, July-August, 1985, 17-18, 23.
"Whose Wedding Is It?" *Gospel Herald*, August 13, 1985, 562.
"Menno Awards Ceremony." Reclassified, *Festival Quarterly*, Fall 1985, 38.
"Reversing the Sexual Revolution." *Gospel Herald*, November 12, 1985, 790.
"Someone I Wish I had Known." *Gospel Herald*, November 26, 1985, 832.

"Five Don'ts For the Religion Writer." *Interlit*, December 1985, 14-15.
"Moving On Up." *Gospel Herald*, December 31, 1985, 920.

Viewpoint
"Churchspeak." Viewpoint, *The Christian Leader,* January 22, 1985, 13.
"The Information Age." Viewpoint, *The Christian Leader*, February 5, 1985, 14.
"Books to Read." Viewpoint, *The Christian Leader*, February 19, 1985, 20.
"Dressed in Doubleknit." Viewpoint, *The Christian Leader*, March 5, 1985, 17.
"Survivors with God." Viewpoint, *The Christian Leader*, March 19, 1985, 20.
"Record Breakers." Viewpoint, *The Christian Leader*, April 2, 1985, 18.
"Harmony Without Any Bulges." Viewpoint, *The Christian Leader*, April 16, 1985, 20.
"The Season of Narcissi." Viewpoint, *The Christian Leader*, April 30, 1985, 15.
"To Delbert Wiens." Viewpoint, *The Christian Leader*, May 14, 1985, 13.
"Not a Pacifist." Viewpoint, *The Christian Leader*, May 28, 1985, 15.
"Whose Wedding is it Anyway?" Viewpoint, *The Christian Leader*, June 25, 1985, 17.
"Rocking Horse Winner." Viewpoint, *The Christian Leader*, July 23, 1985, 17.
"The Farm Crisis." Viewpoint, *The Christian Leader*, August 20, 1985, 16.
"Reversing the Sexual Revolution." Viewpoint, *The Christian Leader*, September 3, 1985, 5.
"What, Me a Theologian?" Viewpoint, *The Christian Leader*, September 17, 1985, 13.
"My Lake Wobegon." Viewpoint, *The Christian Leader*, October 1, 1985, 15.
"Someone I Wish I had Known." Viewpoint, *The Christian Leader*, October 15, 1985, 13.
"Restroom Musings." Viewpoint, *The Christian Leader*, October 29, 1985, 19.
"Moving On Up." Viewpoint, *The Christian Leader*, November 12, 1985, 12.
"Trends to Watch." Viewpoint, *The Christian Leader*, November 26, 1985, 15.
"Tipping over the Tub." Viewpoint, *The Christian Leader*, December 10, 1985, 13.
"Sleeping in the Backseat." Viewpoint, *The Christian Leader*, December 24, 1985, 5.

Book Reviews
Review of *The Brother* by Dorothy Clarke Wilson. *Provident Book Finder*, January-February 1985, 24.
Review of *Stumbling Heavenward: The Extraordinary Life of an Ordinary Man*, by Peter Rempel. *Mennonite Life* 40, no.1 (March 1985): 30.
Review of *The Fire in Their Eyes, Spiritual Mentors for the Christian Life* by Gregory Michael Smith. *Provident Book Finder*, March-April 1985, 11.

Review of *A Widening Light: Poems of the Incarnation* by Luci Shaw. *Provident BookFinder*, March-April 1985, 23.
Review of *When the Aardvark Parked on the Ark* by Calvin Miller. *Provident Book Finder*, March-April 1985, 25.
Review of *Identity* by Ruth Tiffany Barnhouse. *Provident Book Finder*, March-April 1985, 27.
Review of *The God of Sarah, Rebekah, and Rachel* by Barbara Keener Shenk. *Provident Book Finder*, July-August 1985, 1.
Review of *Just Friends?* by Andre Bustanoby. *Provident Book Finder*, September-October 1985, 20.
Review of *Christian Women in a Troubled World* by Monika M. Hellwig. *Provident Book Finder*, September-October, 1985, 28.
Review of *Writing, Reading, and Rage* by Dorothy Fink Ungerleider. *Provident Book Finder*, September-October 1985, 31.

Presentations
"Mapmaking in New Country." Mennonite Biblical Seminaries. Elkhart, Indiana, May 30, 1985.
"Autobiographical Writing." St. Davids Christian Writers' Conference, St. Davids, Pennsylvania, June 16-21, 1985.

1986

Articles and Columns
"Tipping Over the Tub." *Gospel Herald*, February 11, 1986, 94.
"Ten Do's and Don'ts for Religious Writers." *Interlit*, March 1986.
"Family Rituals." *Gospel Herald*, March 4, 1986, 151.
"Twice-Told Tales." Reclassified, *Festival Quarterly*, Spring 1986, 39.
"On Being a Lady." *Gospel Herald*, April 22, 1986, 274.
"Quo Vadis, Church College." *Gospel Herald*, June 3, 1986, 384.
"A Case of Mistaken Identity." Reclassified, *Festival Quarterly*, Summer 1986, 38.
"The Mennonite Identity Crisis." *Gospel Herald*, July 8, 1986, 465.
"Making 'Dear Editor' A Calling." *Window to Mission*, August/September 1986, 5, 15.
"Feminine Gumption." Reclassified, *Festival Quarterly*, Fall 1986, 38.
"Can Faith and Economics Mix?" *Gospel Herald*, September 30, 1986, 664.
"For Grandparents Only: Giftwrap Your Memories." *Christian Reader*, November/December 1986.
"The Power of a Promise." *Gospel Herald*, November 18, 1986, 786.
"We Need Artists in the Church." *Gospel Herald*, December 30, 1986, 896.

Viewpoint

"Crossing Broken Bridges." Viewpoint, *The Christian Leader*, January 21, 1986, 15.

"Family Planning...for Survival." Viewpoint, *The Christian Leader*, February 3, 1986, 13.

"A Debt of Gratitude." Viewpoint, *The Christian Leader*, February 18, 1986, 17.

"The Age of Civility." Viewpoint, *The Christian Leader*, March 4, 1986, 13.

"This Gives Me Hope." Viewpoint, *The Christian Leader*, March 18, 1986, 13.

"On Being a Lady." Viewpoint, *The Christian Leader*, April 1, 1986, 13.

"The Rationalization of Racism." Viewpoint, *The Christian Leader*, April 15, 1986, 15.

"Honor Your Parents." Viewpoint, *The Christian Leader*, April 29, 1986, 5.

"Quo Vadis, Church College?" Viewpoint, *The Christian Leader*, May 13, 1986, 13.

"To You, My Father." Viewpoint, *The Christian Leader*, May 27, 1986, 13.

"The Mennonite Identity Crisis." Viewpoint, *The Christian Leader*, June 24, 1986, 18.

"A Change of Symbols." Viewpoint, *The Christian Leader*, July 22, 1986, 14.

"The Search for Renewal." Viewpoint, *The Christian Leader*, August 19, 1986, 16.

"Thoughts on Labor Day." Viewpoint, *The Christian Leader*, September 2, 1986, 14.

"Can Faith and Economics Mix?" Viewpoint, *The Christian Leader*, September 16, 1986, 13.

"The Right to Speak." Viewpoint, *The Christian Leader*, September 30, 1986, 11.

"The Power of a Promise." Viewpoint, *The Christian Leader*, October 14, 1986, 13.

"A Cloud Bigger Than a Hand." Viewpoint, *The Christian Leader*, October 28, 1986, 15.

"Agreement About Article 15." Viewpoint, *The Christian Leader*, November 11, 1986, 15.

"We Need Artists in the Church." Viewpoint, *The Christian Leader*, November 25, 1986, 13.

"A Lifetime Family Membership." Viewpoint, *The Christian Leader*, December 9, 1986, 13.

"Becoming More Accountable." Viewpoint, *The Christian Leader*, December 23, 1986, 15.

Book Reviews

Review of *Come & Celebrate* by Rev. Hilliard & Beverly Valenti-Hilliard. *Provident Book Finder*, March-April 1986, 3.

Review of *Weeping in Ramah* by J. R. Lucas. *Provident Book Finder*, March-April 1986, 16.

Review of *Steady in an Unsteady World* by Leslie Weatherhead. *Provident Book Finder*, August-September 1986, 6.
Review of *Hillsboro Kansas: The City on the Prairie*. *Mennonite Life* 41, no.3 (September 1986): 30.
Review of *The Legend of the Brotherstone* by Calvin Miller. *Provident Book Finder*, October-December 1986, 7.
Review of *Sighing for Eden* by William H. Willimon. *Provident Book Finder*, October-December, 1986, 27.

Presentations
"Stories I've Never Published." Ninth Annual Writers Conference, People's Place, Intercourse, Pennsylvania, March 7-8, 1986.
"Aspects of Widowhood." Seminar for Widows, Church of the Saviour, Wayne, Pennsylvania, March 22, 1986.
"New Beginnings." Seminar for Widows, Church of the Saviour, Wayne, Pennsylvania, March 22, 1986.
"Journal Keeping and Personal Growth." United States Conference of Mennonite Brethren Churches Conference Convention, Colorado Springs, Colorado, August 5-6, 1986.
"2001: Religious Writing For An Information Age." West Coast Mennonite Writers Conference, Salem, Oregon, October, 17-19, 1986.
"Creativity: Chore or Challenge." West Coast Mennonite Writers' Workshop, Salem, Oregon, October 17-19, 1986.
"Getting the Beginner Started as a Free-lancer." West Coast Mennonite Writers' Workshop, Salem, Oregon, October 17-19, 1986.
"Rhetoric 2001: Role of the Religious Writer in the Information Age." West Coast Mennonite Writers' Workshop, Salem, Oregon, October 17-19, 1986.
"In But Still Out: The New Mennonite Brethren." "Dynamics of Faith and Culture in Mennonite Brethren," Centre for Mennonite Brethren Studies, Winnipeg, Manitoba, November 14-15, 1986.

1987

Books
Alone: A Search for Joy. Winnipeg: Kindred Press, 1987. (Re-issue)

Book Sections
"Ecclesiastes, Song of Solomon and Selected Psalms." *The Adult Quarterly*, 53, no.4 (June/July/August), 1-56. Hillsboro: Mennonite Brethren General Conference Board of Christian Education, 1987.

316 | The Voice of a Writer

Film Script
"Seed Time After Harvest." Winnipeg: David Dueck Film Productions, 1987.

Articles and Columns
"Personal Growth Through Journaling." *The Christian Leader*, January 20, 1987, 7-9.
"Why Isn't It the Thing to Do?" *Gospel Herald*, February 10, 1987, 94.
"The Great Escape: Blessing or Blight?" *The Marketplace*, March/April 1987, 4-9.
"Condemned But Not Guilty." *Rejoice!* March/April/May 1987, 24-27.
"Death on the Cross." *Rejoice!* March/April/May 1987, 28-31.
"Raised from the Dead." *Rejoice!* March/April/May 1987, 32-35.
"Before the Council." *Rejoice* March/April/May 1987, 36-39.
"As Others See Us." Reclassified, *Festival Quarterly*, Spring 1987, 46.
"The Meaning of Lent." *Gospel Herald*, April 7, 1987, 238.
"Overseas Getaways—Boon or Bust?" *The Christian Leader*, May 26, 1987, 8-11
"A Peoplehood Celebration." *Gospel Herald*, June 16, 1987, 436-437.
"The Ubiquitous MCC Quilt." Reclassified, *Festival Quarterly*, Summer 1987, 38.
"The Great Escape: Blessing or Blight?" *Christian Living*, July 1987, 22-25.
"Twenty-five Years Later." *MCC Women's Concerns Report*, July-August 1987, 8-9.
"Deciding Ethics Together." *The Christian Leader*, August 18, 1987, 11-14.
"Where is the Church in Summer?" *Gospel Herald*, August 18, 1987, 591.
"Mr. Swartz and Mr. Druber." Reclassified, *Festival Quarterly*, Fall 1987, 38.
"Does Our Language Affect Our Behavior." *Gospel Herald*, October 20, 1987, 734.
"A Pig for a Pig: A Story of Life and Death." *The Christian Leader*, December 22, 1987, 7-9.

Viewpoint
"Can a Hog Wedding Have Any Value?" Viewpoint, *The Christian Leader*, January 20, 1987, 15.
"Why Isn't It the Thing to Do?" Viewpoint, *The Christian Leader*, February 3, 1987, 13.
"Sufficient Reasons to Begin a SPCBP." Viewpoint, *The Christian Leader*, February 17, 1987, 11.
"Letting Go of Our Oral Law." Viewpoint, *The Christian Leader*, March 3, 1987, 14.
"Do We Need a New Calendar?" Viewpoint, *The Christian Leader*, March 17, 1987, 17.
"Telling the Resurrection Story." Viewpoint, *The Christian Leader*, March 31, 1987, 17.
"What's in a Name?" Viewpoint, *The Christian Leader*, April 14, 1987, 19.

"MCC Sale: A Peoplehood Celebration." Viewpoint, *The Christian Leader*, April 28, 1987, 13.
"Let Yourself be Dissatisfied." Viewpoint, *The Christian Leader*, May 12, 1987, 17.
"Can Men and Women be Friends?" Viewpoint, *The Christian Leader*, May 26, 1987, 14.
"Are Riches a Sign of Right Living?" Viewpoint, *The Christian Leader*, June 23, 1987, 18.
"The Ripening of the Congregation." Viewpoint, *The Christian Leader*, July 21, 1987, 14.
"Where is the Church in Summer?" Viewpoint, *The Christian Leader*, August 18, 1987, 21.
"The Trauma of Self-identity." Viewpoint, *The Christian Leader*, September 1, 1987, 17.
"Too Good to Throw Away." Viewpoint, *The Christian Leader*, September 15, 1987, 14.
"Does Our Language Affect Behavior?" Viewpoint, *The Christian Leader*, September 29, 1987, 14.
"The Year of the Homeless." Viewpoint, *The Christian Leader*, October 13, 1987, 15.
"A Case for Non-monogamy." Viewpoint, *The Christian Leader*, October 27, 1987, 15.
"A Veterans Day Tribute." Viewpoint, *The Christian Leader*, November 10, 1987, 12.
"Mennonite Women are Battered Too." Viewpoint, *The Christian Leader*, November 24, 1987, 14.
"The More We Eat Together." Viewpoint, *The Christian Leader*, December 8, 1987, 12.
"Spread the News—Reading is Not Outdated." Viewpoint, *The Christian Leader*, December 22, 1987, 10

Book Reviews
Review of *Bonded in Christ's Love* by Denise Lardner Carmody and John Tully Carmody. *Provident Book Finder*, March-May 1987, 29-30.
Review of *The Sourcebook For Women Who Create* by Gail Adams, Martha Miles, Linda Yoder. *Provident Book Finder*, March- May 1987, 34.
Review of *Who Said Women Can't Teach?* by Charley Trombley. *The Christian Leader*, May 26, 1987, 18-19.
Review of *Recording Your Family History* by William Fletcher. *Provident Book Finder*, September-October 1987, 19.
Review of *Vital Involvement In Old Age* by Erik Erikson, Joan M. Erikson, Helen Q. Kivnick. *Provident Book Finder*, September-October 1987, 19.

Review of *Household of Freedom* by Letty M. Russell. *Provident Book Finder,* September-October 1987, 31.
Review of *A People Apart: Ethnicity and the Mennonite Brethren* by John H. Redekop. *The Christian Leader,* September 15, 1987, 16-17.
Review of *By Birth Or By Choice: Who Can Become a Mennonite?* by Martha Denlinger Stahl. *The Christian Leader,* September 15, 1987, 16-17.
Review of *Dietrich Bonhoeffer, A Life in Pictures* by Eberhard Bethge, Renate Bethge, Christian Gremmels. *Provident Book Finder,* November-December 1987, 3.
Review of *Inventing the Truth* edited by William Zinsser. *Provident Book Finder,* November-December 1987, 38.

Presentations
"Daily Problems Need Daily Faith." Your Time Radio Broadcast of Mennonite Board of Missions, no. 454, August 1987.
"Risk to Grow." Your Time Radio Broadcast of Mennonite Board of Missions, no. 455, August 1987.
"Help For Your Dreams." Your Time Radio Broadcast of Mennonite Board of Missions, no. 457, August 1987.
"Growing Up After You've Grown Up." Your Time Radio Broadcast of Mennonite Board of Missions, no. 458, August 1987.
"The Glory of the Church Is Love." 57th Session General Conference of Mennonite Brethren Churches of North America, Abbotsford, B.C., August 7-11,1987.
"Response to David Schroeder's Paper, 'Women in Biblical Perspective.'" Mennonite Central Committee (Canada), Special Meeting, September 11, 1987.
"The Bent Woman." Free in Christ Women's Weekend, Columbia Bible Camp, Lindell Beach, B.C., October 23-25, 1987.
"The Displaced Homemaker." Free in Christ Women's Weekend, Columbia Bible Camp, Lindell Beach, B.C., October 23-25, 1987.
"The Anointing Woman." Free in Christ Women's Weekend, Columbia Bible Camp, Lindell Beach, B.C., October 23-25, 1987.
"The Negligent Hostess." Free in Christ Women's Weekend, Columbia Bible Camp, Lindell Beach, B.C., October 23-25, 1987.
"Pilgrimage and Poverty." MCC Ontario Annual Meeting, Markham, Ontario, November 20-21, 1987.

1988

Books
Bless Me Too, My Father. Scottdale: Herald Press, 1988.

Book Sections

"A Tale of Seduction." In *Why I Am A Mennonite: Essays on Mennonite Identity*, edited by Harry Loewen, 324-336. Scottdale: Herald Press, 1988.

"Why I Went to Work When I Was Working." In *Who Am I? What Am I?: Searching for Meaning in Your Work*, edited by Calvin Redekop, 96-105. Grand Rapids: Academie Books, 1988.

Articles and Columns

"Mennonite Changes Wine to—?" Reclassified, *Festival Quarterly*, Winter 1988, 38.

"The More We Eat Together." *Gospel Herald*, January 5, 1988, 6.

"Non-monogamy." *Gospel Herald*, February 2, 1988, 78.

"How I Received Shoes: My Journey as a Communicator." *Mennonite Reporter*, February 29, 1988, 8, 11.

"Menno Appears in Mashed Potatoes." Reclassified, *Festival Quarterly*, Spring 1988, 38.

"When I Wear Purple with a Red Hat, You'll Know." *Gospel Herald*, August 2, 1988, 526.

"Ancient MCC Sale Discovered." Reclassified, *Festival Quarterly*, Fall 1988, 38.

"Is Art the Business of Business?" *The Marketplace*, September/October 1988, 4-8.

"Carrying Our Own Bomb." *Gospel Herald*, November 29, 1988, 826.

Viewpoint

"Going for the Gold." Viewpoint, *The Christian Leader*, January 19, 1988, 15.

"The Velcro Approach." Viewpoint, *The Christian Leader*, February 16, 1988, 17.

"How to Turn the Corner." Viewpoint, *The Christian Leader*, March 15, 1988, 23.

"Men and Women Among the Brethren." Viewpoint, *The Christian Leader*, March 29, 1988, 15.

"The Modern Whalebone Corselet." Viewpoint, *The Christian Leader*, April 12, 1988, 14.

"A Prayer for the Nation and the Church." Viewpoint, *The Christian Leader*, April 26, 1988, 14.

"How Long Since We've Felt Deeply." Viewpoint, *The Christian Leader*, May 10, 1988, 14.

"What Happened to the Unified Budget?" Viewpoint, *The Christian Leader*, May 24, 1988, 18.

"When I Wear Purple with a Red Hat…" Viewpoint, *The Christian Leader*, July 19, 1988, 16.

"Let the Glue Get Thick and Sticky." Viewpoint, *The Christian Leader*, August 16, 1988, 14.

"What I Learned at a Silent Meeting." Viewpoint, *The Christian Leader*, August 30 1988, 12.
"Is Less Still More?" Viewpoint, *The Christian Leader*, September 13, 1988, 12.
"Carrying Our Own Bomb." Viewpoint, *The Christian Leader*, September 27, 1988, 16.
"*Zwieback* Hospitality." Viewpoint, *The Christian Leader*, October 11, 1988, 14.
"Standing in Line for Soup." Viewpoint, *The Christian Leader*, October 25, 1988, 14.
"The Hole in the Picket Fence." Viewpoint, *The Christian Leader*, November 8, 1988, 13.
"Business—Mennonite Style." Viewpoint, *The Christian Leader*, November 22, 1988, 16.
"Love at the Bottom of the Stairs." Viewpoint, *The Christian Leader*, December 20, 1988, 13.

Book Reviews
Review of *The Man Who Was Different: Jesus' Encounters with Women* by Gien Karssen. *Provident Book Finder*, January-March 1988, 10.
Review of *Agatchen* by Peter G. Epp. *Mennonite Life* 43, no.1 (March 1988): 30.
Review of *Humor—God's Gift* by Tal D. Bonham. *Provident Book Finder*, April-May 1988, 5.
Review of *Leaving Home* by Garrison Keillor. *Provident Book Finder*, June-August 1988, 24-25.
Review of *A Cry Like a Bell* by Madeleine L'Engle. *Provident Book Finder*, September-October 1988, 24.
Review of *Call Me Blessed The Emerging Christian Woman* by Faith Martin. *Provident Book Finder*, November-December 1988, 35.

Presentations
"How I Received Shoes: My Journey as a Communicator." Mennonite Publishing
Service, Edmonton, Alberta, February 20, 1988.

1989

Books
Alone: Through Widowhood and Beyond—A Search for Joy. London: Hodder and Stoughton, 1989. (British edition)

Book Sections
"A Real Live Death." In *Liars and Rascals: An Anthology of Mennonite Stories*, edited by Hildi Froese Tiessen, 42-53. Waterloo: University of Waterloo Press, 1989.

Articles

"Oil Paint or Latex?" Reclassified, *Festival Quarterly*, Winter/Spring 1989, 70.

"When I Wear Purple with a Red Hat." *Christian Reader*, January/February 1989, 47-48.

"Never Too Late to Change." *The Christian Leader*, January 31, 1989, 7-9.

"Making Sense of Sex." *Gospel Herald*, March 14, 1989, 182.

"Can the Church Survive the Professionalization of Its Leadership?" *The Mennonite*, March 27, 1990, 124-127.

"Can the Church Survive the Preaching of the Carbonated Gospel?" *The Mennonite*, April 10, 1990, 151-153.

"Yes, the Church Will Survive." *The Mennonite*, April 24, 1990, 174-176.

"The Growing Ministry Gap: Can the Church Survive the Professionalization of Its Leadership?" *The Christian Leader*, May 23, 1989, 8-10.

"Can the Church Survive the Professionalization of Its Leadership?" *Mennonite Brethren Herald*, May 26, 1989, 6-7.

"Can the Church Survive the Preaching of the 'Carbonated' Gospel?" *Mennonite Brethren Herald*, June 9, 1989, 10-11.

"Our 'Fizz' Generation: Can the Church Survive the Preaching of the Carbonated Gospel?" *The Christian Leader*, June 20, 1989, 7-9.

"Yes, the Church Will Survive." *Mennonite Brethren Herald*, June 23, 1989, 10-11.

"At the MEDA Convention." Reclassified, *Festival Quarterly*, Summer 1989, 38.

"Can the Church Survive the Professionalization of Its Leadership?" *Gospel Herald*, July 4, 1989, 482-483.

"Can the Church Survive the Preaching of the Carbonated Gospel?" *Gospel Herald*, July 11, 1989, 501-503.

"A Basis for Hope: The Survival of the Church Rests in a Return to a Simple Trust in God." *The Christian Leader*, July 18, 1989, 14-18.

"Yes, the Church Will Survive." *Gospel Herald*, July 18, 1989, 516-518.

"Mennoorganism and Midianites." Reclassified, *Festival Quarterly*, Fall 1989, 38.

"Sermons I Remember." *Gospel Herald*, October 3, 1989, 702.

"Bless Me Too, My Father." *Christian Reader*, November/December, 1989, 66-81.

"Sex in the Workplace." *The Marketplace*, November/December 1989, 4-9.

Viewpoint

"The Man with the Patched Pants." Viewpoint, *The Christian Leader*, January 17, 1989, 12.

"Making Sense of Sex." Viewpoint, *The Christian Leader*, February 14, 1989, 12.

"A Servant in a Model T." Viewpoint, *The Christian Leader*, February 28, 1989, 13.

"Is Everyone Here Mennonite Brethren?" Viewpoint, *The Christian Leader*, March 14, 1989, 12.

"How Sweet It Is." Viewpoint, *The Christian Leader*, March 28, 1989, 12.
"Table Decorations." Viewpoint, *The Christian Leader*, April 11, 1989, 11.
"What is a Home?" Viewpoint, *The Christian Leader*, April 25, 1989, 13.
"The Price of Radical Faith." Viewpoint, *The Christian Leader*, May 9, 1989, 15.
"Sermons I Remember." Viewpoint, *The Christian Leader*, June 20, 1989, 14.
"Siberia, Land of Hope." Viewpoint, *The Christian Leader*, August 15, 1989, 12.
"Lowering the Fences." Viewpoint, *The Christian Leader*, August 29, 1989, 11.
"Excuses! Excuses! Excuses!" Viewpoint, *The Christian Leader*, September 12, 1989, 15.
"A Homework Assignment." Viewpoint, *The Christian Leader*, September 26, 1989, 11.
"Time for Purple with Red." Viewpoint, *The Christian Leader*, October 10, 1989, 15.
"Mennonite Brethren Annual Awards." Viewpoint, *The Christian Leader*, October 24, 1989, 10.
"Praise Day." Viewpoint, *The Christian Leader*, November 7, 1989, 9.
"TV is Here to Stay." Viewpoint, *The Christian Leader*, November 21, 1989, 3.
"God's Right Names." Viewpoint, *The Christian Leader*, December 6, 1989, 3.
"Who are Our Prophets?" Viewpoint, *The Christian Leader*, December 19, 1989, 3.

Book Reviews

Review of *Godspeed Hitching Home* by Laurel Lee. *Provident Book Finder,* January-February 1989, 2.
Review of *A Mennonite Odyssey* by Rhinehart Friesen. *Provident Book Finder,* January-February 1989, 3.
Review of *Women Take Care* by Tish Sommers and Laurie Shields. *Provident Book Finder,* March-April-May 1989, 9.
Review of *Just a Sister Away* by Renita J. Weems. *Provident Book Finder,* March-April-May 1989, 28.
Review of *To Life* by Ruth Minsky Sender. *Provident Book Finder,* March-April-May 1989, 30.
Review of *A Long Dry Season* by Omar Eby. *Mennonite Reporter*, May 1, 1989, 13.
Review of *Portraits of Healing, Prayers of Wholeness* by Jean Acheson. *Provident Book Finder,* November-December 1989, 4.

Presentations

"Go Ahead, Save the World, But Be Home by Supper." Fresno Pacific College, Fresno, California, May 6, 1989.
"The Back Forty, or the Ordinary Place." MCC Heartland Faith and Farming II Conference, McPherson, Kansas, November 18-20, 1989.

"The Home Place: A Place of Promise." MCC Heartland Faith and Farming II Conference, McPherson, Kansas, November 18-20, 1989.
"The Land, the People, and God: Gift or Grasp." MCC Heartland Faith and Farming II Conference, McPherson, Kansas, November 18-20, 1989.

1990

Book
Yksin. Hämeenlinna: Päivä Osakeyhtiö, 1990. (Finnish edition)

Book Sections
"A Real Live Death." In *Breaking Through: A Canadian Literary Mosaic*, edited by John Borovilos, 115-126. Scarborough: Prentice-Hall, 1990.
"Elizabeth Wiebe." In *The Mennonite Encyclopedia*, vol. 5, edited by Cornelius J. Dyck and Dennis D. Martin, 930. Scottdale: Herald Press, 1990
"Humour." In *The Mennonite Encyclopedia*, vol. 5, edited by Cornelius J. Dyck and Dennis D. Martin, 402-404. Scottdale: Herald Press, 1990.
"Janz, Benjamin B." In *The Mennonite Encyclopedia*, vol. 5, edited by Cornelius J. Dyck and Dennis D. Martin, 461-462. Scottdale, PA: Herald Press, 1990.
"Midwestern Midwife: Sara Block Eitzen." In *The Mennonite Encyclopedia*, vol. 5, edited by Cornelius J. Dyck and Dennis D. Martin, 267. Scottdale: Herald Press, 1990.
"Schellenberg, Katharina Lohrenz." In *The Mennonite Encyclopedia*, vol. 5, edited by Cornelius J. Dyck and Dennis D. Martin, 795. Scottdale: Herald Press, 1990.

Articles and Columns
"Soviet Humor? Da!." Reclassified, *Festival Quarterly*, Winter 1990, 38.
"The Glory of Purple with Red." *Gospel Herald*, January 9, 1990, 21.
"TV is Here to Stay." *Gospel Herald*, March 6, 1990, 165.
"Et Cetera, Et Cetera." Reclassified, *Festival Quarterly*, Spring 1990, 38.
"How I Received Shoes As a Communicator." *The Christian Leader*, April 24, 1990, 14-15.
"A Mennonite Camp Follower." *Gospel Herald*, May 22, 1990, 358.
"Devotional Guide." *WMSC Voice of The Mennonite Church*, July/August 1989-June 1990.
"Yes, Mother, We Had a Tornado." Reclassified, *Festival Quarterly*, Summer 1990, 38.
"Summer Remembrances." *Christian Reader*, July/August 1990, 57-58.
"Older, But Not Old." Reclassified, *Festival Quarterly*, Fall 1990, 38.
"Walking the Ridge Pole." *Gospel Herald*, October 9, 1990, 694.

"The Festival of Peace Needs Celebration." *Mennonite Brethren Herald*, Oct 12, 1990, 4-6.
"The New Immigrants to the Workplace." *The Marketplace*, November/December 1990, 12-16.
"I Have Seen the Face of God." *Mennonite Weekly Review*, December 13, 1990, 1-2.

Viewpoint

"Things Change, Things Stay the Same." Viewpoint, *The Christian Leader*, January 16, 1990, 11.
"The Year of the Dollar." Viewpoint, *The Christian Leader*, January 30, 1990, 15.
"Grace on Tuesdays and Thursdays." Viewpoint, *The Christian Leader*, February 13, 1990, 11.
"I'm Just Fine, Boy, How are You?" Viewpoint, *The Christian Leader*, February 27, 1990, 9.
"A Portrait of Love." Viewpoint, *The Christian Leader*, March 13, 1990, 11.
"At Least be a Mennonite Camp Follower." Viewpoint, *The Christian Leader*, April 10, 1990, 15.
"Waste as a Wrong." Viewpoint, *The Christian Leader*, May 8, 1990, 12.
"Standing at the Back Door." Viewpoint, *The Christian Leader*, June 19, 1990, 9.
"The Original Star Trekkers." Viewpoint, *The Christian Leader*, July 17, 1990, 12.
"Does Faith Mean Walking the Ridge Pole?" Viewpoint, *The Christian Leader*, July 31, 1990, 24.
"A Super-duper Conference." Viewpoint, *The Christian Leader*, August 28, 1990, 21.
"Life According to the Evening News." Viewpoint, *The Christian Leader*, September 11, 1990, 16.
"The Meeting Season." Viewpoint, *The Christian Leader*, September 25, 1990, 19.
"How About Using Plain Words." Viewpoint, *The Christian Leader*, October 9, 1990, 12.
"Forward Toward Greater Unity." Viewpoint, *The Christian Leader*, October 23, 1990, 24.
"Who Should Be Ordained?" Viewpoint, *The Christian Leader*, November 6, 1990, 15.
"Have a Good Day!" Viewpoint, *The Christian Leader*, November 20, 1990, 10.
"The Season of Exchanges." Viewpoint, *The Christian Leader*, December 4, 1990, 13.
"Watch Out: God is at Work." Viewpoint, *The Christian Leader*, December 18, 1990, 11.

Book Reviews

Review of *Letters from Susan* edited by John B. Toews. *Provident Book Finder*, January-February 1990, 28.

Review of *The Faces of Jesus* by Frederick Buechner. *Provident Book Finder*, March-April-May 1990, 7.

Review of *Under the Still Standing Sun* by Dora Dueck. *Direction* 19, no.1 (Spring 1990): 134-135.

Review of *Gender and Grace* by Mary Stewart Van Leeuwen. *Provident Book Finder*, November-December 1990, 34.

Review of *A Leap of Faith: True Stories for Young and Old* by Peter J. Dyck. *Mennonite Weekly Review*, December 27, 1990, 4.

Review of *War-Torn Valley* by Joyce Miller. *Mennonite Weekly Review*, December 27, 1990, 4.

Presentations

Women in Ministry Conference, Fresno, California, March 30-April 1, 1990.

"Writing a Family or Personal History." Climbing the Family Tree Workshop, Center for Mennonite Brethren Studies, Hillsboro, Kansas, April 5, 1990.

"No Deposit, No Return." Eastern Mennonite High School, Lancaster, Pennsylvania, May 1990.

"Creating a Life at Any Age." Senior Adult Week, Laurelville Church Center, Laurelville, Pennsylvania, August 26-31, 1990.

"Getting Started as a Writer." Mennonite Writers' Conference, Hesston, Kansas, September 21-23, 1990.

"Writing Devotionals." Mennonite Writers' Conference, Hesston, Kansas, September 21-23, 1990.

"Connecting Men and Women in the Business World." Northeast Ohio Mennonite Economic Development Associates and WMSC Business and Professional Women, Kidron, Ohio, October 20, 1990.

1991

Books

Und dann war ich allein: Wenn der Partner nicht mehr da ist. Translated by B. Selchert. Giessen/Basel: Brunnen Verlag, 1991. (German edition)

Book Sections

"Genesis." *Mennonite Brethren Bible Study Guide* 57, no.4 (June/July/August), 1-55. Winnipeg: Mennonite Brethren General Conference Board of Resource Ministries, 1991.

"When Faith Comes Under Fire." In *Weathering the Storm: Christian Pacifist Responses to War*, edited by Susan E. Janzen, 149-158. Newton: Faith & Life, 1991.

Unpublished Books
Growing Up in Blaine Lake by Five Who Did. Jack Funk, Katie Funk Wiebe et al. Wichita, 1991.
Neta Janzen Block's Story as told to Katie Funk Wiebe and written in letters. Wichita, 1991.

Articles and Columns
"Real Pacifists." Reclassified, *Festival Quarterly*, Winter 1991, 38.
"'The Understanding of Woman's Place among Mennonite Brethren in Canada: A
Question of Biblical Interpretation.' Katie Funk Wiebe responds to Gloria Neufeld Redekop." *Conrad Grebel Review* 9, no.1 (Winter 1991): 76-78.
"Another Look at Family Worship." *Mennonite Reporter*, March 4, 1991, 8.
"The Nonviolent Approach." Reclassified, *Festival Quarterly*, Spring 1991, 38.
"Give Us the Courage to Feel Pain." *Gospel Herald*, April 2, 1991, 3.
"Families that Pray Together Stay Together." *The Mennonite*, April 9, 1991, 147-148.
"Moved, Seconded, and Carried." *Gospel Herald*, April 23, 1991, 5.
"Your Family's Foundation For Survival: Without Family Worship Are We Becoming Practical Secularists?" *The Christian Leader*, April 23, 1991, 3-5.
"The Strange Ways of Mennonites." Reclassified, *Festival Quarterly*, Summer 1991, 42.
"Drawing the Family Together in Worship." *Mennonite Brethren Herald*, August 23, 1991, 6-8.
"Forbidden Business." *The Christian Leader*, September 24, 1991, 3-6.
"Tips for Staying in Charge." *The Christian Leader*, September 24, 1991, 5.
"This Controversy is About More than Abortion." *Gospel Herald*, October 15, 1991, 8.
"Stories Women Tell." *Gospel Herald*, November 19, 1991, 2-3.
"Rachel Weeps for Her Children in Central America." *Mennonite Reporter*, November 25, 1991, 5.
"The Widows of Guatemala: Who is Hearing Their Cry?" *The Christian Leader*, December 17, 1991, 12-13.

Viewpoint
"A Wish List for the New Year." Viewpoint, *The Christian Leader*, January 15, 1991, 20.

"Why Have We Forgotten So Soon." Viewpoint, *The Christian Leader*, January 29, 1991, 12.
"Funerals are Opportunities." Viewpoint, *The Christian Leader*, February 12, 1991, 21.
"When You Hurt, Laugh." Viewpoint, *The Christian Leader*, February 26, 1991, 11.
"Give Us Courage to Feel Pain." Viewpoint, *The Christian Leader*, March 12, 1991, 12.
"Church Women and Winds of Change." Viewpoint, *The Christian Leader*, March 26, 1991, 20.
"Who is a First-class Mennonite Brethren?" Viewpoint, *The Christian Leader*, April 9, 1991, 14.
"Share the News: Reading is Fun." Viewpoint, *The Christian Leader*, May 7, 1991, 12.
"He Taught Others to Walk." Viewpoint, *The Christian Leader*, June 18, 1991, 15.
"What is the Price of Growth?" Viewpoint, *The Christian Leader*, July 16, 1991, 14.
"Let's Talk to Ourselves First." Viewpoint, *The Christian Leader*, July 30, 1991, 15.
"A Moving Experience." Viewpoint, *The Christian Leader*, August 27, 1991, 17.
"Abortion Activists' Agenda is Multilayered." Viewpoint, *The Christian Leader*, September 10, 1991, 8.
"Prolonged Mental Illness—An Issue for All of Us." Viewpoint, *The Christian Leader*, September 24, 1991, 11.
"Stories Women Tell." Viewpoint, *The Christian Leader*, October 8, 1991, 13.
"Confusion is Grace." Viewpoint, *The Christian Leader*, November 5, 1991, 15.
"Jesus Lives at the Dump." Viewpoint, *The Christian Leader*, November 19, 1991, 14.
"'Retirement': A Progress Report." Viewpoint, *The Christian Leader*, December 3, 1991, 20.
"The Hazards of Travel." Viewpoint, *The Christian Leader*, December 17, 1991, 16.
"After 30 Years, It's Time for a Change." Viewpoint, *The Christian Leader*, December 31, 1991, 9.

Book Reviews

Review of *Celebrating the Seasons of Life* by Mary Batchelor. *Provident Book Finder*, January-February, 1991, 7.
Review of *Let the Waters Roar: Evangelists in the Gulag* compiled by Georgi Vins. *Mennonite Weekly Review*, February 14, 1991, 4.
Review of *Mirror of the Martyrs* by John S. Oyer and Robert S. Kreider. *Mennonite Weekly Review*, February 14, 1991, 4.

Review of *Trackless Wastes and Stars to Steer* by Michael A. King. *Mennonite Weekly Review*, March 14, 1991, 4.

Review of *County Road 13: A Country Philosopher's Homespun Wisdom and Humorous Commentary on Life*, by Robert J. Baker. *Festival Quarterly*, Spring 1991, 30.

Review of *The Kingdom of God is a Party: God's Radical Plan for His Family* by Tony Campolo. *Mennonite Weekly Review*, April 4, 1991, 4.

Review of *And Who is My Neighbor: Poverty, Privilege and the Gospel of Christ* by Gerald W. Schlabach. *Mennonite Weekly Review*, May 9, 1991, 4.

Review of *Mennonite Historical Atlas* by Helmut Huebert. *Mennonite Weekly Review*, May 30, 1991, 4.

Review of *Mennonite Foods and Folkways from South Russia, Vol. 1* by Norma Jost Voth. *Mennonite Weekly Review*, July 4, 1991, 4.

Review of *Surviving Without Romance: African Women Tell Their Stories* by Mary Lou Cummings. *Mennonite Weekly Review*, August 15, 1991, 4.

Review of *A Symphony of Sand* by Calvin Miller. *Mennonite Weekly Review*, September 17, 1991, 4.

Review of *Extending the Table...A World Community Cookbook...Recipes and Stories in the Spirit of More-With-Less* by Joetta Handrich Schlabach. *Mennonite Weekly Review*, October 24, 1991, 4.

Review of *Welcome! A Biblical and Practical Guide to Receiving New Members* by Ervin R. Stutzman. *Mennonite Weekly Review*, November 28, 1991, 4.

Presentations

"Strengthening Roots by Building Memories." Locust Grove Parent-Teacher Fellowship Banquet, March 18, 1991.

"Building in Partnership with Men in the Workplace." Business and Professional Women of the Women's Missionary and Service Commission, Forest Hills, Pennsylvania, March 19, 1991.

"Choosing to Be a Builder." "What Is That in Your Hand?" Annual Lancaster WMSC Meeting, Groffdale Mennonite Church, Leola, Pennsylvania, March 20, 1991.

"Seeing Through New Eyes: Hurting, Forgiving, Healing." Nebraska Mennonite Women's Retreat, Camp Calvin Crest, Fremont, Nebraska, March 23-24, 1991.

"Have a Good Time with Your Old Times." Central Kansas Writing Conference, April 18, 1991.

"When Life Changes Faster Than I Can Manage." Virginia Conference WMSC Annual Day, Stuarts Draft, Virginia, May 2, 1991.

1992

Books
Your Daughters Shall Prophesy: Women in Ministry in the Church, edited by John E. Toews, Valerie Rempel, and Katie Funk Wiebe. Winnipeg: Kindred Press, 1992.

Book Sections
"Women in the Mennonite Brethren Church." In *Your Daughters Shall Prophesy: Women in Ministry in the Church*, edited by John E. Toews, Valerie Rempel, and Katie Funk Wiebe, 173-189. Winnipeg: Kindred Press, 1992.

Articles and Columns
"Confusion is a Grace, Says Salvadoran Priest." *Mennonite Reporter*, February 10, 1992, 7.
"March 2-8." *Rejoice!* March/April/May 1992, 9-15.
"July 20-26." *Rejoice!* March/April/May 1992, 51-57.
"Down with the Mennonites!" Reclassified, *Festival Quarterly*, Spring 1992, 38.
"Katie Funk Wiebe reflects on the conference: 'In a Mennonite Voice: Women Doing Theology,' held at Conrad Grebel College, April 30-May 2, 1992." *Conrad Grebel Review* 10, no.2 (Spring 1992): 209-214.
"To Fix or to Start Over: The Health Care Crisis in The Mennonite Church." *MHA Newsletter*, June 1992, 7-8.
"Bloopers and Whoopers." Reclassified, *Festival Quarterly*, Summer 1992, 38.
"Answers to Questions You Were Afraid to Ask." Reclassified, *Festival Quarterly*, Fall 1992, 38.
"Why We Need a New Name." *The Christian Leader*, September 8, 1992, 15.
"Moving Towards Recovery?" *The Christian Leader*, November 3, 1992, 3-8.
"January 4-10." *Rejoice!* December 1992, January/February 1993, 6-12.

Book Reviews
Review of *Enter His Gates: Fitting Worship Together* by Eleanor Kreider. *Mennonite Weekly Review*, January 16, 1992, 4.
Review of *Born Giving Birth: Creative Expressions of Mennonite Women* edited by Mary H. Schertz and Phyllis Martens. *Mennonite Weekly Review*, February 6, 1992, 4.
Review of *Going Broke: Bankruptcy, Business Ethics and the Bible* by John R. Sutherland. *Mennonite Weekly Review*, February 20, 1992, 4.
Review of *The Best of Mennonite Fellowship Meals* edited by Phyllis Pellman Good and Louise Stoltzfus. *Mennonite Weekly Review*, March 12, 1992, 4.
Review of *Brilliant Idiot* by Abraham Schmitt. *Festival Quarterly*, Spring 1992, 29.

Review of *Great Stories about Parenting* edited by Philip Osborne and Karen Weaver Koppenhaver. *Mennonite Weekly Review*, April 23, 1992, 4.

Review of *Mennonite Furniture: A Migrant Tradition* by Reinhild Kauenhoven Janzen and John M. Janzen. *Mennonite Weekly Review*, May 14, 1992, 4.

Review of *Following Christ in a Consumer Society—Still: The Spirituality of Cultural Resistance* by John F. Kavanaugh. *Mennonite Weekly Review*, July 2, 1992, 4.

Review of *Christ and Narcissus: Prayer in a Self-Centered World* by Warren McWilliams. *Mennonite Weekly Review*, July 11, 1992, 4.

Review of *Seeking Peace: The Stories of Mennonites Around the World, Struggling to Live Their Belief in Peace* by Titus Peachy and Linda Gehman Peachy. *Mennonite Weekly Review*, August 27, 1992, 4.

Review of *Remember Lot's Wife and Other Unnamed Women of the Bible* by April Yamasaki, *Direction* 21, no.2 (Fall 1992): 73-74.

Review of *Assault on God's Image: Domestic Abuse* by Isaac I. Block. *Mennonite Weekly Review*, September 17, 1992, 4.

Review of *The Sign of the Fox* by Sara Stambaugh. *Mennonite Weekly Review*, October 8, 1992, 4.

Review of *Christmas: A Cook's Tour* by Ingebort Relph & Penny Stanway. *Provident Book Finder*, November-December 1992, 2.

Review of *Live is a Zoo —No Matter What Side of the Cage You're On* by Gary Richmond. *Provident Book Finder*, November-December 1992, 6.

Review of *Only the Heart Knows How to Find Them* by Christopher de Vinck. *Provident Book Finder*, November-December 1992, 7.

Review of *Zooful of Animals* selected by William Cole. *Provident Book Finder*, November-December 1992, 18.

Review of *Barry's Sister* by Lois Metzger. *Provident Book Finder*, November-December 1992, 30.

Review of *The Overworked American: The Unexpected Decline of Leisure*. *Mennonite Weekly Review*, November 5, 1992, 4.

Review of *Why America Doesn't Work: How the Decline of the Work Ethic is Hurting Your Family and Future* by Chuck Colson and Jack Eckerd. *Mennonite Weekly Review*, November 5, 1992, 4.

Review of *Jesus and Divorce: A Biblical Guide for Ministry to Divorced Persons* by George R. Ewald. *Mennonite Weekly Review*, December 3, 1992, 4.

Review of *Signposts: Living with Christian Values in an Age of Uncertainty* by Earl Palmer. *Mennonite Weekly Review*, December 31, 1992, 4.

Presentations

"Accepting Responsibility for the Next Generation." Arkansas Valley WMSC, Rocky Ford Mennonite Church, Rocky Ford, Colorado, Spring, 1992.

"What? Me a Theologian?" "In a Mennonite Voice: Women Doing Theology," Conrad Grebel College, Waterloo, Ontario, April 30-May 2, 1992.

"Healthy Gender Relations." MEDA Convention, Denver, Colorado, October 29-November 1, 1992.

1993

Books
Life After 50: A Positive Look at Aging in the Faith Community. Editor. Newton: Faith and Life, 1993.

Book Sections
"If you are Going to Be Old, Now Is the Time." In *Life After 50: A Positive Look at Aging in the Faith Community*, edited by Katie Funk Wiebe, 3-14. Newton: Faith and Life, 1993.
"What the Bible Tells Us About Growing Older." In *Life After 50: A Positive Look at Aging in the Faith Community*, edited by Katie Funk Wiebe, 15-25. Newton: Faith and Life, 1993.
"Media and the Mature Adult: The Image and the Reality." In *Life After 50: A Positive Look at Aging in the Faith Community*, edited by Katie Funk Wiebe, 39-50. Newton: Faith and Life, 1993.
"Retirement: Friend or Foe?" In *Life After 50: A Positive Look at Aging in the Faith Community*, edited by Katie Funk Wiebe, 53-64. Newton: Faith and Life, 1993.
"Turning Losses into Gains: It's Possible!" In *Life After 50: A Positive Look at Aging in the Faith Community*, edited by Katie Funk Wiebe, 65-76. Newton: Faith and Life, 1993.

Articles and Columns
"Living by the Word." Reclassified, *Festival Quarterly*, Winter 1993, 36-37.
"April 5-11." *Rejoice!* March/April/May 1993, 37-43.
"Life after Fifty." *The Mennonite*, March 9, 1993, 3-6.
"The Frugal Mennonite." Reclassified, *Festival Quarterly*, Spring 1993, 38.
"The 'E Word' Meets the 'P word.'" *The Christian Leader*, June 29, 1993, 6-7.
"One- and Two-Handed Mennonites." Reclassified, *Festival Quarterly*, Summer 1993, 42.
"Life's Second Half—It's Never Been Better." *Christian Living*, July 1993, 16-18.
"How to Cross Cultures Without Stumbling." *The Mennonite*, July 27, 1993, 8.
"Another Verse of '606.'" Reclassified, *Festival Quarterly*, Fall 1993, 38.
"New Agenda for Older Adults." *The Christian Leader*, October 5, 1991, 9-11.
"The Rise of the Older American." *The Christian Leader*, October 5, 1993, 4-5
"Challenging Old Assumptions." *The Christian Leader*, October 5, 1993, 6-8.
"Ageless Principles About Aging." *The Christian Leader*, October 5, 1993, 11.
"Stages of Christian Life." *The Christian Leader*, October 5, 1993, 10.

Book Reviews

Review of *Time to be a Friend* by Karen E. Lansing. *Provident Book Finder,* January-February 1993, 20.

Review of *The Overworked American* by Juliet B. Schor. *Provident Book Finder,* January-February 1993, 24-25.

Review of *A Race for Land: Will Ben Be Able to Stake a Claim for his Family in Oklahoma?* by Esther Loewen Vogt. *Mennonite Weekly Review,* January 21, 1993, 4.

Review of *The Trouble with Dreams: The Story of Joseph and His Brothers* by LeeAnn Lewis. *Mennonite Weekly Review,* January 21, 1993, 4.

Review of *Whisper of Love: An Amish Romance on the Moonlit Prairie* by Jewel Miller. *Mennonite Weekly Review,* January 21, 1993, 4.

Review of *Mennonite Community Cookbook: Favorite Family Recipes* by Mary Emma Showalter. *Mennonite Weekly Review,* February 18, 1993, 4.

Review of *Uncommon Decency* by Richard J. Mouw. *Provident Book Finder,* March-April-May 1993, 4.

Review of *A Quiet Strength: the Susanna Roth Krebbiel Story* by Amelia Mueller. *Mennonite Weekly Review,* March 4, 1993, 4.

Review of *Good Friday People* by Sheila Cassidy. *Mennonite Weekly Review,* March 25, 1993, 4.

Review of *Reclaiming Friendship: Relating to Each Other in a Frenzied World* by Ajith Fernando. *Mennonite Weekly Review,* April 8, 1993, 4.

Review of *Peace Theology and Violence Against Women* edited by Elizabeth G. Yoder. *Mennonite Weekly Review,* May 13, 1993, 4.

Review of *Readings from Mennonite Spirituality: New and Old,* compiled by J. Craig Haas. *Mennonite Weekly Review,* July 1, 1993, 4.

Review of *Lord Teach Us to Pray: A New Look at the Lord's Pray* by Arthur Paul Boers. *Mennonite Weekly Review,* July 15, 1993, 4.

Review of *Kneeling in Jerusalem* by Ann Weems. *Provident Book Finder,* August-September 1993, 2.

Review of *A Church for the 21st Century* by Leith Anderson. *Provident Book Finder,* August-September 1993, 7.

Review of *Selling Jesus* by Douglas D. Webster. *Provident Book Finder,* August-September 1993, 8.

Review of *Multiple Choices* by Ruth A. Tucker. *Provident Book Finder,* August-September 1993, 14.

Review of *Shame and Grace* by Lewes B. Smedes. *Provident Book Finder,* August-September 1993, 16.

Review of *Vultures and Butterflies: Living with the Contradictions* by Susan Classen. *Mennonite Weekly Review,* August 19, 1993, 4.

Review of *When Not to Build: An Architect's Unconventional Wisdom for the Growing Church* by Roy Bowman with Eddy Hall. *Mennonite Weekly Review*, September 23, 1993, 4.
Review of *Willing Service Stories of Ontario Mennonite Women* by Lorraine Roth. *Provident Book Finder*, October-November-December 1993, 7.
Review of *Godtalk: The Triteness & Truth of Christian Cliches*, by Randall J. VanderMay. *Provident Book Finder*, October-November-December 1993, 12.
Review of *Mennonite Starter Kit: A Handy Guide for the New Mennonite* by Craig Haas and Steve Nolt. *Mennonite Weekly Review*, November 4, 1993, 4.

Presentations
"Rempel, Redekop and Reflections about Women's Organizations among the Brethren."
"North American Mennonite Brethren at Mid-Century (1940-1960)," Center for Mennonite Brethren Studies, Fresno, California, February 4-6, 1993.
"Life After 50: A Positive Look at Aging in the Faith Community." Bethel College Life Enrichment Series, Bethel College, North Newton, Kansas, April 14, 1993.
"What Is That in Your Hand?" MCC Alberta Women's Concerns Committee Retreat, Water Valley, Alberta, April 23-24, 1993.
"Art—Artificial Implant or Natural Body Part." MCC BC Peace and Arts Festival, Abbotsford, B.C., August 6-8, 1993.
"Stories and Samovars: How to Be Rich When You Are Old." Seventh Annual Friends of Dock Woods Community Dinner, Lansdale, Pennsylvania, November 9, 1993.

1994

Books
Prayers of an Omega: Facing the Transitions of Aging. Scottdale: Herald Press, 1994.

Unpublished Books
My Childhood in South Russia. Abe. J Funk with Katie Funk Wiebe. Wichita, 1994.

Book Sections
"The Dream Movement." (with Christine R. Wiebe) In *A Dry Roof and a Cow: Dreams and Portraits of Our Neighbours - to Commemorate 75 Years of Service in the Name of Christ 1920-1995*, edited by Howard Zehr and Charmayne Denlinger Brubaker, 143-148. Akron: Mennonite Central Committee, 1994.
"Foreword." In *Traces of Treasure: Quest for God in the Commonplace*, Joanne Lehman, 11-13. Scottdale: Herald Press, 1994.

Articles and Columns

"A Pastoral Letter to Mennonite Brethren Women." *Sophia*, Winter 1994, 10-11.
"You Bet We're Special." Reclassified, *Festival Quarterly*, Winter 1994, 36.
"Peace: An Idea for the '90s." *The Christian Leader*, January 1994, 28.
"A Pig For a Pig: A Peacemaking Story for Families." *The Christian Leader*, January 1994, 12-13.
"April 25-May 1." *Rejoice!* March/April/May 1994, 58-64.
"Humor Among Mennonites." Reclassified, *Festival Quarterly*, Spring/Summer 1994, 66.
"The Sign of the Mennonite." Reclassified, *Festival Quarterly*, Fall 1994, 38.
"Tribute to a Colleague: Clarence R. Hiebert." *Direction* 23, no.2 (Fall 1994): 117-120.
"Identity: Sunday School Teacher." *The Christian Leader*, September 1994, 4-7.
"October 24-30." *Rejoice!* September/October/November 1994, 58-64.
"February 20-26." *Rejoice!* December 1994, January/February 1995, 86-92.

Book Reviews

Review of *The Great Alphabet Fight* by Steve Jensen. *Provident Book Finder*, January-February 1994, 13.
Review of *I Never Found That Rocking Chair* by Richard L. Morgan. *Provident Book Finder*, January-February 1994, 28.
Review of *Catch the Age Wave* by Win Arn & Charles Arn. *Provident Book Finder*, January-February 1994, 28-29.
Review of *The Myth of Certainty: Trusting God, Asking Questions, Taking Risks* by Daniel Taylor. *Mennonite Weekly Review*, January 6, 1994, 4.
Review of *Called to Care: A Training Manual for Small Group Leaders* by Palmer Becker. *Mennonite Weekly Review*, February 3, 1994, 4.
Review of *Called to Equip: A Training Manual for Pastors* by Palmer Becker. *Mennonite Weekly Review*, February 3, 1994, 4.
Review of *Amish Country Cookbook Volume III* edited by Bob & Sue Miller. *Provident Book Finder*, March-April-May 1994, 35.
Review of *The Story of Low German and Plautdietsch: Tracing a Language Across the Globe* by Rueben Epp. *Mennonite Weekly Review*, March 3, 1994, 4.
Review of *Our Trek to Central Asia* by Franz Bartsch. *Mennonite Weekly Review*, March 31, 1994, 4.
Review of *Shared Burdens: Stories of Caring Practices Among Mennonites* by Sue V. Schlabacht and Glen A Roth. *Mennonite Weekly Review*, May 5, 1994, 4.
Review of *Torches Extinguished: Memories of a Communal Bruderhof of Childhood in Paraguay, Europe and the USA* by Elizabeth Bohlken-Zumpe. *Mennonite Weekly Review*, June 9, 1994, 4.
Review of *Fabric and Patterns: Portraits of Some Rural Kansas Mennonite Women* by Esther Deckert Sayler. *Mennonite Weekly Review*, July 7, 1994, 4.

Review of *A Mennonite Woman's Life* by Phyllis Pellman Good. *Mennonite Weekly Review*, July 7, 1994, 4.
Review of *What on Earth Can You Do? Making Your Church a Creation Awareness Center* by Donna Lehman. *Mennonite Weekly Review*, July 28, 1994, 4.
Review of *Pain. The Gift Nobody Wants* by Dr. Paul Brand & Philip Yancey. *Provident Book Finder*, August-September 1994,1.
Review of *Footprints* by Margaret Fishback Powers. *Provident Book Finder*, August-September 1994, 2.
Review of *Family Violence: The Compassionate Church Responds*, by Melissa A. Miller. *Mennonite Weekly Review*, August 25, 1994, 4.
Review of *Enter the River: Healing Steps from White Privilege Towards Racial Reconciliation* by Arthur C. Jones. *Mennonite Weekly Review*, October 6, 1994, 4.
Review of *Things They Never Taught You in Seminary* by Deborah and James Bushfield. *Mennonite Weekly Review*, November 10, 1994, 4.
Review of *Mennonite Country Style Recipes and Kitchen Secrets* by Esther H. Shank. *Mennonite Weekly Review*, November 10, 1994, 4.
Review of *Living with Conviction: Germany Army Captain Turns to Cultivating Peace* by Siegfried Bartel. *Mennonite Weekly Review*, December 22, 1994, 4.

Presentations
"Writing Non-Fiction." Kansas Authors Club 90th Annual Convention, Salina, Kansas, October 1-2, 1994.
"How to Write Your Memoirs," Kansas Authors Club 90th Annual Convention, Salina, Kansas, October 1-2, 1994.
"Aging as a Spiritual Journey." Camps With Meaning annual banquet, November 6, 1994.

1995

Books
Border Crossing: A Spiritual Journey. Scottdale: Herald Press, 1995.
Older Adults and Faith: Their Spiritual Development and Relationship to the Church. Newton: Faith and Life, 1995.
Older Adults and Faith: Making New Maps. Newton: Faith and Life Press, 1995.
Prayers of an Omega: Facing the Transitions of Aging. Winnipeg: Kindred Productions, 1995. (Audio book)

Book Sections
"Rempel, Redekop and Reflections about Women's Organizations among the Brethren." In *Bridging Troubled Waters: The Mennonite Brethren at Mid-Twentieth Century*, edited by Paul Toews, 175-180. Winnipeg: Kindred Productions, 1995.

Articles and Columns

"A Menno by Any Other Name Is Just As Sweet." Reclassified, *Festival Quarterly*, Winter 1995, 38.

"Crossbearing in a Cross Culture." Editorial, *The Christian Leader*, February 1995, 32.

"Art: Artificial Implant or Natural Body Part?" *The Christian Leader*, February 1995, 4-8.

"Add Your Piece to the Puzzle." Editorial, *The Christian Leader*, March 1995, 36.

"Our Role in China." *The Christian Leader*, March 1995, 9-10.

"May 15-21." *Rejoice!* March/April/May 1995, 79-85.

"The Big M Stands for Mennonite." Reclassified, *Festival Quarterly*, Spring 1995, 38.

"Can I Grow after 65?" *The Christian Leader*, April 1995, 6-9.

"Older Adults: Tomorrow's Church." Editorial, *The Christian Leader*, April 1995, 36.

"Yes, I am Old!" *The Christian Leader*, April 1995, 10.

"Churchgoing: Upbeat in Wichita." *The Christian Leader*, April 1995, 21-24.

"Grandchildren Without Limits." *The Christian Leader*, April 1995, 18.

"When a Little Recycling Is a Lot—A Prairie Dog Survives Alongside a Mastodon." *Christian Living*, April-May, 1995, 4.

"Developing a Ministry With and for Older Adults." *The Messenger*, May 3, 1995, 2-3.

"Please, God, May We Laugh?" Editorial, *The Christian Leader*, June 1995, 40.

"Envisioning a Rural Future." *The Christian Leader*, July 1995, 20-21.

"The Church's Contract with the Family." *The Christian Leader*, July 1995, 4-10.

"Great Thoughts." Reclassified, *Festival Quarterly*, Fall 1995, 38.

"Growing with the Seasons of Life." *Direction* 24, no.2 (Fall 1995): 75-82.

"Mennonite Brethren Women: Images and Realities of the Early Years." *Direction* 24, no.2 (Fall 1995): 23-35.

"Identity: Sunday School Teacher." *Mennonite Brethren Herald*, September 1, 1995, 6-8.

"To Come Home for the Holidays." *The Christian Leader*, November 1995, 4-6.

"When a Gift Isn't a Gift." *The Christian Leader*, December 1995, 4-5.

Book Reviews

Review of *En Route: The Memoirs of Henry J. Gerbrandt (Hinjawaejis)*. *Mennonite Weekly Review*, January 19, 1995, 4.

Review of *Beyond this Darkness* by Lin Creighton. *Mennonite Weekly Review*, February 8, 1995, 4.

Review of *Jonas and Sally* by Rich Foss. *Mennonite Weekly Review*, March 16, 1995, 4.

Review of *Finding God in the World* by Avery Brooke. *Provident Book Finder*, March-April-May 1995, 8.

Review of *Aging in the Lord* by Mary Hester Valentine. *Provident Book Finder*, March-April-May 1995, 37.

Review of *Beyond the Gold Watch* by Deborah V. Gross. *Provident Book Finder*, March-April-May 1995, 38.

Review of *Amish Women: Lives and Stories* by Lois Stoltzfus. *Mennonite Weekly Review*, April 13, 1995, 4.

Review of *Growing Up Plain* by Shirley Kurtz. *Mennonite Weekly Review*, April 13, 1995, 4.

Review of *Going by the Moon and the Stars: Stories of Two Russian Mennonite Women* by Pamela E. Klassen. *Mennonite Weekly Review*, May 11, 1995, 4.

Review of *Wayside Revelations* by Roy Wilson Henry. *Mennonite Weekly Review*, June 8, 1995, 4.

Review of *Coals of Fire* by Elizabeth Hershberger Bauman. *Mennonite Weekly Review*, June 22, 1995, 4.

Review of *Without Shedding of Blood* by Kevin James Block. *Mennonite Weekly Review*, June 22, 1995, 4.

Review of *When It Hurts to Live* by Kathleen Kern. *The Mennonite*, July 11, 1995, 22.

Review of *The Friesen Mill and Early Milling in Marion County, Kansas* by Peggy Goertzen. *Mennonite Weekly Review*, July 27, 1995, 4.

Review of *We Are the Pharisees* by Kathleeen Kern. *Mennonite Weekly Review*, August 17, 1995, 4.

Review of *Against the Wind: The Story of Four Mennonite Villages* by John Friesen. *Mennonite Weekly Review*, September 14, 1995, 4.

Review of *Mennonite Settlements in Crimea* by H. Goerz. *Mennonite Weekly Review*, September 14, 1995, 4.

Review of *Ready to Live, Prepared to Die* by Amy Harwell. *Provident Book Finder*, October-December, 1995, 16.

Review of *Classic Poems to Read Aloud* selected by James Berry. *Provident Book Finder*, October-December 1995, 26-27.

Review of *Darien: Guardian Angel of Jesus* by Roger Elwood. *Mennonite Weekly Review*, October 12, 1995, 4.

Review of *Gideon's Torch* by Charles Colson and Ellen Vaughan. *Mennonite Weekly Review*, November 2, 1995, 4.

Review of *Runaway Buggy* by Carol Duerksen. *Mennonite Weekly Review*, November 23, 1995, 4.

Presentations

"Seniors and Church Ministry." Steinbach Bible College Conference Seminar, Steinbach, Manitoba, March 17, 1995.

"Growth Through Change." Indiana-Michigan WMSC Inspirational Meeting, Goshen, Indiana, May 6, 1995.
"Stories from My Russian Roots." Bethel College Life Enrichment Series, Bethel College, North Newton, Kansas, May 10, 1995.
"Writing the Magazine Article." The Kansas Authors Club Writing Conference and State Convention, Wichita, Kansas, October 7-8, 1995.
"Spirituality and Aging." 40th Anniversary Lecture Series, United Mennonite Home, Vineland, Ontario, November 1, 1995.

1996

Unpublished Books
Anna Janzen Funk's Story: Childhood to Coming to Canada as told her daughter Katie Funk Wiebe over a period of years. Wichita, 1996.

Book Sections
"Frieda Marie Kaufman: Builder of Institutions and Lives." In *Entrepreneurs in the Faith Community: Profiles of Mennonites in Business*, edited by Calvin W. Redekop and Benjamin W. Redekop, 145-165. Scottdale: Herald Press, 1996.
"Lost and Found." In *Godward: Personal Stories of Grace*, edited by Ted Koontz, 181-187. Scottdale: Herald Press, 1996.
"Love Walks Through Doors." In *All Are Witnesses: A Collection of Sermons by Mennonite Brethren Women*, edited by Delores Friesen, 137-141. Winnipeg: Kindred Productions, 1996.

Articles
"Peter Had Come Home." *Journal of Mennonite Studies* 14 (1996): 172-190.
"About Hookers, Hairstyles, and Heaven." Reclassified, *Festival Quarterly*, Winter 1996, 38.
"Who? Us, Racist?" *The Christian Leader*, January 1996, 9-11.
"Reflections." *MCC Women's Concerns Report*, January-February, 1996, 11-12.
"Crossing the Line." *The Christian Leader*, February 1996, 11-13.
"July 15-21." *Rejoice!* June/July/August 1996, 53-59.
"A Pig for a Pig." *Mennonite Brethren Herald*, September 27, 1996, 4-5.
"Giving Our Promises Integrity." *The Christian Leader*, October 1996, 4-6.

Book Reviews
Review of *Katie and the Lemon Tree* by Esther Bender. *Mennonite Weekly Review*, February 15, 1996, 4.
Review of *Barbara: Sarah's Legacy* by James D. Yoder. *Mennonite Weekly Review*, February 15, 1996, 4.

Review of *Lost River Conspiracy* by Dave Jackson. *Mennonite Weekly Review*, February 15, 1996, 4.

Review of *Aging Without Apology*, by Robert E. Seymour. *Provident Book Finder*, March-April-May 1996, 33.

Review of *And a Time to Die: The Pain and Love of a Journey Home With AIDS* by Frances Bontrager Greaser. *Mennonite Weekly Review*, March 21, 1996, 4.

Review of *Godward: Personal Stories of Grace* edited by Ted Koontz. *Mennonite Weekly Review*, April 11, 1996, 4.

Review of *The End of the Age* by Pat Robertson. *Mennonite Weekly Review*, May 9, 1996, 4.

Review of *JB: A Twentieth- Century Mennonite Pilgrim* by J.B. Toews. *Mennonite Weekly Review*, June 6, 1996, 5.

Review of *The Jesus I Never Knew* by Philip Yancey. *Mennonite Weekly Review*, June 27, 1996, 4.

Review of *Russia Letters: A Collection of Letters Written Mostly from Russia to Edward Esau and His Family in Kansas and from Central Asia to Gerhard Esau II and His Family in Nebraska* translated and annotated by Elma E. Esau. *Mennonite Weekly Review*, July 18, 1996, 4.

Review of *Toward Holy Ground* by Margaret Guenther. *Provident Book Finder*, August-September 1996, 32-33.

Review of *Mennonite Women of Lancaster County: A Story in Photographs from 1855-1935* by Joanne Hess Siegrist. *Mennonite Weekly Review*, August 15, 1996, 4.

Review of *Drink from the Stream: Essay by Bethel College Faculty and Staff* edited by John K. Sheriff and Heather Esau. *Mennonite Weekly Review*, September 19, 1996, 4.

Review of *Fire on the Mountain*, *Pulling the Lion's Tail*, and *Miro in the Kingdom of the Sun* by Jane Kurtz. *Mennonite Weekly Review*, October 24, 1996, 5.

Review of *Abdi and the Elephants* by Mary W. Gehman. *Mennonite Weekly Review*, October 24, 1996, 5.

Review of *Entrepreneurs in the Faith Community: Profiles of Mennonites in Business* by Calvin Redekop and Benjamin W. Redekop. *Mennonite Weekly Review*, October 31, 1996,

Review of *Hitched* by Carol Duerksen and Maynard Knepp. *Mennonite Weekly Review*, November 21, 1996, 4.

Review of *Preacher* by Carol Duerksen and Maynard Knepp. *Mennonite Weekly Review*, November 21, 1996, 4.

Review of *MadeleineL'Engle, Suncatcher* by Carole F. Chase. *Provident Book Finder*, August-September 1996, 2.

Presentations

"Spirituality and the Elderly: Issues for the 21st Century." Maple Lawn Homes and Meadows Mennonite Retirement Community, Eureka, Illinois, September 19, 1996.

"Stories of Healing and Humor." "Have a Good Time with Your Old Times," Life Education and Development Storytelling Weekend, Hesston College, Hesston, Kansas, October 4-5, 1996.

"Aging As a Spiritual Frontier." Commission on Aging of Lancaster Mennonite Conference Annual Meeting, Landisville, Pennsylvania, October 19, 1996.

"Donate Your Rocking Chair to the Thrift Shop." Annual Senior Emphasis Day, Senior Concerns Committee of First Mennonite Church, Bluffton, Ohio, October 22, 1996.

"Livelong and Keep Growing." Annual Senior Emphasis Day, Senior Concerns Committee of First Mennonite Church, Bluffton, Ohio, October 22, 1996.

1997

Books
The Storekeeper's Daughter: A Memoir. Scottdale: Herald Press, 1997.

Unpublished Books
Born Out of Season: A Short Biography of Walter William Wiebe 1918-62. Wichita, 1997.

Articles and Columns
"Beyond Common Cents: When Stewardship Has Integrity." *The Christian Leader*. February 1997, 4-6.

"June 9-15." *Rejoice!* June/July/August 1997, 18-24.

"A Name of My Own." *Christian Living*, Summer, 1997, 4-7.

"Giving Our Promises Integrity." *Mennonite Brethren Herald*, September 26, 1997, 9-10.

"Subversive Faith." *The Christian Leader*, October 1997, 7-9.

"When I Am Old, I Want to be an Elder." *MCC Women's Concerns Report*, September-October 1997, 10-12.

"Donner de l'integrite a nos promesses." *Le Lien*, December 1997, 1-3.

Book Reviews
Review of *A Harvest of Memories: Illustrations and Recollections* by Randy Penner. *Mennonite Weekly Review*, January 2, 1997, 4.

Review of *To Have a Home: The Centennial History of Messiah Village* by Ray M. Zercher. *Mennonite Weekly Review*, February 13, 1997, 4.

Review of *The Work of Their Hands: Mennonite Women's Societies in Canada* by Gloria Neufeld. *Mennonite Reporter*, March 3, 1997, 10.
Review of *Gifts Handed Down* by J. Daniel Hess. *Mennonite Weekly Review*, March 13, 1997, 4.
Review of *Profiles of Anabaptist Women: 16th Century Reforming Pioneers*, edited by C. Arnold Snyder and Linda Huebert Hecht. *Mennonite Weekly Review*, April 10, 1997, 4.
Review of *Doing Life: Reflections of Men and Women Serving Life Sentence* by Howard Zehr. *Mennonite Weekly Review*, May 8, 1997, 4.
Review of *Aging: God's Challenge to Church and Synagogue* by Richard H. Gentzler Jr. and Donald F. Clingan. *Mennonite Weekly Review*, May 22, 1997, 4.
Review of *Hill Station Teacher: A Life With India in It* by Ruth Unrau. *Mennonite Weekly Review*, June 12, 1997, 4.
Review of *Dust Between My Toes: An Amish Boy's Journey* by Wayne M. Weaver. *Mennonite Weekly Review*, July 3, 1997, 6.
Review of *No Strange Fire* by Ted Wojtasik. *Mennonite Weekly Review*, July 3, 1997, 6.
Review of *With Our Own Eyes: The Dramatic Story of a Christian Response to the Wounds of War, Racism and Oppression* by Don Mosley. *Mennonite Weekly Review*, July 17, 1997, 4.
Review of *The 11th Commandment: Wisdom from our Children* by The Children of America. *Mennonite Weekly Review*, August 7, 1997, 4.
Review of *Selina and the Bear Claw Print* by Barbara Smucker. *Mennonite Weekly Review*, August 7, 1997, 4.
Review of *Let's Make A Garden* by Tamara Awad Lobe. *Mennonite Weekly Review*, August 7, 1997, 4.
Review of *More Little Stories for Little Children: A Worship Resource* by Donna McKee. *Mennonite Weekly Review*, August 7, 1997, 4.
Review of *In Her Own Voice: Childbirth Stories by Mennonite Women* edited by Katherine Martens and Heidi Harms. *Mennonite Weekly Review*, August 21, 1997, 4.
Review of *Prayer Book for Ernest Christians: A Spiritually Rich Anabaptist Resource*, translated and edited by Leonard Gross. *Mennonite Weekly Review*, September 18, 1997, 4.
Review of *Just in Time: Stories of God's Extravagance* by Lynn A. Miller. *Mennonite Weekly Review*, November 6, 1997, 4.
Review of *North Americans and Telugus: The Mennonite Brethren Mission in India, 1885-1975* by Peter Penner. *Mennonite Weekly Review*, November 27, 1997, 4.
Review of *Images of the Church in Mission* by John Driver. *Mennonite Weekly Review*, December 25, 1997, 4.

Presentations

"She Sits in the Pew with Other Widows: Aging, Gender, and Public Images." "Conscious Aging: A Creative Spiritual Journey," Lifelong Education and Development Program, Hesston College, Hesston, Kansas, April 3-4, 1997.

"What the Bible Teaches about Aging." "Conscious Aging: A Creative Spiritual Journey," Lifelong Education and Development Program, Hesston College, Hesston, Kansas, April 3-4, 1997.

"A Feminist Critique of *The Mennonite Experience in America* Series." Response to Dianne Zimmerman Umble, "Mennonite Experience in America Conference,"Bethel College and Tabor College, Kansas, April 25-26, 1997.

"The Future Belongs to the Old." "Aging Issues for the 21st Century," Greencroft Senior Center, Goshen, Indiana, May 5, 1997.

"What Determines Quality of Life in Old Age?" "Aging Issues for the 21st Century," Greencroft Senior Center, Goshen, Indiana, May 5, 1997.

"Exploring Your Life Story." Elderhostel at Spruce Lake Retreat, Canadensis, Pennsylvania, October 5-10, 1997.

1998

Book Sections

"Gender and Aging, Male or Female—What Difference Does It Make?" In *Women & Men: Gender in the Church*, edited by Carol Penner, 84-95. Scottdale: Herald Press, 1998.

"When I Am Old, I Want to Be an Elder, Not a Senior." In *What Mennonites Are Thinking –1998*, edited by Merle Good and Phyllis Pellman Good, 125-132. Intercourse: Good Books, 1998.

Articles

"The Handprint on the Hat—How Humor Keeps Us Honest." (with Melanie Zuercher) *MCC Women's Concerns Report*. January-February 1998, 2-3.

"Journey to India: Passage to Forgiveness." *Sophia*, Spring 1998, 22-23, 26.

"July 27-August 2." *Rejoice!* June/July/August 1998, 60-66.

Book Reviews

Review of *Comanches and Mennonites on the Oklahoma Plains: A. J. and Magdalena Becker and the Post Oak Mission* by Marvin E. Kroeker. *Mennonite Weekly Review*, January 15, 1998, 4.

Review of *Faith Dilemmas for Marketplace Christians* by Ben Sprunger, et al. *Mennonite Weekly Review*, February 5, 1998, 4.

Review of *Saints, Sinners and Angels* by Danny Unrau. *Mennonite Weekly Review*, April 2, 1998, 4.

Review of *A Symphony of Frogs: An Autobiography* by Mary (Troyer) Bergey. *Mennonite Weekly Review*, April 23, 1998, 4.
Review of *God and the American Writer* by Alfred Kazin. *Mennonite Brethren Herald*, May 1, 1998, 26-27.
Review of *Through Fire and Water: An Overview of Mennonite History* by Harry Loewen and Steven Nolt. *Mennonite Weekly Review*, May 14, 1998, 4.
Review of *Little Foxes That Spoil the Vines* by W. Barry Miller. *Mennonite Weekly Review*, June 4, 1998, 4.
Review of *Seduction of the Lesser Gods* by Leslie Williams. *Mennonite Weekly Review*, June 4, 1998, 4.
Review of *Martyrs Mirror: The Story of 17 Centuries of Christian Martyrdom from the Time of Christ to A.D. 1660* by Thieleman J. Van Braght. *Mennonite WeeklyReview*, June 18, 1998, 4.
Review of *Journeys: Mennonite Stories of Faith and Survival in Stalin's Russia*, edited and translated by John B. Toews. *Mennonite Weekly Review*, July 9, 1998, 4.
Review of *Heaven's Not a Crying Place* by Joey O'Connor. *Provident Book Finder*, August-September 1998, 21-22.
Review of *A Weaver's Source Book: Up Home with Jonas and Emma* by Mary Lou Weaver Houser. *Mennonite Weekly Review*, August 6, 1998, 4.
Review of *The Blumenstein Legacy: A Six-Generation Family Saga* by Leland D. Harder and Samuel W. Harder. *Mennonite Weekly Review*, August 27, 1998, 4.
Review of *Oracle of the Heart: Selected Poems* by Muriel T. Stackley. *Mennonite Weekly Review*, September 17, 1998, 4.
Review of *Parents: Passing the Torch of Faith*. *Mennonite Weekly Review*, October 8, 1998, 4.
Review of *The Odyssey of Escape From Russia: The Saga of Anna K.* by Wilmer A. Harms. *Mennonite Weekly Review*, November 5, 1998. 4.
Review of *Greeting the Dawn: An Anthology of New Mennonite Writing* edited by Stephen Yutzy. *Mennonite Weekly Review*, November 19, 1998, 4.
Review of *A Simple Christmas: Hundreds of Ways to Bring Christ and Joy Back into Christmas in the Spirit of More-with-Less* by Alice Chapin. *Mennonite Weekly Review*, December 17, 1998, 4.

Presentations

"Facing the Fear of Death." Rockhill Mennonite Retirement Center, Rockhill, Pennsylvania, March 3, 1998.
"Me Tarzan, Son of Menno, You Jane, Mennonite Mama." "EnGendering the Past: Women and Men in Mennonite History," University of Winnipeg, Chair of Mennonite Studies, Winnipeg, Manitoba, October 16-17, 1998.
"Am I My Mother's Keeper?" Bethania Retirement Center, Winnipeg, Manitoba, October 19, 1998.

1999

Articles

"Me Tarzan, Son of Menno—You Jane, Mennonite Mama." *Journal of Mennonite Studies* 17 (1999): 9-21.
"When I Survey the Empty Cross." *Mennonite Weekly Review*, March 4, 1999, 6.
"May 31-June 6." *Rejoice!* June/July/August 1999, 4-10.
"Telling Our Stories." *The Christian Leader*, July 1999, 14-16.
"'Spiritual Security' for the Older Adult." *The Christian Leader*, September 1999, 10-12.

Book Reviews

Review of *Profiles of Anabaptist Women: 16th Century Reforming Pioneers*, edited by C. Arnold Snyder and Linda Huebert Hecht. In *What Mennonites Are Thinking: 1999*, edited by Merle Good and Phyllis Pellman Good, 280-282. Intercourse: Good Books, 1999.
Review of *From Wounded Hearts: Faith Stories or Lesbian, Gay and Transgendered People and Those Who Love Them* compiled by Roberta Showalter Kreider. *Mennonite Weekly Review*, January 7, 1999, 4.
Review of *God's Week Has Seven Days: Monday Musing for Marketplace Christians* by Wally Kroeker. *Mennonite Weekly Review*, February 4, 1999, 4.
Review of *Blessed Is the Meadow: Stories of the Spiritual Lives of People with Developmental Disability* by Barbara Esch Shisler. *Mennonite Weekly Review*, March 11, 1999, 4.
Review of *Service with a Smile: 52 Humorous Sketches for Sunday Worship* by Daniel Wray. *Mennonite Weekly Review*, April 1, 1999, 4.
Review of *Pregnant and Single: Help for the Tough Choices* by Linda Roggow and Carolyn Owens. *Mennonite Weekly Review*, May 13 1999, 4.
Review of *The Storyteller's Beads* by Jane Kurtz. *Mennonite Weekly Review*, June 3,1999, 4.
Review of *Gadding About Gypsum Creek* by Roy Wilson Henry. *Mennonite Weekly Review*, July 8, 1999, 4.
Review of *On the Pilgrim's Way: Conversations on Christian Discipleship on the 12-Day Walk Across England* by J. Nelson Kraybill. *Mennonite Weekly Review*, August 19, 1999, 4.
Review of *Holy Hunger: A Memoir of Desire* by Margaret Bullitt-Jones. *Mennonite Weekly Review*, September 9, 1999, 4.
Review of *Meditations for Meetings: Thoughtful Meditations for Board Meets and for Leaders* compiled by Edgar Stoesz. *Mennonite Weekly Review*, October 21, 1999, 4 .
Review of *Painful Questions: Facing Struggles with Faith* by Gary L. Watts. *Mennonite Weekly Review*, December 9, 1999, 4.

Presentations

"You are All Children of the Light, Children of the Day." WEB Day at Bethel College, North Newton, Kansas, January 16, 1999.

2000

Book Sections

"Foreword." In *A Little Left of Center: An Editor Reflects on His Mennonite Experience.* by Daniel Hertzler, 9-10. Telford: Pandora Press, 2000.

Articles

"When I Survey the Empty Cross." *Mennonite Brethren Herald*, March 31, 2000, 7.
"Esther Hiebert Ebel: A Biography." *CMBS Newsletter*, Fall 2000, 1-5.

Book Reviews

Review of *Garden in the Wilderness: Mennonite Communities in the Paraguayan Chaco 1987-1997* by Edgar Stoesz and Muriel T. Stackley. *Provident Book Finder,* 2000.

Review of *What Mennonites Are Thinking-1999* edited by Merle Good and Phyllis Pellman Good. *Mennonite Weekly Review,* January 13, 2000, 6.

Review of *Another Country: Navigating the Emotional Terrain of Our Elders* by Mary Pipher. *Mennonite Weekly Review*, February 24, 2000, 4.

Review of *Sexuality: God's Gift* edited by Anne Krabill Hershberger. *Mennonite Weekly Review*, April 20, 2000, 4.

Review of *Quilts from Two Valleys: Amish quilts from the Big Valley and Mennonite Quilts from the Shenandoah Valley* by Phyllis Pellman Good. *Mennonite Weekly Review,* May 25, 2000, 4.

Review of *Mennonite Recipes from the Shenandoah Valley* by Phyllis Pellman Good and Katie Good. *Mennonite Weekly Review*, May 25, 2000, 4.

Review of *The Hammer Rings Hope: Photos and Stories from Fifty Years of Mennonite Disaster Service* by Lowell Detweiler. *Mennonite Weekly Review,* June 6, 2000, 6.

Review of *The Life and Times of William Jennings* by Merrill and Boots Raber. *Mennonite Weekly Review*, June 29, 2000, 6.

Review of *Christ Plays in Ten Thousand Places* by Eugene H. Peterson. *Direction* 29, no.2 (Fall 2000): 200-201.

Review of *Friends and Enemies* by Lousann Gaeddert. *Mennonite Weekly Review*, September 7, 2000, 6.

Review of *Liberty in Confinement: A Story of Faith in the Red Army* by Johannes Reimer. *Mennonite Weekly Review*, September 7, 2000.

Review of *A Separate People: An Insider's View of Old Order Mennonite Customs and Traditions* by Isaac R. Horst. *Mennonite Weekly Review*, November 9, 2000, 6.

Review of *Lucy of the Trail of Tears* by James D. Yoder. *Mennonite Weekly Review*, November 30, 2000, 4.

Presentations
"Aging with Spirit." Senior Retreat, Association of Retired Persons and Mennonite Health Services, Laurelville, Pennsylvania, September 29-October 1, 2000.

2001

Books
Bridging the Generations. Scottdale: Herald Press, 2001.

Book Sections
"Foreword." In *Tobias of the Amish* by Ervin R. Stutzman, 9-11. Scottdale: Herald Press, 2001.

Articles
"Reinvent Your Life at Any Age." *The Christian Leader,* June 2001, 7-11.

Book Reviews
Review of *When Life Hurts: A Three-fold Path to Healing* by Brian C. Stiller. *Mennonite Weekly Review,* January 18, 2001, 6.
Review of *Amish Children* by Phyllis Pellman Good. *Mennonite Weekly Review,* February 15, 2001, 4.
Review of *Growing up Religious: Christians and Jews and Their Journeys of Faith* by Robert Wuthnow. *Mennonite Weekly Review,* April 19, 2001, 4.
Review of *Getting Home Before Dark: Stories of Wisdom for all Ages* by Peter J. Dyck. *Mennonite Weekly Review,* May 31, 2001, 4.
Review of *Women Without Men: Mennonite Refugees of the Second World War* by Marlene Epp. *Mennonite Weekly Review,* August 16, 2001, 4.
Review of *Healing the Wounds: One Family's Journey Among the Northern Cheyenne* by Esther and Malcolm Wenger with Ann Wenger. *Mennonite Weekly Review,* September 13, 2001, 4.
Review of *Christ and the Powers* by Hendrik Berkhof, *Mennonite Weekly Review,* November 1, 2001, 6.
Review of *Why Are You Still Alive? A German in the Gulag* by Georg Hildebrandt. *Mennonite Weekly Review,* December 6, 2001, 4.

Presentations
"From the Sunny Steppes of the Ukraine to the Cold Hell of Siberia: One Woman's Story." Center for Mennonite Brethren Studies, Hillsboro, Kansas, May 2001.
"From the Sunny Steppes of the Ukraine to the Cold Hell of Siberia: One Woman's Story." Fairview, Oklahoma, October 2001.

"Journaling and Memoir Writing." Eighth Annual Marion County Women's Wellness Workshop, Marion, Kansas, November 3, 2001.

2002

Book Sections
"The Dilemma of The Mennonite Brethren Writer: Having One Soul or Two?" In *For Everything a Season: Mennonite Brethren in North America, 1874-2002: An Informal History*, edited by Paul Toews and Kevin Enns-Rempel, 109-119. Winnipeg: Kindred Productions, 2002.

Articles
"Surveying the Empty Cross." *The Christian Leader*, March 2002, 4-6.
"A Gift of Poetry from Siberia." *Sophia*, Spring 2002, 18-20.
"A Story Sampler from Siberia." *Sophia*, Summer 2002, 16-17.
"Galloping, Naked, in the Night." *DreamSeeker Magazine*, Summer 2002, 16-23.
"A Conversion Story." *Sophia*, Fall 2002, 18-19.
"Like-minded Travelers." *The Christian Leader*, September 2002, 16.
"Dad's Store." *The Marketplace*, November-December 2002, 12-15.

Book Reviews
Review of *Transcending: Portraits of Crime Victims* by Howard Zehr. *Mennonite Weekly Review*, February 4, 2002, 6.
Review of *Crossing the Divide: Language Transitions Among Canadian Mennonite Brethren, 1940-70* by Gerald C. Ediger. *Mennonite Weekly Review*, March 11, 2002, 6.
Review of *From Bolshevik Russia to America: A Mennonite Family Story* by Henry D. Remple. *Mennonite Weekly Review*, July 8, 2002, 4.
Review of *Jacob J. Dyck: Am Trakt to America: A History and Genealogy for the Descendants of Jacob J. Dyck and Marie G. Harder* by D. Frederick Dyck. *Mennonite Weekly Review*, August 26, 2002, 4.
Review of *Sixty Years of Silence: The Dyck Family in Soviet Russia* by Alice Sitler Dyck, *Mennonite Weekly Review*, August 26, 2002, 4.
Review of *Nickel and Dimed: On (Not) Getting By in America* by Barbara Ehrenreich and Henry Holt. *Mennonite Weekly Review*, October 21, 2002, 4.
Review of *The Wisdom of Daughters: Two Decades of the Voice of Christian Feminism*, edited by Reta Halteman Finger and Kari Sandhaas. *Mennonite Weekly Review*, November 18, 2002, 4.

Presentations
"Watch Out! The Crowd of Witnesses Is Not Only Above You But Also Behind You." National Older Adult Conference of the Church of the Brethren, Lake Junaluska, North Carolina, September 2-6, 2002.

2003

Books

Border Crossing: A Spiritual Journey, rev. ed.. DreamSeeker Books: Telford: 2003.

Articles

"The Curriculum Is Changing." *Mennonite Brethren Herald*, August 22, 2003, 6-7, 9.

Book Reviews

Review of *Neu-Samara: A Mennonite Settlement East of the Volga* compiled by Jacob H. Brucks and Henry P. Hooge, edited by Tena Wiebe. *Mennonite Weekly Review*, February 10, 2003, 4.

Review of *David Toews Was Here: 1870-1949* by Helmut Harder. *Mennonite Weekly Review*, March 10, 2003, 4.

Review of *Calm Before the Storm* by Janice L. Dick. *Mennonite Weekly Review*, June 2, 2003, 4.

Review of *Celebrating Women's Stories: Faith Through Life's Seasons*, edited by Rebecca L. Ebersole. *MCC Women's Concerns Report*, July-August, 2003, 114-116.

Review of *Mennonite Alternative Service in Russia* by Lawrence Klippenstein and Jacob Dick. *Mennonite Weekly Review*, July 14, 2003, 4.

Review of *The Story of Abram Dueck and His Colleagues, 1911-1917* by Lawrence Klippenstein and Jacob Dick. *Mennonite Weekly Review*, July 14, 2003.

Review of *Celebrating Women's Stories: Faith Through Life's Seasons* by Rebecca L. Ebersole et al. *Brethren in Christ History and Life*, August 2003.

Review of *My Early Years: An Autobiography* by Robert S. Kreider. *Mennonite Weekly Review*, August 11, 2003, 4.

Review of *Pioneers in Ministry: Women Pastors in Ontario Mennonite Churches 1973-2003* by Mary A. Schiedel. *Mennonite Weekly Review*, October 6, 2003, 4.

Review of *A Mennonite Family in Tsarist Russia and the Soviet Union 1789-1923* by David G. Rempel with Cornelia Rempel Carlson. *Mennonite Weekly Review*, December 15, 2003, 4.

Presentations

"Aging Is Not a Sin." Southern District Mennonite Brethren Senior Retreat, Branson, Missouri, October 2003.

"Let's Catch the Boomers Before They Fall Over the Cliff." Canadian Conference Mennonite Brethren Senior Retreat, Banff, Alberta, 2003.

"Spiritual Tasks of the Later Years." Camp Friedenswald, Cassopolis, Michigan, October 2003.

2004

Articles
"Touching the Future." *The Christian Leader*, April 2004, 7-10.
"Mentoring Across the Generations." *The Christian Leader*, April 2004, 10.

Book Reviews
Review of *Eyes at the Window* by Evie Yoder Miller. *Mennonite Weekly Review*, January 26, 2004, 4.
Review of *Keeper of Hearts* by Dianne Christner. *Mennonite Weekly Review*, March 1, 2004, 4.
Review of *Speak to Her Kindly: A Novel of the Anabaptists* by Jonathan Rainbow. *Mennonite Weekly Review*, March 1, 2004, 4.
Review of *Strangers at Home: Amish and Mennonite Women in History* edited by Kimberly D. Schmidt, Diane Zimmerman Umble, and Steven D. Reschly. *Direction* 33, no.1 (Spring 2004): 107-108.
Review of *A Family Torn Apart* by Justina D. Neufeldt. *Mennonite Weekly Review*, April 12, 2004, 6.
Review of *Reinventing Aging* by Shirley Yoder Brubaker. *Mennonite Weekly Review*, August 16, 2004, 4.
Review of *Who's Grace? A John Smyth Mystery* by James R. Coggins. *Mennonite Weekly Review*, October 4, 2004, 4.
Review of *MennoFolk: Mennonite & Amish Folk Traditions* by Ervin Beck. *Mennonite Weekly Review*, October 18, 2004, 6.

Presentations
"Spiritual Invitations and Hazards of the Older Years." Mennonite Conference of Eastern Ontario Annual Workshop, Kitchener, Ontario, January 10, 2004,
"Learning to Value Our Age As We Age." Shepherd's Centers of America Conference at Lake Junaluska, North Carolina, October 2004.

2005

Articles
"My Impressions of the Early Years of the Women's Task Force." *Conrad Grebel Review* 23, no.1 (Winter 2005): 83-87.
"Retirees Need a Mentor." *Mennonite Brethren Herald*, November 25, 2005, 8.

Book Reviews
Review of *The Children's Blizzard* by David Laskin. *Mennonite Weekly Review*, January 3, 2005, 4.

Review of *God's Shalom Project* by Bernhard Ott. *Mennonite Weekly Review*, March 7, 2005, 7.
Review of *Echoes Along the Sweetbriar* by James D. Yoder. *Mennonite Weekly Review*, April 25, 2005, 4.
Review of *Passing the Comfort: The War, the Quilts, and the Women Who Made a Difference* by Ann Keuning-Tichelaar and Lynn Kaplanian-Buller. *Mennonite Weekly Review*, June 11, 2005, 6.
Review of *An Introduction to the Russian Mennonites* by Wally Kroeker. *Mennonite Weekly Review*, August 29, 2005, 4.
Review of *Rolling Down Black Stockings: A Passage Out of the Old Order Mennonite Religion* by Esther Royer Ayers. *Mennonite Weekly Review*, October 24, 2005, 4.

Presentations
"What I've Learned As a Writer." Emerging Writers, Project Barclay Press, Wichita, Kansas, September 10, 2005.
55+ Retreat, Canadian Conference of MB Churches Adult Ministry, Ste-Adèle, Quebec, October 20-23, 2005.

2006

Articles
"Who? Me? A Fundamentalist?" *DreamSeeker Magazine*, Autumn 2006, 24-29.
"Faith Is a Journey, Not Just a Beginning." *Mennonite Brethren Herald*, September 22, 2006, 8-10.
"Faith is a Journey." *The Christian Leader*, October 2006, 16-18.

Book Reviews
Review of *Without the Loss of One: The Story of Nevin and Esther Bender and Its Implications for the Church Today* by Don, Mildred and Titus Bender. *Mennonite Weekly Review*, January 23, 2006, 4.
Review of *Walker in the Fog: On Mennonite Writing* by Jeff Bundy. *Mennonite Weekly Review*, April 10, 2006, 4.
Review of *Touched by Grace: From Secrecy to New Life* by Ann Showalter. *Mennonite Weekly Review*, May 22, 2006, 4.
Review of *Sound in the Land: Essays on Mennonites and Music*, edited by Maureen Epp and Carol Anne Weaver. *Mennonite Weekly Review*, July 24, 2006, 4.
Review of *Between Worlds: Reflections of a Soviet-born Canadian Mennonite* by Harry Loewen. *Mennonite Weekly Review*, November 27, 2006, 5.

Presentations
"Your Child's Faith, Your Faith, Your Mother's Faith." Mennonite Women USA and Women in Conversation Workshops, Wichita, Kansas, March 31-April 2, 2006.
"Late Life Creativity: Chore or Challenge?" Shepherd's Centers of America Conference, Little Rock, Arkansas, October 2006.

2007

Unpublished Books
"Into the Twilight Zone: Family Stories My Father and Others Told Me— Too Good to Throw Out." Wichita, 2007.

Articles
"The Quest for a Proper Burial: How My Family Buried Their Dead." *Journal of Mennonite Studies* 25 (2007): 215-227.
"Words to Live By." *The Christian Leader*, November 2007, 18.
"Face to Face: Recognizing the Christ." *The Christian Leader*, December 2007, 12-14.

Book Reviews
Review of *Telling Our Stories: Personal Accounts of Engagement with Scripture* edited by Ray Gingrich and Earl Zimmerman. *Mennonite Weekly Review*, January 22, 2007, 6.
Review of *Grief and Sexuality: Life After Losing a Spouse* by Rachel Nafziger Hartzler. *Mennonite Weekly Review*. March 19, 2007, 5.
Review of *Even the Demons Submit: Continuing Jesus Ministry of Deliverance* edited by Loren L. Johns and James R. Krabill. *Mennonite Weekly Review*, June 18, 2007, 6.
Review of *Amish Grace: How Forgiveness Transcended Tragedy* by Donald B. Kraybill et al. *Mennonite Weekly Review*, August 20, 2007, 4.
Review of *Forgiveness: Legacy of the West Nickel Mines Amish School* by John L. Ruth. *Mennonite Weekly Review*, August 20, 1007, 4.
Review of *Diaspora in the Countryside: Two Mennonite Communities and Mid-Twentieth Century Rural Disjuncture* by Royden Loewen. *Mennonite Weekly Review*, November 12 2007, 6.

Presentations
"Who am I when I am Retired?" Spring conference, Menno Haven Retirement Communities, Chambersburg, Pennsylvania, March 24-28, 2007.

2008

Book Reviews

Review of *A Widow Among the Amish* by Ervin R. Stutzman. *Mennonite Weekly Review*, February 11, 2008. 4.

Review of *Remember Us: Letters from Stalin's Gulag (1930-37), Vol. 1: The Regehr Family* by Ruth Derksen Siemens. *Mennonite Weekly Review*, June 23, 2008, 6.

Review of *Powwowing Among the Pennsylvania Dutch: A Traditional Medical Practice in the Modern World* by David W. Kriebel. *Mennonite Weekly Review*, October 20, 2008, 6.

Review of *Lost Sons* by Judy Clemens. *Mennonite Weekly Review*, December 15, 2008, 6.

2009

Books

You Never Gave Me a Name: One Mennonite Woman's Story. Telford: DreamSeeker Books, 2009.

How to Write Your Personal or Family History: If You Don't Do It, Who Will? Intercourse: Good Books, 2009.

Articles

"Beginning a Marriage, Beginning a Dream." *Mennonite Brethren Herald*, August 2009, 12-13.

"A Pig for a Pig." *The Chronicle*, September 2009, 4-6.

"The Frugal Christian." *The Christian Leader*, October/November, 2009, 13-15.

Book Reviews

Review of *The Amish and the Media* edited by Diane Zimmerman Umble and David L. Weaver-Zercher. *Mennonite Weekly Review*, February 23, 2009, 5.

Review of *Mennonite Women in Canada: A History* by Marlene Epp. *Mennonite Weekly Review*, April 13, 2009, 4.

Review of *The Houses I Lived In: Memoirs of My Life* by Leland Harder. *Mennonite Weekly Review*, June 15, 2009, 4.

Review of *The Secret, The Longing,* and *The Forbidden* by Beverly Lewis. *Mennonite Weekly Review*, August 24, 2009, 6.

Review of *The Dark Night: A Gift of God* by Daniel P. Schrock. *Mennonite Weekly Review*, October 12, 2009, 5.

Review of *A Generation of Vigilance: The Lives and Work of Johannes and Tina Harder* by T.D. Regehr. *Mennonite Weekly Review*, November 30, 2009, 4-5.

Contributors

Lorraine Dick has been a pastor in three Canadian Mennonite Brethren Churches, most recently at Lendrum M.B. Church in Edmonton, Alberta. Currently she serves the wider constituency on the Canadian Board of Faith and Life and lives in Langley, B.C.

Marlene Epp teaches History and Peace & Conflict Studies at Conrad Grebel University College at the University of Waterloo in Ontario, Canada. Her main areas of research are Mennonites, gender, and immigration and ethnicity. In 2008, she published *Mennonite Women in Canada: A History* (University of Manitoba Press).

Delores Friesen is Professor of Pastoral Counseling at the Mennonite Brethren Biblical Seminary in Fresno, California, a position she has held since 1988. She is a licensed Marriage and Family Therapist with specialties in aging, grief, sexuality, and marriage and family issues. Delores and her husband Stanley spent thirteen years in West Africa, where she taught in three theological schools as well as in the African Independent Churches.

Peggy Goertzen is Director of the Center for Mennonite Brethren Studies in Hillsboro, Kansas. As an archivist, she is passionate about preserving, recording, and communicating the Mennonite story. Peggy and her husband Gaylord have been the pastoral couple at the Ebenfeld MB Church since 1988.

Doug Heidebrecht is Director for the Centre for Mennonite Brethren Studies and lives with his wife Sherry in Winnipeg, Manitoba. Previously he was an instructor in Biblical and Theological Studies at Bethany College in Hepburn, Saskatchewan (1992-2008), where he also served as Academic Dean for several years.

Daniel Hertzler, former editor of *Christian Living* (1960-73) and the *Gospel Herald* (1973-90), is now retired and living in Scottdale, Pennsylvania. He is author of *A Little Left of Center* (DreamSeeker Books) and a part-time instructor at Associated Mennonite Biblical Seminary in Elkhart, Indiana.

Don Isaac is professor emeritus, Tabor College, having taught and chaired the Business Department for 24 years. He has published articles in *The Christian Leader, Direction*, and chapters in several books. His recent work includes the restoration of hundreds of audio recordings for the Center for Mennonite Brethren Studies, where he serves as an advisory board member. Don lives in Hillsboro, Kansas with his wife Connie Wiebe Isaac.

Harold Jantz has spent much of his life in publications, serving as editor of the *Mennonite Brethren Herald* for twenty years. In 1987 he founded *ChristianWeek*, a national evangelical fortnightly of news and comment. He is editor of the book, *Leaders Who Shaped Us: Canadian Mennonite Brethren, 1910-2010* (Kindred Productions). Harold and his wife Neoma live in Winnipeg, Manitoba.

Darlene Klassen, former Children's Pastor at West Portal Church in Saskatoon, Saskatchewan, is currently involved in the Saskatoon Children's Ministry Network. She is an adjunct instructor at Bethany College, and loves to watch her children explore life. Darlene and her husband Randy are looking forward to the new adventure of grandparenting.

Wally Kroeker has spent more than 40 years as a reporter and editor, specializing in business and faith. Former editor of *The Christian Leader* (1975-85) he currently edits *The Marketplace*, a magazine of Mennonite Economic Development Associates (MEDA). His books include *God's Week has Seven Days* (Herald) and *An Introduction to the Russian Mennonites* (Good Books). Wally and his wife Millie live in Winnipeg, Manitoba.

Valerie Rempel is Dean of Students and Enrollment and Associate Professor of History and Theology at Mennonite Brethren Biblical Seminary in Fresno, California. She has taught at the Seminary since 1996 and currently serves on the Faith and Life Commission of the Mennonite World Conference.

Joanna Wiebe lives in Evanston, Illinois and is an information architect and interaction designer with Orbitz Worldwide. Joanna and her husband, Tim Baer, are active in the Evanston Home Educators (EHE) community, and facilitate outdoor and spiritual retreats and workshops for young people and adults.